Children Without a State

Children Without a State

A Global Human Rights Challenge

Edited by Jacqueline Bhabha

The MIT Press
Cambridge, Massachusetts
London, England

© 2011 Massachusetts Institute of Technology

For information about special quantity discounts, please email special_sales@ mitpress.mit.edu.

This book was set in Sabon by Toppan Best-set Premedia Limited. Printed and bound in the United States of America.

Library of Congress Cataloging-in-Publication Data

Children without a state : a global human rights challenge / edited by Jacqueline Bhabha.
    p.   cm.
Includes bibliographical references and index.
ISBN 978-0-262-01527-1 (hardcover : alk. paper)
1. Immigrant children—Civil rights. 2. Immigrant children—Legal status, laws, etc. 3. Human rights. I. Bhabha, Jacqueline.
JV6344.C45   2011
323.3'2912—dc22

                                                        2010030453

10 9 8 7 6 5 4 3 2 1

Never let anyone tell you that you cannot make a difference. You can. What's more—*you must*.

—Albina du Boisrouvray, Founder and chair, François-Xavier Bagnoud Foundation, UNESCO opening address, December 4, 2009

Contents

Foreword

Mary Robinson

For close to a century, with growing focus and specificity, the international community has recognized states' obligations toward vulnerable children, including those who are stateless. In 1924, the League of Nations adopted the Geneva Declaration of the Rights of the Child and proclaimed that "mankind owes to the Child the best that it has to give." A quarter century later, the United Nations signed the Universal Declaration of Human Rights, agreeing that "childhood [is] entitled to special care and assistance." And in 1989, the United Nations Convention on the Rights of the Child mandated that "the child shall be registered immediately after birth and shall have . . . the right to acquire a nationality." The Convention went on to instruct states parties to "ensure implementation of these rights . . . in particular where the child would otherwise be stateless." This is as it should be. More than virtually any other section of the population, children need state protection—for enjoyment of their basic rights to education and health care and for surrogate protection when their families fail them.

Stateless children have a double claim to this protection because they have no effective recourse to the default provider—the state. And yet despite international legal obligations, public consensus that children deserve protection and care, and growing awareness of the effects of migration on the lives of millions of children, the needs of stateless children are largely unattended to, and the needs of stateless children in the twenty-first century are inadequately understood. It is shocking to learn that one-third of the world's children do not have their birth registered and that they risk exclusion from essential state services as a result. It is also disturbing to acknowledge that growing numbers of children, including those who have undocumented immigration status or who belong to marginalized communities such as the Roma or the Rohingya, face similar problems as a result of their inability to prove a legal identity.

to deliver on their entitlements to state protection despite the absence of powerful advocacy lobbies pressing their case.

This book grows out of a conference with the same name held at Harvard University in May 2008. About two-thirds of the chapters build on paper presentations. In my opening remarks at the conference, I described the meeting as "something akin to an unlikely and unexpected wedding, the celebration of a marriage with a dubious prognosis." I pointed out that the bride and groom hailed from very different backgrounds and had little previous mutual understanding. Their spheres of operation and their histories scarcely overlapped. On one side of the church aisle were experts in birth registration and birth certification. These demographers, statisticians, public health experts, and economists working with census data and surveys conduct field work in developing countries such as Nepal, the Dominican Republic, and Mozambique. On the other side of the aisle were experts in migration, voluntary and forced population movements, and national and local state responses to undocumented and irregular populations. These sociologists, education and international relations experts, historians, lawyers, scholars, and advocates work in the richest countries in the world—the industrialized states that form the destination of much contemporary migration. And yet the two parties shared a common interest in children's civil and political rights (to a legal identity and respect for their family life) and their economic and social rights (to education, health care, and shelter). There was also a common preoccupation with the marginalization of children's issues, particularly for the populations of stateless children under consideration. And despite the disciplinary divides, many of the participants straddled the world of theory and practice, scholarship and advocacy. They were interested in conducting careful empirical research and then translating it into effective policy through targeted engagement with public discussion and opinion forming. It is for the reader to decide whether the marriage worked and whether our claim that child statelessness needs to be rethought in broader and deeper terms across disciplines and geographical areas is substantiated by the chapters that follow.

Any joint venture such as this relies on much collaboration and team spirit. This book is no exception. Without the conference, there would have been no book, and without the unflagging support of many partners, there would have been no conference. Many Harvard colleagues disproved the accepted wisdom that the only *modus operandi* here is "each tub on its own bottom." We had generous collaboration from the Graduate School of Education (and Fernando Reimers, in particular), the Yenching Institute in the Center for Asian Studies, and the Carr Center for Human Rights Policy at the Harvard Kennedy School (particularly Andrea Rossi, who contributed the original idea of including questions of birth registration within the children's-rights agenda). Elizabeth Bartholet and Gerald Neuman at Harvard Law School, Mary Waters at the Harvard department of sociology, and Kenneth Hill at the Harvard School of Public Health participated in the discussions, and the Swiss government and consulate in Boston, Swissnex (and Deputy Consul Emil Wyss, in particular), provided enthusiastic and generous support for developing the children's-rights agenda in the direction we suggested.

The conference organizer from the University Committee on Human Rights Studies, Lauren Herman, contributed with flawless organization, obsessive but never oppressive attention to every detail, and meticulous follow through. A successful conference is not a sufficient condition for a good book. I am very grateful to all the contributors to the book—scholars, policy makers, and advocates—for agreeing to suspend their disbelief, join in this new configuration of the concept of child statelessness, and incorporate it into their thinking and writing. Several contributors graciously succumbed to my persistent pleading and agreed to write chapters despite other obligations and commitments. The book is immeasurably richer as a result, and I am grateful for this. Other contributors defied the challenges of pressing advocacy deadlines and travel schedules to carve out time to write at night and on weekends, and again we are the grateful beneficiaries. Securing the contributions of people working in the field rather than in the academy is crucial for the success and credibility of a project such as this. It is not just the wealth of individual ideas and arguments that I am thankful for. Seeing the contributors generously engage with each others' work and agendas has been one of the real pleasures of completing this book. I am also grateful to Clay Morgan and his colleagues at the MIT Press. I could not have hoped for a more supportive and flexible publisher. They agreed to support this unconventional and ambitious volume and provided solutions and encouragement throughout the process. Four anonymous readers suggested excellent changes, and I hope they see the fruits of their labors reflected in the final version of the manuscript. Two research assistants, Beth Maclin and Kelsey Quigley, also provided invaluable support during the editing process. And as usual, I am the immensely fortunate recipient of sustained intellectual challenges from my husband, Homi Bhabha. They have refined my thinking throughout this project and indeed had lasting effects on most areas of my life over the last three decades. Last and probably most, I would like to thank my indefatigable and invaluable research assistant and now colleague, Christina Alfirev, who shepherded the contributors toward deadlines with unfailing tact and tenacity. As one of our contributors remarked, she deserves, in addition to praise and gratitude in abundance, an award for diplomacy.

Jacqueline Bhabha
Cambridge, Massachusetts

1

From Citizen to Migrant: The Scope of Child Statelessness in the Twenty-First Century

Jacqueline Bhabha

The Algerian coast guard rescued on 10 April the corpses of 13 migrants that set sail from the beach of Mers the Hdjadj, in the coast of Oran, in the direction of Spain. "On board were 16 youths, from 17 to 25 years old, and after their shipwreck three of them were still missing."[1]
—A routine Mediterranean press report

Cristina (13) and Violetta (10) gave their fingerprints [to the Italian police implementing compulsory fingerprinting of all Roma including children] shortly before they died. Violetta was upset. She ran away and started crying. She thought the police were coming to take her away. Cristina was angry and scrubbed the ink from her thumb. She understood everything. She knew we were being treated like animals. She died knowing she had no real hope of a better life.
—Mariana, mother of two Roma girls who drowned on an Italian beach while summer beach life resumed around their bodies[2]

Legal identity does not guarantee a good life, but its absence is a serious impediment to it. An absence of legal identity interferes with many fundamental encounters between the individual and the state. It affects the individual's capacity to make claims on the state, and it disrupts the state's ability to plan and provide resources and services to the individual. This problem takes two conceptually distinct forms—the lack of legal identity and the inability to prove the legal identity that one does have. The former, the lack of legal identity, characterizes both *de jure* (or *legally*) *stateless* people (people without the nationality of any state, the literally stateless) and also *de facto stateless* people (people who have a nationality but whose status where they reside is not legal because they are illegal, irregular, or undocumented migrants in their current location). Both these groups lack legal identity. The latter, the inability to prove the legal identity that one has, affects people who are legal citizens but who lack the documents necessary to assert their legitimate claim to state services. These are people whose birth, family affiliation, or connection to society is not registered or otherwise provable. They may, despite their possession of nationality and a legal status, find themselves *effectively stateless*. Together, these three constituencies represent different aspects of twenty-first-century statelessness, a form of disenfranchisement that is familiar to European historians of the twentieth century and yet is distinctive and neglected in its contemporary aspects. As one scholar observes, "It is not easy to reconcile twenty-first-century challenges and problems with twentieth-century resources and nineteenth-century models."[3]

Twenty-first-century statelessness has significant human-rights repercussions for children in today's world, jeopardizing their access to fundamental social protections and entitlements that many take for granted. It can result in dramatic abuses, such as the detention or deportation of very young unaccompanied child migrants,[4] or the acute rights violations against accompanied European Union (EU) citizen children in Italy (fully described later in this volume by Elena Rozzi). But contemporary statelessness also causes more endemic quotidian deprivations, such as the lack of access to education and primary health care of rural migrant children in China[5] (described in Kirsten Di Martino's chapter) and of Rohingya refugee children (noted in Brad K. Blitz's chapter).

Until recently, human-rights scholars, advocates, and policy makers have underestimated the problem of statelessness,[6] ignored its serious effects on children, and completely missed the important and revealing connections between the different types of statelessness just outlined. One of the central arguments of this book is that analyzing key contemporary children's-rights violations in terms of statelessness helps to explain their genesis and suggests clues to their solution. A focus on statelessness draws attention to important but neglected dynamics that generate rightlessness for many different groups of marginalized children.

At first glance, the two categories of stateless children—those without a legal identity (whether *de jure* or *de facto* stateless) and those with a legal identity that they cannot prove (the effectively stateless)—seem radically different, not only conceptually but in practice. One category lacks a legal identity; the other category includes people who cannot provide documentary proof of the legal identity that they do have. One category consists of outsiders, whether foreigners or internal migrants; the other group consists of nationals and locals. One category can, as a matter of law,[7] be forced to leave the place of residence; the other category is immune from such treatment. From a human-rights advocate's perspective, these might seem to be immensely significant differences.

There are also marked divisions from the perspective of scholarship and policy. Detention and deportation are concerns of immigration and children's-rights advocates and legal scholars. Lack of birth registration is a topic for demographers, statisticians, and development economists. Although the links between states' interests in controlling migration and "the development of techniques for uniquely and unambiguously identifying each and every person on the face of the globe"[8] have been commented on,[9] the effects of irregular migration and lack of birth registration on the rights of children have never, to our knowledge, been considered together. So what is the justification for linking them? And why is the topic of statelessness important as an overarching framework for considering the legal and moral claims of very large groups of disadvantaged children?

A *stateless person* is defined in international law as "a person who is *not considered* as a national by any State."[10] This book argues that statelessness has several different contemporary manifestations, with comparable effects on children's access to key human-rights protections. *De jure* or *legal statelessness* is the absence of any nationality—what could be called statelessness *stricto sensu*. Examples of this form of statelessness include Palestinian children (see the chapter by Christina O. Alfirev) and, as discussed below, unregistered children born to Haitian parents in the Dominican Republic or Burmese Rohingya children. *De facto statelessness* is the absence of a legal migration status despite a legal nationality. Examples include undocumented children in the European Union (see chapters by Jyothi Kanics, Luca Bicocchi, and Daniel Senovilla Hernández) or the United States who are nationals of a country other than their country of residence (see chapters by Stephen H. Legomsky and David B. Thronson) and rural Chinese child migrants residing without the requisite *hukou* (permit) in urban conurbations. Finally, we consider *effective statelessness*, which is the inability to prove formal nationality and legal immigration status despite having both. This type of statelessness affects children who are living within their own countries but whose birth has never been registered (see chapters by Bela Hovy and Caroline Vandenabeele) or legally present but unregistered Roma children living in the EU (see the chapter by Elena Rozzi). Any of these types of statelessness (any case where there is an absence of demonstrable legal identity) is potentially devastating for a child because it jeopardizes the child's automatic claim to inclusion by and attention from the state. It is therefore a key indicator of vulnerability, a proxy for problematic access to essential resources, services, and protections. Statelessness in children, we suggest, has profound human-rights repercussions.

exacerbated when routine bureaucratic requirements, such as production of a valid passport to effectuate border crossing, are not complied with. A long-term stateless U.S. resident provides a clear example of the interplay of migration and lack of legal identity documents:

[I] became stateless as a young child when the Soviet Union collapsed. I have been stateless for 17 years. . . . In the former Soviet Union, permanent residency and citizenship documents were issued at the age of 16. I left the Soviet Union when I was only seven. . . . Being stateless is a psychologically crippling condition. I have spent years at a time without access to health care, the right to drive, attend college.[26]

Although the precise mechanisms that generate these obstacles vary from country to country, the general principle is clear. As Caroline Vandenabeele points out, "Identity documentation has a clear and direct link to overseas travel and employment and the opportunities that these bring." There are other close links between the statelessness resulting from irregular migration status and from lack of birth registration. As Luca Bicocchi, Elena Rozzi, and Jyothi Kanics point out in their chapters, children born to irregular migrants are at considerable, perhaps growing risk of statelessness.[27] One reason for this is that access to birthright citizenship is increasingly qualified by conditions relating to length and status of parents' residence,[28] with the result that children born to irregular migrants are less likely to acquire the nationality of their country of birth. Another reason is that the risk of detection and deportation acts as a disincentive to come into contact with officialdom for irregular migrants, including as a disincentive to register their children at birth. As one scholar puts it, "There are many obstacles in the way of ensuring that children born to irregular migrants are registered at birth: problems of law, logistics and attitudes."[29] A compelling example of this dynamic is described in Elena Rozzi's chapter, where she reflects on the circumstances of undocumented Roma children in Italy:

Italian law provides that all undocumented children, simply by virtue of their minority, be issued a residence permit "for minor age," valid until the age of eighteen. However, in practice, this has a very different effect on the two groups of children. Children accompanied by undocumented parents are generally not issued any residence permit because only the parents can make the relevant application (no guardians are appointed for accompanied children). But since undocumented parents risk expulsion if they come into contact with the police, these applications are rarely made.

Children born to undocumented Colombian refugees in Ecuador lose their entitlement to Ecuadorian citizenship by birth for the same reason: their parents fail to register them for fear of deportation.[30]

The lack of birth registration is particularly significant for children of irregular migrants. Not only does it deprive them of access to the nationality of their place of birth, but absence of a birth certificate may also disqualify a child from eligibility for his or her parents' nationality, thus increasing the risk of *de jure* statelessness.[31] Parental failure to register children's birth is not the only reason for this. According to the United High Commissioner for Refugees (UNHCR), "statelessness is often caused by States' deliberate policies not to confer nationality to children born to refugees."[32] These policies do not apply only refugees, one might add. In her chapter, Jyothi Kanics describes the plight of many different groups of migrant children and children of migrants born in Europe who are denied appropriate identity documents. For example, quoting a 2007 U.S. State Department report, she notes that in Greece, even legal immigrants (in addition to significant numbers of undocumented migrants) are denied birth certificates for children born in Greece. If these children are not able to secure their parents' citizenship by descent, then they are likely to become *de jure* stateless.

Beyond the close connection between birth registration and *de jure* statelessness is the much broader link between birth registration and effective statelessness, which may directly affect children's entitlement to economic and social rights. It is worth articulating the links in this process. Birth registration is critical to obtaining a birth certificate with full information about date and place of birth and names of parents. This certificate, in turn, is a key part of the evidence of legal identity. And evidence of legal identity is a common prerequisite to the enjoyment of public services. As a child-rights researcher remarked at a conference: "Lack of a birth certificate places a child outside the community of citizens." [33] Remarkably, given its potentially devastating consequences, this is a commonplace situation. According to the United Nations Children's Fund (UNICEF), 36 percent of all births are not registered, leaving more than 48 million children under age five without a legal identity.[34] Other statistics are equally dramatic: one-third of developing countries have birth registration rates of less than 50 percent, and 55 percent of Sub-Saharan and 63 percent of South Asian children are unregistered children from ethnic or indigenous groups. Internally displaced persons (IDPs), refugees, and orphaned children (including those orphaned by AIDS) are particularly at risk of nonregistration. Children in remote rural areas are more likely to be unregistered than their urban counterparts. In Macedonia, for example, birth registration in the capital is reported to be 99 percent, but in an outlying region it is only 68 percent.[35] Single unmarried mothers in traditional societies are less likely than married mothers to register the birth of their children. The same is true of families that are caught up in armed conflict and civil war.

On the basis of extensive research, UNICEF asserts that there is *a clear link* between birth registration and access to state benefits.[36] The evidence has led UNICEF and nongovernmental organizations (NGOs) such as PLAN International to launch high-profile campaigns calling on governments to promote energetic efforts to increase birth registration. Their argument is that since lack of birth registration is responsible for serious rights deprivations, particularly among the poorest of the poor, promoting registration can be expected to reduce these deprivations. UNICEF has suggested that this is true not only in peacetime but also in societies emerging from war: "Birth registration can play a key role in peace agreements and in the establishment of stable post-conflict transition."[37] If birth registration is the ticket to (or a crucial prerequisite of) access to benefits and services, then this rallying call makes good sense. Analogously, calls for amnesty for undocumented migrants accurately reflect the reality that regular legal status is a crucial ticket for accessing important social and legal benefits and for securing guarantees of permanence within a society.

There certainly are situations that justify UNICEF's emphasis on the importance of birth registration. A recent example is the predicament facing a number of Burmese refugees in India trying to resettle in New Zealand. According to an advocate involved in their case:

The major problem is the fact that they do not have identity documents the New Zealand High Commission would accept—either a birth certificate, passport or the national identity card. . . . All Burmese nationals, however, have the "Family Chart" . . . , a document that is drawn up for all families in Burma, which gives information about the number of people, their age, sex, occupation, address. This document is issued under the seal of the Department of Immigration of the Union of Myanmar. This seems to me to be sufficient if all that the New Zealand High Commission wants to do is to verify the authenticity of the applicant. I am however told that this has not been accepted by the people in the High Commission in Delhi.[38]

But birth registration may not be *the* ticket to legal identity in the way that a regular immigration status is *the* ticket for inclusion for the *de facto* stateless. As Caroline Vandenabeele points out in her chapter in this book: "Many documents can confirm a person's legal identity. . . . an overreliance on birth registration as the sole means for establishing legal identity and as a prerequisite for accessing other rights and protections risks exacerbating poor and vulnerable groups' patterns of exclusion." Unlike the New Zealand authorities in the example just cited, societies may have a range of effective credentialing mechanisms for establishing legal identity. Advocates need to ascertain what these mechanisms are before they insist on the indispensability of birth registration.

As Vandenabeee rightly says, a clear link between birth registration and access to social benefits does not mean a causal link. The link might simply highlight the correlation between a failure to register birth and other factors leading to social disadvantage, such as poverty, illiteracy, or minority status. Drawing on empirical data from Nepal, Bangladesh, and Cambodia, Vandenabeele disentangles the nature of this link, demonstrating complex connections between access to services and identity registration and the multiple credentialing mechanisms in use for establishing legal identity. In her analysis of the right to education in Nepal, she deconstructs access to basic education into various elements: "the narrow sense of being allowed to sit in a classroom when teaching is going on," her research suggests, is "sometimes, but not always, dependent on possession of a birth certificate." But other critical elements of the right to education *are* conditional on registration: "being eligible for government scholarships and free schoolbooks, being allowed to sit for the school-leaving certificate, and having access to higher education are usually conditional on possessing a birth certificate." Those who do not have a birth certificate are effectively stateless for the purposes of these crucial educational entitlements.

Kirsten Di Martino also scrutinizes the underlying causes of the educational handicaps facing citizen children in the developing world—in her case, rural migrants in China. Because they migrate from villages to urban areas and lack the required official permit (*hukuo*), rural children in cities are irregular migrants (albeit nationals) and face some of the same exclusions that *de facto* (noncitizen) stateless children face in other countries. In contrast to the United States (see Stephen H. Legomsky's chapter in this book), access to primary and secondary education in China presents greater obstacles than access to the meritocratic higher-education system: "Expenditures are tilted toward higher-education institutions at the expense of the institutions providing compulsory education" (see Di Martino's chapter in this book). Di Martino reports that according to a 2003 UNICEF survey, 47 percent of migrant children do not enter school at age six, the official school age, and notes that financial problems also bedevil access to public education for these *de facto* stateless Chinese children. Thirty-eight percent of migrant children in Beijing cannot attend public school and have to fall back on lower-quality high-cost alternatives.

Compare this situation in developing countries to the one that confronts irregular migrant children in Europe or undocumented migrant youngsters in the United States—populations that are *de facto* stateless. The similarities are remarkable. A complaint lodged by Defense for Children International against the Netherlands and cited by Jyothi Kanics in her chapter claims that Dutch legislation deprives undocumented child residents of key economic and social rights. In his chapter on undocumented children in the EU, Luca Bicocchi also criticizes the practical failure to protect all children within the jurisdiction equally, despite contrary norms. He contrasts the generally enabling approach of national legislation toward the education of undocumented children (some countries, such as Belgium, make explicit legislative references to the educational rights of undocumented children) with the situation on the ground. His chapter describes multiple examples of practical barriers, including a requirement to produce identification documents before enrolling in school, difficulties paying for books and school transportation, and discrimination against undocumented children demonstrated by a refusal to issue graduation diplomas. The net result is captured by a quotation that he cites from a French NGO: "The simple task of registering in school becomes a kind of war between, on the one side, parents and students, and on the other, the administrative system, the latter of whom has the power to hijack this right."[39] When the state has the power to hijack rights because of the precarious status of the rights holder and when the inevitability of nondiscriminatory access to fundamental social rights is absent, then one is in a condition of statelessness.

Elena Rozzi points out similar difficulties facing undocumented children in Italy who lack legal permission to reside within the country. She cites data that show that in 2006, 20,000 Roma children were estimated to be outside the compulsory school system altogether.[40] This situation was further exacerbated when "In December 2007, the Municipality of Milan issued an ordinance preventing children of irregular migrants from enrolling in kindergarten" (see Rozzi's chapter in this book), a measure that was eventually struck down by the courts.[41] Despite this legal victory, she notes, "undocumented children are often not accepted outside the compulsory school system, particularly in vocational training courses."[42] Far from being legally stateless, however, some of these Roma children are Italian and some are of Romanian nationality and citizens of the EU. As a matter of European community law, all nationals of EU member states are EU citizens. This common citizenship raises the expectation of equal treatment regardless of specific member-state citizenship at least in theory or maybe as a future aspiration.[43] Indeed, EU citizenship was developed to incorporate notions of choice and membership that are cardinal principles of liberal political theory. In practice, however, the potential of a radically inclusive status has yet to be realized. It has eluded undocumented Roma children in Italy, a sobering demonstration of the complex relationship between politically driven frameworks for inclusion and bureaucratically controlled practical mechanisms that translate those structures into human realities.

The chasm between general principles of inclusion and practical rights is also illustrated by the situation in the United States, particularly the elusiveness of comprehensive educational entitlements for *de facto* stateless populations, such as children with irregular immigration status. Despite a landmark U.S. Supreme Court decision a quarter century ago guaranteeing the right to free elementary and secondary education for all children in the United States, irrespective of their immigration status or nationality,[44] the culmination of an educational experience (college or university education) remains elusive for undocumented populations. Again, it is generally not the case that these would-be students are legally barred from attending tertiary educational institutions. Instead, practical barriers, particularly financial ones, constitute the primary impediment. This is not accidental. As Stephen H. Legomsky points out in his chapter in this volume:

These barriers are not merely a result of their frequently low family income. They are also a product of deliberate policy decisions enshrined in law. Two of these barriers are particularly noteworthy. First, undocumented students are legally ineligible for all federal and state educational financial aid. Second, the laws of at least forty states require undocumented students who attend public postsecondary educational institutions to pay tuition at the higher rate reserved for nonstate residents.

Given the high cost of U.S. higher education, these financial hurdles act as effective bars to access. So *de facto* stateless and effectively stateless children face similar educational hurdles, whether they are undocumented populations in the United States, irregular migrant children in Europe, or unregistered children in Nepal. Despite differences in formal nationality or immigration status, the access of these diverse populations to fundamental social rights is similarly flawed: they lack the effective protection of a state.

De jure or legally stateless populations—those without any nationality at all—face similar handicaps across a range of jurisdictions. Absence of state protection is as devastating for the legally stateless, despite international legal measures to combat this, as it is for *de facto* or effectively stateless populations who are not covered by international legislation on statelessness. In her chapter in this volume, Christina O. Alfirev provides a compelling account of the hurdles that confront children born to Israeli Palestinians. Like their parents, they face complex legal barriers to the most fundamental of rights, starting with access to a legal identity. As Alfirev points out, many members of this community are presented with a harsh choice. They can either exercise their right of residence in their home country at the expense of family unity with immediate relatives disqualified from joining them, or they can enjoy the right to family life at the price of exile from their country. Alfirev, therefore concludes that "Israel's nationality laws, taken together, have a harmful effect on Palestinian children."

Other *de jure* stateless populations also face difficulties that recall those described for the *de facto* stateless. Brad K. Blitz comments on this at some length in his chapter, citing the position of the Rohingya as a particularly acute example of the perils of legal statelessness. A *de jure* stateless Kuwaiti Bidun, for example, describes a situation identical to that documented by Legomsky: "I was one of the lucky few to finish high school, but my effort was really in vain because I'm not allowed to attend Kuwait University."[45] Syrian Kurds present another example of the exclusionary impact of *de jure* statelessness. Classified by law as *Ajanibi* (foreigner), they are subject to persistent discrimination. A recent report by Refugees International cites a touching first-person account:

As a stateless Kurd, I was seen as a *persona non grata* because I was an outsider in the eyes of the Syrian authorities. When I traveled from my hometown to Damascus for study, Syrian security officers stopped vehicles on the highway asking for IDs. The moment they saw my "Foreigners" red ID, they detained me so long that I missed the bus. At that point, I was at their mercy. They slapped and interrogated me. There is nothing worse than to be classified as a "Foreigner" in one's country of birth. It really is a catastrophe.[46]

Another frequently cited example is the situation of the Haitian population in the Dominican Republic. Though the Dominican Republic has a *jus soli* system of nationality attribution (birthright citizenship), the state operates an arbitrary and discriminatory rule that excludes children of Haitians residing in the country from nationality because their parents are held to be "in transit" and therefore, under a recently passed law, "illegal."[47] The sentiment behind this discriminatory law was pithily summarized by Manuel Polanco, head of the Dominican Army: "An illegal person cannot produce a legal person."[48] As a result, hundreds of thousands of children born in the Dominican Republic to long-settled Haitian families find themselves legally stateless, relegated to second-class status with respect to a range of services, benefits, and documentary protection. Educational access is problematic, too, just as it is for the *de facto* and effectively stateless populations discussed earlier:

As well as the risk of expulsion, Dominican children of Haitian descent face barriers when they try to obtain a birth certificate from the Civil Registrar Office. Without a birth certificate (the identification document for minors), they are unable to study beyond primary level.[49]

To summarize the reasoning so far: A central argument of this book is that the millions whose births have never been registered (the effectively stateless) and the millions who have an irregular, illegal immigration status (the *de facto* stateless) or who are without any nationality (the *de jure* or legally stateless) challenge the professed liberal and democratic commitment to nondiscrimination and social equality in fundamental and similar ways. Despite the optimistic rhetoric of universal rights proclaimed in international legal instruments and despite the best efforts of human-rights advocates, international jurists, and civil society organizations, claims for the enjoyment of human citizenship and its associated benefits are increasingly mediated by proof of legal identity, nationality, or immigration status, and as Hannah Arendt first noted over half a century ago, "bare personhood" does not suffice for this purpose. The absence of demonstrable legal identity is a grave handicap in today's world.

But this book makes an additional claim that, to our knowledge, has never been directly and comprehensively addressed. Statelessness is a particularly important social and political *child-rights issue* because children are peculiarly dependent on states. There are two aspects to this dependency: all children depend on states for basic services, and many children depend on states when their families fail them.

First, children are inherently dependent on states for crucial aspects of their lives. Educational access has already been discussed. But several chapters in this book show that children without demonstrable legal identity may also be excluded from other state services that are essential for survival—primary health care and shelter, for example. Elena Rozzi quotes a poignant vignette about a Romanian Roma twelve-year-old in Italy that captures the exclusionary essence of statelessness:

Rebecca is a Romanian girl of the Roma ethnic group, and she has spent half of her life out on the street. She has slept in a van, in a makeshift shelter, and on the floor. On some days, she has begged on the streets of Spain and Italy with her parents. At other times, she has seen her makeshift shelter destroyed. She has been attacked by Italian police officers. She listened (hiding under a blanket) as her father was beaten up after he attempted to defend her. She has seen babies and children die due to a lack of medicines. She shared the fear of the Roma people fleeing from Ponticelli (Naples) when their camp was set fire to. . . . The family had not slept under a proper roof for five years. "In Romania, we had a home, but we had nothing to eat," explains Rebecca. "We ate thanks to charity from our neighbors. Then in Milan, my parents were unable to find work," she continues, "and we had to go out and beg."[50]

Destitution and homelessness are rights violations that stateless children encounter repeatedly, as Brad K. Blitz also illustrates in his chapter. But some stateless children face another serious human-rights violation—the deprivation of the right to family unity. In her chapter, Jyothi Kanics notes the perverse separation of *de facto* stateless children from their parents, merely because of the parents' destitution or immigration problems, a practice that renders the children "social orphans."[51] She questions the legitimacy of these psychologically damaging forced separations of children, including very young children, from their parents. Measures such as these appear to violate one of the obligations of the Convention on the Rights of the Child (CRC)—the article prohibiting the separation of child from parents unless the separation is deemed "necessary for the best interests of the child."[52] Despite their possession of a nationality, these children are effectively in the same position of statelessness as the Palestinian children described by Alfirev, who also encounter grave threats to the right to family unity.

There is a second aspect to children's dependency on states that makes statelessness particularly devastating for children. Children rely on the state for surrogate protection when the family—their primary source of protection—fails them. Without demonstrable legal identity, however, this insurance against social hazards is much more elusive because the chances of effective state engagement with the child are compromised. Luca Bicocchi reports on the widespread gap in European countries between a theoretical entitlement to education irrespective of legal status and extensive practical barriers for unaccompanied and irregular child migrants in access on the ground (see Bicocchi's chapter in this book). Another disturbing and clear illustration of the potential for discrimination is the situation in Ireland, described by Jyothi Kanics: not only are undocumented children who are unaccompanied or separated from their parents frequently detained, but even when they are placed in the custody of child welfare authorities, the care that they receive is inferior to that provided to citizen children (see Kanics's chapter in this book). The same is true elsewhere. In the United Kingdom, according to material cited by Bicocchi, *de facto* stateless children have access to medical care only in emergencies (see Bicocchi's chapter in this book).

It is worth listening to some first-person accounts of this situation from separated children. An unauthorized Romanian fifteen-year-old living rough in Paris had this to say: "It was eleven at night. Four police cars came after us. I did eighteen hours of detention. They don't touch your face. They beat you in the ribs, on the legs, the feet, everywhere."[53] Meanwhile, in the United Kingdom, a sixteen-year-old unaccompanied asylum seeker from Chad told this disturbing story:

[I] claimed asylum on a Friday, and the Asylum Screening Unit in Croydon told [me] that they did not believe that [I] was a child. It referred [me] to the Refugee Council's Children's Panel in Brixton. The Panel referred [me] on to the local social services department, who had closed their offices by the time [I] arrived there. [I] returned to the Refugee Council to discover that it too was closed. [I] spent the weekend living on the street.[54]

The problem is not confined to northern Europe. In his chapter, Daniel Senovilla Hernández cites an official UN report on Spain's treatment of undocumented migrant children who are facing expulsion back to their country of origin against their wishes—*reunification*. The report illustrates what it is like to be an unaccompanied or separated child without a state and subject to rights violations inflicted by both the Spanish and Moroccan governments. Writing in 2004, the UN High Commission for Human Rights had this to say:

The Special Rapporteur believes that because of the way in which some family "reunifications" have been carried out, allegedly leaving the minor in the hands of the Moroccan police without the presence of his family or the social services, these reunifications are interpreted [by the children] as expulsions. [M]any "reunited" minors return to Spain and some speak of ill-treatment by the Moroccan police.[55]

All these groups of children were denied state protection and shelter and had no alternative provider and no immediate legal recourse. Although the children were not legally stateless, they could not rely on any authority to make their best interests a primary consideration during encounters with the state. By contrast with these *de facto* stateless children, citizen children held in arbitrary detention or denied shelter would have had legally enforceable claims to the protection of social welfare agencies.[56]

Since the invention of childhood[57] as a distinct phase of human life, society has accepted an obligation to protect the youngest members of its population. This book hopes to demonstrate that stateless children have a peculiarly strong claim to that public protection. Children, particularly those who are unaccompanied or separated, are also vulnerable to the coercive power of the state, especially when the social position they occupy is irregular and gives him the status of outsiders. Small children who are smuggled across a border to join undocumented relatives or who are trafficked by exploiters do not know who can help them. Older children who smuggle themselves across borders to secure a livelihood (legal or illegal) and unregistered children who are denied legal identity and therefore travel documents find themselves in a dangerous limbo—because they do not exist as persons before the law. But in addition to the general vulnerability that they share with similarly situated stateless adults is the acute need that comes from deprivation of key elements of childhood—a consistent education, a secure home, and a supportive family and community. This makes them peculiarly defenseless.

Like all children, stateless children are vulnerable and dependent, but they have the added handicaps that come from legal and social disenfranchisement. Unlike citizen or otherwise legal children, their claim to protection as minors is in tension with their excludability as outsiders. In this sense, their membership in the broader community of citizens, including noncitizen residents and others legally present on the territory, is always marginal and precarious. The reaction of a Mexican child trying to cross into the United States through the Arizona desert illustrates the emotional correlate of that legal limbo: "My first impression when I ran into the officials [as I was crossing the border] was that they thought I had robbed a bank or was a criminal. They yelled at me not to move, and that made me very nervous. We were questioned individually."[58] Some state practices violate children's rights in the opposite way—by failing to question them in detail and by denying them a right to a hearing. To cite Senovilla Hernández: "Some children are returned without even an attempt by the authorities to locate their family. Others do not receive a hearing or are never informed of the repatriation process."[59]

What is more, repatriation techniques can be brutal. Senovilla Hernández writes:

Sometimes police forces come to a reception center in the middle of the night and pull a child out of bed and drive the child directly to the airport without allowing the child to take his or her personal belongings. Other children living in the center witness these practices, and the threat of being the next victim causes them extreme stress and mistrust. At other times, police have come to schools or vocational training centers, taken children from their lessons, and treated them as delinquents in front of their colleagues.[60]

The long waiting time to obtain a residence permit and "the confiscation of the children's passports [while they are in state custody] are other common forms of mistreatment" (see Senovilla's chapter in this book). Although lack of a regular migration status is not a criminal offense, statelessness renders these children liable to be treated as delinquents who are outside the regulatory framework of the juvenile justice system. This presents particular risks for the children implicated.

Another tension aggravates the conflict between states' child-protection obligations and their border-control or national-security responsibilities. Children, particularly young children, are not held to be responsible for the decisions that have led to their irregular status, but punitive approaches to their parents, who are considered culpable (for having agreed to their being trafficked, for having brought them in illegally, or for having given birth to them while undocumented) directly affect the children. A case in point is the detention of accompanied migrant children pending deportation of families, a phenomenon that has in recent years been on the rise in the United States. Some immigrant family-detention policies are so harsh that they have attracted repeated public criticism. A privately run detention center, the T. Don Hutto Residential Center in Taylor, Texas, had such poor living conditions for its inmate families that it became the object of litigation: "The children were dressed in prison garb like their parents. . . . The only children who weren't wearing prison clothing were the infants because they couldn't find prison uniforms small enough." According to the University of Texas School of Law's Immigration Clinic, "Families were counted seven times a day and children spent most of their time inside prison cells."[61] These practices were discontinued as a result of the lawsuit.

The perverse transfer of culpability from adult to child is not limited to situations where children are *de jure* or *de facto* stateless. It also occurs in situations of effective statelessness when children are citizens or legal residents of the country they are in although their parents are not. Because of the parents' irregular status, children are denied fundamental rights. The *de facto* statelessness of the parents is transferred to the children, rendering their citizenship ineffective as a channel to rights. David B. Thronson provides a compelling illustration of this situation in his chapter, demonstrating that U.S. citizen children can become effectively stateless by being denied the right to enjoy security of residence in their country with their parents. As he says: "the very connection between children and parents that family law works to create and protect can result in a diminished connection between children and state as a variety of formal and informal barriers assimilate them to the status of noncitizen." He describes the harsh rules that apply to these so-called mixed-status families in the U.S. context to deprive citizen children of the right to family unity, as if it were natural or inevitable that children's citizenship would have no effect on parents' status. But there is nothing inevitable about this. European law, for example, approaches the problem differently.[62] The European Court of Justice (ECJ) has ruled in favor of a citizen child's right to use her Irish nationality to secure residence rights for her mother, even if—as in the case—that nationality had been acquired solely for this purpose.[63] By contrast, Thronson shows that "the devaluation of children and their interests in immigration law often operates to deny U.S. citizen children in mixed-status families (that is, families in which all family members do not share the same immigration or citizenship status) the full social benefits of citizenship" (see Thronson's chapter in this book).

The noncitizen parent's outsider position effectively cancels out the child's citizenship status. The state here not only fails to protect children from harm but actively provokes the hardships that they are subjected to. Far from being an authority to which these children can turn for enforcement of their rights, the state is a source of oppression. These children therefore, like *de jure* or *de facto* stateless children, lack a state that they can rely on, a state that acts in their best interests.

But why does this occur? Given all its devastating consequences, why is statelessness among children, even among legal or citizen children, pervasive? Many have suggested a simple explanation—invisibility. Children are stateless in many cases because they are not seen and therefore their needs are not attended to. A typical account is the following: "Unregistered children are ignored by statistics and neglected by city and state planners. They are *invisible* when policy decisions and budgetary choices are made."[64] The claim is that invisibility is not just the consequence of statelessness, although it certainly is that. Failure to register birth can obliterate the child's civic existence, denying the child the fundamental right to be "a person before the law," a sure route to invisibility in relation to officialdom. Avoidance of state authorities because of undocumented status, as Bicocchi observes, can literally prevent children from being seen by the social service providers they need. But the dominant explanation is that invisibility is also *the cause* of the persistence of the problem. In other words, it is claimed that the pervasive reality of child statelessness is the product of oversight or myopia[65] on the part of policy makers—what could be called *reverse ageism* or *adult centrism.* Using phrases like *invisibility, hiddenness, slipping between the cracks,* and *void,*[66] it has been suggested that states have innocently overlooked the problems of migrant children and their correlative duties because of a dual perception lacuna: for issues of migration, they have focused on adults, and for issues of child welfare, they have focused on citizens. The implication is that states are well intentioned in their concern for and commitment to migrant children but have been incompetent, unperceptive, unprepared. Adults make policy and in the process ignore or overlook the interests of children, especially when these are not related to other interests they are pursuing. UNICEF, for example, suggests that "[t]he value of birth registration as a fundamental human right is often *overlooked* due to the continuing lack of awareness that registration is a critical measure."[67] Despite the somewhat tautological nature of this explanation (the value of birth registration is overlooked because the value of birth registration is overlooked), there are reasons for its popularity. If the consequences of nonregistration are invisible, by definition they are not on the political map, and so they do not lead to political pressure for reform. If the "victims" of nonregistration have no legal identity, they are in no position to exert political pressure. As Saudamini Siegrist pithily puts it, "a child who is not counted does not count."[68]

The same argument that has been used to explain the problems facing the unregistered (the effectively stateless) that Caroline Vandenabeele explores (invisibility causes lack of rights) is also used to account for the destitution and lack of protection of irregular child migrants (the *de facto* stateless) (invisibility causes lack of rights). The explanation implies that increasing visibility and recognition of their presence would bring with it improved access to protection. Greater visibility, it is claimed, would produce more engagement with these children's distinctive situation. This in turn would lead to status enhancements, which would reduce the vulnerability to exclusion and repression.

The strategy of much recent advocacy has been driven by this perspective. It has focused on making the problems of effectively and *de facto* stateless children visible and on drawing attention to their invidious exclusion and deprivation—by trying to bring them into the same legal and institutional framework as child citizens (for example, demands for access to education, health care, and shelter), as registered children (such as campaigns for increasing access to documentary proof of legal identity), and as legal child migrants (for example, demands for access to permanent residence, to adequate legal representation, and to protection from detention). Has the strategy been successful? Have advocates been able to reap human-rights yields from publicity and greater social and political awareness of the circumstances of these stateless children? Is their analysis of the problem correct?

Some continue to suggest that invisibility is the root of the problem of rights exclusion for stateless children. As Elena Rozzi discusses in her chapter, Silvio Berlusconi, the current prime minister of Italy and head of one of the most xenophobic contemporary European governments, recently claimed that his policy of mandatory fingerprinting of all Roma in Italy, including children, did not constitute a flagrant violation of human rights but was a means for tackling invisibility, a justifiable social-planning measure. Accused of providing ammunition for blatantly discriminatory mass state deportations of legal EU migrants and violating EU principles of social integration, the Italian premier replied: "We also need to know who these [Roma] children are to guarantee that they can go to school. What we are doing is defending the right [of children] to go to school."[69]

But recent developments raise several questions regarding the invisibility thesis. First, how convincing is it given current political and legal realities? With the Inter American Court's ruling about Haitian and Dominican children,[70] the May 2008 anti-Roma pogroms and subsequent legislative developments in Italy,[71] the resurgence of aggressive anti-immigrant policies in France,[72] and the recent raids on undocumented migrant families in the United States,[73] can we really argue that the legal problems of child migrants or unregistered children are caused by their invisibility? Haven't they more and more been catapulted into the headlines?[74] The condition of stateless children, particularly *de facto* stateless child migrants, is an increasingly central preoccupation of less instantaneous or journalistic social reflection, too, as witnessed by contemporary cultural work in theater, art, and film.[75] Not since the Elian Gonzalez saga has public attention been this focused on the problems raised for and by this section of our society. But something is different this time. The simple image of child innocence captured by pictures of the photogenic five-year-old Cuban Elian Gonzalez rescued from the waves or of tearful child detainees with handcuffs falling off their tiny wrists now shares the space with a more complex and threatening portrait of the stateless but pubescent Palestinian suicide bomber, the disenfranchised but evil Roma teenage child snatcher, the marginalized but lethal British adolescent Islamic jihadist, the disadvantaged but antisocial Hispanic tattoo-covered gang member, and lurking behind these images the omnipresent young illegal other.

There is a second problem with the invisibility thesis. Is its empirical claim accurate? Turning from public attention to quantitative information, it is not clear that accessing data about *de jure* stateless populations really is as elusive as sometimes suggested. In his chapter in this volume, Bela Hovy illustrates various strategies, using population census information, for capturing levels, trends, and basic characteristics of stateless persons, including children. He suggests that available data are underutilized rather than nonexistent, demonstrating a failure of political will rather than of raw material. In other words, we do not need to wait for more comprehensive and reliable census systems or better state overview of legally stateless communities to generate data for policy makers who are committed to providing services to legally stateless children. And for *de facto* and effectively stateless populations, similar doubts arise. Creative statistical analysis and alternative information gathering techniques can already generate data on undocumented and unregistered populations that could justify economic and social rights access that are sorely lacking.

The authors of this book generally disagree with the invisibility thesis as an explanation for children's statelessness and their resulting lack of access to rights.[76] We argue that children do not *in the main* end up without a state by accident or oversight. These factors may account for some problems of *de facto* stateless children—for example, the failure to establish mechanisms for child guardianship for the unaccompanied migrant children described in Jyothi Kanics's chapter, where citizen children would have this protection. But invisibility fails to capture the more complex dynamics that are in play for many others groups of stateless children. After they are identified as victims of trafficking, trafficked children without legal immigration status (*de facto* stateless) are not as a rule considered for forms of long-term protection such as asylum but instead tend to be repatriated "home," even where home is a place where retrafficking is likely and caring family is nonexistent. This policy is driven by immigration control considerations and is not an approach that is stymied by lack of information.[77] Again, undocumented migrant children who are associated with gangs or forms of petty delinquency or antisocial behavior *who enter the asylum process* are routinely excluded from asylum protection (they never lose their *de facto* stateless status), irrespective of the evidence of serious risk presented.[78] These children's vulnerability and needs are not hidden. We see them: many groups of professionals (detention facility staff, immigration officials, adjudicators, and social workers) come into contact with them.

As a general explanation, it does not seem accurate to say that stateless children are invisible. A better explanation is that we (policy makers and administrators) see but are torn over how to act. We are ambivalent. The pressure to protect the vulnerable child is in ongoing tension with the drive to punish and exclude the young tribal, rural, or ethnic outsider, the threatening juvenile, or the dangerous young terrorist. Rather than seeing them as vulnerable children in need of protection on a continuum with our children, we tend to view them as disruptive juvenile outsiders who are in need of discipline and punishment—young adults in essence if not in age. Accordingly, we fail to engage effectively with their manifest problems. States' failure to adequately address the needs of these stateless children arises out of a cognitive, not a perception, deficit: we see, but we do not have a clear strategy for acting. We legislate the children's right to public education and health care irrespective of their legal status, but at the same time we erect practical obstacles preventing access to these services—demanding documents, proof of residence, and social ties. We accept obligations to protect the children from exploitation and abuse, creating—in our legislative chambers and international congresses—antitrafficking visa protections for them and criminal sanctions for their exploiters. But on the ground, at the borders, on the streets, and in the police stations, we blame them for the risks they pose to our social fabric and look for ways of removing them from circulation in our societies.

Children who are stateless end up without a state for a reason: they are considered dispensable, undeserving, threatening, or dangerous. Insofar as their rights conflict with government priorities (whether immigration control, the enforcement of national security, majoritarian dominance, or responsiveness to xenophobic public opinion), they are placed in disenfranchised legal or *de facto* situations. Daniel Senovilla Hernández makes a strong case illustrating this point. In his chapter in this book, discussing the situation of *de facto* statelessness in Spain, he writes:

For over a decade, national and regional authorities in Spain have chosen to return migrant children to their home country in preference to other options. Return to the country of origin is viewed as the best durable solution to the situation of unaccompanied and separated children and has been used to justify deterrent policies and practices targeted at potential new migrants to Spain.

In three summer months in 2001, the Spanish authorities are reported to have carried out expulsions of at least thirty-two *de facto* stateless, unaccompanied children from Spain to Melilla, the Spanish enclave on the northern coast of Morocco.[79] This policy, which contradicts Spain's obligations under the CRC to consider the child's best interests prior to the implementation of its policies, has attracted international criticism. For example, a 2002 observation by the UN Committee on the Rights of the Child, quoted by Senovilla Hernández, expresses concern "at reports of summary expulsions of children without ensuring that they are effectively returned to family or social welfare agencies in their country of origin."[80]

It is not just migrant children who are the targets of oppressive or negligent government procedures. Citizen children, too, can be targeted for exclusion from protection because of government policy. Kirsten Di Martino illustrates the mechanism in relation to the Chinese context, showing how invisibility is actively generated. She writes: "Many [rural child migrants] are not registered in their new place of residence and remain invisible to the local authorities as there is no requirement to collect data and register children under sixteen years of age in their new place of residence" (see Di Martino's chapter in this book). This is not a real but a manufactured invisibility—a product of the decision to ignore the migrant children in cities by not collecting relevant data on them. Because the children are not registered, they lack the requisite *hukuo*, or legal permission to reside where they are. As we have seen, this has serious consequences for education, shelter, and access to medical care. It places the children outside the community of citizens. This exclusion reflects government opposition to the migration of children to the cities, just as the Spanish government's expulsion policy reflects its immigration-control agenda.

Invisibility is not the *cause* of child statelessness but the *result* of state strategy toward particular groups of children. This is demonstrated by the evidence just cited of intentional state conduct that deprives children of rights, surely caused by acknowledging and not ignoring their presence. It is also demonstrated by the opposite situation—by state conduct that accords children rights despite their lack of birth registration or other identity qualifications. So where there is no political agenda to exclude or penalize particular groups of children, then legal invisibility per se does not automatically result in rights denial. Instead, creative solutions around it are found. For example, in the case of unregistered majority ethnic children, Caroline Vandenabeele shows that the simple lack of birth-registration documents leads not to effective statelessness but to the substitution of alternative credentialing mechanisms: "In Bangladesh, a statement by a local official who knows a child's family may be enough, in some locations, to enroll a child in school. In Nepal, traditional Hindu religious documents (such as astrologic charts that note the time and place of birth) have been used to establish age and thus to allow access to basic education" (see Vandenabeele's chapter in this book). Conversely, formal citizenship alone does not guarantee rights enjoyment, as the situation of EU citizen Roma children in Italy today demonstrates.

The larger point here is that effective rights access does not flow simply from purely formal solutions. The gap between legislation and practice in Spain, for example (described in Senovilla Hernández's chapter) illustrates that clearly. Practical effects on individual lives and on state policy are the product of complex negotiations and moves implicating norms and procedures, legislators, judges, and, probably most important of all, members of the executive, particularly those working at the coal face. As has been pointed out: "Purely formal solutions . . . might reduce the number of stateless persons but not the number of unprotected persons. They might lead to a shifting from statelessness *de jure* to statelessness *de facto*."[81]

For children, it is not simply lack of a set of documents that produces statelessness. Rather, the obstacle to rights realization is a more complex absence of a legal identity, however caused. An additional point needs to be made. Just as invisibility may not cause statelessness, so visibility may not guarantee enfranchised citizenship. States require identity documentation to develop their economic and social policies. But the state's monopolistic role in documenting its inhabitants' presence also provides an opportunity for surveillance and control that may particularly endanger some groups of children. Undocumented child migrants trying to escape *la migra* know this well. There is a long history to this darker side of state investment in identity documentation. As Simon Szreter argues in his chapter, state- rather than individual-serving functions and Foucaultian control rather than Fabian provision of services were the primary reasons behind early state identification projects:

Systems for recording the existence of persons have existed throughout history for a number of reasons, the most well-known being military and tax-related censuses. These include the census taken over two thousand years ago by the Roman occupiers of what is today Israel and the census in operation in the

Andean empire of the Incas when the Spanish arrived there.[82] This kind of registration was conducted for purposes of state or imperial administration.

In fact, as Szreter demonstrates, surveillance often gave way to more oppressive state conduct, which directly depended on states' abilities to document the population under their jurisdiction:

The European imperial powers, motivated by colonizing projects of economic extraction and political subjugation, created a diverse range of registration systems . . . often for labor-regulation purposes. This was also true of the tsarist empire in continental Russia, which wished to regulate the geographical movement of laborers without granting them full citizenship rights.

Herein lies one of the central dilemmas of social-justice advocacy today. For all the talk of globalization and regional integration, the state remains the key dispenser of the means to rights realization (hence the crucial significance of identity registration) and the key dispenser of the means to rights repression (hence the perils of excessive surveillance). James Scott famously argued that "seeing like a state" is a mixed blessing that the human-rights movement advocates at its peril.[83] By calling for more engagement, one is also opening oneself up to more scrutiny. Would more data on China's migrant children in major cities enhance their access to public education, or would it increase the likelihood of government sanctions, including perhaps expulsion? Bela Hovy suggests that governments frequently fail to collect data on migrant populations consistently but that even when they have adequate data, they "may use indicators that are not well suited for protection purposes" (see Hovy's chapter in this book).

Human-rights and child-migrant advocates who insist on the importance of legal identity documentation have to make the sometimes perilous assumption that the populations they serve are going to be advantaged by greater state engagement with and scrutiny of their lives. This may be relatively unproblematic for effectively stateless child populations, minorities, or marginalized ethnic groups in urgent need of educational and health services, particularly in societies that still have rudimentary systems of data storage and recovery. But in developed societies, the risks may be substantial. Even mainstream citizens who have perfectly straightforward claims to citizenship and legal status are wary of the risks of "privacy invasion"—as is evident in the heated debate about mandatory identity cards. As one scholar comments: "as ID cards become ubiquitous, a *de facto* necessity even when not required *de jure*, the card becomes the visible instantiation of a large, otherwise unseen, set of databases. If each use of the card also creates a data trail, the resulting profile becomes an ongoing temptation to both ordinary and predictive profiling."[84] For *de jure* and *de facto* stateless children, who are noncitizens more likely to be exposed to the harsh and repressive than the protective side of the controlling state, calls for greater visibility by government presuppose inclusive and pro-immigrant political climates, which are currently not much in evidence.

Difference can elicit control and repression. The complex and dual state role is nowhere more evident than in the case of stateless children. Reference has already been made to the dangers lurking behind the seemingly well intentioned call for mandatory fingerprinting of Roma children by the Berlusconi government in Italy. David B. Thronson describes the traumatic effects that immigration raids designed to identify illegal aliens have had on immigrant communities, including citizen children in the United States over the past few years. Citing a recent report, he writes in his chapter in this book:

Mass immigration raids cause "crisis scenarios in terms of the care arrangements for the hundreds of children who temporarily lose their parents." . . . [Some] families have hidden "in their basements or closets for days."

One of the most pervasive uses of procedures to establish legal identity is age determination—the process by which state authorities purport to establish the age of children who arrive without acceptable[85] identity documents. Whatever the situation on the ground, as a matter of law children are usually in a more privileged position than their adult counterparts in detention, deportation, and other harsh aspects of state migration-control policy. So there is at least a theoretical benefit to be derived from being classified a minor by the authorities. For this reason, establishing a distinction between a seventeen-year-old and an eighteen-year-old can be a critical but also a vexed issue for stateless children. Being wrongly classified as an adult can result in months or even years of detention pending determination of a claim to asylum or some other legal immigration status (see Daniel Senovilla Hernández's chapter in this volume). It can also increase the chances of summary removal without access to legal representation, social services intervention, or any scrutiny of best-interest considerations.[86] Disputes about age can even undermine a child's credibility as a truthful witness if in the process of being questioned to establish age, the child provides seemingly inconsistent answers. The protective potential of identity determination may thus turn into a repressive instrument.

Large numbers of *de facto* stateless children are affected by age-determination procedures. A recent study of unaccompanied and separated children seeking asylum in the United Kingdom noted that in 2004, 37 percent of child applicants had their cases age disputed. In one council, about 50 percent of those age disputed were eventually found to be children. Being "age disputed" has serious consequences.[87] A child who was denied welfare services until the authorities secured medical confirmation of her age commented:

Social services treated me like a dog —they didn't ask me any questions at the beginning because they wouldn't bother with it because the Home Office [the authority responsible for Immigration] said I was not under 18. They just told me to go away. I was so sad.[88]

Many immigration destination states use medically unconvincing methods to ascertain the accurate age of undocumented migrants suspected of falsely claiming to be children. This methodology is a contested issue between immigration authorities and child advocates. For the authorities, scientific tests provide black and white answers that are welcome for implementing the sharp legal distinction between who is and who is not a child. For the medical and child-welfare community, current practices are inappropriate and flawed. As the British Royal College of Paediatrics and Child Health noted: "an age determination is extremely difficult to do with certainty, and no single approach to this can be relied on. Moreover, for young people aged 15 to18, it is even less possible to be certain about age. "Age determination is an inexact science and the margin of error can sometimes be as much as 5 years either side [and] estimates of a child's physical age from his or her dental development are accurate [only] to within + or − 2 years for 95 percent of the population."[89] The Royal College therefore recommended a holistic approach to age assessment rather than one based on a single test such as a dental or shoulder or wrist X-ray. Yet single-procedure age-determination tests are still widely used, often with deleterious results.

Birth certificates or other identity-documentation techniques have a role to play in facilitating accurate age determination. But if the political climate is one of mistrust or xenophobia, the value of even genuine birth certificates can be undermined. Advocates report frequent cases where immigration authorities prejudicially assume that all documents from certain countries are forgeries.[90] This complex balance— between the protective role of identity documentation as a ticket to social benefits and its repressive role as an instrument of surveillance and exclusion—

therefore needs to be carefully measured and assessed. That is the task this book sets itself.

Conclusion

This book investigates the paradox that although children's rights are widely upheld in theory irrespective of a child's status, access to these rights in practice is uncertain and conditional on proof of legal identity. Simple visibility will not solve the problem. As others have also concluded, we need a new twenty-first-century notion of citizenship that reconceptualizes the ticket to full entry into the community:

Upholding the principle of democratic inclusion and placing political members on a more egalitarian plateau in the new millennium may . . . require . . . a willingness to explore new ways of articulating the alliance between citizenship and democracy.[91]

Indeed, our critique suggests a radical rethinking of mainstream advocacy strategy regarding *de jure*, *de facto*, and effectively stateless children. In David B. Thronson's chapter, for example, the denial of rights to citizen children—whether through raids on immigrant workplaces or through court decisions regarding deportation appeals—is shown not to be accidental or a result of oversight. It is a product of state policy. Similarly, Elena Rozzi's description of the brutal policies of the Italian state toward Roma children does not suggest ignorance about the problem but rather a determined policy. We suggest that children's rights urgently need to be brought into the flourishing discussion over citizenship and its boundaries. In this book, we propose a meticulous and empirically grounded deconstruction of the concepts of citizenship and legal identity as they apply to children. Our hope is that—through an examination of the meaning of citizenship for children and their access to its benefits—we can clarify why in an age when children's rights are vaunted[92] they are also flaunted and we can begin to develop corrective strategies.

In a xenophobic climate with economic uncertainty and political polarization, visibility may be counterproductive. We therefore propose a more complex approach that does not presume universal sympathy toward stateless children but rather takes realistic note of the widespread ambivalence toward this group. Policy makers and advocates need to be equipped to tackle the complex obstacles to rights enforcement with cogency. Why should undocumented, "illegal"children have a right to free public education? Why should irregular migrant children not be promptly repatriated to their homes abroad? Why should populations that do not comply with birth-registration requirements be assisted with alternative forms of certification? Why should children of irregular migrants not accompany their parents when they are deported? The answers and the political clout to implement them require engagement with two factors that complicate the simple protection mandate—first, the suspicion and hostility toward stateless populations including (and sometimes particularly) children and second, the realization that protection must be complemented with respect, including respect for different, unorthodox, challenging solutions.

Elements of this more complex approach to child statelessness are set out in various chapters. They include detailed empirical analyses of country-specific situations to explain the genesis and effects of child statelessness. There are, for example, significant legal and political differences driving the circumstances of *de facto* stateless children in Spain (Daniel Senovilla Hernández 's chapter), in Italy (Elena Rozzi's chapter), and in other EU member states (Luca Bicocchi's chapter). So, too, the modalities of effective statelessness, as Caroline Vandenabeele shows, are different in Nepal, Bangladesh, Cambodia, and China, as Kirsten di Martino details. Understanding the differences contributes to forging the solutions, since the historical role of identity documentation and immigration control in the different countries varies. As Christina O. Alfirev, Simon Szreter, and Linda K. Kerber illustrate, state structures leading to statelessness and exclusion are the product of multiple complex determinants, often an archeology of diverse interests and goals that produce layered structures of exclusion and inclusion. Family books in Cambodia, as Vandenabeele shows, are the product of a tyrannical, compulsively intrusive regime of control and surveillance, but today the family book functions as an effective mechanism for identity documentation. It may not make sense to call for birth registration and birth certification to substitute for this functioning system of inclusion, at least not at this stage of Cambodian economic development (although Simon Szreter advances a powerful counterargument in favor of a comprehensive birth registration requirement).

A second element of the approach to child statelessness that we advocate is a more energetic engagement with the diversity of stateless children's interests, leading to more active embrace of the tension between protection and respect. Childhood, to be sure, is a unitary category in international law—"every human being below the age of 18"[93]—but a hugely diverse grouping physically, psychologically, and socially. For example, the young stateless children (as documented by Jyothi Kanics) who are abusively detained in harsh facilities in Ireland require nurturing in a family context, whether through fostering or other welfare means. They should not be prematurely treated as self-sufficient adults just because of their harsh life experiences. By contrast, independent adolescent migrants want an opportunity to work and, as Senovilla and Bicocchi explain, often demonstrate, by their disappearance, a radical rejection of the infantilizing care facilities in which they are placed. In Ireland, for example, over three hundred unaccompanied children have gone missing from the care of local authorities in recent years.[94] By imposing a reductive, culturally inapposite calculus that considers "childhood" a uniform, work-free zone, current social responses avoid the complex challenge of engaging with the dilemmas and limited strategic options facing stateless children. Current interventions misclassify the risks and needs that drive these children's behavior, wrongly assuming that family, school, play, and home are fixed and necessary points of reference for all children.

This book is not a purely scholarly project. In connecting the work of academics from various disciplines with the work of writers engaged in international or nongovernmental organizations, we hope to contribute to the development of policies that improve the current situation of stateless children. All the chapters in this book take this on in some way. Some argue in favor of more creative uses of statistical data already available or identity documentation mechanisms already in place, to assist countries in promoting the protection needs of stateless children. Others suggest greater scrutiny of administrative procedures that violate domestic and international obligations. Yet others advocate legal challenges and the mobilization of political constituencies to correct "the scandal of invisibility"[95] and discredit the comfortable myth that rights deprivation is inevitable for stateless children. Implicitly if not explicitly, all advocate a more inclusive, plastic notion of citizenship that recognizes the importance of children's current residence as a justified basis for claim making and state protection. After all, "everyone should have the right to citizenship somewhere,"[96] most of all children.

Notes

1. Platform for International Cooperation on Undocumented Migrants (PICUM), *Newsletter*, May 2008, <http://www.picum.org> (accessed July 30, 2009).

2. Dan McDougall, "Why Do the Italians Hate Us?," *Observer Magazine*, August 17, 2008, 14–25.

3. Dora Kostakopoulou, *The Future Governance of Citizenship* (Cambridge: Cambridge University Press, 2008), 2.

4. See, for example, the egregious case of five-year-old Tabitha, who was detained and deported alone back to the Democratic Republic of the Congo (DRC) by the Belgian authorities. *Mubilanzila Mayeka and Kaniki Mitunga v. Belgium*, application no. 13178/03, <http://www.coe.int> (accessed July 30, 2009). The following is a U.S. example. Eight immigrant teenagers who were held at a detention facility for unaccompanied minors sued the U.S. government over alleged abuse and denial of access to attorneys. They alleged that they were beaten and subjected to other rights abuses while in custody at the 122-bed Houston facility run by Cornell Companies, Inc. Michelle Roberts, "Detention Facility for Immigrant Kids Sued for Abuse," Associated Press, April 3, 2008. Undocumented children who are held in "secure facilities" (juvenile jails) are still routinely brought to court shackled and handcuffed in San Francisco, despite vigorous protests over this practice for years. Aryah Somers, Vera Institute, personal communication to the author, June 18, 2009.

5. According to Kirsten Di Martino, 38 percent of migrant children in Beijing are excluded from the public school system (see Di Martino's chapter in this volume). There is also evidence of higher neonatal and infant mortality among migrant children and differential access to health care between migrant and nonmigrant children. According to UNICEF's research, only 48 percent of migrant children in China have regular physical examination cards compared to over 90 percent of nonmigrant children in Beijing.

6. This general statement needs some qualification. For interesting recent work on statelessness that has a direct bearing on the argument being advanced here, see Audrey Macklin, "Who Is the Citizen's Other? Considering the Heft of Citizenship," *Theoretical Inquiries in Law* 8, no. (July 2007): 333–366; Laura van Waas, *Nationality Matters: Statelessness under International Law* (Antwerp: Intersentia, 2008).

7. This qualifier is important. As David B. Thronson shows in his chapter on U.S. citizen children of undocumented migrants, citizen children who have the same right as adult citizens to stay permanently in their own country might nevertheless find themselves "constructively" deported—forced to leave their home country because their parents or other sole caregivers are deported (see Thronson's chapter in this volume).

8. John Torpey, *The Invention of the Passport: Surveillance, Citizenship and the State* (Cambridge: Cambridge University Press, 2000), 7.

9. Van Waas, *Nationality Matters*.

10. United Nations (UN) General Assembly, Convention Relating to the Status of Stateless Persons, art. 1, September 28, 1954, United Nations, *Treaty Series*, vol. 360, p. 117, <http://www.unhcr.org> (accessed August 1, 2009).

11. Article 6 states: "Everyone has the right to recognition everywhere before the law." Article 7 states: "All are equal before the law and are entitled without any discrimination to equal protection of the law. All are entitled to equal protection against any discrimination in violation of this Declaration and

against any incitement to such discrimination." UN General Assembly, Universal Declaration of Human Rights, December 10, 1948, <http://www.unhcr.org> (accessed August 1, 2009).

12. Hannah Arendt, *The Origins of Totalitarianism* (New York: Harcourt, 1951).

13. Acknowledgment of the mismatch between the current reality of millions and the framework of nation-state citizenship has prompted many suggestions for new bases for affiliation, including easier and nondiscretionary access to naturalization (Rainer Bauböck, "Citizenship and National Identities in the European Union," Harvard Jean Monnet Working Papers, Harvard Law School, Cambridge, Mass., 1997); constitutional patriotism (Craig Calhoun, "Constitutional Patriotism and the Public Sphere: Interests, Identity, and Solidarity in the Integration of Europe," in Pablo De Greiff and Ciaran P. Cronin, eds., *Global Justice and Transnational Politics: Essays on the Moral and Political Challenges of Globalization* (Cambridge: MIT Press, 2002)); cosmopolitan solidarity (Seyla Benhabib, *The Rights of Others: Aliens, Residents and Citizens* (Cambridge: Cambridge University Press, 2004)). But it has generally taken as given an undifferentiated "disadvantage" flowing from otherness rather than probing its specific manifestations.

14. Siofra O'Leary, *European Union Citizenship: The Options for Reform* (London: Institute for Public Policy Research, 1996).

15. Will Kymlicka, *Multicultural Citizenship* (Oxford: Oxford University Press, 1995).

16. Bauböck, "Citizenship and National Identities in the European Union," 1.

17. Yasemin Soysal, *Limits of Citizenship: Migrants and Postnational Membership in Europe* (Chicago: University of Chicago Press, 1994); David Jacobson, *Rights across Borders: Immigration and the Decline of Citizenship* (Baltimore: Johns Hopkins University, 1996).

18. Peter Spiro, *Beyond Citizenship: American Identity after Globalization* (New York: Oxford University Press, 2008).

19. The preeminent legal authority on legal statelessness is Paul Weis, who was commissioned by the United Nations Department of Social Affairs to issue "A Study of Statelessness," United Nations document E/1112, February 1, 1949, document E/1112/add., May 19, 1949, prior to the adoption of the 1954 Statelessness Convention. See also Paul Weis, *Nationality and Statelessness in International Law* (Alphen aan den Rijn: Sijthoff & Noordhoff, 1979). Several studies have adopted a regional focus. See, for example, Tang Lay Lee, *Statelessness, Human Rights and Gender: Irregular Migrant Workers from Burma in Thailand* (Leiden: Martinus Nijhoff, 2005); P. R. Chari et al., *Missing Boundaries: Refugees, Migrants, Stateless and Internally Displaced Persons in South Asia* (New Delhi: Manohar, 2003); Tang Lay Lee, "Refugees from Bhutan: Nationality, Statelessness and the Right to Return," *International Journal of Refugee Law* 10 (1998): 118–155; Amnesty International, *Bhutan: Nationality, Expulsion, Statelessness and the Right to Return*, ASA 14/001/2000, London, September 2000; Tibet Justice Center, *Tibet's Stateless Nationals: Tibetan Refugees in*

Nepal (Berkeley: Tibet Justice Center, June 2002); Sumit Sen, "Stateless Refugees and the Right to Return: The Bihari Refugees of South Asia" (Parts 1–2), *International Journal of Refugee Law* 11, no. 4 (1999): 625–645 and 12, no. 1 (2000): 41–70; Médecins sans Frontières Holland, *Ten Years for the Rohingya Refugees in Bangladesh: Past, Present and Future*, MSF Holland, March 2002; Susan M. Akram, "Palestinian Refugees and Their Legal Status: Rights, Politics and Implications for a Just Solution," *Journal of Palestine Studies* 31, no. 3 (Spring 2002): 36–51; Curtis F. Doebbler, "A Human Rights Approach to Statelessness in the Middle East," *Leiden Journal of International Law* 15 (2002): 527–552; Patrick Barbieri, "About Being Without: Bidun," Refugees International, October 2007; Andras Fehervary, "Citizenship, Statelessness and Human Rights: Recent Developments in the Baltic States,"_International Journal of Refugee Law* 5 (1993): 392–423. For a useful overview, see *Forced Migration Review* special issue on statelessness, issue 32, April 2009.

20. The public health importance of birth registration is addressed in Philip W. Setel, Sarah B. Macfalane, Simon Szreter, Lene Mikkelsen, Prabhat Jha, Susan Stout, and Carla Abouzahr, "A Scandal of Invisibility: Making Everyone Count by Counting Everyone," *Lancet* 370 (October 2007): 1569–1577; Prasanta Mahapatra, Kenji Shibuya, Alan D. Lopez, Francesca Coullare, Francis C. Notzon, Chalapati Rao, and Simon Szreter, "Civil Registration and Vital Statistics: Successes and Missed Opportunities," *Lancet* 370 (November 10, 2007): 1653–1663.

21. United Nations Children's Fund (UNICEF) has researched the relationship between statelessness and armed conflict. See UNICEF, "Birth Registration and Armed Conflict," *Innocenti Insight* (Florence: Innocenti Research Centre, 2007); UNICEF, "Birth Registration: Right from the Start," *Innocenti Insight* (Florence: Innocenti Research Centre, March 2002).

22. Katherine Southwick and Maureen Lynch, "Nationality Rights for All: A Progress Report and Global Survey on Statelessness," Refugees International, March 2009, 7, <http://www.refugeesinternational.org> (accessed August 1, 2009).

23. Laura van Waas identifies deficient birth registration and migration as the two "new" sources of statelessness and argues that by not addressing these issues, the 1961 Convention on the Reduction of Statelessness has become outdated. See van Waas, *Nationality Matters*, 152.

24. Kostakopoulou, *The Future Governance of Citizenship*, 33.

25. Torpcy, *The Invention of the Passport*, 244.

26. Southwick and Lynch, "Nationality Rights for All," 9.

27. See also Laura van Waas, "The Children of Irregular Migrants: A Stateless Generation?," *Netherlands Quarterly of Human Rights* 25, no. 3 (2007): 437–458.

28. See T. Alexander Aleinikoff and Douglas B. Klusmeyer, eds., *Citizenship Today: Global Perspectives and Practices* (Washington, D.C.: Carnegie Endowment for International Peace, 2001).

29. Van Waas, "The Children of Irregular Migrants," 2.

30. Ibid., 12.

31. Ibid., 8.

32. United Nations High Commissioner for Refugees (UNHCR), "Refugee Children: Guidelines on Protection and Care," UNHCR, 1994, cited in Saudamini Siegrist, UNICEF representative, paper presented at the conference on Children without a State, Harvard University, Cambridge, May 5, 2008, available from the author.

33. Siegrist, paper presented at Harvard University, May 5, 2008.

34. UNICEF, "The 'Rights' Start to Life: A Statistical Analysis of Birth Registration," UNICEF, 2005, 3, <http://www.unicef.org> (accessed August 1, 2009).

35. Siegrist, paper presented at Harvard University, May 5, 2008, 3.

36. UNICEF, *The "Rights" Start to Life.*

37. Siegrist, paper presented at Harvard University, May 5, 2008, 7.

38. Personal communication with Sahana Basavapatba, who can be reached at sahana.basvapatba@gmail.org.

39. Alexandre Le Cleve, Hors la Rue, France, cited in Luca Bicocchi's chapter in this volume.

40. European Commission against Racism and Intolerance (ECRI), "Third Report on Italy, Adopted on 16 December 2005," Strasbourg, sec. 97, cited in Elena Rozzi's chapter in this volume.

41. Court of Justice of Milan, 1st Civil Section, Ordinance no. 2380/2008, <http://www.asgi.it> (accessed August 1, 2009).

42. A recent attempt by the Milan city council to prevent irregular migrants from enrolling their children in state kindergartens was overruled by a court, which held that insisting on a valid residence permit as a precondition for enrollment "unduly subordinate[d] children's rights to their parents' residence status." Milan Tribunal, 1st Civil Section, no. 2380/08 R.G., February 11, 2008 (see Elena Rozzi's chapter in this volume). It is interesting to compare this rights enhancing judgment with the U.S. Supreme Court's decision in *Plyler v. Doe*, 457 U.S. 202 (1982) (reference in the next paragraph of the text).

43. Although all Romanian children, including the Roma, are citizens, their legal status may expire after three months in Italy if they are dependent on public funds for their support. In this case, their claim to equal treatment as a citizen is compromised and may simply become a future aspiration. See also E. Meehan, "Rethinking the Path to European Citizenship," in William J. V. Neill and Hanns-Uve Schwedler, eds., *Migration and Cultural Inclusion in the European City* (Basingstoke, England: Palgrave Macmillan, 2007).

44. *Plyler v. Doe*, 457 U.S.202 (1982).

45. Southwick and Lynch, "Nationality Rights for All," 15. *Bidun*, the report explains, is the Arabic word for "without" and in this context is an abbreviation of *bidun jinsiya*, which means "without citizenship."

46. Ibid., 11.

47. See Human Rights Watch, ""'Illegal People': Haitians and Dominico-Haitians in the Dominican Republic," April 4, 2002, B1401, <http://www.unhcr.org> (accessed August 1, 2009). Even though the Inter-American Commission on Human Rights ruled that equating "in transit" with "illegal" is unconstitutional and a violation of the American Convention on Human Rights in *Case of the Girls Yean and Bosico v. Dominican Republic* (2005) I/A Court HR (Series C), no. 134, recent investigations by Refugees International and the Robert F. Kennedy Memorial Center found that the Dominican authorities continue to exclude from Dominican nationality children born to Haitian parents. See Haiti Innovation, "Dominico-Haitians: Stateless in the Dominican Republic," Inter-American Court of Human Rights Series C, no. 130; see also Open Society Institute Justice Initiative, "Inter American Court Affirms the Human Rights to Nationality," October 17, 2005, <http://www.justiceinitiative.org> (accessed August 1, 2009).

48. Human Rights Watch, *Illegal People,* cited in Van Waas, "The Children of Irregular Migrants."

49. Amnesty International, *Dominican Republic: A Life in Transit—The Plight of Haitian Migrants and Dominicans of Haitian Descent*, March 22, 2007, AMR 27/001/2007, <http://www.unhcr.org> (accessed August 1, 2009).

50. "Querida Europa," *El País,* July 13, 2008, <http://www.elpais.com> (accessed August 1, 2009); see also Elena Rozzi's chapter in this volume.

51. See chapters by Jyothi Kanics and Luca Bicocchi in this volume. These practices are generally confined to *de facto* stateless children in Europe because citizen and resident families are entitled to state accommodation when they have minor children within the household. In the United States, however, this is not the case, and the major predictor of mother-child separation is homelessness, Kirsten Cowal et al., "Mother-Child Separations among Homeless and Housed Families Receiving Public Assistance in New York City," *American Journal of Community Psychology* 30, no. 5 (October 2002), cited in Kelsey Quigley, Research Proposal Abstract, April 2009, available from the author.

52. UN General Assembly, Convention on the Rights of the Child (CRC), art. 9, November 20, 1989, United Nations, *Treaty Series*, vol. 1577, p. 3, <http://www.unhcr.org> (accessed 3 August 2009).

53. Marine Vassort, *Paroles d'errance* (Marseille: Editions P'tits Papiers, 2006),13 (translation by the author).

54. Jacqueline Bhabha and Nadine Finch, *Seeking Asylum Alone: Unaccompanied and Separated Children and Refugee Protection in the U.K.* (Cambridge: President and Fellows of Harvard College, 2006), 56, <http://www.humanrights.harvard.edu> (accessed August 1, 2009).

55. "Report submitted by Ms. Gabriela Rodríguez Pizarro, Special Rapporteur, in Conformity with Resolution 2003/46 of the Commission on Human Rights: Addendum. Visit to Spain," United Nations Commission on Human Rights, 60th

session, E/CN.4/2004/76/Add.2, January 14, 2004, <http://www.unhchr.ch> (accessed August 1, 2009).

56. Whether citizen children could secure effective legal representation to translate the legal entitlement into a practical reality is another matter. But the absence of a legal entitlement eliminates a prerequisite for state protection.

57. Philippe Aries, *Centuries of Childhood,* trans. Robert Baldick (London: Pimlico, 1996).

58. Jacqueline Bhabha and Susan Schmidt, *Seeking Asylum Alone: Unaccompanied and Separated Children and Refugee Protection in the U.S.* (Cambridge: President and Fellows of Harvard College, 2006), 4.

59. See Amnesty International, "Amnistía Internacional denuncia expulsiones encubiertas de menores no acompañados," October 25, 2007, <http://www.es.amnesty.org> (accessed August 1, 2009).

60. See P. Perez, "De náufragos y navegantes: Los menores y jóvenes no acompañados," *Boletín Puntos de Vista, Juventud e Inmigración,* no. 10 (2007): 12.

61. Melissa del Bosque, "Children of the State: The Feds and Texas Quarrel over Custody of Undocumented Kids," *Texas Observer,* May 16, 2008, <http://www.texasobserver.org> (accessed August 1, 2009).

62. Kostakopoulou, "The Future Governance of Citizenship," 138–139; Jacqueline Bhabha, "Get Back to Where You Once Belonged: Identity, Citizenship and Exclusion in Europe," *Human Rights Quarterly* 20 (1998): 592–627.

63. European Court of Justice, *Chen & Others v. United Kingdom,* no. C-200/02, 2002.

64. Siegrist, paper presented at Harvard University, May 5, 2008.

65. I used the phrase "Adult-centered myopia," for example, in "Not a Sack of Potatoes: Moving and Removing Children across Borders," *Boston University Public Interest Law Journal* 15, no. 2 (2006): 197, 209. For a recent report on *de facto* stateless child migrants that invokes this perspective, see Save the Children, *Our Broken Dreams: Child Migration in Southern Africa* (Maputo: Mozambique: Save the Children UK and Norway, 2008). Speaking of "a culture of silence and invisibility," the country director of Save the Children in Mozambique says: "Unaccompanied child migrants are extremely vulnerable to abuse and exploitation, but this is an issue which has *slipped through the cracks* of public concern in southern Africa and around the world." Integrated Regional Information Networks (IRIN), *Southern Africa Child Migrants Tell All,* April 29, 2008, <http://www.unhcr.org> (accessed August 1, 2009).

66. Bhabha and Schmidt, *Seeking Asylum Alone,* 7. For a similar approach, see also Jacqueline Bhabha and Wendy Young, "Not Adults in Miniature: Unaccompanied Child Asylum Seekers and the New U.S. Guidelines," 11 *IJRL* 84 (1999): 87–88; Jacqueline Bhabha and Wendy Young, "Children Seeking Asylum Held in Detention," *Women's Commission News* (Women's Commission for Refugee Women and Children, New York) (Summer/Fall 2001): 10, <http://www.womenscommission.org> (accessed August 1, 2009). See generally Simon

Russell, "Most Vulnerable of All: The Treatment of Unaccompanied Refugee Children in the U.K," *Amnesty International*, 1999; Christopher Nugent and Steven Schulman, "Giving Voice to the Vulnerable: On Representing Detained Immigrant and Refugee Children," *Interpreter Releases* 1569 (October 8, 2001); Human Rights Watch, "Detained and Deprived of Rights: Children in the Custody of the U.S. Immigration and Naturalization Service," 1998, sec. 4, <http://www.hrw.org> (accessed August 1, 2009).

67. UNICEF, *The "Rights" Start to Life*, 3.

68. Siegrist, paper presented at Harvard University, May 5, 2008.

69. Deutsche Presse Agentur, "Barroso: Confident Italy Is in Line with EU Immigration Principles," July 15, 2008, <http://www.monstersandcritics.com> (accessed August 5, 2008).

70. *Case of the Girls Yean and Bosico v. Dominican Republic.* See Southwick and Lynch, *Nationality Rights for All*, 7.

71. Christina Fraser, "Italy Police to Protect Gypsies," *BBC News*, May 14, 2008 (see Elena Rozzi's chapter in this volume for details).

72. Miguel Benasayag, in *La chasse aux enfants: L'effet miroir de l'expulsion des sans-papiers* (Paris: Decouverte, 2008), documents the traumatic effects on families and children of discriminatory state policies in France.

73. Urban Institute, *Paying the Price: The Impact of Immigration Raids on America's Children* (Washington, D.C.: Urban Institute. 2007). See also David B. Thronson's chapter in this volume.

74. Erika Haysaki, "Mayor Criticizes Raid for Disrupting Families: Immigration Arrests in Massachusetts Stranded 140 Youths," *L.A. Times*, March 9, 2007, A16; Ali Noorani, "U.S. Immigration System at Its Worst," *Boston Globe*, March 9, 2007, <http://www.boston.com> (accessed August 1, 2009); Pierre Avril, "L'Europe prête à incarcérer tous les mineurs illégaux," *Le Figaro*, April 25, 2008, <http://www.lefigaro.fr> (accessed August 1, 2009).

75. See, for example, films such as *The Lost Boys of Sudan, In this World*, and *The Visitor*; plays such as *Edgar Chocoy*, a documentary theater piece by Jeffrey Solomon's Half Moon Theater Company about the murder of a deported Guatemalan child migrant, <http://www.detentionwatchnetwork.org> (accessed August 1, 2009); and contemporary art works on displacement, marginalization, exclusion, and illegality, such as *Guests*, the installation art work by Krzysztof Wodiczko, representing Poland at the 2009 Venice Biennale art show. This piece depicts the blurry figures of immigrant youth filmed through the opaque windows they are washing, "within arms reach" and at the same time "on the other side," a metaphor for their ambiguous status. See Bozena Czubak, catalog essay, in *Fare Mondi, Making Worlds: Fifty-third International Art Exhibition* (Venice: 2009 Fondazione La Biennale di Venezia, 100.

76. Not all authors have a uniform view, and invisibility is not always dismissed as an irrelevance. Luca Bicocchi, in his chapter in this volume, refers to invisibility as a relevant factor in understanding child statelessness and its implications.

77. Jacqueline Bhabha and Christina Alfirev, "The Identification and Referral of Victims of Trafficking to Procedures for Determining International Protection Needs," UN High Commissioner for Refugees, October 2009, PPLAS/2009/03, <http://www.unhcr.org> (accessed November 1, 2009).

78. Personal communication, Barbara Hines, Radcliffe Institute Exploratory Seminar on Unaccompanied and Separated Children, Harvard University, Cambridge, June 17–20, 2009.

79. Human Rights Watch, "Nowhere to Turn: State Abuses of Unaccompanied Migrant Children by Spain and Morocco," May 7, 2002, D1404, 28–32, <http://www.unhcr.org> (accessed August 1, 2009).

80. UN Committee on the Rights of the Child (CRC), "UN Committee on the Rights of the Child: Concluding Observations: Spain," June 13, 2002, CRC/C/15/Add.185, sec. 45(e), <http://www.unhcr.org> (accessed August 3, 2009).

81. Manley Hudson, special rapporteur for the International Law Commission, cited in Carol A. Batchelor, "Stateless Persons: Some Gaps in International Protection," *International Journal of Refugee Law* 7, no. 2 (1995): 234.

82. P. Granville Edge, "Vital Registration in Europe. The Development of Official Statistics and Some Differences in Practice," *Journal of the Royal Statistical Society* (1928): 346–79, 354–355.

83. James C. Scott, *Seeing Like a State: How Certain Schemes to Improve the Human Condition Have Failed* (New Haven: Yale University Press, 1998).

84. Michael Froomkin, *Identity Cards and Identity Romanticism* (New York: Oxford University Press, 2009).

85. Sometimes, the judgment that an identity document is unacceptable appears to be arbitrary and irregular. See Bhabha and Schmidt, *Seeking Asylum Alone,* 57.

86. See Bhabha and Schmidt, *Seeking Asylum Alone*; Mary Crock, *Seeking Asylum Alone: Australia* (Sydney: Themis Press, 2006).

87. Bhabha and Finch, *Seeking Asylum Alone,* 56.

88. Ibid., note 29.

89. Cited in ibid., 61.

90. For a case in point, see ibid., 57.

91. Kostakopoulou, *The Future Governance of Citizenship,* 8.

92. Preparations are already afoot for international celebrations of the twentieth anniversary of the 1989 UN Convention on the Rights of the Child, the most comprehensively and rapidly ratified of all international human rights instruments. See, for example, the UNICEF Web site, <http://www.unicef.org>; Movement, Socialist Educational International Web site, <http://www.ifm-sei.org>; and the Web site of the Office for Standards in Education, Children's Services and Skills, <http://ofstednews.ofsted.gov.uk> (accessed August 1, 2009).

93. CRC, art. 1.

94. Over the last seven years, 388 children placed in the care of the Irish authorities as suspected victims of trafficking have gone missing and have never been traced. See Sr. Stanislaus Kennedy, "Who Cares About the Disappeared Children?," <http://www.ireland.com> (accessed May 23, 2008).

95. Setel et al., "A Scandal of Invisibility."

96. Matthew J. Gibney, "Statelessness and the Right to Citizenship," *Forced Migration Review* 32 (April 2009): 50.

I

Legal Statelessness

(Democratic Republic of the Congo), and Asia (Myanmar). It concludes with a series of recommendations for enhancing protection.

Stateless Children under International Law

Under international law, all people (including children) are guaranteed protection of their human rights, irrespective of their nationality status. The UN Charter, Universal Declaration of Human Rights (UDHR), and subsequent documents speak of "all people"—not "nationals" or "citizens"—as the basis for enjoyment of human rights. In the context of stateless minorities, the situation is no different: persons belonging to minority groups equally enjoy human rights, irrespective of their nationality status. This is noted in article 27 of the 1966 International Covenant on Civil and Political Rights (ICCPR) and the very similar article 30 in the CRC. The rights of minorities are especially elaborated over the entirety of the 1965 Convention on the Elimination of All Forms of Racial Discrimination (CERD). In practice, however, governments often use nationality and citizenship status to restrict access to state resources, a strategy that introduces the danger of discriminatory treatment against nonnationals. The rights of all are not uniformly respected.

Although citizenship is frequently defined in national legislation, within international law citizenship has generally been understood in the context of nationality. A substantial body of international jurisprudence establishes that nationality laws must be consistent with general principles of international law as noted in the 1923 decision by the Permanent Court of International Justice[2] and under article 1 of the 1930 Hague Convention on Certain Questions Relating to the Conflict of Nationality Laws.[3] Within the UN system, nationality is situated unequivocally within the framework of universal human rights. Article 15 of the UDHR recognizes that nationality ensures individuals access to the enjoyment of human rights and prohibits the arbitrary removal of this right.[4] Although the UDHR does not itself specify what constitutes arbitrary deprivation, accepted definitions of *arbitrariness* usefully describe the limitations placed on states. *Arbitrariness* covers practices that do not follow a fair procedure or due process, and the term is used to refer to actions where states cannot be held to account.[5]

While it is accepted that states may withdraw citizenship rights under certain conditions, provided they are reasonable and meet the test of nonarbitrariness, in general such conditions do not apply to children.[6] Article 15 of the UDHR establishes several principles that reaffirm the centrality of universal protection and also guard against the forced assimilation of children of minorities.[7] These provisions are reinforced by subsequent articles that are of direct relevance to children. For example, article 25(1) states in subsection (1) that "Everyone has the right to a standard of living adequate for the health and well-being of himself and of his family, including food, clothing, housing and medical care and necessary social services" and in subsection (2) that "Motherhood and childhood are entitled to special care and assistance." Finally, the UDHR includes rights to education under article 26. Thus, irrespective of states' rights to determine the criteria for nationality, international law stipulates that stateless children should enjoy a host of rights irrespective of their nationality status.

The ICCPR restates the principle of universal coverage, includes protections against arbitrary expulsion (article 13) and equality before law (article 26), and further sets out obligations to prevent the denial of citizenship by insisting on birth registration and reaffirming a child's right to nationality under articles 24(2) and (3). Also noteworthy is the introduction of article 27 on minority rights, which may be taken to prohibit both the forced assimilation of children[8] and the denial of citizenship on arbitrarily defined grounds that relate to linguistic and cultural backgrounds.[9] The related 1966 International Covenant on Economic, Social, and Cultural Rights (ICESCR) explicitly prohibits the creation of conditions that undermine the social and economic survival of an individual and their family members and specifically sets out principles to protect children.[10] Under article 10(3), children and young persons are to be protected from economic and social exploitation. Further, under article 13(2), the Convention sets out the universal right of access and entitlement to free primary education.

Most important for the purposes of this chapter is the CRC, which restates the universal protections and provisions on matters of nationality and elaborates on the rights of children. Under article 7(1), the CRC declares that every child has a right to acquire a name and nationality and stipulates that states should register births to ensure that this happens. Under article 7(2), it draws attention to the prospect of statelessness in the event that births are not recorded and nationality not formally transmitted. The CRC also introduces a clause regarding unlawful interference that firms up the principle of arbitrariness described above. Under article 8(1), it declares that "States Parties undertake to respect the right of the child to preserve his or her identity, including nationality, name and family relations as recognized by law without unlawful interference."

It also mentions the possible deprivation of elements of a child's identity and calls on states to reestablish a child's identity in such cases under article 8(2). This clause may be taken to extend the prohibition on the deprivation of citizenship, given the essential relationship between citizenship and personal identity. These clauses in the CRC add further weight to claims regarding the prohibition of arbitrary denial and deprivation of citizenship toward children, not least because this instrument has been ratified by almost every state.

Finally, other international conventions further reaffirm the principle of universal protection and include other groups, among them women and children.[11] The 1990 International Convention on the Protection of the Rights of All Migrant Workers and Members of Their Families (hereafter Migrant Rights Convention) also reiterates the principle of universal protection. Although only thirty-five states have signed onto this convention, it is significant because it acknowledges the role that the migration of workers plays in the global economy and is directly relevant to the concepts of *de facto* and effectively stateless people, as set out in the introduction to this volume.

Nondiscrimination and the Rights of Children

A significant body of international law has elaborated the principle of nondiscrimination on the basis of race, ethnicity, and related criteria that further limit state action and includes provisions regarding the rights of children to nationality. These include the CERD, the 1979 Convention on the Elimination of All Forms of Discrimination against Women (CEDAW), the 1992 Declaration on the Rights of Persons Belonging to National or Ethnic, Religious and Linguistic Minorities, and the 1990 Migrant Rights Convention.

One of the most noteworthy instruments is the CERD. Article 1 of the CERD provides a precise definition of *racial discrimination* and is particularly relevant to the problem of denial or deprivation of citizenship to children because it addresses the issue of motivation and also highlights the liabilities of states that create conditions that exacerbate the vulnerability of minority populations. The CERD affirms that differential treatment between groups of noncitizens may constitute discrimination[12] and reaffirms under article 5 the universal provision that state parties are obliged to guarantee equality for all in the enjoyment of civil, political, economic, social, and cultural rights to the extent recognized under international law.

In 2004, the Committee on the Elimination of Racial Discrimination (hereafter the Committee) published its General Recommendation Number 30 on the theme of discrimination against noncitizens. In this document, the Committee reaffirmed the need to tighten loopholes that might lead to discrimination on the basis of citizenship and nationality. This recommendation called on states to take measures to ensure that noncitizens enjoyed protection before the law; had access to education, housing, employment, and health; and were protected against forced expulsions. It further sought to clarify the prohibitions regulating states under international law. Under section IV, it recommended that states "pay due attention to possible barriers to naturalization that may exist for long-term or permanent residents" and called on states to reduce statelessness among children by, for example, encouraging their parents to apply for citizenship on their behalf and allowing both parents to transmit their citizenship to their children.[13] The Committee has generated an important body of country-specific recommendations on the issue of discrimination in relation to the acquisition of citizenship, some of which make explicit reference to children. For example, the Committee called on Mauritania to respect the principle of nondiscrimination in children's access to nationality.[14]

The denial or deprivation of citizenship is also prohibited under the 1954 Statelessness Convention and the 1961 Statelessness Convention. Although these conventions have not been ratified by large numbers of states, they have made a significant contribution to the human-rights regime regarding the treatment of noncitizens. For example, the 1954 Convention provides for equality of treatment under articles 7 and 8. Otherwise, this instrument puts stateless persons on an equal footing with noncitizens residing in the country. Under articles 20 through 24, the 1954 Statelessness Convention includes provisions that cover children by calling on states to treat stateless persons no less favorably than nationals with respect to rationing, housing, public education, public relief, and social security.

In addition to these UN conventions, a growing body of regional treaties and conventions has called attention to the principle of nondiscrimination and equal treatment of noncitizens, including children. For example, in the context of Africa, the 1981 African Charter on Human and People's Rights includes several articles that apply the principles of nondiscrimination, equality before the law, and the rights of equal access. Together these articles severely restrict the conditions under which nationality may be denied.

The 1999 African Charter on the Rights and Welfare of the Child has been ratified by only a small number of states, but it contains additional provisions that seek to protect children from some of the consequences associated with the arbitrary denial of citizenship and the vulnerability that such practices create. The charter aims to protect the private life of the child and safeguard the child against all forms of economic exploitation and against work that is hazardous, interferes with the child's education, or compromises his or her health or physical, social, mental, spiritual, and moral development.

Within the European system, a number of central conventions and related instruments have been introduced that prohibit the denial and deprivation of citizenship and significantly advance international jurisprudence in this area. The most important sources of law on this region include the 1950 European Convention for the Protection of Human Rights and Fundamental Freedoms (hereafter the European Convention) and its five protocols, corresponding rulings from the European Court of Human Rights, and the Consolidated Treaties of the European Union. The European Convention is the only international human-rights agreement providing such a high degree of individual protection. The European Convention contains several provisions that constrain states' actions to deny or deprive eligible individuals of the right to citizenship including article 14, which sets out a universal prohibition against discrimination, and article 17, which prohibits the abuse of rights. The 1963 European Convention on the Reduction of Cases of Multiple Nationality and on Military Obligations in Cases of Multiple Nationality establishes rules to reduce multiple nationalities in the case of the acquisition or renunciation of a nationality. It also addresses the legal consequences of loss of nationality for persons concerned, including children.

Most important is the 1997 European Convention on Nationality (hereafter European Nationality Convention). The main principles of this Convention are the prevention of statelessness, nondiscrimination in questions of nationality, as well as nondiscrimination in matters of sex, religion, race, color, national, or ethnic origin. The European Nationality Convention also calls for respect for the rights of persons "habitually resident" on the territories concerned and thus may apply to individuals who, in the terminology adopted in this study, are defined as effectively stateless. In the context of post-cold war Europe, the European Nationality Convention also establishes principles concerning persons in danger of becoming stateless as a result of state succession. One of the most significant expressions of concern about the arbitrary denial of citizenship is found in the brief article 4, which sets out the rules on nationality and guiding principles, including that (1) everyone has the right to a nationality, (2) statelessness shall be avoided, (3) no one shall be arbitrarily deprived of his or her nationality, and (4) neither marriage, the dissolution of a marriage between a national of a state party and an alien nor the change of nationality by one of the spouses during marriage shall automatically affect the nationality of the other spouse. The 2006 European Convention on the Avoidance of Statelessness in Relation to State Succession also sets out important protections, including the granting of citizenship to all who had it at the time of state succession, on condition of residence and historic connection.

Within the European Union (EU), the prohibition of discrimination on the basis of nationality is at the very heart of the Union and is recorded under article 12 of the 2006 EU Treaty. With the exception of immigration, there are ever fewer points of distinction between citizens and noncitizens living within the EU. Indeed, the EU is one arena where national identity and the privileges of citizenship have been notably disassociated. EU member states are required to permit the entry and residence of the family members of those citizens and to provide education for their children on the same basis as that of their own nationals' children.

A significant body of case law is emanating from national and regional courts and treaty bodies. One of the most widely cited is the case of Judge *Unity Dow v. Attorney-General* in Botswana. Dow, a distinguished human-rights activist, successfully challenged the legitimacy of the Citizenship Act, which denied Botswana citizenship to her children because her husband was a foreigner. The High Court and later the Court of Appeal found that the gender discrimination inherent within the Botswana Citizenship Act was in violation of the constitution.[15]

More recently, the prohibition on arbitrary deprivation and denial of citizenship to children has been reiterated by the Inter-American Court of Human Rights, which ruled that "states' discretion must be limited by international human rights that exist to protect individuals against arbitrary state actions." In *Dilcia Yean and Violeta Bosico v. Dominican Republic,* the Inter-American Court concluded that the Dominican Republic's discriminatory application of nationality and birth-registration laws and regulations rendered children of Haitian descent stateless and unable to access other critical rights, such as the right to education, the right to recognition of juridical personality, the right to a name, and the right to equal protection before the law. In so doing, it affirmed the human right to nationality as the gateway to the equal enjoyment of all rights as civic members of a state. The ruling recognizes that statelessness makes impossible the recognition of a juridical personality and the enjoyment of civil and political rights and that it produces a condition of extreme vulnerability. It also affirms that states cannot base the denial of nationality to children on the immigration status of their parents and that the proof required by governments to establish that an individual was born on a state's territory must be reasonable.

Statelessness in Context

In spite of the substantial development of international law outlined above, children are particularly affected by statelessness. The denial of the right to nationality is often accompanied by a series of deprivations that have longstanding consequences in terms of children's social, economic, and personal development. In its most extreme form, the total exclusion of children from state services such as education and health care and the denial of the right to identity that may result from discriminatory policies can leave children vulnerable to the compound ills of poverty, infant mortality, chronic morbidity, and exploitation in the labor market, in the sex industry, and by organized criminals including human traffickers and armed gangs. The following section explores the effects of statelessness on the lives of children in three regional contexts.

Europe

Although the European region is the site of some of the world's most extensive laws prohibiting statelessness, European states have redefined their immigration laws and obligations under the international agreements noted above, including the 1951 Convention. As a result, several European states have contributed to the creation of a protection gap where people who have reached their shores in search of protection have been denied this right. In addition, the breakup of Yugoslavia and the former Soviet Union was followed by a reorganization that did not automatically give nationals of former federations the nationality of the independent states in which they were located. These two processes have left approximately half a million individuals—including former migrants and their descendants—effectively stateless. Although children should be among the most protected category of people in the EU, some have been denied the benefits and protections that come with nationality and that follow from the principle of nondiscrimination. Two contrasting cases are offered below. In the first case, the United Kingdom withdrew its powers to protect, and in the second, Slovenia undermined children's rights and ultimately removed them from its territory.

United Kingdom

It is difficult to estimate the number and profile of stateless children in the United Kingdom. Although the United Nations High Commissioner for Refugees (UNHCR) estimates that there were only 205 stateless people in the United Kingdom at the end of 2005, children tend to be treated as a separate category excluded from these figures.[16] In practice, many refused child asylum seekers are (to use the terminology proposed by Jacqueline Bhabha in the introduction to this volume) *de facto* stateless, so the official stateless estimates represent a significant underestimate of the magnitude of the problem of statelessness among children in the United Kingdom. Recent research on the problem of refused asylum seekers in the United Kingdom has started to paint a harrowing picture of destitution and associated mental health problems.[17] Further, as suggested by the Still Human Still Here Campaign initiated by refugee support organizations, destitution itself appears to be a means of forcing people to leave the UK.

Although the situations of stateless people and asylum seekers are legally distinct, the growing contraction of benefits and support to asylum seekers contributes to serious problems in the ways in which vulnerable populations access their human rights to educate their children, secure decent housing, and receive health care.[18] A further consequence of recent policy measures has been the stigmatization of asylum seekers into categories of those "deserving" and "undeserving" protection,[19] a fact equally relevant to stateless populations in general and children in particular.

One episode illustrates the coercive way in which UK immigration and asylum policies have been applied to the detriment of stateless children. In summer 2004, Thames Valley police officers and the UK immigration authorities arrested a number of declared Pakistani refugee families in Oxford as part of Operation Iowa. The incident led to a criminal trial and an immigration inquiry, which resulted in the cancellation of refugee status and subsequent withdrawal of state protection that had been given to a group of stateless children. The families concerned claimed to be not Pakistani but in fact Kashmiri, their nationality status having been disputed by the British, Indian, and Pakistani governments.

Although Kashmiris born in India are entitled to the same rights as citizens, India has consistently denied citizenship to Punjabi Muslims who have been living in Kashmir for more than sixty years. The situation has been further complicated by the geography of Kashmir and the history of conflict in the region. India reportedly amended its Citizenship Act of 1955 and Citizen Rule of 1965, authorizing the district magistrate of Jaisalmer to grant Indian citizenship to Pakistanis who had been living in the border district for the last five years. This effort was aimed at some of the Kashmiri Pandits who represented approximately 12 percent of the population in the valley in 1947 but since 1989 have been expelled (as many as 300,000 families have been forced out). In 2003, the Ministry of Home Affairs asked states to provide identity cards to displaced Kashmiri Pandits to regularize the situation of at least 50,000 displaced persons who were not registered as migrants when they left the Kashmir Valley after 1990. However, for over 100,000 Punjabi refugees who fled to Jammu and Kashmir from neighboring Sialkot district of Punjab province (now in Pakistan) in 1947, both they and their descendants have been denied the right to citizenship in India, and their exclusion has been a source of recent protests and unrest.[20]

The refugees who settled in Oxford claimed to be from Kashmir, although they had ties to Pakistan and their ancestral home was described to the author as Sialkot. Yet their nationality status became an academic matter following police Operation Iowa, which brought the families to court and began a process whereby their right to remain in the United Kingdom was called into question. In the 2005 criminal case *R. v. Faruq and Others* (Operation Iowa), the Crown Prosecution Service claimed that there had been a conspiracy to contravene the Immigration Act by bringing relatives into the UK under false pretenses and then falsely claiming asylum as a prelude to falsely claiming benefits from government departments and local authorities. As a result of this criminal hearing, the Home Office revoked the status of several of the parties concerned, including the children of the families involved in the criminal act. It was argued that if the families had lied during their asylum application, then other information could no longer be considered credible, including the ages of some of the children.

Interviews conducted in winter 2008 with some of the older children of family members revealed the extent to which the governmental action undermined their well-being and personal identity. One nineteen-year-old who was allowed to continue his further education studies because he enrolled before the 2004 Immigration Act came into effect claimed that his home life was dominated by arguments. As a consequence of his unhappy domestic environment, he spent time "on the streets, hanging around parks, fighting and in trouble" and claimed that he would not have done so if he had been permitted to work. He said that he currently spent most of his time playing computer games and was otherwise idle. He noted that as a result of his lack of documentation, he was unable to drive, open a bank account, obtain a mobile phone contract, or go to clubs like other young people. His friend described a similar situation and explained how the loss of his identity card (ID) card and cancellation of his refugee status in 2004 affected his life:

Without ID, you can't do anything. You can't get anything. I used to get £30 from Social Services, but this stopped when I was 18. They said I have to work, but I said I couldn't. They said, "It's not our problem."

He then described his life as a stateless person in the UK:

I can't work because of paperwork. I can't go to different countries. I tried [to work] in a restaurant, but I couldn't. If papers arrived, I would be like normal people. They can do whatever they want. I think there is something missing. I don't have my ID to prove who I am. Sometimes I question that. My identity is missing. Everyone has their identity.

By the end of 2009, the plight of the two Kashmiri interviewees remained unchanged. Both were still without status and existed precariously by depending on charitable organizations and the good will of professionals in the absence of state protection.

Slovenia

With the creation of the independent state of Slovenia in 1991, its government was faced with the task of defining formal citizenship policies. Ethnic Slovenes were to receive citizenship on the basis of *jus sanguinis*, which effectively meant the transfer of Slovenian nationality under the former Yugoslav system. Under the principle of *jus soli*, nonethnic Slovenes who were considered autochthonous minorities were allowed to naturalize if they were born on the territory. The remaining issue to be resolved concerned the 221,321 foreigners who could not be classified as either ethnic Slovenes or recognized minorities.

Prior to independence, there were many indications that Slovenia's secession from the Federal Republic of Yugoslavia would be met with protection arrangements for nonethnic Slovenes who were not covered by the existing constitutional provisions given to the autochthonous minorities from the Hungarian and Italian communities.[21] One means of protection was the offer of citizenship to all foreigners who had resided permanently on Slovenian soil at the time of the plebiscite. To this end, the Act Governing Citizenship was introduced in June 1991 providing the nonautochthonous minorities with the opportunity of naturalization. According to article 40, former Yugoslav nationals who were resident on the territory of Slovenia could apply to naturalize but were restricted to a six-month period. More than 170,000 were granted citizenship in this way, but thousands of others who either did not know about the law or who simply failed to apply were denied status. At this point, more than 25,000 Slovenian residents were disenfranchised, and the policy known as the *erasure* began.

In February 1992, article 81 of the Aliens Act came into force and designated new categories of noncitizens. In effect, all those who had been registered by means of the Aliens Act were deregistered and lost their residency rights and the social and economic privileges that came with residency status. The erased included a wide range of individuals with different histories—approximately five hundred officers from the Yugoslav National Army (JNA), many of whom had never participated in active service and had intermarried with Slovenes; Bosniaks, Croats, Serbs, and Roma who had migrated to Slovenia for work (especially in the mines); and civilians born in Slovenia whose birth had been registered in one of the other republics. The only unifying factor was that these individuals were perceived as southerners and thus exogenous to the Slovene nation.[22]

As evidenced by the documents now released by the Ministry of the Interior, there was a concerted effort to ignore the acquired rights of the residents who became erased.[23] Hence, the blame for the erasure must lie with the Slovenian government of the time. Residents were asked to present their documents to state agencies and appear before the town hall or local administrative unit. According to Jasminka Dedic, Vlasta Jalušic, and Jelka Zorn,[24] there was considerable uniformity of practice. Official authorities notified residents to appear in person, at which point their documents were often confiscated or destroyed—punched, defaced, cut up—in front of them. Those who lost their residency status became official foreigners—effectively stateless persons who automatically lost access to the social and political privileges they had enjoyed for decades.[25] The cancellation of their status left them especially vulnerable.

Several of the erased were subject to arbitrary removal and were deported from Slovenia.[26] One estimate is that approximately twenty people were expelled.[27] The *Helsinki Monitor*, a quarterly on security and cooperation in Europe, contends that the number is far greater and that people were handcuffed and transported to Croatia, Macedonia, and Montenegro by bus, plane, and ferry, respectively, without the knowledge of the destination states.[28] The expulsions also affected children and those who had just reached the age of majority.

The erasure broke up families and separated parents from their children.[29] Those who were able to work in Slovenia claimed that their lack of status made them liable to exploitation and subject to intensive and family-unfriendly work schedules. One participant explained that during the period when he was erased, he could not afford to be ill and could visit his child only once every two weeks. He did not have time for family, charging "they made mental invalids of us. I worked for 350 hours a month driving a taxi."[30]

One family of Bosnian refugees explained how their children had been removed from Slovenia at the insistence of the state, in spite of their refugee status and long-standing connection to Slovenia.[31] The daughter was born in Doboj, Bosnia, in 1980, and the father began working in mines in Slovenia in 1981. When the wife came to Slovenia in 1992 with their three children (age twelve, ten, and two and a half) as refugees, the father had temporary residency, and the wife and children received a residence permit. In 1995, the father filed papers for permanent residency but was turned down by the ministry because it was found that he had been outside the country for thirteen days. Officially, the five family members were refugees from 1992 to 1996, when the father received permanent residency. He received Slovene citizenship in 2002.

From 1992 to 1998, his daughter lived with the family in Valenje, Slovenia, on the basis of temporary residency. In January 1998, her father sought to extend her residency but was told that this would not be possible because she would turn eighteen in two months (March 1998) and would have to leave the country at that time. A few days before her birthday, as instructed, he took her back to Bosnia where she stayed with a family in Gracanica. The Slovene government merely gave her notice that she could return in 2001. Since 1998 the daughter has been able to visit her family in Slovenia on one-month tourist visas. Although the family became Slovene citizens in 2004, the daughter has been repeatedly refused a temporary residence permit.

In another case, a woman who was erased with her daughter explained how the erasure and the abuse she suffered at the hands of the state affected her family life and children.[32] In 1992, she placed her older daughter, who was mentally ill, in a special daycare unit. The costs were enormous, and her Bosnian father therefore offered to take the child with him to Bosnia and then send her to a relative in Germany. However, the war in Bosnia interrupted the family's plans, making it impossible to leave Bosnia until 1995. After the war ended in 1995, the woman brought her daughter back to Slovenia, where she unsuccessfully tried to obtain documents to enroll her child in school. Slovenian officials told her that if she herself had no documents, then the child could not obtain any either. Since 1996, the daughter has been living in Bosnia, unable to rejoin her mother.

Africa: Democratic Republic of the Congo

The conflicts in the Democratic Republic of the Congo have multiple sources, but one relates to the problem of statelessness—particularly the denial and deprivation of citizenship to the ethnic-Rwandan members of the Banyamulenge community. Although the Banyamulenge arrived in the territory of what is now the Democratic Republic of the Congo from Rwanda centuries ago, they have often been excluded from full participation in the country. At issue is the nature of Congolese identity. Some crucial markers are 1885, when King Leopold II of Belgium made the region his personal property; 1908, when the Belgium parliament took over the region as a colony; and 1960, when the country achieved independence.[33]

It is generally accepted that the Banyamulenge settled in the Mulenge hills between the towns of Uvira and Bukavu in what is now South Kivu. Several thousand were also forcibly migrated and settled in the region by the Belgian colonial forces, which enlisted the Banyamulenge as forced laborers on rubber and agricultural plantations. Living in the border region, they have since been collectively identified with ethnic interests both internal and external to the Congolese state, which has repeatedly sought to exclude them from full membership, including access to state resources. The exclusion of the Banyumulenge is illustrated by the personal testimony that a seventeen-year-old boy, now in detention in Egypt, gave to the Equal Rights Trust:[34]

We were not wanted in Congo. The people on the street treated us as if we were not Congolese. They treated us as if we were foreigners. This is because we are Banyumulenge. All Banyumulenge people in Congo are treated this way. Like my parents, many Banyunulenge people are living without papers. My sister and I never got Congolese nationality. People were always telling us we were not real Congolese. My mother taught us at home because I was not allowed to go to a public school. The Congolese government used to tell us that if we wanted to study, we should go to where our grandfathers came from in Rwanda.[35]

Relations between the Congo's main ethnic groups grew strained during the period following independence, when the Banyamulenge were charged with helping the Congolese National Army crush a rebellion in the Kivu region in 1964. The rebellion had aimed to install a communist style of government in which property, land, and cattle were to be shared among the local people. In January 1972, Joseph Désiré Mobutu, the president of Zaire (the country was known as Zaire from 1971 to 1997), signed a decree collectively granting Zairian citizenship to all Rwandan and Burundian natives who had settled in Zaire prior to 1950. However, this decree was retroactively invalidated by the parliament in 1981, effectively rendering the people of Rwandan origin stateless.

Preparations for elections in 1991 included the completion of a census, which again raised the question of the rights of the Banyamulenge to full political participation. As Mobutu reexamined the composition of the Zairian state under the auspices of a new "sovereign national conference," the place of the Banyamulenge attracted further attention. Unfortunately for the Banyamulenge, they were ultimately excluded, again on the grounds that they were nonindigenous. A few years later, the genocide in Rwanda and unrest in Burundi quickly drew the Banyamulenge and then state of Zaire into the wider ethnic conflicts. During the Rwandan genocide in 1994, thousands of Banyamulenge crossed back to neighboring Rwanda and joined the Tutsi-led rebels (the Rwandan Patriotic Front) to topple the Hutu-dominated government there. The transnational nature of the conflict continued after the genocide. For over fifteen years, the Democratic Forces for the Liberation of Rwanda[36] "preyed on Congolese civilians in the mountainous provinces of North and South Kivu," including children.[37]

In 1996, a local Zairian official warned all Banyamulenge that they must leave Zaire within a week and threatened to confiscate their property. Armed Banyamulenge repelled the Zairian offensive and were joined by rebel forces under the leadership of the future Zairian president, Laurent Kabila. The Banyamulenge were considered to have played an essential role in the overthrow of Mobutu, but their relationship with Kabila quickly eroded in 1998 when the new leader decided to expel Rwandan and Ugandan contingents from his army. In the name of defending Tutsis against oppression in North Kivu, a rebel army consisting primarily of Banyamulenge and commanded until recently by General Laurent Nkunda, has been fighting the DRC government. Despite a 2004 citizenship law granting citizenship to all those born on the territory that became the DRC, several hundred thousand of the Banyamulenge community have been unable to obtain nationality documents. As noted by the UK Home Office, "in practice, there are no examples of cases of Banyamulenge who have successfully obtained Congolese nationality."[38]

protection, the Bangladeshi government has repeatedly engaged in repatriation drives, forcing the Rohingya refugees back over the border into Myanmar. In spite of some internationally mediated initiatives—including the signing of a formal Memorandum of Understanding between UNHCR and the Myanmar government in November 1993, which enabled UNHCR to establish a presence on the ground in Rakhine state—the repatriation initiatives conducted in collaboration with the Bangladeshi authorities have raised many questions about the forced nature of these returns. Others have challenged that these repatriation initiatives violate international human-rights laws. In 1995, the United Nations assisted the Bangladeshi government in a repatriation process characterized by excessive use of force, including killings perpetrated by the Bangladeshi security forces and also by the Burmese troops receiving the Rohingya.[48]

Although the Bangladeshi authorities have returned hundreds of thousands of Rohingya to Arakan state in Myanmar, new refugee movements continue unabated, fueled by the ongoing repression of the Rohingya in Myanmar. Unfortunately, recently arrived Rohingya refugees from Myanmar have been denied access to UNHCR-supported refugee camps in Cox's Bazaar because the Bangladeshi authorities have described new arrivals as "economic migrants." Furthermore, the Bangladeshi government has recently stepped up efforts to return large numbers of Rohingya in the wake of new conflicts over the 320 kilometer maritime border between Myanmar and Bangladesh. The latest conflict was exacerbated following an agreement between the government of Myanmar and South Korea's Daewoo International Corporation, which was granted oil and gas exploration rights in an area of contested waters. Since then, Bangladeshi border forces have expelled Rohingya living in the border area. Tensions worsened following the rejection of a repatriation plan by the Burmese junta in 2008 and the recent news that it had started construction of a 200 kilometer fence to prevent future "push backs" of Rohingya into Myanmar.[49] One consequence of the tensions between Myanmar and Bangladesh over the maritime border has been an influx of Rohingya refugees to recognized camps, which has created a strain on resources.[50] A recent decision by the European Commission on the financing of humanitarian assistance to Bangladesh noted that the numbers of Rohingya in Cox's Bazaar had increased dramatically in just one year as a result of the internal flows of Rohingya seeking safety:[51]

DG ECHO[52] mission in September 2008 identified a spontaneous settlement of around 5,000 undocumented Rohingyas, living in very poor conditions, directly adjacent to Kutupalong UNHCR camp; a further DG ECHO mission in February 2009 observed that this spontaneous settlement had grown considerably; most of the inhabitants seem to have been expelled from Bangladeshi villages.

Recent humanitarian assessments carried out by DG ECHO partners between March and April 2009 revealed that there are now approximately 20,500 people in this spontaneous settlement and their living conditions have deteriorated: they have very basic shelters with no access to healthcare, sanitation or safe water, and are excluded from official camp services.[53]

Recent arrests by Bangladeshi forces have further discouraged Rohingya from leaving the relative safety of camps in search of work and food.

The problems facing stateless Rohingya children, a disproportionately large section of this refugee population, are especially daunting. Those outside of the handful of UNHCR refugee camps cannot access education and are subject to malnutrition, ill health, and chronic poverty.[54] Before the latest border dispute resulted in the collective confinement of large numbers of Rohingya refugees, Rohingya children were left to wander the streets unaccompanied, which put them at considerable risk of abuse, including drug use, exploitation, and trafficking. Indeed, reports of Rohingya children in Malaysia[55] and elsewhere demonstrate how such children may be "groomed for a life of abuse."

The Obligation to Protect and the Right to Nationality

The above case studies provide a brief illustration of forms of abuse that result from the deprivation of and the loss of a right to nationality. These include arbitrary expulsion, child exploitation in war, and the denial of the right to work, be educated, and secure decent housing. Although the states described vary in the degree to which they are party to particular human-rights instruments, they are all guilty of mistreatment of children by virtue of the prohibitions in international law described at the outset of this chapter. In this context, the academic distinction between state action where rights are denied (for example, cases where such children are deemed to be outside the polity) and situations where the rights of children are directly violated by states and third parties (for example, through expulsions and enlistment in armed units) is arguably of little legal value. It does, however, raise an important issue regarding membership and the effects of exclusion on the basis of nationality.

Status matters. In situations where stateless children had some formal status (for example, as refugees in one of the select camps in Bangladesh), they enjoyed considerably greater access to rights (education, health care, housing) than children without status. Having a recognized immigration and nationality status may determine whether one can access resources to address basic needs. Yet even in other situations (for example, in developed states such as the United Kingdom and Slovenia, where there is the added layer of European protection), status is essential to personal identity and security. The lack of formal status was a less predictable indicator of the personal fortunes of the Kashmiri children in the UK or the erased in Slovenia since some of the interviewees were able to enjoy education and had access to other rights before they turned eighteen, and some were able to remain in their country of residence after turning eighteen while others faced removal. Nonetheless, being legally stateless in Europe raised a number of fears and presented challenges that prevented young people from enjoying a reasonable quality of life. Above all, the arbitrariness of their situation and the inconsistent application of laws left them vulnerable to exploitation, psychological distress, and other illnesses.

For human-rights advocates, there are a number of conclusions to be drawn from the above discussion. The fact that some states may instigate abuse against children and create conditions of rightlessness requires further attention. As illustrated in the cases of the Rohingya in Myanmar and the erased in Slovenia, people who are excluded from censuses or deliberately removed from formal registers are susceptible to subsequent abuse on the grounds of nationality. The fact that legislation can be created subsequently (as in the Democratic Republic of the Congo and Slovenia) or applied retroactively (as in Myanmar) illustrates the fragility of nationality as a cornerstone of human-rights protection. As the above case studies demonstrate, nationality is a long-standing issue at the heart of geopolitical tensions and thus an issue that may be activated with potentially devastating human impacts during periods of political uncertainty.

Conclusion

The rights of children are among the most elaborated within contemporary international law. Children, however, may be exposed to gaps in the human-rights architecture regarding the implementation of such protection in the event that states do not recognize these rights under international law.

Unfortunately, neither the right to nationality nor many of the rights elaborated in the CRC and associated human-rights instruments are sufficient to prevent states from reinterpreting their obligations and deciding whom they should protect. Yet even though the right of children to a nationality is not sufficient to guarantee their protection from abuse by the state, respect for the right to nationality may nonetheless act as an important line of defense (for example, against expulsion, especially in the European context). Moreover, since nationality disputes may give rise to unrest and the violation of children's rights, as shown most emphatically in the Congolese case, it is essential that the protection of the right to nationality be considered a key element of conflict prevention. The mistreatment of minorities should send up early warning flags. To protect stateless children effectively, stringent efforts are required to shore up the right to nationality and to tie it more explicitly to widely accepted prohibitions against discrimination.

Notes

1. For a comprehensive review of the literature, see Brad K. Blitz, *Statelessness, Protection, and Equality*, UK Department of International Development and University of Oxford, Refugee Studies Centre Policy Brief, September 2009, <http://www.rsc.ox.ac.uk> (accessed January 5, 2010).

2. International Court of Justice (ICJ), "Nationality Decrees Issued in Tunis and Morocco," Advisory Opinion no. 4, February 7, 1923, <http://www.unhcr.org> (accessed February 2, 2010).

3. League of Nations, Convention on Certain Questions Relating to the Conflict of Nationality Law, April 13, 1930, League of Nations, *Treaty Series*, vol. 179, p. 89, no. 4137, <http://www.unhcr.org> (accessed February 2, 2010).

4. UN General Assembly, "Universal Declaration of Human Rights," December 10, 1948, 217A(III), art. 15(2), <http://www.unhcr.org> (accessed February 2, 2010).

5. The Human Rights Committee has suggested that the concept of arbitrariness should be interpreted more broadly to include actions that might be described as "inappropriate" and "unjust" as well. For a good discussion on this point, see Open Society Justice Initiative, "Human Rights and Legal Identity: Approaches to Combating Statelessness and Arbitrary Deprivation of Nationality," paper presented at conference in New York, May 2006.

6. Examples acquiring by fraudulent means, voluntarily acquiring another nationality, or serving in a foreign military force. Other criteria that might be relied on include settlement in another country, no genuine link to the declared country or nationality that would support a claim to citizenship, and the placement of the national security or interests of a state at considerable risk.

7. The UN Committee on Economic, Social, and Cultural Rights' General Comment 4 makes a formal connection among survival, housing, and the preservation of cultural identities. See UN Committee on Economic, Social, and Cultural Rights (CESCR), "General Comment No. 4: The Right to Adequate

Housing (Art. 11(1) of the Covenant)," December 13, 1991, E/1992/23, <http://www.unhcr.org> (accessed February 2, 2010).

8. Under article 27, the Covenant declares that "In those States in which ethnic, religious or linguistic minorities exist, persons belonging to such minorities shall not be denied the right, in community with the other members of their group, to enjoy their own culture, to profess and practice their own religion, or to use their own language."

9. Although states may insist on language tests as a condition for the acquisition of citizenship, the article 27 affirms the rights of minorities to maintain and preserve their cultural identity and thus prohibits attempts to deny nationality on the grounds that minorities may speak another language or engage in different cultural practices.

10. See UN General Assembly, International Covenant on Economic, Social and Cultural Rights, December 16, 1966, A/RES/2200, art. 11(1), <http://www.unhcr.org> (accessed February 2, 2010).

11. For example, the nationality of married women and children is first mentioned in the 1930 Hague Convention on Certain Questions Relating to the Conflict of Nationality Laws under chapters III and IV, respectively. The rights of married women have been further elaborated in the 1957 Convention on the Nationality of Married Women. These principles are expressed even more strongly in article 9 of the 1979 Convention on the Elimination of All Forms of Discrimination against Women, December 18, 1979.

12. See David Weissbrodt, "Final Report on the Rights of Non-Citizens," UN Doc. E/CN.4/Sub.2/2003/23 UNHCR, 2003.

13. See UN Committee on the Elimination of Racial Discrimination (CERD), "CERD General Recommendation XXX on Discrimination against Non Citizens," October 1, 2002, <http://www.unhcr.org> (accessed February 2, 2010).

14. See "Concluding Observations of the Committee on the Elimination of Racial Discrimination: Mauritania," CERD/C/65/CO/5, December 10, 2004, par. 18, <http://www.unhchr.ch> (accessed July 7, 2010).

15. See High Court (Botswana), *Attorney General v. Unity Dow*, CA No. 4/91, July 3, 1992, <http://www.law-lib.utoronto.ca> (accessed January 5, 2010).

16. UN High Commissioner for the Rights of Refugees (UNHCR), *Statistical Online Population Database*, 2009, <http://apps.who.int> (accessed January 5, 2010).

17. See, for example, the 2007 Still Human Still Here campaign by British NGOs, which highlighted the destitution of tens of thousands of refused asylum seekers in the United Kingdom, <http://stillhumanstillhere.wordpress.com> (accessed July 7, 2010).

18. See A. Bloch, "Refugee Settlement in Britain: The Impact of Policy on Participation," *Journal of Ethnic and Migration Studies* 26, no. 1 (2006): 75–88; J. A. Dennis, *A Case for Change: How Refugee Children in England Are Missing Out* (London: Children's Society, Refugee Council, and Save the Children, 2002); and R. Sales, "The Deserving and Undeserving? Refugees, Asylum Seekers and Welfare in Britain," *Critical Social Policy* 22, no. 3 (2002): 456–478.

19. Sales, "The Deserving and Undeserving?"

20. In spite of large demonstrations in 2007, the State Assembly of the Jammu and Kashmir rejected a bill in May 2007 seeking to grant citizenship and other rights for the refugees of west Pakistan in the Jammu and Kashmir states.

21. Brad K. Blitz, "Statelessness and the Social (De)Construction of Citizenship: Political Restructuring and Ethnic Discrimination In Slovenia," *Journal of Human Rights* 5, no. 4 (2006): 1–27.

22. Ibid.

23. Jelka Zorn and rsula Lipovec ebron, *Once upon an Erasure: From Citizens to Illegal Residents in the Republic of Slovenia* (Ljubljana: Študentska Založba, 2008), <http://www.izbrisan17let.si> (accessed July 7, 2010).

24. J. Dedic, V. Jalušic, and J. Zorn, *The Erased: Organized Innocence and the Politics of Exclusion* (Ljubljana: Peace Institute, 2003).

25. Amnesty International, "Slovenia: Amnesty International's Briefing to the UN Committee on Economic, Social and Cultural Rights," 35th Session, November 2005.

26. European Commission against Racism and Intolerance (ECRI), "Second Report on Slovenia, adopted 13 December 2002," Document CRI (2003), 39, July 8, 2003.

27. Matevz Krivic, interview with the author, June 9, 2004.

28. Helsinki Monitor of Slovenia, "Human Rights Problems in Slovenia," Statement No. 1, February 11, 1998, <http://www.fortunecity.com> (accessed January 5, 2010).

29. See Dedic, Jalušic, and Zorn, *The Erased*.

30. Focus group with author, June 14, 2004, Velenje, Slovenia.

31. Interview with Beslagic family, June 14, 2004, Velenje, Slovenia

32. Focus group, Ljubljana, June 10, 2004; Dragica Lukic, Bosnian Catholic (that is how she described herself).

33. B. Manby, *Struggles for Citizenship in Africa* (London: Zed Books, 2009), 8.

34. Equal Rights Trust, "Testimony of a Stateless Child in Detention in Egypt," *Equal Rights Trust Review* 3 (2009): 56–62.

35. Ibid., 57.

36. Les Forces Démocratiques de Libération du Rwanda (FDLR).

37. Human Rights Watch, "You Will Be Punished: Attacks on Civilians in Eastern Congo," *Human Rights Watch* (December 2009), <http://www.hrw.org> (accessed January 5, 2010).

38. Home Office, "Operational Guidance Note: Democratic Republic of Congo (DRC)," OGN V8.0, August 20, 2007, 12, <http://www.unhcr.org>.

39. See Manby, *Struggles for Citizenship in Africa*.

40. See Pax Christi International, "Human Insecurity in DRC: Examining the Causes and Effects," February 28, 2006, <http://storage.paxchristi.net> (accessed January 5, 2010).

41. See UN General Assembly, "Children and Armed Conflict: Report of the Secretary-General," December 21, 2007, A/62/609–S/2007/757, <http://www.unhcr.org> (accessed February 2, 2010).

42. Human Rights Watch, "You Will Be Punished," 109.

43. Ibid., 93.

44. Amnesty International, "Perilous Plight: Burma's Rohingya Take to the Seas," May 2009, <http://www.hrw.org> (accessed January 5, 2010).

45. C. Grundy-Warr and E. Wong, "Sanctuary under a Plastic Sheet: The Unresolved Problem of Rohingya Refugees," IBRU Boundary and Security Bulletin 5, no. 3 (Autumn 1997): 79–91.

46. Amnesty International, "Perilous Plight," 6.

47. Lawi Weng, "Rohingya Issue to Be Focus of Talks," The Irradwaddy, December 28, 2009, <http://www.irrawaddy.org> (accessed January 5, 2010).

48. Amnesty International, "Perilous Plight."

49. See Alex Ellgee, "The Vise Tightens on Rohingya in Bangladesh," The Irrawaddy, November 7, 2009, <http://www.irrawaddy.org>.

50. See Weng, "Rohingya Issue to Be Focus of Talks."

51. Commission of the European Communities, "Commission Decision on the Financing of Emergency Humanitarian Actions from the General Budget of the European Communities in Bangladesh," ECHO/BGD/BUD/2009/02000, <http://ec.europa.eu> (accessed January 5, 2010).

52. Ibid.

53. Commission of the European Communities, "Commission Decision," 2.

54. Ibid.

55. J. Allchin, "Rohingya Children Groomed for a Life of Abuse," Democratic Voice of Burma, November 4, 2009, <http://english.dvb.no> (accessed January 5, 2010).

3

Volatile Citizenship or Statelessness? Citizen Children of Palestinian Descent and the Loss of Nationality in Israel

Christina O. Alfirev

"On our wedding day, I was alone," Kifah explains, reenacting the occasion by dancing without the bridegroom across the screen of Ayelet Bechar's 2005 documentary film *Just Married*. Kifah, a Palestinian Israeli citizen, married Yazid, a Palestinian man from the Gaza Strip. They had first met in Germany, and she eventually returned to live in Germany after the wedding ceremony so she could be with her husband, even though this meant giving up her high-ranking position at Israel's ministry of culture. Kifah returns to Israel when she is pregnant to arrange the necessary paperwork for her unborn child. The social security officer advises her to remain in Israel for the birth of her child to avoid the risk of them both losing Israeli citizenship for being abroad too long. Unable to constrain her frustration any longer, Kifah bursts out in Hebrew: "I won't lose my citizenship!" In the end, Kifah chooses to give birth where her husband can be present, and so their child is born in a German hospital.

Like many others, this young family faces an uncertain situation. In 2003, the Knesset, the Israeli parliament, enacted the Citizenship and Entry into Israel Law as a temporary order (hereafter Temporary Order).[1] According to the law, legal residence and naturalization in Israel are denied to all persons hailing from the Gaza Strip, the West Bank, Lebanon, Syria, Iran, or Iraq. The law effectively prevents family reunification and residence in Israel. According to a 2008 article in the British newspaper *The Guardian*, the Interior Ministry declared that some 4,600 Palestinians were waiting for the Temporary Order to be lifted to have their residence status renewed.[2] In addition to Palestinians from the Occupied Palestinian Territories (OPT), the law disproportionately affects the roughly 20 percent of Israeli citizens who are Palestinians[3] and who marry Palestinians from those areas.

As an Israeli citizen, Kifah may also be affected by the Nationality Law, particularly section 11, which deals with the annulment of nationality[4] after taking up residence in several Arab countries and regions. Since the law was enacted in 1952, it has undergone several amendments, most recently in October 2008. This amendment was meant to be less intransigent than its predecessors because a safeguard against *legal statelessness*[5] on the loss of nationality was built into the law. Yet this safeguard is nullified due to the vagueness of its wording.

Core considerations of this chapter are the volatility of Israeli citizenship for Palestinian Israelis, the risk of legal statelessness flowing from an involuntary loss of citizenship, and the disproportionate effect of this type of statelessness on children. Israel's state practice is analyzed in the light of international legal norms and, to a lesser extent, national security concerns. For Israel's Palestinian minority, the principle cause of involuntary loss of citizenship is the conflict of nationality laws. In addition, Palestinian children also risk becoming stateless as a result of the revocation of a parent's legal status. The parent's withdrawal of nationality and, more so, the derivative loss of children's citizenship, I argue, are contrary to widely accepted international human-rights norms, particularly the obligation to respect a child's best interest. Concerns such as national security, I contend, do not outweigh the duty to respect the best interests of children.

If considered individually, neither the most recent amendment to Israel's nationality law nor the Temporary Order necessarily cause statelessness. Moreover, neither law explicitly refers to Israel's Palestinian minority, although the Temporary Order and the Citizenship Law refer to regions inhabited by Arabs. Yet Jewish Israeli citizens as well as Jewish immigrants are not in practice affected because they are eligible for Israeli citizenship under another law regulating Israeli nationality, the 1950 Law of Return. So it is the citizenship rights of Israel's Palestinian minority that are at stake as they are negatively impacted by the Temporary Order and the latest amendment to the Nationality Law just discussed.

The combination of these laws confronts Israeli citizens such as Kifah with some tough choices. Kifah can either live abroad with her Gazan husband, risking statelessness if she takes up residence in one of the disqualifying countries listed in the nationality laws; she can stay in Israel unmarried; or she can return to Israel following her marriage without her husband to raise their child there alone. Kifah's dilemma is a result of Israel's violation of binding international legal norms, particularly norms regarding family unity and nationality.

I compare Israeli national law to international standards regarding children's best interests in terms of their right to acquire a nationality, protection from the loss of citizenship, family unity, and the avoidance of statelessness. I then discuss the conflict of nationality laws leading to children's volatile citizenship and their risk of derivative statelessness after a parent's involuntary loss of citizenship.

Torn between Citizenship and Family: Israel's Laws on Nationality and International Legal Norms

Israel has an ethnocentric, Janus-faced conception of citizenship. Persons of Jewish faith can immigrate to Israel and be granted citizenship any time. As a result of Israeli laws, Jews are therefore potential Israeli citizens, even if they have spent no time at all in the country. As a result of other Israeli laws, non-Jewish Israeli citizens risk losing their citizenship through no fault or disloyalty of their own, especially if they find themselves caught in a conflict of laws—Israel's Nationality Law and the Temporary Order on family reunification. Palestinian children are particularly at risk of this loss of citizenship because any withdrawal of nationality from their parents may be transmitted to them. Under certain circumstances, children of Palestinian parents may end up stateless.

Israel has ratified several international human-rights instruments referring to children's rights, including the Convention on the Rights of the Child (CRC).[6] Since the CRC has been ratified by all states except the United States and Somalia, it reflects a near international consensus on states' obligations toward children within their jurisdiction. At the core of the CRC is the "best-interest" principle. According to article 3(1) of the CRC, "the best interests of the child shall be a primary consideration." As Jacqueline Bhabha has noted, this does not mean that the best interests of the child are the "paramount or trumping consideration."[7] However, the principle does imply, at a minimum, that states cannot simply disregard the child's best interest. On the contrary, they are required to take it into account and weigh the consequences of policies that conflict with these interests,[8] such as family separation on grounds of national security concerns. It follows that Israel, as a ratifying state, is bound to protect key rights enshrined in the Convention, such as the right to acquire a nationality (a critical method for avoiding statelessness) and the child's right to family unity. To comply with its international obligations, Israel is therefore bound to prevent the derivative statelessness that flows to children from their parents' loss of nationality.

Children's Right to a Nationality
In public international law, the state has discretionary powers in terms of conferment and withdrawal of nationality.[9] Indeed, this is widely

tive of whether there had been any (other) breach of allegiance, constitutes a breach of loyalty. The relevant countries are Afghanistan, Iran, Lebanon, Libya, Sudan, Syria, Iraq, Pakistan, Yemen, and the Gaza Strip.[30] Permanent residence or receipt of citizenship in any of these states is now deemed a breach of loyalty, tantamount to an act of terror or treason. To mitigate the sweeping scope of this amendment, the revocation of citizenship based on a breach of loyalty was made conditional on the person affected not ending up stateless. Yet this safeguard is compromised by the fact that the same article envisages statelessness in some cases: where the individual will end up stateless, the article stipulates, residence in Israel will be granted. Moreover, the law "assumes" that a person permanently residing outside Israel will not remain stateless. Unlike in previous amendments, the consequence of a parent's revocation of citizenship on a child is not specified. However, given that the possibility of statelessness is not entirely excluded in this amendment, it may well be presumed that the child's loss of citizenship is conditional on the parent's.

In practice, Israel has never stripped Jewish citizens of their citizenship and rarely, if ever, revoked the nationality of citizens belonging to a minority. However, in view of the successive amendments of Israel's Nationality Law, it is likely that citizenship for non-Jews will become progressively easier to lose, especially for Palestinian citizens. Residence abroad is more likely to lead to unilateral withdrawal of citizenship, thanks to the recent amendments, and safeguards against statelessness are not absolute and rely on the unverified assumption that persons residing abroad have an alternative nationality.

Children's Right to Family Unity

The right to family unity is central to our understanding of a child's best interests. Although this right is protected by several human-rights treaties,[31] the CRC gives the most expansive gloss on the scope of this protection. It states that the right to family unity includes within it the right not to be separated, the right to reunification, and a state's obligation to process family-reunion applications by a migrant child or his parents "in a positive, humane and expeditious manner."[32]

In 2003, the Israeli Knesset passed the Citizenship and Entry into Israel Law (Temporary Order) 5763-2003.[33] This law prevents family unification in Israel between Israeli citizens and Palestinian residents of the West Bank and Gaza Strip because the latter are barred from attaining permanent residence status or citizenship in Israel. Subsequent amendments were passed to soften the effects of the law on affected families. In 2005, the law was amended to grant the minister of the interior discretionary powers to issue a residence permit to the immediate family of an Israeli citizen.[34] The minister was also authorized to make decisions about granting residence permits to minors from the Gaza Strip and the West Bank on a case-by-case basis.[35] Furthermore, in 2007, the law was amended to enable a humanitarian committee to examine family-unification requests in exceptional cases. But at the same time as these measures were enacted, the scope of government interference with family unification was extended beyond the Gaza Strip and the West Bank. Lebanon, Iraq, Iran, and Syria are now all listed as countries subject to a prohibition on family unifications.[36] Although initially conceived as a temporary measure, the law has been continually renewed.

In 2006, the law, as amended in 2005, was reviewed for its constitutionality and compliance with international law by the Israeli Supreme Court. The case was submitted by Adalah, an organization advocating for the rights of Israel's Palestinian minority, along with other civil society associations. Given the difficulties of promoting the rights of Palestinians who have no formal right to be in the country, Adalah first focused on the violation of constitutional rights for Israeli citizens, especially the right to family life and the right to equality.[37] In particular, Adalah emphasized the discriminatory denial of rights.[38] It highlighted the fact that since Israelis of Jewish origin rarely marry a person from the Gaza Strip and the West Bank,[39] the law (without making any explicit reference to national origin) overwhelmingly targeted the 1 million Palestinian Israelis.[40] The advocacy group also referred to violations of human rights (the right to marriage, family life, and the reunification of families) under international law.[41]

Conversely, the government defended the law on grounds of national security. Its justification was based on the facts following the outbreak of the second Intifada in 2000, when thirty-eight terrorist attacks were perpetrated or aided and abetted by Palestinian men who had received residence status through marriage and reunification with their families within Israel.[42] Daphne Barak-Erez observes that the law is based on an assumption that "all Palestinians residing in Israel would uniformly place loyalty to their people above loyalty to the state."[43] The government further denied that reasons other than those of national security constituted the basis for instituting the law. Consequently, it claimed that the law "is not based on any demographic purpose of restricting the increase of the Palestinian population in Israel."[44] The government also stressed the temporary character of the law, claiming that it would be abandoned once the reasons for enacting it (the terrorist attacks) subsided.[45]

These government justifications did not convince Adalah. Relying on the parliamentary debates preceding the enactment of the law to establish that demographic considerations were behind it, Adalah claimed that the number of people who had abused the right to family unification for terrorist purposes was too minimal to justify the imposition of a blanket policy on the entire Palestinian Israeli minority.[46] Instead, given the disproportionately severe discriminatory impact of the law on a subset of the population, Adalah called for the abolition of the blanket policy and a case-by-case investigation of all terrorist attacks.[47]

Ultimately, the High Court of Justice narrowly ruled in favor of the government. The majority agreed with the government's argument that since the "Palestinian Authority [was] *de facto* waging war or quasi-war against Israel," this made the residents of the territory enemy nationals.[48] Justice Adiel, acknowledging that the law violated a constitutional right to family life, nevertheless claimed that "in view of the bloody conflict between the Palestinians and Israel, the violation of the constitutional right is proportionate."[49] Hence, Adalah's petition was rejected because of the security situation in Israel. The law was also justified because of its temporary character. Justice Levy admonished that if changes were not made to the law, however, the latter would be unlikely to "satisfy judicial scrutiny in the future."[50]

In spite of the fact that the majority of the court sided with the view of the government, specific attention was paid to a child's right to family unity. Presenting the opinion of the minority, Chief Justice Aharon Barak held that the right to family life has a dual aspect. He argued that it includes the parent's right to raise a child in the parent's own country and a child's right to be raised in his or her own family:

Respect for family unity has, therefore, two aspects. The *first* aspect is the right of the Israeli parent to raise his child in his country. This is the right of the Israeli parent to realize his parenthood in its entirety, the right to enjoy his relationship with his child and not be severed from him. This is the right to raise his child in his home, in his country. This is the right of the parent not to be compelled to emigrate from Israel, as a condition for realizing his parenthood. It is based on the autonomy and privacy of the family unit. This right is violated if we do not allow the minor child of the Israeli parent to live with him in Israel. The *second* aspect is the right of the child to family life. It is based on the independent recognition of the human rights of children. These rights are given in essence to every human being . . . , whether adult or minor. The child "is a human being with rights and needs of his own." . . . The child has the right to grow up in a complete and stable family unit.[51]

Israel's Conflict of Laws: A Sign of Statelessness or Volatile Citizenship?

Israel's nationality laws, taken together, have a harmful effect on Palestinian children. At best, children's citizenship is volatile, perpetually at risk of being undermined by legislative constraints. At worst, children are subject to derivative statelessness by losing their nationality when their parents lose theirs. International norms to which Israel has adhered should preempt the creation of stateless children. States, including Israel, evidently enjoy discretionary powers to regulate the conferment and withdrawal of citizenship by weighing national security concerns against individual protections, but these powers are constrained by the state's obligations under international law, which include attention to the avoidance of statelessness and the protection of children.

Statelessness can occur at birth or through loss of citizenship. Paul Weis distinguishes between "original or absolute statelessness for persons being born stateless and subsequent or relative statelessness for persons who lose their citizenship."[52] At birth, a child can end up stateless if he or she does not acquire nationality on the basis of *jus soli* (birth in the territory) or *jus sanguinis* (descent by blood).[53] Loss of citizenship results in statelessness if the individual has no second nationality to fall back on or if the loss of nationality occurs before a new nationality is granted. Hannah Arendt provided the most harrowing account of Nazi Germany's political motives in creating statelessness through mass denationalizations in Eastern Europe during World War II:

> The Jews in these newly annexed areas were always denied the status of nationals; they automatically became stateless and therefore suffered the same fate as the refugees in Western Europe—they were invariably the first to be deported and liquidated.[54]

It is likely that U.S. Supreme Court Chief Justice Earl Warren had Arendt's images in mind when he ruled in *Trop v. Dulles* that "denationalization . . . constituted cruel and unusual punishment . . . because it rendered the expatriate stateless."[55] Yet this statement applies only when the loss of citizenship actually does leave a person stateless and not when it simply eliminates one of multiple possible nationalities to which the person is entitled. Furthermore, his assertion that citizenship is "the right to have rights . . . [and a] priceless possession . . . [the removal of which leaves a person stateless, and thus] disgraced and degraded in the eyes of his countrymen,"[56] ignores stateless persons' rights under the emerging human-rights regime of the 1950s. As David

Weissbrodt has pointedly observed, rather than being a citizen, it is "being human [that brings with it] . . . the right to have rights."[57]

Protection and Its Limits under the Human-Rights Regime

The 1954 Convention Relating to the Status of Stateless Persons (hereafter 1954 Statelessness Convention) consolidated a range of civil, social, economic, and cultural rights for stateless persons by drawing on existing human-rights conventions, including the 1951 Convention Relating to the Status of Refugees (hereafter 1951 Refugee Convention). Among other rights, the latter includes the rights to education, health care, and work.[58]

In addition to the 1954 Statelessness Convention, other human-rights treaties implicitly grant rights to stateless persons. Of particular relevance are the nondiscrimination clauses of the ICCPR and the International Covenant on Economic, Social, and Cultural Rights (ICESCR).[59] The former, for instance, exhorts states to

respect and to ensure to all individuals within its territory and subject to its jurisdiction the rights recognized in the present Covenant, without distinction of any kind, such as race, colour, sex, language, religion, political or other opinion, national or social origin, property, birth or other status.

Hannah Arendt questioned the efficacy of the concept of human rights by pointing out how, in twentieth-century Europe, "the Rights of Man, supposedly inalienable, proved to be unenforceable."[60] The interwoven web of states' human-rights obligations to citizens and noncitizens alike is stronger today than it was at the time of Arendt's writing. Numerous treaty bodies, Special Rapporteurs, and human-rights organizations monitor states' implementation of human rights. Robyn Linde, for instance, has documented the leverage exercised by international organizations on the Czech Republic to persuade it to change its citizenship law in 1999 and enable some 10,000 to 25,000 formerly stateless Roma residing in the country to access citizenship.[61] Stateless people today are therefore not as rightless as Arendt believed them to be. Moreover, as Jyothi Kanics argues elsewhere in this volume, litigation can be a powerful tool for asserting the rights of marginalized populations, including the stateless.[62] In addition to this legal strategy, the human-rights system provides a mechanism through which stateless persons can have their voices heard.

Nevertheless, statelessness remains an all too real and undesirable status. Several general observations serve to emphasize this point. First, despite the fact that stateless persons' eligibility for basic human-rights protections is no longer in question as a matter of international law, some rights remain reserved for citizens. Thus, although the ICCPR applies to all human beings equally, political rights (such as the right to vote and stand for office) are rights that states may grant only to citizens.[63] In addition, states typically provide diplomatic protection only to citizens. Most critically, only noncitizens can be deported. Second, apart from disparities in rights access, stateless persons are *de facto* among the most vulnerable people in society. Even in states where they are legally recognized, stateless people often encounter difficulties accessing rights to which they are entitled. And they may avoid asserting their rights for fear of retributions or arbitrary detention.[64] To be legally recognized as a stateless person is therefore an incomplete solution.

Palestinian Children's Difficulties in Accessing an Effective Nationality

The natural remedy for statelessness is the conferment of nationality. This is reflected in both the United Nations Study of Statelessness and the 1954 Statelessness Convention. The former lists remedies to eliminate statelessness,[65] and the latter calls on states to facilitate the naturalization process and confer nationality on stateless persons living in the country.[66] The goal of *eradicating* all statelessness was considerably weakened by the second convention on statelessness—the 1961 Convention on the Reduction of Statelessness (hereafter the 1961 Statelessness Convention)— which focused on *reduction* of the phenomenon. According to Carol Batchelor, the drafters of that Convention felt that elimination would be too far-reaching a goal because it might interfere with states' prerogative in matters of nationality. Reflecting these concerns, the 1961 Statelessness Convention aims at avoiding statelessness at birth but does not exclude the possibility of subsequent withdrawals of citizenship under certain circumstances.[67]

State practice, as born out by a Supreme Court decision,[68] suggests that Israel considers citizenship to be a fundamental right that cannot easily be withdrawn. To date, no Israeli citizen has ever, according to my research, been stripped of his or her nationality, a fact that is at least consistent with Israeli support for the principle of a right to a nationality in international law. Moreover, Israel is bound to respect all international instruments that are part of customary international law, including the nationality provisions set out in the Universal Declaration of Human Rights (UDHR). Yet it is not clear that Israel accepts these provisions to be binding on its practice. Although the attribution and revocation of nationality represent cardinal pillars of state sovereignty, international treaties are not self-executing in Israel and have to be both ratified and incorporated into national law to be legally binding.[69] Israel has ratified the 1954 Statelessness Convention and signed the 1961 Statelessness Convention,[70] but neither convention is directly applicable in national law because Israel has not passed any national legislation addressing the problem of statelessness. As a result, the impact of customary international law on statelessness is weak in terms of practical effect within Israel.

Although weak, it is not completely ineffective. In a case decided in 2007, the Tel Aviv Administrative Court concurred with the Association for Civil Rights in Israel (ACRI) that the government failed to accord stateless people residence permits or access to services. Recognizing the precarious situation of stateless persons, the court instructed the interior ministry to establish procedures to register stateless persons and grant them *temporary residence permits*. But the court's decision went only part of the way to recognizing the needs of stateless people; it turned down the petitioners' request for access to permanent status in Israel.[71]

ACRI has also highlighted the potential statelessness of Palestinian children subjected to the Temporary Order. The latter, as amended in 2005, enabled Palestinian children with an Israeli citizen parent to be granted residence (but not citizenship) status when they returned to Israel from one of the prohibited territories listed in the law. However, ACRI noted that this residence permit was often not sufficient to access health and social services.[72] Therefore, Palestinian children who are allowed to stay in Israel on a temporary residence permit but who have no alternative nationality are stateless, and they are unable to access the services to which they are entitled as stateless residents. The circumstances of these Palestinian children clearly contravene Israel's duty to naturalize stateless persons and to consider a child's best interests.[73]

Consequences of the Conflict of Laws for Palestinian Children

Because of Israel's nationality laws, Jewish and Palestinian citizen children do not risk statelessness to the same extent. Israeli children of Jewish descent are guaranteed access to Israeli citizenship at all times thanks to the Law of Return. In fact, it is renunciation, not acquisition of citizenship, that presents a hurdle for Jewish citizens. Their place of birth and the length of their residence in Israel are irrelevant.

The disparity between this situation and the circumstances facing Palestinian citizen children is sharp. If the parents of Palestinian Israeli children have their Israeli nationality withdrawn, then the Palestinian children risk losing or never acquiring Israeli citizenship. Because their status depends on their mother's or father's due to the *jus sanguinis* rule in Israel, they are subject to derivative statelessness.

Even though one of its stated goals is to avoid statelessness, the 1952 Nationality Law allows admits the possibility that Palestinian children can become legally stateless.[74] A parent's nationality can be revoked if he or she has "been disloyal" by obtaining citizenship or permanent residence status in the Gaza Strip, Iran, Afghanistan, Lebanon, Libya, Sudan, Syria, Iraq, Pakistan, or Yemen. A true safeguard against statelessness would be a stipulation that citizenship can be revoked only with reliable evidence that nationality of another state granting citizenship rights has been achieved. Simply acquiring permanent residence is no guarantee of nationality, and yet (when it occurs in the countries listed), it is considered a breach of loyalty and a disqualification as regards Israeli citizenship. What happens to a child when a parent thus becomes stateless is not clear.

According to the Temporary Order, residents of a certain age range[75] from the West Bank, Gaza, and, since 2007, Iran, Iraq, Syria, and Lebanon are prohibited from attaining a residence permit in Israel for purposes of unification with their Israeli spouses. Although some children may receive a residence permit to be with their Israeli parent, this permit does not necessarily entail access to social and health services. Although the 2007 amendment permits exceptions on humanitarian grounds, the mere fact of having shared children does not count as one such humanitarian exception and does not therefore justify the grant of family unification or access to legal status in Israel.

When these nationality regulations are reviewed together, a conflict of laws emerges. The Temporary Order prohibits an Israeli parent married to a citizen or resident of the Gaza Strip, Iran, Iraq, Lebanon, or Syria from living together with his or her family in Israel. But under the 1952 Nationality Law, the Israeli parent cannot move to any of those regions or countries to live with his or her family without jeopardizing his or her (and possibly the child's) Israeli citizenship.

It follows that, under present laws, some Israeli parents face an inhuman choice.[76] They can choose to live in Israel but be separated from their families, or they can elect to live with their families if they give up living in their home country. If they choose the former alternative, then their children may get a residence permit, but their non-Israeli spouse will not. If they choose the second alternative, then the parent and possibly by default the child risk ending up stateless if the country where they take up residence is one of those on the list set out above.

From the state's perspective, the parents' dilemma, however regrettable, is necessary because of the threat to national security posed by the ongoing armed conflict in the region. Whereas actions that strengthen the position of the Jewish community are considered justified and in the interests of the Israeli state, measures that might improve the status of Palestinians are considered national security threats.[77] In Nadim Rouhana's words, "national interests of the state [have] become equated with the interests of the dominant ideology or the dominant group."[78]

Despite this sectarian government position, the Israeli Supreme Court has, on several occasions, applied tests aimed at balancing the derogation from individual liberties and the strengthening of state security concerns.[79] But if this balancing exercise were to be applied with the interests of Palestinian citizen children in mind, it would be difficult to advance a convincing case for pitting the risk of statelessness and family separation against national security concerns. First of all, an argument for discriminating against one whole group of Israeli citizens without any attention to individual behavior or affiliation in relation to a fundamental human right would have to be made. Second, a justification would have to be proposed for effectively (or constructively) deporting these citizen children to a place where their life is endangered, a distinct risk if the only place that the parents can live together is war-ravaged Gaza. Third, the inescapable tension between two cardinal state interests—national security and promotion of the best interests of the child— would have to be confronted. Ignoring the best interests of the child by summarily imposing a ban on family reunification contradicts the obligation to take into account the child's best interests. Finally, since Palestinian citizen children constitute one of Israel's national minorities, any national security measures that especially impinge on this group should be subject to strict scrutiny to prevent discrimination against a minority.

Kifah, Yazid, and their child can live united in neither Israel nor Gaza and choose to live in Germany due to the father's residence status there. Given that living in Germany is not considered a breach of loyalty, neither Kifah nor her child will end up stateless. However, many Palestinian families do not have the luxury of finding a place where they can live in unity. Moreover, Kifah's family cannot take this relatively secure situation for granted. Since 1952, Israel's nationality law has been amended nine times. For example, under the 1968 amendment, Kifah could have ended up stateless because *any* residence abroad could lead to the revocation of citizenship. Moreover, the Temporary Order has been persistently renewed since 2003 and has been amended twice, extending the list of prohibited countries as described above. Families never know for certain when the law will be amended again, whether it will be to their advantage or detriment, and whether it will render one or more family members, in particular children, stateless.

To my knowledge, no cases of derivative child statelessness based on a parent's loss of Israeli nationality have occurred so far. So the issue at stake is whether the unpredictability of future nationality laws will increase the risk of derivative statelessness for children. At present, Palestinian Israelis enjoy at best a volatile, second-class citizenship that is mired in the haunting uncertainty of never knowing whether rights will be lost or gained. Horrendous acts by a few suicide bombers or other terrorists (such as the attacks carried out by the group of Palestinians who gained residence in Israel through the family-unification mechanism) have consequences for the entire Palestinian population in Israel. This situation is a far cry from the one to which U.S. Supreme Court Chief Justice Earl Warren referred when describing citizenship as the "right to have rights." Whatever this complex and much-cited phrase means, it certainly includes the right not to be deprived of a cardinal set of protections by arbitrary and generic procedures that take no account of individual circumstances. Perhaps Chief Justice Warren had in mind precisely the sort of situation that exists in Israel when he called for a prohibition on Congress' powers to withdraw a citizen's nationality unilaterally. Although Israel may never have denationalized a person, the Interior Minister's discretion to do so detracts from the sense that citizenship is a "priceless right." A state that misuses its prerogative to regulate citizenship can undermine the meaning of citizenship altogether.

Conclusion

Israeli citizenship is defined by a unique, three-pronged nationality regulation. At face value, an Israeli passport confers the same rights to all citizens, but after all the relevant nationality laws are taken into consideration, a different meaning of citizenship emerges, with distinct consequences for children. Under the Law of Return, the gate to Israeli citizenship always remains open for Jewish children. Moreover, Jewish children tend to retain their Israeli nationality even when their parents voluntarily renounce it.

By contrast, the Israeli citizenship of non-Jewish children, especially children of Palestinian descent, is much more volatile. It is closely linked to the nationality of the child's parents. If a parent's citizenship is revoked against his or her will because he or she opted to raise the child in family unity outside Israel, the fate of the child's nationality depends on the way the government exercises its discretion. There is a real risk of statelessness for a Palestinian child whose parent loses his or her Israeli citizenship, a risk that does not exist for a Jewish child. Moreover, the frequent changes to Israeli nationality law enacted in response to high-profile political events add yet another element of volatility and uncertainty to the Palestinian Israeli citizenship package.

The heated debate about the extent to which such evident discrimination on grounds of national origin is appropriate in the face of Israel's security situation will no doubt continue to rage. But so will deep concerns about the lack of enforcement of a range of international human-rights norms relating to the right to a nationality, the rights of stateless persons, and the rights of children to family unity. These fundamental rights are binding on Israel, define democratic statehood, and are crucial safeguards against complete rightlessness. Although many international human-rights norms apply to all individuals, irrespective of their nationality, these generic human rights cannot replace the rights to which only citizens are entitled—most critically, the protection from deportation and the right to participate in a state's political life. Granting meaningful citizenship that is not subject to perpetual volatility remains the ultimate measure for eradicating statelessness. Depriving children of one basic right at the expense of another—citizenship at the expense of the right to enjoyment of family life—is an untenable option.

Notes

1. Citizenship and Entry into Israel Law (Temporary Order), 5763–2003, amend. 1 (2005), art. 1 (translated by the Legal Center for Arab Minority Rights in Israel), <http://www.adalah.org> (accessed May 1, 2009).

2. However, some organizations argued that the number was much higher. "Forced Apart by Law," *guardian.co.uk*, June 20, 2008, <http://www.guardian .co.uk> (accessed May 15, 2009).

3. According to Israel's Central Bureau of Statistics, out of a population of 7.3 million, 1.5 million people (nearly 20 percent) in Israel are Israeli citizens of Palestinian origin. See Israel's Central Bureau of Statistics, <http://www1.cbs .gov.il/www/yarhon/b1_e.htm> (accessed May 14, 2009).

4. For the purposes of this chapter, *nationality* and *citizenship* are used interchangeably as both terms refer to a legal status.

5. *Legal* or *de jure* statelessness in international law refers to a person "who is not considered as a national by any State under the operation of its law." United Nations (UN) General Assembly, "Convention Relating to the Status of Stateless Persons," September 28, 1954, United Nations, *Treaty Series*, vol. 360, art. 1, p. 117, <http://www.unhcr.org> (accessed July 30, 2009).

6. At the international level, Israel is bound to respect all international standards that are part of customary international law and appear in international treaties ratified by Israel. According to Israel's domestic legal system, international customary law is directly binding unless it conflicts with domestic legal provisions. International treaties are not self-executing, which means that they have to be incorporated (transposed) into domestic legislation prior to their implementation. Yet in the case of international treaties that codify preexisting international customs, they are directly applicable within Israel. See Katharina Penev, *Minderheitenrechte der Araber in Israel* (Berlin: Duncker und Humblot, 2004), 52–53.

7. Jacqueline Bhabha, "Un 'Vide Juridique'? Migrant Children: The Rights and Wrongs," in *Realizing the Rights of the Child*, ed. Carol Bellamy et al., Swiss Human Rights Book vol. 2 (Zurich: Rüffer & Rub, 2007), 213.

8. Ibid.

9. The concept of nationality was first defined in the 1930 Convention on Certain Questions Relating to the Conflict of Nationality Laws (hereafter Nationality Convention) by the Hague Conference for the Codification of International Law. The first article of the Convention determined that "it is for each State to determine under its own law who are its nationals." Article 2 specifies that "any question as to whether a person possesses the nationality of a particular State shall be determined in accordance with the law of the State." See League of Nations, Convention on Certain Questions Relating to the Conflict of Nationality Law, April 13, 1930, League of Nations, *Treaty Series*, vol. 179, p. 89, no. 4137, <http://www.unhcr.org> (accessed May 5, 2009).

10. See Kay Hailbronner, "Nationality," in T. Alexander Aleinikoff and Vincent Chetail, eds., *Migration and International Legal Norms* (The Hague: T.M.C. Asser, 2003), 75.

11. Manley O. Hudson, "Report on Nationality Including Statelessness," A/CN.4/50, *Yearbook of the International Law Commission*, vol. 2 (1952), 7–9.

12. Jaap E. Doek, "The CRC and the Right to Acquire and to Preserve a Nationality," *Refugee Survey Quarterly* 24, no. 3 (2006): 26.

13. UN Human Rights Committee (HRC), "CCPR General Comment No. 17: Article 24 (Rights of the Child)," April 7, 1989, par. 8, <http://www.unhcr.org> (accessed June 13, 2009).

14. Doek, "The CRC and the Right to Acquire and to Preserve a Nationality," 27; see also Elena Rozzi, Kirsten Di Martino, and Caroline Vandenabeele's chapters on birth registration.

15. The Law of Return, 5710-1950 (Israel), July 5, 1950, art. 1, <http://www .unhcr.org> (accessed May 1, 2009).

16. Citizenship Law 5712-1952 (Israel), amend. 4, LSI XXXIV, sec. 2, p. 254.

17. David Kretzmer, *The Legal Status of the Arabs in Israel* (Boulder: Westview Press, 1990), 36.

18. See Ayelet Shachar, "Citizenship and Membership in the Israeli Polity," in T. Alexander Aleinikoff and Douglas Klusmeyer, eds., *From Migrants to Citizens: Membership in a Changing World* (Washington, D.C.: Carnegie Endowment for International Peace, 2000), 387.

19. Ibid., 387.

20. Citizenship Law, 5712-1952 (Israel), amend. 4 (1980), LSI XXXIV, sec. 4(a) (1), p. 256.

21. Shachar, "Citizenship and Membership in the Israeli Polity," 420.

22. Ibid., 422–423; see also Citizenship Law, 5712–1952 , sec. 10(e)–(g), p. 260.

23. Citizenship Law, 5712-1952, amend. 4 (1980), sec. 10(g).

24. Ibid., sec. 11(a)(2), p. 243.

25. Ibid., sec. 11(c).

26. In 2007, however, in the case of two Palestinian Israeli parliamentarians, the Supreme Court ruled that the revocation of nationality of citizens who visited Syria without authorization was not automatic. The Minister of the Interior had to act on it. "Israeli Court Rejects Petition to Revoke Arab Knesset Member's Citizenship," *Jerusalem Post,* September 19, 2007.

27. Prevention of Infiltration (Offenses and Jurisdiction) Law, 5714-1954 (Israel), LSI VIII, p. 133.

28. Citizenship Law, 5712-1952, sec. 11(a), amend. 4 (1980).

29. Ibid., amend. 9, SH 146, 2008, p. 521.

30. The West Bank is excluded from the list.

31. See Universal Declaration of Human Rights (UDHR), art. 16; CRC, art. 9(1); International Covenant on Economic, Social and Cultural Rights (ICESCR), art. 10(1); ICCPR, art. 23; and European Convention on Human Rights (ECHR), art. 8.

32. CRC, art. 10(1).

33. The Nationality and Entry into Israel Law (Israel) (Temporary Order), 5763-2003, amend. 1 (2005) (translated by the Legal Center for Arab Minority Rights in Israel), <http://www.adalah.org> (accessed May 1, 2009).

34. Henceforth, residence permits could be issued to an Israeli citizen's husband over age thirty-five, wife over age twenty-five, and child below age fourteen, and in some cases below age eighteen. Ibid., amend. 1 (2005), art. 3, 3A.

35. Ibid., art. 3(a).

36. UN Committee on the Elimination of Racial Discrimination (CERD), Reports submitted by states parties under article 9 of the Convention: Interna-

tional Convention on the Elimination of All Forms of Racial Discrimination, information received from the government of Israel on the implementation of the concluding observations of the Committee on the Elimination of Racial Discrimination, December 16, 2008,CERD/C/ISR/CO/13/Add.1, <http://www .unhcr.org> (accessed March 1, 2009).

37. Daphne Barak-Erez, "Israel: Citizenship and Immigration Law in the Vise of Security, Nationality, and Human Rights," *International Journal of Constitutional Law* 6 (January 2008): 186.

38. *Adalah Legal Centre for Arab Minority Rights in Israel and Others v. Minister of Interior*, HCJ 7052/03 (Israel High Court of Justice, 2006), 9.

39. Apart from cultural reasons, this is partly due to the fact that interreligious couples have difficulties getting married in Israel. Civil weddings are not accepted in Israel, and national law prohibits religious authorities from marrying Jews to non-Jews. For a Jewish and Palestinian marriage to be recognized in Israel, one partner would have to convert to the other religion prior to the wedding, or a civil wedding would have to be performed abroad, which would be registered in Israel under international law. See Immigration and Refugee Board of Canada, "Israel: Mixed-marriage couples and families (particularly of an Arab husband and a Jewish wife); reports of such couples being targeted by Orthodox Jewish groups or any difficulties they may face; protection and recourse available," August 17, 2004, ISR42896.E, <http://www.unhcr.org> (accessed June 13, 2009).

40. Amnesty International, "Israel and the Occupied Territories: Torn Apart— Families Split by Discriminatory Policies," July 1, 2004, MDE 15/063/2004, p. 2, <http://www.unhcr.org> (accessed May 1, 2009).

41. Ibid.

42. Ibid., 12.

43. Barak-Erez, "Israel," 185.

44. *Adalah Legal Centre v. Minister of Interior*, 14.

45. Ibid., 15.

46. Ibid., 10.

47. Ibid.

48. Ibid., 3.

49. Ibid.

50. In March 2009, the Supreme Court held hearings to review the case after the submission of petitions by Adalah and other civil-rights organizations. Ibid.; see also "Court Deliberates on Family Unification," *Jerusalem Post*, March 15, 2009, <http://www.jpost.com> (accessed May 10, 2009).

51. *Adalah Legal Centre v. Minister of Interior*, sec. 28.

52. Weis refers to relative statelessness insofar as the stateless person's link to the former state in which he or she possessed citizenship is of legal relevance. Paul Weis, *Nationality and Statelessness in International Law* (Alphen aan den Rijn: Sijthoff & Noordhoff, 1979), 162.

53. In Paul Weis's words, it is considered "obvious that *jus sanguinis* is more apt to lead to statelessness since it makes it hereditary." Yet the case of *Dilcia Yean and Violeta Bosico v. Dominican Republic* before the Inter-American Court of Human Rights in 2005 proved this to be a flawed assumption. Even though nationality in the Dominican Republic is granted on a *jus soli* basis, children of Haitian immigrants have been rendered stateless because they were deprived of birth certificates that would prove their birth and thus their eligibility for citizenship in the Dominican Republic. *Dilcia Yean and Violeta Bosico v. Dominican Republic*, I/A Court HR (ser. C), no. 134 (2005), sec. 3.

54. Hannah Arendt, *Eichmann in Jerusalem: A Report on the Banality of Evil* (New York: Penguin Books, 1992), 182.

55. Cited in Alexander Aleinikoff, "Theories of Loss of Citizenship," *Michigan Law Review* 84 (June 1986): 1481.

56. *Perez v. Brownell*, 356 U.S. 4 (1958), cited in Aleinikoff, "Theories of Loss of Citizenship," 1480.

57. David Weissbrodt, *The Human Rights of Non-Citizens* (New York: Oxford University Press, 2008), 248.

58. Carol A. Batchelor, "Stateless Persons: Some Gaps in International Protection," *International Journal of Refugee Law* 7 (1995): 246.

59. ICCPR, art. 2; ICESCR, art. 2(2).

60. Hannah Arendt, *The Origins of Totalitarianism* (New York: Harcourt, 1951), 290.

61. Robyn Linde, "Statelessness and Roma Communities in the Czech Republic: Competing Theories of State Compliance," *International Journal on Minority and Group Rights* 13 (2006): 1–2.

62. See Jyothi Kanics's chapter in this volume.

63. See ICCPR, art. 25. Some states have passed legislations that allow noncitizens to vote. For example, New Zealand granted permanent residents the right to vote in general elections in 1975. In the United Kingdom, nationals of the former Commonwealth states can vote in elections at all levels since 1949. In some Scandinavian countries, foreign residents can vote in local elections nationwide. In federal states such as Switzerland and the United States, noncitizens' right to vote at the local level is restricted to some cantons (Jura and Neuchâtel) or certain municipalities (in Maryland). Finally, in Israel, persons eligible for but refusing to acquire citizenship under the Law of Return can vote in local elections. See Thomas Alexander Aleinikoff and Douglas B. Klusmeyer, *Citizenship Policies for an Age of Migration* (Washington, D.C.: Carnegie Endowment for International Peace, 2002), 48–49.

64. Weissbrodt, *The Human Rights of Non-Citizens*, 3–4.

65. UN Department of Social Affairs, *A Study of Statelessness*, E/1112, February 1, 1949, E/1112/add. 1, May 19, 1949 (Lake Success: United Nations, 1949), 131–144.

66. Under article 32 of the 1954 Statelessness Convention, which Israel ratified, "[t]he Contracting States shall as far as possible facilitate the assimilation and naturalization of stateless persons."

67. See Batchelor, "Stateless Persons," 257. Only the European Convention on Nationality (hereafter European Nationality Convention) and the Council of Europe's Convention on the Avoidance of Statelessness Following State Successions (hereafter COE Statelessness Convention) prohibit the withdrawal of citizenship if the result would be statelessness. See European Nationality Convention, art. 7(3); COE Statelessness Convention, art. 6.

68. In the case of *Hilla Alrai v. Minister of Interior*, the Supreme Court rejected the request by a third party to revoke the nationality of Yigal Amir, the Jewish Israeli citizen who had assassinated Prime Minister Yitzhak Rabin. See *Hilla Alrai v. Minister of Interior et al..*, H.C. 2757/96, Supr. Ct. Rpt. 50 (2) 18; Nimer Sultany, *Citizens without Citizenship* (Haifa: Arab Center for Applied Social Research, 2003), 91.

69. According to Israel's domestic legal system, provisions of international treaties can be directly applied only if they are considered to be part of customary international law. The latter is directly binding unless it conflicts with domestic legal provisions. See Katharina Penev, *Minderheitenrechte der Araber in Israel* (Berlin: Duncker und Humblot, 2004), 52–53.

70. As of October 2009, Israel had signed but had not ratified the 1961 Statelessness Convention. See <http://www.unhcr.org/3bbb24d54.html> (accessed November 15, 2009).

71. "Judge Orders State to Set Procedure for Handling Stateless Persons," *Haaretz*, January 31, 2007, <http://www.haaretz.com> (accessed May 10, 2009).

72. Oded Feller, "No Place to Go: Statelessness in Israel," *Forced Migration Review* 32 (April 2009): 36.

73. See 1954 Statelessness Convention, art. 32; CRC, art. 3.

74. See Citizenship Law, 5712-1952 (Israel), amend. 9, SH 146, 2008, p. 521.

75. See note 34 above.

76. For a similar Hobson's choice confronting American citizen children with noncitizen parents, see the chapter by David B. Thronson in this volume.

77. Kretzmer, *The Legal Status of the Arabs in Israel*, 136.

78. Nadim N. Rouhana, *Palestinian Citizens in an Ethnic Jewish State* (New Haven: Yale University Press, 1997), 57.

79. Ibid., 139–141.

4

Human Rights and Citizenship: The Need for Better Data and What to Do about It

Bela Hovy[1]

The protection of noncitizens is a joint responsibility implicating both the country of citizenship and the country of residence. The latter is responsible for guaranteeing basic human, economic, and social rights while the former retains the obligation to grant legal protection and to protect political rights, including the right to vote. Despite these two sets of obligations and duty bearers, noncitizens face numerous protection challenges that are well illustrated by the circumstances of migrant workers and their families. As the 2009 United Nations Human Development Report, *Overcoming Barriers: Human Mobility and Development*, documents, this population remains vulnerable to exploitation in the labor market, discrimination in the housing market, and exclusion from education and health care despite a half century of human-rights treaty signing and ratification.[2] Diplomas awarded in the country of origin may not be recognized in the destination country, and pension contributions earned in the destination country may not be accessible when migrants return to the country of origin. Being vulnerable to abuse does not imply that all noncitizens are victims, however. Millions of people continue to live and work outside their country of citizenship without discrimination. But a sizeable minority encounters persistent problems, including those who experience statelessness of one form or another.

Some noncitizen groups require no protections beyond those that are the inherent responsibility of the countries of residence and citizenship—fundamental economic and social rights for the former and civil and political rights for the latter. But other noncitizen groups *do* require special protection. A case in point are refugees: they are fleeing persecution in their country of citizenship and seeking protection abroad and therefore cannot, by definition, exercise their rights as citizens. Every refugee needs international protection. Asylum seekers—persons who have applied for refugee status but have not yet been recognized as refugees—are even more vulnerable. Without refugee status, their legal status in the host country remains precarious. Persons in refugee-like situations who are allowed to remain for humanitarian reasons face a similar predicament.

Another noncitizen group with distinctive protection needs are stateless persons without any legal nationality[3]—those termed *legally stateless* in Jacqueline Bhabha's introduction to this book. These noncitizens may, as residents, enjoy the basic forms of protection and access to economic and social rights provided by their host country, but they frequently encounter obstacles accessing other key rights, such as the right to vote or obtain travel documents. In some crucial ways, the plight of the legally stateless resembles that of refugees as they struggle to obtain legal documentation of their identity and to exercise political rights. As the introduction to this book points out, it is not just legally stateless populations who struggle to obtain proof of their legal identity. People who reside in their country of birth, have never crossed a border, but have never had their birth registered by the state—the *effectively stateless*, in Jacqueline Bhabha's terminology—also resemble refugees in their relative rightlessness. In countries that lack adequate birth registration or that exclude certain groups from the birth registration system, children are especially vulnerable to becoming effectively stateless.

A first step to protect and assist vulnerable populations and to improve their plight is to ensure that they are counted and identified. Without being registered, it is more likely that individuals and families will be unable to access their rights under national or international law. As other chapters in this volume demonstrate, this is true for legally stateless populations, for those who are not identified because they are undocumented and thus *de facto stateless*, and for those who are not registered or counted even within their own country and are thus effectively stateless. Quantitative data are also essential to assess needs and target interventions. Some basic questions—"How many vulnerable persons and families are living the country?" "How do they fare compared to the local population?" "Where do they live?" "What are their needs?"—can be answered only if quantitative information is available.

This chapter assesses the quality and availability of statistical data on persons who are vulnerable because of their citizenship status—refugees, asylum seekers, stateless persons, and migrant workers, including children. It examines the data reported by states signatories to relevant United Nations (UN) human rights conventions. Most international legal instruments have mechanisms that require state parties to report on their implementation. Generally, however, the reporting of quantitative data is inadequate for evidence-based monitoring. This chapter argues that statisticians should be involved in developing guidelines for the reports that countries as well as special rapporteurs prepare in the context of international human-rights instruments. For example, refugee statistics collected by the United Nations High Commissioner for Refugees (UNHCR) as part of its responsibility to supervise the implementation of the 1951 Convention Relating to the Status of Refugees (hereafter the 1951 Refugee Convention) are considered good practice that could be replicated for other international conventions.

In addition to improving the reports submitted to the human-rights committees, what else should be done to improve access to evidence? The chapter next discusses the various national statistical sources that are available to assess the situation of groups that are of concern due to their citizenship status. These sources are generally ignored by the human-rights community. The chapter highlights the opportunities for using population statistics and administrative sources to assess the number, characteristics, and needs of persons who are outside their country of citizenship or who are without any nationality. By using the example of legal statelessness, this chapter demonstrates that important progress in improving the evidence base can be made without significant additional resources. The chapter concludes that closer cooperation between statisticians and the human-rights community will strengthen the protection regime for vulnerable groups and contribute to addressing their plight.

The Quality of Statistics in Human-Rights Reporting

The main international human-rights instruments relevant for the protection of persons who are vulnerable due to their citizenship status include the 1951 Refugee Convention, the 1954 Convention Relating to the Status of Stateless Persons (hereafter the 1954 Statelessness Convention), the 1961 Convention on the Reduction of Statelessness (hereafter the 1961 Statelessness Convention),[4] the 1985 Declaration on the Human Rights of Individuals Who Are Not Nationals of the Country in Which They Live,[5] the 1989 Convention on the Rights of the Child (CRC), and the 1990 International Convention on the Protection of the Rights of All Migrant Workers and Members of Their Families (hereafter the Migrant Workers Convention).[6] This section evaluates the statistical reporting guidelines for these international instruments. What instructions exist, if any, for the collection of quantitative information required for the objective measurement of progress and gaps in their implementation?

The 1951 Convention Relating to the Status of Refugees

According to article 1(A) of the Refugee Convention and its 1967 Protocol,[7] a refugee is someone who

owing to well-founded fear of being persecuted for reasons of race, religion, nationality, membership of a particular social group or political opinion, is outside the country of his nationality and is unable, or owing to such fear, is unwilling to avail himself of the protection of that country; or who, not having a nationality and being outside the country of his former habitual residence as a result of such events, is unable or, owing to such fear, is unwilling to return to it.

Refugees have fled from persecution in their country of citizenship in search of alternative state protection. In the country of asylum, refugees are granted certain rights but not the full set of rights enjoyed by citizens. In many countries, noncitizens, including refugees, are not allowed to vote in elections or to run for political office. After commission of a serious nonpolitical crime, all noncitizens, including refugees,[8] are subject to deportation. Although deportation of "ordinary" noncitizens is lawful, provided that basic standards have been met, returning refugees to their country of origin where their life continues to be at risk amounts to *refoulement*, a violation of international humanitarian and refugee law.

In finding durable solutions for refugees, citizenship plays a critical role. The most common solution for refugees is voluntary repatriation. When the situation in the country of origin has improved, refugees, if willing, can return in safety and dignity to reavail themselves of the national protection of their country of citizenship. Voluntary repatriation is also the preferred durable solution (see Figure 4.1). Local integration is the second most common option. In many countries of asylum (although more so in the industrialized world), noncitizens, including refugees, become eligible for naturalization after a stipulated minimum period of residence and after fulfilling other obligations. Local integration is a gradual process. Refugees have access to some basic rights immediately on arrival, the main one being the right to *nonrefoulement*. However, full local integration, including all political and legal rights, occurs only after refugees become citizens of their new country of habitual residence. The third durable solution, resettlement, is numerically the least significant. Resettlement involves a transfer of refugees from a first country of temporary asylum to a third country, where they have the

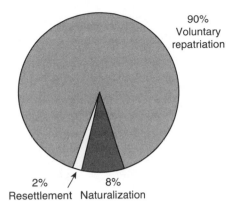

90%
Voluntary
repatriation

2%   8%
Resettlement Naturalization

Figure 4.1
Durable solutions for refugees, 1996 to 2005 (total = 14.4 million). *Source*: UNHCR.

right to permanent residence and eventually naturalization. The large majority of resettlement places are offered by the traditional immigration countries as part of their immigration programs. From the perspective of national protection, resettlement and local integration are similar solutions. The refugee is able to restore his or her full access to rights by adopting a new nationality.

As long as refugees retain their temporary refugee status, they are unable to exercise the rights of citizens anywhere in the world. That is why refugees become of concern to UNHCR, which provides them with international protection. UNHCR has the mandate to intervene on behalf of refugees, whether or not the country has acceded to the international refugee instruments.

Article 35 of the Refugee Convention requests states to provide UNHCR with information and *statistical data*. In 1993, more than forty years after its establishment, UNHCR created the post of statistician to satisfy the growing demand for accurate refugee statistics. Since then, the availability of refugee statistics has gradually improved.[9] UNHCR's *Annual Statistical Report*, submitted for all countries hosting persons of concern to UNHCR, provides a global framework for the reporting of statistics. The decision of High Commissioner Ruud Lubbers in 2001 to issue a *Statistical Yearbook* provided further impetus to collect and analyze global refugee data. In addition, the office prepares reports on asylum applications submitted in industrialized countries, global refugee status determination outcomes, detailed profiles of refugees living in camps, and unaccompanied and separated children seeking asylum.

The fact that the Refugee Convention includes an explicit requirement to report statistical data is evidence of its drafters' foresight. The requirement was included in article 35, which regulates the cooperation of the national authorities with UNHCR. Evidently the drafters of the Convention felt that it was impossible to supervise the implementation of the Convention without statistical information.

As highlighted in the text quoted above, the Refugee Convention also refers to stateless persons who have become refugees. Anyone can be a refugee, whether with or without the formal nationality of a country. However, distinguishing legally stateless refugees who seek asylum from other refugees is a challenge. Due to a lack of documentation and cooperation by the authorities of the country of origin, it is often not clear that a refugee has the citizenship of the country he or she fled. From a protection perspective, this distinction between a stateless and a non-stateless refugee is of secondary importance since both lack the protection of their country of habitual residence. The distinction becomes more significant, however, when refugees exercise their rights to return to their country of origin because stateless persons without appropriate documentary proof of identity typically face obstacles in being readmitted.

Children are not specifically mentioned in the Refugee Convention, but guidelines to protect refugee children have existed for many years. The identification of children is particularly relevant in refugee camps where children under five and infants receive special care. Age is also critical in exercising the right to family reunion, since refugees who reach the legal age of adulthood may be disqualified from joining resettled parents.

The 1954 and 1961 Statelessness Conventions

Possession of a nationality is essential for full participation in society and for the enjoyment of rights. Legally stateless persons are by definition vulnerable because they cannot exercise their rights as citizens in any country in the world. As already suggested, from a legal perspective, the plight of stateless persons, whether or not they are refugees, resembles that of refugees.

Statelessness has a significant impact on the lives of individuals. Although human rights are to be enjoyed by everyone, rights such as the right to vote and to enter and reside in a state may be limited to nationals. In the absence of a nationality, stateless persons may be detained, denied access to education and health services, or blocked from obtaining employment.[10] As other essays in this volume illustrate, these problems are not confined to the legally stateless. *De facto* and effectively stateless populations may also experience such human-rights violations.

As Christina O. Alfirev also notes in her chapter on Palestinian children, the two leading international conventions on statelessness have different emphases and functions. The 1954 Statelessness Convention focuses on the *consequences* of statelessness, whereas the 1961 Statelessness Convention seeks to *prevent* statelessness from occurring in the first place. Although the two conventions are not as widely ratified as the Refugee Convention, the pace of ratification has picked up in recent years.[11] As stateless persons face similar protection challenges to those facing refugees, it may not come as a surprise that the UN General Assembly requested UNHCR to monitor the implementation of both Statelessness Conventions.

By contrast with the now satisfactory documentation of refugee statistics and the detailed data on refugee stocks, flows, and characteristics, the collection of data on stateless persons who are not refugees poses significant challenges. Neither of the two conventions requires the contracting states to submit statistical reports to the United Nations. Although article 33 of the 1954 Convention requests states to submit information on laws and regulations, the 1961 Convention is silent on any obligation to share information with the UN. The lack of attention to data in the reporting requirements for the contracting states is reflected in UNHCR's continued struggle to provide credible statistical information. Regrettably, data on stateless persons are limited to the total number of persons once per year and to only selected countries.

The absence of a provision to report statistical data to the United Nations in the two statelessness conventions may well be related to the inherent differences between stateless persons and refugees. Whereas the UN has the responsibility to provide international protection to each and every refugee, those stateless persons remaining in their country of habitual residence are presumed to still benefit from some form of protection provided by the country in which they reside.

There are also practical obstacles to identifying stateless persons. Refugees cross an international border and therefore become of immediate interest to a receiving state. The receiving state wants to know who is coming in and why. In contrast, stateless persons continue to live in their country of habitual residence. From a state's security perspective, the need to identify noncitizens is significantly greater than the need to identify habitual residents, even if some of the latter are not recognized as citizens by the state.

In 2006, UNHCR's Executive Committee adopted a Conclusion on the Identification, Prevention, and Reduction of Statelessness and Protection of Stateless Persons that encourages "those States which are in possession of statistics on stateless persons or individuals with undetermined nationality to share those statistics with UNHCR." It also calls on UNHCR to establish a more "formal, systematic methodology for information gathering, updating, and sharing." Considering the low level of registration of stateless persons, the main avenue for UNHCR to implement the 2006 Conclusion is to ensure that population censuses include a question on the country of citizenship and that *statelessness* is provided as a response category to this question.[12]

The 1990 International Convention on the Protection of the Rights of All Migrant Workers and Members of Their Families

The 1990 International Convention on the Protection of the Rights of All Migrant Workers and Members of Their Families details the rights of migrant workers and members of their families, including those in an irregular situation (who, in this book, are referred to as *de facto stateless* populations). The Migrant workers Convention does not cover the rights of noncitizens in general. The Convention established a committee[13] to supervise the implementation of the Convention's provisions. Under article 73, state parties to the Convention submit a report to the committee every five years. Countries are requested to submit disaggregated "information on the characteristics of migratory flows (immigration, transit and emigration) in which the state party involved is concerned." The Committee is allowed to provide additional guidelines on the drafting of country reports, particularly in respect to the provision of statistical data. Article 29 calls for the registration of migrant children at birth to reduce and avoid situations of statelessness. Nevertheless, the absence of a standard reporting format for migrant statistics coupled with the five-year reporting cycle complicate compilation of up-to-date and comparable data on number, composition, and condition of migrant workers and members of their families.

The 1985 Declaration on the Human Rights of Individuals Who Are Not Nationals of the Country in Which They Live

The Declaration on the Human Rights of Individuals Who Are Not Nationals of the Country in Which They Live, adopted by the UN General Assembly in 1985, seeks to protect the rights of noncitizens. The Declaration lists the various human rights to which noncitizens are entitled. Migrant children are mentioned in the context of family reunification for the spouse and dependent minor children. However, declarations are not binding on state parties and do not imply any reporting obligations.

The 1989 Convention on the Rights of the Child

The 1989 Convention on the Rights of the Child is one of the most widely ratified international instruments. The CRC contains only two references to noncitizen children. Article 7 of the CRC describes the child's right to acquire a nationality, while article 22 refers to the rights of unaccompanied minors seeking asylum. The CRC, like the Migrant Workers Convention, created a committee that issues guidelines for state parties governing periodic reporting obligations.[14] But the guidelines from the committee overseeing the CRC are much more precise than those from the Migrant Workers Committee and request *disaggregated data* at multiple locations.[15] The two sets of guidelines are similar, however, to the extent that neither of them includes standardized tables, which are essential for cross-sectional and longitudinal comparison.

The United Nations Children's Fund (UNICEF) supports the work of the committee by promoting and protecting child rights. In addition to contributing advice and assistance to the Committee, UNICEF facilitates broad consultations within states to maximize the accuracy and impact of reports to the committee.[16]

Outstanding Data Reporting Needs

This review has indicated that the reporting requirements for state parties to the human-rights instruments governing the rights of noncitizens and stateless persons do not allow for the compilation and analysis of comparative statistical information among countries or within countries over time. Even in cases where an oversight committee is mandated to provide additional reporting guidelines, there are no prescribed tables or reporting formats.

A cursory assessment of country reports suggest that data are rarely presented in the form of standardized tables. References to country of citizenship are generally limited to specific contexts, such as adoption, right to a nationality at birth, and unaccompanied minors seeking asylum. Typically, the statistical data are subsumed in narrative country reports and limited to a description of the numerator ("x number of children were affected"). To make comparisons, however, the use of percentages is essential. Although it is useful to know that 100 stateless persons were issued nationality documents during a particular calendar year, it is much more effective from the perspective of impacting policy to know that these 100 stateless persons represented 1 percent (or 99 percent) of the total number of stateless persons in a particular region. The usefulness of absolute numbers (*incidence reporting*) without the denominator is limited.

In this respect, UNHCR constitutes an exception.[17] Each year, UNHCR requests member states to prepare a detailed statistical report. Over the years, these reports have significantly improved in terms of accuracy, coverage, and completeness. The successful experience in respect to the collection of global refugee statistics may be due to three critical factors. First, every refugee counts. Because of its protection mandate, UNHCR literally has to know each refugee. No analogous responsibility exists for persons who are legally stateless. Many staff member are involved in collecting information on the number and condition of refugees. Protection officers conduct interviews and adjudicate refugee claims, program officers need beneficiary figures for their budgets, and field officers register and deregister refugees on a daily basis. Again, no analog either regarding field staff responsibility or legal obligations exists for those who are legally stateless. Second, UNHCR offices, located in more than 120 countries, maintain a close relationship with ministries of the interior, immigration agencies, refugee status determination bodies, and other critical institutions. This facilitates accurate information exchange and monitoring. Third, refugee statistics are the subject of separate reporting instructions and are overseen by the UNHCR statistician working in headquarters.

National Data Sources on Noncitizens and Citizenship

The previous section assessed the quality of statistical information contained in the reports submitted by countries to monitor compliance with their international human-rights obligations. It looked at the legal instruments through a "statistical lens." The current section takes the opposite approach. Taking a human-rights perspective, what is the contribution of official statistics to providing information relevant for the monitoring of the status and condition of vulnerable groups?

Globally, information on groups that are vulnerable to exploitation and abuse due to their citizenship status is included in two main statistical sources—the decennial population and housing census and data on the inflow and outflow of noncitizens. Most countries in the world count their population once every ten years. By contrast, information on the annual flow of noncitizens is available for only some thirty industrialized countries in the world. The United Nations has published recommendations on how to compile international migration statistics based on these sources. Properly implemented, these sources can provide invaluable information on the various groups in need of protection.

The Population Census

The decennial population and housing census is the main source of statistical information on the size and basic composition of a country's population. The purpose of the census is to collect reliable and detailed data on the size, distribution, and composition of all persons residing within a country to facilitate government interventions, including resource allocation.

According to UN recommendations,[18] the population census should be carried out on a *de facto* basis. Everyone who meets the definition of a resident should be counted as part of the resident population and included in the census tabulations, irrespective of their legal status. Vulnerable groups—such as refugees, migrant workers, asylum seekers, irregular migrants, and stateless persons—are to be included if they meet the definition of a resident. Legal status should not be a reason for including or excluding persons from the census.

Once groups of concern are included and identified, the potential of the population census to provide statistical information is almost limitless. Typically, topics covered by the census include age, gender, family structure, current place of residence, education, health, employment, socioeconomic status, housing conditions, previous place of residence, and many more. The only limitation to the sharing of disaggregated statistical data is the requirement to maintain the anonymity of respondents. If the numbers in the tables become too small, there is a risk that individuals can be identified on the basis of the characteristics provided.

The United Nations recommends that censuses include a question on the respondent's country of citizenship. The census should list all the possible countries of citizenship and include the category *stateless* for persons without a legal nationality.[19]

Although most countries in the world include a question on citizenship, there are significant differences between regions (see table 4.1). The number of UN member states reporting data by citizenship increased

Table 4.1
Countries reporting data on citizenship by census round

Region	1975–1984	1985–1994	1995–2004	Total number of countries
Africa	40	41	27	53
Asia	23	34	36	47
Europe	20	36	37	43
Latin America and the Caribbean	18	18	20	33
Northern America	2	2	2	2
Oceania	9	9	11	14
Total	112	140	133	192

Source: *United Nations Global Migration Database*, <http://www.unmigration.org>.

from 112 during the 1980 census to some 140 during the 1990 round but fell to 133 during the 2000 round. During the 2000 census round, the number of countries reporting on country of citizenship increased in Asia, Europe, Latin America, the Caribbean, and Oceania but fell dramatically in Africa. The highest compliance rates with the UN recommendation were recorded in Northern America (100 percent) and Europe (86 percent), regions with the most developed statistical systems. Country of citizenship was also collected by most countries in Oceania (79 percent) and Asia (77 percent). In Latin America, 61 percent of the countries collected citizenship during the latest census round, whereas the proportion was only 51 percent in Africa.

What are the prospects for collecting information on subsets of the foreign population? As noted earlier, once groups are included and identified in the census, the possibilities for obtaining statistical data are almost boundless. If the country of citizenship is included in the census, the number of persons with foreign nationality can be cross-tabulated by age to extract the number of noncitizen children. Data on noncitizen children could be presented with other relevant indicators, such as place of residence, family structure, education, housing conditions, socioeconomic situation, and so on. If provision was made to record the different forms of statelessness, a complete statistical profile of the stateless population could be extracted, including their detailed place of residence, socioeconomic status, ethnicity (if collected), and housing situation. The same data can be collected for migrant workers.

By cross-tabulating country of citizenship with employment status, a detailed profile can be established on migrant workers and members of their family.

Identifying refugees through the population census is less straight-forward. First, trying to count persons with a particular legal status is at odds with the census principle of self-declaration. Legal documents are not required to answer census questions. Second, respondents, despite assurances of anonymity by the census takers, may be afraid to identify themselves as refugees.

Despite these obstacles, there is growing interest in distinguishing forced migrants from economic migrants in the population census. Several countries in Central and Eastern Europe and sub-Saharan Africa with high levels of forced migration have questioned the need for migration data in their census. The 2010 census recommendations issued by the United Nations Economic Commission for Europe provide detailed guidance in this regard.[20] If refugees cannot be identified in the census, indirect methods may be used to determine their approximate number. By combining several indicators, such as year of arrival and country of citizenship, the number of refugees can be estimated based on the assumption that most noncitizens arriving from a particular country during a particular period were refugees.

The census is not a good vehicle for collecting data on irregular migrants, a group of foreign citizens who have a high risk of facing protection problems. Although irregular migrants should be included in the census if they meet the residence criteria, they cannot be identified separately as a group. As noted above, censuses seek to include all residents, regardless of their legal status. Asking a question on legal status would lead to high levels of nonresponse. Although the census can provide useful information on migrant workers, it can do so for migrant workers only in general. It cannot separate out regular and irregular migrant workers.

Although the inclusion and identification of groups in the census is a necessary condition for obtaining statistical information, it is not a sufficient condition. One cannot guarantee that all the required statistical information will be readily available. In practice, much of the data collected are, if at all, not disseminated in sufficient detail. Too often, confidentiality is invoked to prevent the dissemination of information on noncitizens, as their size, location, and basic characteristics are considered sensitive data. A second issue that hinders data dissemination is data quality. Statistical offices may be reluctant to share data because of limited reliability. Third, data dissemination is often a source of income for statistical offices.

Even if data on noncitizens become available, they may not include all those who are residing in the country. Despite the UN recommendation to conduct the census on a *de facto* basis, many countries continue to limit the census to the *de jure* population—those who have the right of residence. Noncitizens who are unable to produce proper documentation are excluded from the official population count, leading to a considerable undercount.

In sum, the population census can be a valuable source of statistical information about the various groups who may be in need of protection due to their citizenship status, provided that it includes country of citizenship (including statelessness) and reasons for migration. These questions are a necessary but not sufficient precondition for collecting statistical information on vulnerable groups. National statistical offices should also ensure that all persons living in the country, regardless of their legal status, are included in the census. Finally, cross-tabulations should be made available quickly and in sufficient detail to target protection and assistance to vulnerable groups.

Data on the Inflows and Outflows of Noncitizens

Various countries collect data on citizenship when noncitizens change their country of residence. Currently, statistics on the annual inflows and outflows of non citizens are available for some thirty countries.[21]

Data on the issuance of entry or exit visa, residence permits, work permits, asylum requests, and other immigration statuses can be a useful source for ascertaining the number and basic characteristics of noncitizens entering or leaving the countries. Unfortunately, some countries are hesitant to disseminate statistical information from administrative registers.

One successful project that uses administrative sources for monitoring populations in need of international protection is the collection of asylum statistics by UNHCR. Since the late 1990s, industrialized countries have provided UNHCR with monthly statistics on the number of persons applying for asylum by country of citizenship. Such information is compiled and disseminated on a regular basis. UNHCR also publishes statistics on the outcome of the refugee status-determination procedures by countries of citizenship in more than 100 asylum countries. Dissemination of this information has helped to standardize some aspects of refugee status-determination procedures as asylum seekers from the same country of origin are expected to have similar recognition rates in different countries of asylum. Collection and dissemination of comparable information on stateless populations would likely also have a beneficial effect on improving and harmonizing rights protections across states for this population. Improvements in these statistical engagements could be particularly useful for developing policy for stateless children whose claims to protection are otherwise unlikely to be attended to.

Three Steps to Fill the Evidence Gap for Stateless Persons
As noted above, 133 out of 192 UN member states included a citizenship question in the population census during the 2000 census round. Of the 133 countries that provided statistical information on country of citizenship, fifty-four countries reported data on stateless persons.[22] What can be done to address this significant gap in statistical information on stateless persons? As a first step, UNHCR, in collaboration with civil society, should convince the national statistical offices located in these fifty-four countries to provide detailed tables on stateless persons. This would fill an important data gap in the short run.

The second, more difficult step is to ensure that the seventy-nine countries that included country of citizenship in their population census but did not report the number of stateless persons during the 2000 census round do so during the 2010 round of censuses. All concerned parties should advocate for the inclusion of statelessness in the census and ascertain that the data are tabulated and disseminated.

The third step would be to ensure that the fifty-nine United Nations member states that did not collect data on citizenship during the 2000 census do so from the 2010 census round onward. This requires a significant advocacy effort by all parties concerned.

Although these three steps may sound ambitious, they do not go beyond the UN census recommendations. As pointed out earlier, these recommendations requested countries to include the question on citizenship in the census, to report on all countries of citizenship separately, and to ensure that statelessness is included as a reply category. Closing the evidence gap for stateless persons thus requires a close collaboration between the global statistical community, humanitarian agencies, and civil society.

Conclusion

This chapter has reviewed the availability of statistical information on population groups who are vulnerable due to their citizenship status—

refugees and asylum seekers, legally stateless persons, and other non-citizens, including migrant workers and children. Several conclusions can be drawn from the evidence presented.

First, the reports submitted to monitor state compliance under the various human-rights instruments are weak on data. Although the narrative reports contain numerical information, statistical analysis is impossible due to the absence of standardized tabulations and indicators. The guidelines for drafting these reports should therefore include standardized statistical tables and indicators.

Second, the absence of a dedicated statistical unit has a pervasive effect on data collection. A statistical unit to develop indicators, prepare formats, compile and analyze statistical information, and present data for policy purposes should be created by the various committees and agencies overseeing the implementation of the conventions. UNHCR's experience in collecting and using statistics to monitor the implementation of the Refugee Convention could serve as a model. As already indicated, since the creation of a statistical unit in 1993, the quality and availability of global refugee statistics has improved significantly.

Third, the requirement in some conventions that country reports should be submitted only every five years is not conducive to evidence-based assessments. The design of brief annual reports by all states parties, including key statistical data and indicators, should be considered.

Fourth, the population census is a rich but often underutilized source of statistical information. Although most countries included a question on citizenship in their national population during the 2000 census round, large gaps remain in the dissemination of tabulations.

The 2010 round of censuses, which is currently underway, is an important opportunity to advocate for the implementation of the UN census recommendations. Countries and funding agencies alike should ensure that all countries include a question on the country of citizenship in the census, that all countries of citizenship are listed, and that the response categories include statelessness for those who do not have any country of citizenship. Equally important is the requirement that countries ensure the timely processing, tabulation, and dissemination of statistical information. Africa, Latin America, and the Caribbean were the regions with the greatest gap in providing data on citizenship. To distinguish refugees and asylum seekers from other noncitizens, countries should include a question on the reasons for migration in their population census.

The human-rights community has much to gain from working with the statistical community to develop evidence-based reporting for international human-rights instruments. Similarly, the statistical community needs to cooperate more closely with the human-rights community to promote the implementation of the UN census recommendations.

Notes

1. Chief, Migration Section, Population Division, Department of Economic and Social Affairs, United Nations, New York. From 1993 to 2006, Bela Hovy was in charge of statistics at UNHCR in Geneva. The views expressed are those of the author and do not necessarily reflect those of the United Nations.

2. "Human Development Report 2009," <http://hdr.undp.org> (accessed July 24, 2009).

3. See article 1 of the 1954 Convention Relating to the Status of Stateless Persons for the legal definition. UN General Assembly, "Convention Relating to the Status of Stateless Persons," September 28, 1954, United Nations, *Treaty Series*, vol. 360, p. 117, <http://www.unhcr.org> (accessed July 24, 2009).

4. UN General Assembly, "Convention on the Reduction of Statelessness," August 30, 1961, United Nations, *Treaty Series*, vol. 989, p. 175, <http://www.unhcr.org> (accessed July 24, 2009).

5. UN General Assembly, "Declaration on the Human Rights of Individuals Who Are Not Nationals of the Country in Which They Live," December 13, 1985, <http://www.unhcr.org> (accessed July 24, 2009).

6. UN General Assembly, "International Convention on the Protection of the Rights of All Migrant Workers and Members of Their Families: Resolution Adopted by the General Assembly," December 18, 1990, A/RES/45/158, <http://www.unhcr.org> (accessed July 24, 2009).

7. The 1967 Protocol removed the temporal limitation from the Refugee Convention. See UN General Assembly, Convention Relating to the Status of Refugees, July 28, 1951, United Nations, *Treaty Series*, vol. 189, p. 137, <http://www.unhcr.org> (accessed July 24, 2009); and UN General Assembly, Protocol Relating to the Status of Refugees, January 30, 1967, United Nations, *Treaty Series*, vol. 606, p. 267, <http://www.unhcr.org> (accessed July 24, 2009).

8. See Refugee Convention, art. 1(F)(b).

9. See the UNHCR Statistics Web site at <http://www.unhcr.org> (accessed July 22, 2009).

10. See the UNHCR Web site, <http://www.unhcr.org/protect/3b8265c7a.html> (accessed April 30, 2009).

11. See the UN Treaty Collection Web site, <http://treaties.un.org/Pages/Treaties.aspx?id=5&subid=A&lang=en> (accessed July 24, 2009).

12. See the following section on national data sources.

13. Committee on the Protection of the Rights of All Migrant Workers and Members of Their Families.

14. See CRC, arts. 43–44.

15. The statistical reporting requirements provided in the guidelines issued by the Committee on the Rights of the Child are contained in the document UN High Commissioner for Human Rights (UNHCHR), "General Guidelines regarding the Form and Contents of Periodic Reports to be Submitted by States Parties under Article 44, Paragraph 1 (b), of the Convention," <http://www.unhchr.ch> (accessed July 24, 2009).

16. See the UNICEF Web site, <http://www.unicef.org/crc/index_30210.html> (accessed July 24, 2009).

17. UNICEF has a significant capacity to collect data on the rights and well-being of children, which could serve as another model for reporting on human-rights-related issues. Considering the limited attention that has been paid to noncitizen children in the CRC and in UNICEF's work, this chapter does not focus on them.

18. UN Statistics Division, "Principles and Recommendations for Population and Housing Censuses Revision 2," United Nations, New York, 2008 (ST/ESA/STAT/SER.M/67/Rev.2), <http://unstats.un.org> (accessed July 24, 2009).

19. "[F]or the purpose of preparing tabulations on citizenship, all countries should be shown separately to the extent possible and a category of stateless persons should be presented." See "Principles and Recommendations for Population and Housing Censuses Revision 2," United Nations, New York, 2008, 127.

20. "CES Recommendations for the 2010 Round of Population and Housing Censuses," UN Economic Commission for Europe Web site, <http://www.unece.org> (accessed July 24, 2009).

21. United Nations, Department of Economic and Social Affairs, Population Division, "International Migration Flows to and from Selected Countries: The 2008 Revision" (United Nations database, POP/DB/MIG/FL/Rev.2008) (2009).

22. *United Nations Global Migration Database*, <http://www.unmigration.org> (accessed July 24, 2009).

II

De Facto Statelessness

Irregular but accompanied children do not always fare better than their unaccompanied counterparts. In some cases, as members of undocumented migrant families, the children are placed with their parents in detention facilities. This disturbing practice is increasingly common in many European countries. In other cases, children—with or without their families—are repatriated in circumstances that have raised the concerns of nongovernmental organizations (NGOs) and public institutions such as the European Court of Human Rights (ECtHR).[5] Even where migrant children are granted a lawful status, this frequently expires when they reach the age of majority, forcing those who are unable to return home into situations of prolonged irregularity and clandestinity.[6]

This complex package of rightlessness and compromised access to the protection of family or state renders undocumented migrant children *de facto* stateless, to use the helpful terminology suggested by Jacqueline Bhabha in her introduction to this volume. In the majority of cases, these children are not literally or legally stateless because they have the nationality of their country of origin. But the lack of a legal migration status makes it impossible for them to access social rights that are generally thought to be the entitlement of all children or to make demands on their country of nationality. These children also are not in a position to take advantage of the generally protective obligations toward children that apply to the state in which they reside.[7]

I suggest in what follows that the condition of *de facto* statelessness affects all aspects of the lives of undocumented migrant children, ranging from access to health care to education and decent housing. Indeed, the problem goes further. It is widely assumed by policy makers and the general public alike that if the parents of an undocumented child are deported because of their irregular status, it is in the child's best interest to be returned together with the parents. But this assumption may be faulty. Although the right to family unity and respect for family life are of fundamental importance when assessing what is in the "best interests" of a child, so too are other cardinal factors such as access to adequate health care, to education, and to the enjoyment of adequate living conditions.[8]

Despite increased recent attention by civil society and international organizations to the protection needs of undocumented children and despite concerted appeals for enhanced rights protections for this population, governments have so far failed to react consistently or adequately. In fact, as a result of increasingly restrictive and aggressive policies to control irregular immigration, there has been a general lowering of the protection level for minors. This deteriorating situation has led nongovernmental advocacy organizations to adopt a range of innovative strategies to document what *de facto* statelessness means in practice for affected child migrants. Although they cannot substitute for the state in providing essential and fundamental services, these civil society entities have a critical role in bearing public witness to the lives of a population that is otherwise largely ignored. One of the most diligent and effective of these civil society organizations over the last few years has been PICUM, a model collaborative entity that has built on the strengths and experiences of multiple nongovernmental stakeholders across Europe to compile reliable and previously unavailable data about irregular migrant populations, including children. A good and relevant example of PICUM's innovative approach is a project entitled "Fighting Discrimination-based Violence against Undocumented Children," which was carried out between February 2007 and February 2009. The project focused on discrimination-based violence against undocumented children in the areas of health care, housing, and education in nine EU member states—Belgium, France, Hungary, Italy, Malta, the Netherlands, Poland, Spain, and the United Kingdom.

PICUM's research is trend setting because it is the first time that the impact of *de facto* statelessness on children in Europe has been systematically studied. The project focused primarily on in-depth investigation of concrete examples of undocumented children's social exclusion. PICUM's research included three primary data sources—a thorough analysis of applicable domestic and international legislation; interviews conducted in each country with all relevant stakeholders (government agencies, service providers, civil society organizations, and child migrants); and detailed country-based reports presented by experts at two specially convened international workshops held by PICUM during the course of the project.[9] The lack of systematic, published research on this topic by government or other entities made the interviews essential. PICUM's research documents a range of problems associated with access to education, health care, and shelter for child migrants across the EU member states studied. However, in addition to the problems with and lacunae in effective protection, the research also highlights useful examples of good practice instituted to enhance the rights of undocumented migrant children by NGOs across Europe.

The Triple Vulnerability of Undocumented Children

All migrants face a risk of poverty and social exclusion, and these dangers are exacerbated for those who lack proper immigration status.[10]

Among this group, children, whether they have migrated alone or are accompanied by their parents or caregivers, occupy an especially vulnerable position in terms of their ability to access rights and protection. In January 2008, the Social Protection Committee of the European Commission released a report on "Child Poverty and Well-Being in the EU" in which it referred to the situation of migrant children and their risk of poverty in the EU:

Children living in a migrant household face a much higher risk of poverty than children whose parents were born in the host country. In most countries, undocumented children face at least a 30 percent higher chance of living below the poverty line than children whose parents were born in the country of residence.[11]

Undocumented children are in a situation of triple vulnerability—as children, as migrants, and—their major vulnerability—as undocumented migrants. Anecdotally, the particular vulnerability of these minors is reported on daily by relevant NGOs and has been widely recognized on the European and international level. More systematic attention and intervention, however, have been slow in coming.

As the commissioner for human rights of the Council of Europe, Thomas Hammarberg, recently pointed out in one of his "viewpoints":

Migrant children are one of the most vulnerable groups in Europe today. Some of them have fled persecution or war; others have run away from poverty and destitution. There are also those who are victims of trafficking. At particular risk are those who are separated from their families and have no—or only a temporary—residence permit. Many of these children suffer exploitation and abuse. Their situation is a major challenge to the humanitarian principles we advocate.[12]

The data deficit is a central impediment to effective governmental enforcement of applicable social protections for undocumented children in Europe. This difficulty is compounded by the fact that undocumented children constitute a complex, mobile, and varied group requiring a nuanced and varied range of interventions to achieve effective results. Statistical data on migrants in Europe is virtually nonexistent; available official figures are approximate. These indicate that the undocumented migrant population in Europe as a whole is estimated at between 4.5 to 8 million.[13] No equivalent (even approximate) figure exists for the percentage of this population that is under age eighteen. The data situation is not better if one switches attention from the European Union to the national picture. Although considerable work has been done to document the numbers of separated children,[14] little or no attention has so far been paid to the category of undocumented children as a whole, a group that includes separated and accompanied children.[15]

One of the key difficulties in monitoring and compiling statistics on the social exclusion and discrimination of undocumented minors is their radical neglect by responsible institutions in the host societies. Hostility to them as undocumented migrants trumps protective concern about their vulnerable social circumstances. As a result of this pervasive social attitude, families (including children) report being reluctant to register official complaints about discrimination that they experience because of the likely negative consequences of such complaints, particularly the risk of detention and expulsion. Lack of access to essential state services and benefits is therefore compounded by the ever-present risk of racism and discriminatory violence, a situation of radical insecurity and double victimhood.[16]

Aside from the *de facto* invisibility caused by migrants' enforced clandestinity, there is another state-driven type of willful state neglect at play. It is the routine official failure to collect systematic empirical data that would ground an objective evaluation of the effect of their immigration-control measures on children, including the wide range of rights violations to which undocumented child migrants are routinely subjected. The second Joint Chief Inspectors' Report on arrangements to safeguard children conducted in the United Kingdom in 2005 reported that "the lack of available information about the range of children in the UK who are subject to immigration control itself raises considerable concern about safeguarding arrangements."[17]

Current EU control policies directed against irregular migration[18] have dramatically diverted public and official attention away from the acute child protection needs of these young immigrants to control of their irregular situation. Some have considered the impact of harsh migration control policies on irregular immigrants as a whole, but there is no comprehensive evaluation of the effect of these policies on undocumented children.

Access to Education

School helps to shape a child's formation and social integration. School is where a child acquires the knowledge necessary for growth and begins the social and cultural integration that is necessary to become a full citizen of the society in which he or she lives.[19]

For undocumented children, access to education also represents the principal means for their introduction to society and for initiating the process of obtaining regular residence permits once they reach eighteen years of age. In some countries, regular school attendance is the driver of access to legal residence at age eighteen. In Italy[20] and France,[21] for example, conferment of a permanent residence permit on reaching adulthood is directly tied to proof of physical presence in the territory for a certain number of years and school attendance.

International and European Legislation
The importance of education for children is affirmed and codified by a wide range of international conventions. All of the main international conventions on human rights recognize the right of instruction as a fundamental right of every child.[22]

Among them is the Convention on the Rights of the Child[23] (CRC). Article 28 states that "States Parties recognize the right of the child to education, and with a view to achieving this right progressively and on the basis of equal opportunity. They shall, in particular: (a) Make primary education compulsory and available free to all."

At the European level, both the Council of Europe (COE) and the EU have adopted instruments for the protection of the right to education for *all children*. Article 17 of the European Social Charter (ESC) and article 2 of the first Protocol of the European Convention on Human Rights and Freedoms (ECHR) clearly state that no person shall be denied the right to education and that the state has a duty to render this right effective. The EU has adopted the Charter of Fundamental Rights of the European Union,[24] which states in chapter 2, article 14, that "everyone has the right to education and to have access to vocational and continuing training; this right includes the possibility to receive free compulsory education." EU legislation protects the right to education for all children who are regularly present in the territory, but there is no analogous or clear provision protecting the right to educational inclusion for undocumented children in Europe.

National Legislation
A thorough examination of national legislation in the countries reviewed produced no evidence of direct discrimination against undocumented children.[25] In no case did the law explicitly forbid access to education for undocumented children, nor were there reports of direct legislative discrimination explicitly prohibiting undocumented children's access to education. Nevertheless, the level of protection given to noncitizen and undocumented children varies from country to country.

It is helpful to group the legislation of the states in which PICUM conducted its research according to the different levels of protection granted to undocumented children. Three general groups are discernible. In one group including Belgium, Italy, and the Netherlands, the legislation contains a specific reference to the right to education for irregular children. In a second group including France, Spain, Poland, and the United Kingdom, there is no specific reference in the legislation, but the right to education is extended to all children, implicitly including irregular children. Finally, in a third group including Hungary and Malta, the law covers only the right to education for migrant children in a regular immigration status.[26]

The Situation on the Ground

The simple task of registering in school becomes a kind of war between, on the one side, parents and students, and on the other, the administrative system, the latter of whom has the power to hijack this right.[27]

It seems evident that the right to education for undocumented children is protected by law (or at least not explicitly prohibited) in all the countries reviewed. However, by shifting attention to the reality that young immigrants face in European schools and the practical barriers to education, a much more complex picture emerges.

At the second multilateral workshop on "Fighting Discrimination-based Violence against Undocumented Children" organized by PICUM in April 2008,[28] many participants emphasized the significant gap between theoretical entitlements granted by law to all children, including undocumented children, and the concrete barriers that these children experience.[29] The discrepancy between the inclusive provisions of international and domestic law and the reality of exclusion experienced by undocumented children was an underlying theme of the workshop and of all the interviews conducted in the education and broader social rights sectors.

Examples of the practical barriers to educational access documented by interviewed NGOs include the requirement to produce identification documents before enrolling in school, as well as the real risks of detention and related sanctions experienced by parents of undocumented children when registering their children at school. Nontuition-related expenses such as books and transportation are directly tied to the child's education and were also identified as a barrier. The nonissuance of diplomas at the end of their scholastic career represents a serious aspect of discrimination against undocumented children.[30]

Precarious living conditions also impede access to education. Only by guaranteeing access to decent living quarters can these minors be assured consistent access to education. Conversely, undermining access to housing inevitably impinges on the enjoyment of the right to education and on other basic social rights, such as health care. Several interviewed NGOs noted that irregular families, either for economic reasons or out of fear of being tracked down by the authorities, change their place of residence frequently, thus making it impossible for their children to complete an entire year of school in one place.

Box 5.1
"Let Them Grow Up Here": Promoting the Education of Undocumented Children in France with the Education without Borders Network (RESF)

On June 26, 2004, at the Bourse du Travail in Paris, teachers, staff from the national education system, parents of students, youth workers, and members of associations, trade unions, and human-rights organizations met to discuss the situation of undocumented pupils in nursery schools through universities. The group initially intended to mobilize protests against the arrest and expulsion of two young people over the age of eighteen who were enrolled in secondary schools. Beginning with this meeting, a support network grew—Réseau Éducation Sans Frontières (RESF) or Education without Borders Network.

The group called on teachers and other staff members at school institutions at all levels to inform their pupils that they were ready to mobilize to help normalize their situation. RESF's slogan—"Let them grow up here"—refers to the group's belief that if a child starts his or her education in France, then he or she should finish it there, even if the student is in school until the age of thirty.

The education without Borders Network usually begins in schools with petitions, parent rallies, and teacher strikes. The network also offers drop-in legal sessions to advise undocumented families on their rights and to help them complete official documents. RESF currently has more than two hundred local branches, but it does not have a hierarchy and central structure that would define it as an organization.[a]

Note

a. For more info, go to the Web site of Réseau Éducation Sans Frontières (RESF) or Education without Borders Network, <http://www.educationsansfrontieres.org> (accessed February 1, 2009).

Access to Health Care

Undocumented migrants in Europe face serious problems gaining access to health care. Their physical and mental health tends to deteriorate because of poor access to health-care services and the continual fear of being discovered and expelled.[31] Undocumented children encounter similar difficulties in accessing a high standard of health care in terms of bureaucratic impediments, a lack of adequate information, and the fear of being caught.

International and European Legislation

The right to health care is protected on the international level by a variety of international instruments.[32] Article 24 of the CRC states that

States Parties recognise the right of the child to the enjoyment of the highest attainable standard of health and to facilities for the treatment of illness and rehabilitation of health. States Parties shall strive to ensure that no child is deprived of his or her right of access to such health care services.

At the European level, references to the right to health care for undocumented children can be found in article 13 of the ESC and in article 3 of the ECHR. The ECtHR ruled that article 3 of the ECHR—which prohibits torture and inhumane or degrading treatment—may in certain exceptional circumstances protect those denied health care if they may as a consequence suffer inhumane or degrading treatment or punishment.[33]

National Legislation

A comparative analysis of the different laws in force in the countries where PICUM conducted its research reveals both commonalities and differences in their legislative positions on undocumented child migrants' access to health care. Spain is the only country where the legislation fully conforms with the international standards guaranteed by the CRC. In Spain, the provision of health care for undocumented children is equal to the provision of health care granted to Spanish children.

In Italy,[34] Belgium, and France, the law provides separated children with completely equal health-care protections to those available for native children. However, accompanied undocumented children (children who are living irregularly in the country with their parents) are worse off than their unaccompanied or separated counterparts. These children, like their parents, are entitled only to primary health care. They do not have access to nonemergency, ongoing medical facilities or to regular health care for chronic diseases. The discrimination between accompanied and other irregular child migrants appears to be irrational. In a third group of countries, including the United Kingdom and the Netherlands, the law neither forbids nor permits complete access to health care but instead leaves the decision about whether the care is essential to the general practitioners. Finally, in Hungary, Poland, and Malta, the law does not provide any special safeguards for undocumented children, and therefore guaranteed access is limited to essential health care as it is for undocumented adults. As noted in the next section, NGOs working in these countries have found the boundaries of essential and emergency health care to be unclear and confusing.

The Situation on the Ground

If you've got health needs, you should be seen by a medical practitioner. That's particularly so for children. If you're undocumented, then it's very difficult to register with a doctor. In practice, they'll only be seen if they've got an emergency.[35]

In most interviews, NGOs emphasized the fact that undocumented children generally have access only to essential and urgent care, without regular supervision by a general practitioner and with stringent limits on specialist care. Nonetheless, the interpretation of urgent care differs from country to country, ranging from the situation in Italy (where the interpretation is rather open and allows continuous care for all)[36] to Poland or Hungary (where the interpretation is much more restrictive). Within countries, there are also local variations concerning the meaning of *urgent care*. Some doctors, for example, include mental health, and others do not.

The most worrying consequence of this arbitrary interpretation is the discretionary power that general practitioners and hospitals exercise over the decision to accept or refuse care to undocumented migrants and their children. According to many interviewees, appropriate access to care often depends more on the goodwill of the doctor than on a uniform and universally accepted interpretation of the law. Training of medical staff and administrators on this complex but critical aspect of medical entitlement was reportedly nonexistent.

In addition to problems of legal interpretation, there are practical barriers that interfere with the implementation of legal entitlements. In the majority of cases, access to health care for undocumented children differs little from that of undocumented migrants in general. Both groups encounter similar difficulties caused by bureaucratic impediments, lack of adequate information, and reluctance to make use of public health services because of the known consequences of having irregular migration status detected.[37]

Besides these practical barriers, the research interviews revealed a widespread concern with issues related to mental health, including the difficulties that undocumented children experience in accessing adequate care. Some of the interviews focused on the connection between undocumented children's precarious daily living conditions and their vulnerability to mental-health problems. Other interviews analyzed the specific difficulties of accessing appropriate and responsive mental-health care. Rian Ederveen of the NGO Stichting LOS in the Netherlands, for example, pointed out that the burden of their families' irregular status is often too much for young children to bear:

Children take a lot of responsibilities for their parents because they speak the language earlier and understand the system more easily, so often it's the children who take on the responsibility, and for them there is no support network. You see parents who are traumatised and don't have the strength to go on, and you see children who are traumatised. They become too old too soon.[38]

Finally, reference is often made to the interdependence of the right to health care with other rights. Many have highlighted the relationship between poor housing conditions and the health of undocumented children. Various NGOs[39] have documented repeated cases of infant lead poisoning caused by poor housing conditions or the psychological effects on children living in unhealthy quarters, without privacy, and in conditions encouraging promiscuity with adults.

Access to Housing

Throughout PICUM's research, the subject of housing emerged as one of the most significant quotidian problems for undocumented children. NGO respondents noted their inability to assist the majority of undocumented families. Even where families with children live in extremely poor conditions, the fact that they are irregular excludes them from access to social housing.[40]

International and European Legislation
The right to housing is explicitly recognized as a basic human right in a wide range of international instruments. The UDHR and the Interna-

Box 5.2
Promoting Access to Health Care for Undocumented Children by Working within the Health Provider Community: Medact Refugee Health Network

The British Medact Refugee Health Network devotes a large proportion of its resources to finding general practitioners who will treat undocumented migrants, focusing on maternity care and health care for children. The Network's advocacy for undocumented children has taken the form of awareness raising in the health community (for instance through talks at the Royal College of Paediatrics and Child Health) and recruiting high-profile members of the medical community. The group has also worked on publicizing the National Health Service scheme that allows a "care first, pay later" approach for immediate necessary care. This scheme has been inadequately publicized in government documents and is therefore ineffective in clarifying the obligations of medical practitioners.[a]

Note

a. This network of health professionals, many of whom have considerable professional experience, campaign and lobby with governments, international bodies, and other influential organizations, calling on them to take positive actions to prevent violent conflict, improve health, and raise the standards of health care worldwide. Members of the network share information and resources and offer mutual support. The network currently has 280 members. See Medact Refugee Health Network, <http://www.medact.org> (accessed April 20, 2009).

tional Covenant of Economic, Social, and Cultural Rights (ICESCR) call for an "adequate standard of living." This right is applicable to all persons irrespective of nationality or legal status.[41] According to article 27 of CRC:

States Parties, in accordance with national conditions and within their means, shall take appropriate measures to assist parents and others responsible for the child to implement this right and shall in case of need provide material assistance and support programs, particularly with regard to nutrition, clothing and housing.

At the European level, the ECHR can be invoked to protect the right to housing of undocumented children. The jurisprudence of the ECtHR has clearly affirmed the right to be free from degrading treatment (ECHR, art. 3) and the right to respect for one's private and family life, home and correspondence (ECHR, art. 8). The latter may be invoked to impose a positive obligation on the state to protect persons from particularly intolerable housing conditions.[42]

What Right to Housing Exists for Undocumented Children without National Protection?

Even if the right to adequate housing exists at the international level, national legislation makes no specific reference to the protection of this right for all undocumented children. Unaccompanied or separated children are entitled to state protection (including the right to adequate housing).[43] However, undocumented children living with their families have no legal entitlement to public housing.

In many cases, local authorities (who are generally responsible for separated children) do not accept irregular immigrants in reception centers and do not guarantee them any assistance. A limited exception, for short periods of time, is sometimes made for the most vulnerable groups, such as mothers with newborn or small babies. As a result of these policies, children living with undocumented parents generally do not have access to housing or to assistance with shelter and often subsist in inadequate living conditions (such as dilapidated and overcrowded lodging, abandoned factories, and shacks along rivers).

The only legal obligation to provide housing for undocumented children in the countries researched arises from the children's status as minors. However, even here, in practice the assistance that undocumented children can draw on is limited because what is typically offered is accommodation in a shelter that excludes the child's family. Such policies present children and their families with a difficult and unsatisfactory choice—access to living conditions guaranteed for children by international law but without protection of the right to family unity or the enjoyment of family life in circumstances of radical housing deficit.[44]

The Situation on the Ground

What we are increasingly finding is that for certain categories of people from abroad who apply for housing assistance, the local authorities say that they won't house the family, but they only accept that they have duties to house the child. So the family is faced with the situation that they either become homeless or they have to give up the child to the social care.[45]

Across all the countries researched, access to housing for undocumented children was problematic. As previously documented, [46] families with irregular immigration status have problems gaining access to the private housing market and are excluded from social housing. A family's irregular status results in serious obstacles to securing housing and often translates into forms of exclusion or discrimination against the family, with repercussions on the child. It is hard to imagine a clearer demonstration of the impact of *de facto* statelessness than this radical social exclusion confronting undocumented children every day.

The right to housing for undocumented children is also closely linked to the more general social exclusion that irregular immigrant families face. For these families, access to regular work is limited, and the children's parents often have no choice but to enter the informal labor market, where they routinely experience underpayment, exploitation, and abuse.

A family's poor economic condition also dramatically affects their living conditions, as well. Besides being excluded from public housing due to their lack of a residence permit, they are relegated to the margins of the private housing market, where harassment and atrocious safety and health standards are rampant. Unsanitary facilities, pest infestation, inadequate heating, fire hazards, overcrowding, and dampness are only some of the chronic environmental hazards that arise. Even in the face of these precarious and often exploitative situations, just as with denial of basic educational or health access, irregular families rarely turn to the authorities to denounce their landlords for fear of retaliatory measures directed at their irregular immigration status.

Finally, numerous NGOs have reported that unaccompanied children are *de facto* excluded from appropriate and much needed social services provisions that specifically cater to them because they end up living in situations of radical social exclusion. These circumstances mirror those just described for undocumented family groups. In the case of undocumented children who are without family caregivers, two main scenarios are described—unaccompanied children subsisting outside any form of shelter and minors leaving designated reception centers and choosing to return to life on the streets. Both situations were observed in each of the countries reviewed.

Conclusion

The overall findings emerging from this research point to commonalities and differences in the impact of *de facto* statelessness on undocumented children's access to economic and social rights across the countries surveyed. An important first commonality is that rights accorded to all children irrespective of their status under international legislation are often not implemented. All EU member states have ratified the CRC, which includes basic principles and detailed provisions that, when implemented, should ensure equal access to services and education as well as

Box 5.3
Helping Children Who Have Abandoned the "System": The Experience of Synergie 14 in Belgium

Minors who have left the shelters are often completely abandoned. For these children, who typically are between the ages of sixteen and eighteen, leaving the shelter means ending up on the streets at serious risk of many forms of exploitation. For many child migrants in these situations, past negative experiences lead them to distrust of guardianship institutions and complicate the task of NGOs that seek to provide them with a protective environment.

In Belgium, the NGO Synergie 14 has for a number of years provided shelter and tried to build up relations with unaccompanied minors who are outside the shelter system. Synergie 14 was born as an initiative of a multicultural and multidisciplinary team of political refugees and others interested in migration, including teachers, professors, nurses, judges, students, and social workers.

Community outreach workers from this organization establish initial contact with street children and offer accommodation as well as company for those who already have accommodation but are looking for a place to socialize. "Apart from those who are sheltered, we also give hospitality to street kids who are not staying here. So a youth can come here, take a shower, do laundry, and eat. The independent ones, who go to school, can always come to a safe place where they can meet and talk with an adult," said one of the organization's staff.

Besides providing accommodation, the association takes care of all the administrative procedures related to obtaining a residence permit for the child. Finally, importance is given to entertainment, and many Belgian volunteers are involved in promoting cultural exchanges between Belgians and unaccompanied children.[a]

Note

a. For more info, go to the Synergie 14 Web site at <http://www.synergie14.be> (accessed July 1, 2010).

equitable treatment and protection of all children. Yet the needs of undocumented migrant children are often neglected or ignored, and as a result, these children face a variety of barriers in accessing their rights.

A second general finding is that practical barriers rather than direct legal discrimination are often the main impediment to the realization of migrant children's social rights. These barriers include bureaucratic practices impeding access to social services for some groups (for example, accompanied as opposed to unaccompanied child migrants or asylum-seeking as opposed to other children), arbitrary documentary identification requirements, and the unfettered and unsupervised abuse of discretionary power by local administrators who control access to social services.

Finally, the research highlighted the profound interdependence of social rights. To ensure the healthy development of undocumented migrant children, basic access to education, health care, and housing must all be guaranteed. To deny access to one of these rights is to affect enjoyment of all the others. All types of discrimination represent a form of violence against both the victims of the discrimination and also indirectly against society as a whole. The denial of access to basic social rights that afford dignity to each human being constitutes violence against the most fundamental principles of social solidarity. This is particularly the case when vulnerable groups such as undocumented children are targeted.[47]

Notes

1. This article is based on research conducted by the Platform for International Cooperation on Undocumented Migrants (PICUM) on the access to basic social rights for undocumented children. PICUM, *Undocumented Children in Europe: Invisible Victims of Immigration Restrictions* (Brussels: PICUM, 2008), <http://www.picum.org> (accessed April 18, 2009).

2. The term *children* in this chapter refers to all human beings under the age of eighteen as acknowledged in international human-rights instruments, such as article 1 of the Convention on the Rights of the Child (CRC).

3. The Committee on the Rights of the Child defines *unaccompanied minors* as children "who have been separated from both parents and other relatives and are is not being cared for by an adult who, by law or custom, is responsible for doing so." Separated children, in turn, are described as "children . . . separated from both parents, or from their previous legal or customary caregiver . . . not necessarily from other relatives to social services as a result of the minor's choice (out of fear of being repatriated) or more simply because they do not know about the social support system set up for them." See UN Committee on the Rights of

the Child (CRC), "CRC General Comment No. 6 (2005): Treatment of Unaccompanied and Separated Children outside Their Country of Origin," September 1, 2005, CRC/GC/2005/6, <http://www.unhcr.org> (accessed December 10, 2009).

4. See, for example, PICUM's report, "PICUM's Main Concerns about the Fundamental Rights of Undocumented Migrants in Europe in 2006," <http://picum.org> (accessed April 18, 2009).

5. See the recent European Court of Human Rights (ECtHR) case of Tabitha Mitunga, in which the Belgian government was condemned for inhumane treatment regarding a child. *Mubilanzila Mayeka and Kaniki Mitunga v. Belgium*, no. 13178/03, judgment, Strasbourg, October 12, 2006, <http://www.coe.int> (accessed April 20, 2009).

6. See, for example, the respective legislative changes recently introduced in Italy and France (detailed further in the paragraph on education).

7. The state of residence, even if not the actual nationality of the child, has a duty to protect undocumented children. In the case of children in irregular situations, however, the state faces a contradiction between the duty to protect every child and the policies fighting irregular migration, which more and more are criminalizing undocumented migrants, regardless of their age.

8. See E. Rozzi, "Minori stranieri e comunitari accompagnati da genitori irregolari: Quali diritti?," *Minori Giustizia*, no. 3 (2008): 218–228.

9. Both workshops were held in Brussels. Each included over 100 participants (representatives of NGOs, local authorities, ministerial and other government actors, and professionals from fields such as health care, education, employment, migrants' and children's-rights organizations. Participants shared experiences that had never previously been presented in an EU-wide forum and discussed strategies for increasing rights access for the affected population. Reports of the workshops are available at <http://www.picum.org>.

10. The same argument is advanced by United Nations Development Program, *Human Development Report 2009: Overcoming Barriers — Human Mobility and Development* (New York: Palgrave Macmillan, 2009).

11. It goes without saying that these statistics are even higher for migrants with irregular status. See European Commission Directorate-General for Employment, Social Affairs and Equal Opportunities Report, "Child Poverty and Well-Being in the EU: Current Status and Way Forward," January 2008, 63–65, <http://ec.europa.eu> (accessed April 20, 2009).

12. See Commissioner Viewpoint, "Children in Migration Should Get Better Protection," <http://www.coe.int> (accessed April 20, 2009).

13. See Global Commission on International Migration, "Migration in an Interconnected World: New Directions for Action. Report of the Global Commission on International Migration," October 2005, 32, <http://www.gcim.org> (accessed April 20, 2009).

14. See, for example, reports issued by the Separated Children in Europe Program (SCEP), such as SCEP, "Children in Migration: Conference Report, Warsaw,"

2007; "Position Paper on Preventing and Responding to Trafficking in Europe," 2007; "How to Make Children Visible in Migration: Seminar Report," 2006.

15. The term *undocumented children* generally refers to those children who are present in Europe without a valid residence permit. In contrast, the term *separated or unaccompanied children* refers to migrant children who are not with any family members. In some cases, the two groups can be overlapping: separated children can arrive and stay in Europe without a valid residence permit and also be undocumented.

16. A number of NGOs reported this fear in different contexts. Many highlighted that even when the families are in contact with an NGO that is ready to help and even offer free legal assistance, they mostly prefer not to proceed with their complaint. See PICUM, *Undocumented Children in Europe,* 79.

17. See Joint Chief Inspectors, "Safeguarding Children: The Second Joint Chief Inspectors' Report on Arrangements to Safeguard Children," Commission for Social Care Inspection, 2005, <http://www.hmica.gov.uk> (accessed April 20, 2009).

18. As one of many examples of the extent to which repression of irregular migration is a priority of the EU policy, see Europe Parliament, "Policy Priorities in the Fight against Illegal Immigration of Third-Country Nationals," <http://www.europarl.europa.eu> (accessed April 20, 2009).

19. In an article about the integration of migrants, Walter Kälin, representative of the United Nations (UN) secretary-general on the human rights of internally displaced persons, affirms that social integration is realized by integration in the educational system through nonsegregated primary and secondary schools, as well as higher education. He considers equality of treatment as one of the keys of integration, as well as respect of the nondiscrimination principle. See A. Guimont, Office of the High Commissioner for Human Rights (OHCHR), "Le droit a l'éducation des enfants migrants," March 2007, 2, <http://www2.ohchr.org> (accessed April 20, 2009).

20. See Law no. 286/98, art. 32, as modified by no. 189/2002, art. 25, <http://www.parlamento.it> (accessed April 20, 2009). The law states that to obtain a residence permit after turning eighteen, the child must be present in Italy for at least three years and have followed a "social integration process" (which includes school enrollment and vocational courses) for two years.

21. In France until November 2003, undocumented children monitored by the child welfare services were entitled to apply for French nationality when they turned eighteen. But the Act of November 26, 2003, on controlling migration flows (the so-called Sarkozy Act) has ended this. After reaching the age of majority, young people may apply for French nationality only if they have been on the child welfare service's registers (schools, for example) for three years—that is, if they were younger than fifteen when they arrived. See Loi no. 2003-1119 of November 26, 2003, Relative à la maîtrise de l'immigration, au séjour des étrangers en France et à la nationalité, art. 14, <http://www.droit.org> (accessed April 20, 2009). See also Circular no. Nor/Int/D/04/00006/C of January 20, 2004, Application of Law no. 2003-1119 of November 26, 2003, Relative à la maîtrise

de l'immigration, au séjour des étrangers en France et à la nationalité, which explains that the change is intended to restrict the "illegal immigration of unaccompanied minors," <http://www.vie-publique.fr> (accessed April 20, 2009).

22. Among others we can recall here Universal Declaration of Human Rights (UDHR), art. 26; International Convention on Economic, Social and Cultural Rights (ICESCR), arts. 13–14; International Convention on the Elimination of All Forms of Racial Discrimination (ICERD), art. 5; and International Convention on the Protection of the Rights of All Migrant Workers and Members of Their Families (ICRMW), art. 30. For a list of all of the international instruments that have been ratified by EU member states that offer protection to undocumented children, see PICUM, "Undocumented Migrants Have Rights! A Guide to the International Human Rights Framework," Brussels, 2007, p. 8, <http://www.picum.org> (accessed April 20, 2009).

23. The CRC has been ratified by all the members of the UN General Assembly except the United States and Somalia.

24. The Charter of Fundamental Rights of the European Union lists the fundamental rights under six major headings—dignity, freedoms, equality, solidarity, citizens' rights, and justice. The charter has been incorporated into the second part of the draft European constitution, but the constitution itself has not been ratified by the twenty-seven member states of the European Union. The Charter of Fundamental Rights of the European Union is therefore not a legally binding document. For general information on the Charter of Fundamental Rights of the EU, see <http://europa.eu.int> (accessed April 20, 2009).

25. "Almost all European countries comply fully with th[e] . . . basic right [to education], extending it to all immigrant children, irrespective of their residential status. In other words, families of refugees or asylum seekers or those who are irregularly resident, no less than those with long term residential status, may all enroll their children at a school in the host country." See the European Commission Directorate General for Education and Culture, "Integrating Immigrant Children into Schools in Europe," Eurydice, 2004, 67, <http://eacea.ec.europa.eu> (accessed April 20, 2009).

26. For a more detailed analysis of the legislation see PICUM, *Undocumented Children in Europe*, 16–21.

27. Interview with Alexandre Le Cleve in Paris in August 2007 and cited in PICUM, "Undocumented Children in Europe," 26.

28. See the report of the second workshop, PICUM, "Fighting Discrimination-Based Violence against Undocumented Children," Brussels, April 4, 2008, 12–15, <http://picum.org> (accessed April 20, 2009).

29. For examples of these barriers and how these are linked to *de facto* statelessness, see the chapter on access to education of PICUM, "Undocumented Children in Europe," 23–27.

30. In Spain and Italy, for example, countries where universal access to schooling irrespective of migration status is cited by NGOs as an example of good practice, serious problems in guaranteeing undocumented children a diploma have been reported. See PICUM, "Undocumented Children in Europe," 35.

6

Realizing the Rights of Undocumented Children in Europe

Jyothi Kanics

International human-rights law has evolved to offer many entitlements and protections to undocumented migrant children. Most notably, the United Nations Convention on the Rights of the Child (CRC), which is nearly universally ratified, includes basic principles and detailed provisions that, when implemented, should ensure equal access to services and education as well as equitable treatment and protection to all children. Additionally, at both the European and national levels, legislative and policy measures have been taken to further the rights of all children.

Despite these protective measures, undocumented migrant children, who may indeed have some documentation but who lack the legal entitlement to reside where they live, are usually ignored and face various barriers in accessing their rights. They are, as Jacqueline Bhabha argues in the introduction to this volume, *de facto* stateless.

Children and families may become undocumented or "irregular" in a variety of ways. Research in Ireland[1] has identified several categories of irregular migrants, including those who (1) entered the country irregularly, (2) overstayed or otherwise violated the conditions of their visa, (3) were trafficked to Ireland, (4) were not granted refugee status after making an asylum application but stayed in the country, and (5) joined legal resident family members but lacked an independent right of residence themselves.

Because of the serious social and legal problems that arise, it is important to document both the circumstances of undocumented children and the good-practice measures that might enable improved access to human-rights protections. Empowering undocumented children requires strengthening the relevant legal framework, implementing it more effectively, and addressing prevailing attitudes and lack of awareness.

to observe and develop international law, including respect for the principles of the United Nations Charter.[8]

Council of Europe

The ECHR established the ECtHR, which gives legal recourse to individuals to enforce the wide range of human rights guaranteed by the convention if they are victims of a violation of rights. Children can be given assistance in bringing complaints. The case law of the ECtHR reflects decisions made on the individual cases brought to the court, but as with all courts, it also indicates the interpretative standards set by the ECHR and the remedies needed to avoid future violations.

Additionally, the European Social Charter (ESC) guarantees social and economic human rights. Complaints regarding violations of the charter may be lodged with the European Committee of Social Rights. Nongovernmental organizations (NGOs) that have participatory status with the Council of Europe are entitled to lodge complaints with the Committee.

The Council of Europe Convention on Action against Trafficking in Human Beings also includes a variety of measures to ensure respect for the best interests of the child. Of particular note is the provision that child victims "shall not be returned to a State," if there is indication, following "a risk and security assessment" that such return would not be in the best interests of the child.[9]

Finally, the Committee of Ministers and the Parliamentary Assembly of the Council of Europe have also adopted recommendations and resolutions related to the protection of children's rights, in particular the rights of child migrants and separated children who are seeking asylum.[10]

National Commitments

At the national level, many European governments have adopted legislation and policies to promote and to protect the rights of children. Such provisions are often included in national constitutions as well as specific legislation. National strategies and action plans for the promotion of children's rights further address implementation of standards. Most recently, many European governments have drafted National Action Plans to combat child trafficking and to protect child victims of trafficking. In addition, independent children's-rights institutions such as children's ombudspersons, commissioners for children, or focal points on children's rights in national human-rights institutions or general ombudsman offices exist in many European countries.[11]

Human-Rights Problems Faced by Undocumented Children in Europe

Despite the obligations outlined in international human-rights law, most states focus more on undocumented migrant children's immigration status than their needs as children. Although systematic research in this area is scarce, useful reports by the press and by NGOs highlight some concerns and document violations that seriously hamper these children's access to protection.

Deprived of Identity and Nationality

In some European countries, the children of undocumented migrants are not registered at birth. Thus, in addition to their *de facto* statelessness as undocumented migrants, these children also become *effectively stateless* in the sense advanced in this volume—unable to prove their nationality. In some cases, as explained below, they may even become *legally stateless* if they are not entitled to nationality by descent through their parents. This lack of birth registration has been attributed to a range of factors, including the parents' fear of being discovered,[12] fees or overly bureaucratic procedures associated with the birth registration procedure, and irregular migrants' (and even, in some cases, regular noncitizens') ineligibility for birth registration or certification.

For example, in Greece, registration is possible in theory, but in practice even legal immigrants are not issued with a birth certificate. In its *Country Reports on Human Rights Practices 2007*, the United States (U.S.) State Department noted:

The [Greek] government does not issue birth certificates for immigrant children born in Greece. In July, the ombudsman for human rights urged the government to start issuing special birth certificates for immigrant children and to accept them in all education, social security and social protection-related services. Without a birth certificate, immigrant children face difficulties registering for school and have to apply for residence permits when they reach the age of 18.[13]

According to current Greek citizenship law, immigrants are not eligible for a birth certificate because this document is issued only to babies whose parents are registered on a municipal roll (*dimotologio*) and only Greek citizens may be entered into such rolls.[14] This leads to serious problems of social exclusion for immigrant children: a birth certificate is a requirement for school enrollment as well as for registration with health insurance foundations.[15] These children are thus *de facto* stateless and may, depending on the nationality laws of their parents' countries of origin, even end up *de jure* stateless[16] if birthright citizenship cannot be transmitted to them by descent (*jus sanguinis*).

Although some undocumented children are not registered at birth and remain undocumented because of their parents' reluctance to interface with state authorities, other migrant children, such as those separated from their families, may remain unregistered and without proper identification documents even after they have been taken into state care. This is the situation in Ireland, where there is no legal requirement for children to be registered until they are sixteen. Social workers receive no guidance on how to deal with unregistered children under age sixteen, which leaves many of these children vulnerable to long-term irregular status. In Norway, children who are unable to prove the identity of at least one of their parents are denied citizenship even if the children were born and have always lived in Norway. Apparently this legal barrier has affected as many as 1,500 children in 2007 and 2008, mainly of Iraqi, Somali, and Afghan origin.[17] Some children find it impossible to regularize their status at any stage and end up classified as *de jure* stateless[18] even if they return to their parents' country of origin.[19]

Deprived of Liberty and Freedom of Movement

The criminalization of children who are not charged with any criminal wrongdoing is an egregious human-rights violation. Both the UN Committee on the Rights of the Child and the European Network of Ombudspeople for Children[20] have provided authoritative guidance stating that children should not be penalized and detained for immigration-related offenses.[21] Yet this is a common occurrence for undocumented children who, in many different European countries and for a range of reasons, can find themselves subject to detention, sometimes for extensive periods.[22] Even in cases where children have been trafficked and have a strong defense against any criminal charges for activities that flow from having been trafficked,[23] states continue to apply punitive measures, which further stigmatize and traumatize trafficked children.[24]

Denied Basic Social Rights: Health Care, Education, and Housing

Undocumented children who manage to live in the community face many challenges in accessing basic social rights. They have to wrestle daily with their *de facto* statelessness. Typically, they are eligible only for emergency medical services under national legislation. Even where, as in Spain and Italy, they are legally entitled to all forms of medical care, in practice they encounter serious difficulties accessing these services.[25] With regards to education, in some countries, such as Sweden, undocumented children are even denied access to primary and secondary education. In most European countries, education is compulsory for all children as a matter of domestic law, but many practical difficulties arise in practice. As for shelter, most European countries have legislation requiring local authorities to offer accommodation to undocumented children who are separated from their parents. By contrast, children living with their families arc rarely entitled to any state housing provision.[26]

Separated from Parents

According to the CRC, in certain decision-making situations, the best interests of the child should not only be a *primary* but rather the *paramount* consideration. In other words, the best interests of the child should trump other considerations such as immigration control or fiscal constraints. One such instance is the decision to separate a child from his or her parents. In some countries, like Ireland, respect for family unity is also a fundamental provision in the Constitution.[27]

Despite these obligations, many states employ draconian measures to enforce immigration control, resulting in the effective separation of families. In Ireland, this occurs at the predeportation stage when a parent is detained and the children are placed in state care. Such measures have been known to last up to two months. The effect of this separation on young children has not been documented.

In its recent exchange with the UN Human Rights Committee, the Irish government conceded that children had been separated from their parents as a consequence of deportation:

The practice is that where, following a full consideration of the circumstances of the case with particular reference to Ireland's human rights obligations, it is determined that adult persons should be deported, they will be accompanied by their children. Exceptions to this are extremely rare and arise only where the parents have made a deliberate choice to separate themselves from their children in an attempt to have the deportation order revoked. A recent case has arisen where this occurred. The outcome was that some of the children returned to their country of origin with their mother while others remained on in their community in Ireland. The decision in this case to separate the children from their mother was ultimately made by the family itself in that the State imposed no restriction on the children returning with their parent.[28]

The fact that citizen children can be deprived of their parents' care in their country of birth because parents are deported as a direct consequence of state immigration policies is a serious rights violation. Unfortunately, Ireland is not the only country where deportations have led to temporary or permanent separation of families, even families with citizen children. Faced with this Hobson's choice, some families choose to take their children with them, removing them from the only home they have ever known and where they hold citizenship. This becomes a form of constructive deportation.[29] Undocumented families in the United States, as David B. Thronson demonstrates in another chapter in this volume, face similar difficult choices and practices.[30]

Undocumented children are also sometimes separated from their parents on child-protection grounds. Although such measures generally have a stronger legal basis than the cases just described and usually include court oversight, they may be evidence of discrimination in instances where there has been no neglect or abuse—where the only basis for the child's removal is abject poverty and homelessness.[31] Undocumented parents are unable to rely on social welfare benefits. In some cases, because of this economic hardship, their children are viewed as "social orphans," separated from the parents, and placed into care. Tactics such as the denial of social welfare benefits to rejected asylum seekers and threats to separate families are also used by states to pressure undocumented families to leave the country. It is hard to envisage a clearer example of *de facto* statelessness than this.

Denied Family Reunification

For some children, there are other barriers to family unity. Families separated during refugee flight have been denied reunification,[32] and procedures that could be applied in the best interests of the child to promote and secure family unity (such as the more positive aspects of the Dublin II regulation) are neglected in practice.[33]

In many European countries, even applicants who are legally entitled to family reunification are denied a timely resolution to their separation. For example, in Ireland, refugees must wait an average of two years for their families to be able to join them. In practice, this means that many children take the risk of traveling to Ireland alone. In fact, over 50 percent of the separated children who arrive irregularly in Ireland come to seek family reunification. Many of these children are undocumented and risk being denied permission to enter the country legally.

Apart from the procedural delays, some European countries have instituted immigration-control measures that create legal barriers to family reunification. In Ireland, for example, a scheme that was developed for the parents of Irish-born children[34] prevented them from bringing other children still living abroad to Ireland. As a result, family reunification was undermined. Some families in this situation have arranged for their children abroad to travel to Ireland to join them, but these children typically remain undocumented despite having lived in Ireland with their families for years.[35] As David B. Thronson describes for the United States, these families end up with a *mixed status*.[36] The citizenship rights of the children who are born in the country are jeopardized by the precarious status of other members of their immediate family.

Denied Equitable Treatment and Care: Denied Child-Protection Measures

Policies and practices for undocumented children who are separated from their families vary greatly across Europe. In some cases, as discussed above, these children are detained by immigration officials; in other cases, they are placed in the care of child welfare authorities. Even when placed in care, these children frequently receive lower levels of care than domestic children in care, a clear example of the prioritization of immigration over childhood status in the state's consideration of its *parens patriae* obligations. This is the current situation in Ireland. Given the low standard of care because the primary needs of the children (to earn, to be mentored, and to be offered training, career alternatives, or a legal status) are ignored, many separated children go missing from state care every year.[37]

Denied Access to Asylum and International Protection

When children are traveling with their families, their individual claims for protection are typically not individually assessed. Consideration of the child's circumstances is simply subsumed within the parent's claim, and if that claim is rejected, the child's claim for protection fails, too, without any independent scrutiny. In such circumstances, children remain dependent and undocumented and are likely to be deported along with their parent.

It is not only accompanied children who encounter difficulties securing access to a system where their protection needs are carefully assessed. Even separated children seeking asylum on their own are sometimes denied this possibility. Their rights to have their views listened to[38] and to seek asylum[39] are ignored. Children may also encounter difficulties securing asylum even once they have been admitted to the asylum process because their stated grounds for seeking protection may not be recognized. States may not recognize that a child is capable of being considered to emergency accommodation such as a homeless shelter. These provisions also completely exclude some children from the protective mantel of the law, a radical situation of rightlessness.

An effective legal and policy framework for protecting rights should also ensure *reliable complaints and monitoring mechanisms*. Ombudsman institutions can play a key role in this regard. In practice, though, while some ombudsmen for children are actively engaged in promoting and defending the rights of undocumented children, others face challenges in doing so. Ireland exemplifies these difficulties. The Ombudsman for Children Act of 2002 includes a provision excluding the Ombudsman for Children from investigating any action by or on behalf of a public body, school, or voluntary hospital "taken in the administration of the law relating to asylum, immigration, naturalisation or citizenship[46] as well as any decision taken in the administration of the prisons or other places for the custody or detention of children."[47]

Complaints and monitoring mechanisms provide a critical tool for correcting problematic administrative practices. But equally important are "clear definitions and guidelines" that prevent abuses in the first place. In practice, however, both these critical tools are frequently underdeveloped, and as a result, domestic immigration law provisions across Europe frequently clash with basic child-protection or child-welfare laws. This means that the best interests of the child routinely fail to be a primary consideration in relevant decision making affecting the child, a central determinant of the persistence of rights abuses against migrant children.

Practical Barriers

Apart from the legal and procedural defects already described, there are also concrete barriers that block undocumented children's access to fundamental rights enshrined in law. Again, these barriers directly reflect the political failures to adequately prioritize the problems of this section of the population rather than any more innocent phenomenon of ignorance or invisibility. By far the most overwhelming problem is the dramatic lack of material resources, an impediment that decades of human-rights legislation has been designed to neutralize. Access to education is often limited by bureaucratic and financial barriers. To ensure access to services and complaints mechanisms, translation of materials and qualified interpreters are needed. Additionally, in many cases, access to free legal aid is urgently required to ensure fair procedures.

Prevailing Stereotypes and Attitudes: Lack of Political Will

Finally, discrimination and prejudice will persist unless attitudes are changed—until influential policy makers challenge rather than perpetuate prevailing stereotypes and attitudes. As long as undocumented migrant children are primarily thought of as juvenile delinquents and antisocial youth rather than neglected or abused children, official hostility and discrimination are likely to persist. Relevant actors such as immigration officials, law enforcement officers, social workers, policy makers, and judges urgently require training. Concerted efforts by senior administrators need to be directed to media coverage of these topics, as well as to briefings of high-level policy makers to correct the current drift into increasing xenophobia and exclusion.

What Needs to Be Done?

One way of improving the current situation of documented children is to increase their own awareness of rights and entitlements by *creative outreach*. Some European cities have achieved good results using cultural mediators for this work. An example is the Leanbh project for children and families who beg, run by the Irish Society for the Prevention of Cruelty to Children (ISPCC) in Dublin.[48] Another example is the work of Save the Children Italy and the Center against Begging in Rome.[49]

In addition to outreach work on the streets and in the community, some anonymous services like Save the Children Sweden's telephone and Internet helpline[50] appear to be successful in reaching and responding to the needs of seldom-heard undocumented children. Following on this example, Save the Children Norway has set up a Web site and hotline for trafficked children.[51] Outreach work can also encourage input directly from undocumented children, which helps to inform and improve priorities and future efforts for change. These efforts can be assessed and disseminated by targeted, participatory research to make them more effective.

Another familiar strategy is to target policy makers and other opinion formers to *shift popular consensus* in favor of greater rights protection for undocumented child migrants. NGOs have used these tactics for some time. In January 2008, a group of lawyers and members of child-rights organizations created an "Opinion Court" to pass judgment on the Belgian state for detaining foreign children in closed detention centers.[52] The court had both an adult jury and a children's jury. Both juries issued public judgments condemning the Belgian state's practice and recommending changes.

In theory, national legislation should always reflect a state's international obligations, and domestic policy should then implement these domestic legal provisions. But as shown above, the reality on the ground does not always produce this result. So *lobbying to produce legislative change* that translates into specific regulations is essential. An ongoing campaign in Ireland addresses this precise issue. It is focused on amending the Constitution to include children's rights and involve actively engaged NGOs in this process by having them contribute to debates in Parliament[53] and publish related advocacy materials targeting both the public and decision makers. Advocacy efforts in Ireland also seek to ensure that the principle of the best interests of the child will be included in the Immigration, Residence and Protection Bill[54] and that the bill includes provisions to protect separated and unaccompanied children.

Perhaps one of the most effective ways to advocate for change is through *the courts*. A recent UK case concerns asylum seekers who have remained in the country after their application was rejected. In 2006, the UK government issued guidelines denying refused asylum seekers access to free medical care, including treatment for long-term conditions such as HIV. But this instruction was reversed by the UK High Court in April 2008.[55] The court held that asylum seekers who have been refused refugee status but remain in the United Kingdom because they have no safe route home should be granted free health care under the National Health Service. This decision may benefit over 11,000 refused asylum seekers who cannot safely return home.

NGOs also have an important role to play in *monitoring* official practices and policies. Some European NGOs contribute information to relevant UN treaty bodies such as the CRC, CEDAW, and CERD, commenting on reports submitted by states party to those conventions. This is an example of good practice because such NGO reports complement and often expand on the evidence submitted officially, giving the UN investigators a more comprehensive sense of the factual situation as it plays out in practice. For example in Ireland, the Children's Rights Alliance presented both a shadow report to the Committee on the Rights of the Child and a children's report entitled *Our Voices, Our Realities,* which included the opinions and concerns of asylum-seeking children.

Additionally, NGOs actively lobby other monitoring mechanisms that publish national assessment reports following country visits such as the Commissioner for Human Rights and the Council of Europe's Committee for the Prevention of Torture and Inhuman or Degrading Treatment or Punishment. Such processes provide NGOs with an opportunity to engage in constructive dialog with governments and provide a record and recommendations that can be used for future advocacy and practical work. The European Committee of Social Rights recently accepted a complaint from Defense for Children International against the Netherlands alleging that Dutch legislation deprives children residing illegally in the Netherlands of key economic and social rights, reducing them to a situation of *de facto* statelessness by excluding them from fundamental state protections.[56]

To impinge effectively on situations of this kind, existing guidelines about the treatment of migrant children need to be improved, with more attention given to the identification of child-specific persecution and more detailed guidance on the complex process of arriving at a formal best-interests determination that takes the multiple competing factors into account. To quote UNHCR:

The best interests of the child will rarely be determined by a single, overriding factor. In most cases, the result of the formal Best Interests Determination will take into account the entire range of the child's rights. Decision-makers need to determine which of the available options better secures the attainment of the child's rights.[57]

To arrive at a convincing decision, a variety of factors need to be considered, including the views of the child and family members, the family environment or possible alternative care and developmental needs of the child, and considerations of safety. In addition, resources need to be allocated to provide ongoing training to relevant authorities.

Conclusion

The challenges and good practices noted above provide a partial account of some of the supports and barriers encountered by undocumented children across Europe. Building on the rights-respecting elements already included in this framework could allow interested stakeholders to better assess what their potential role could be in realizing the rights of undocumented children here and now.

Notes

1. Migrant Rights Centre Ireland, *Living in the Shadows: An Exploration of Irregular Migration in Ireland* (Dublin: Migrant Rights Centre Ireland, December 2007). Irish Refugee Council (IRC) staff has also had contact with individuals in these categories—particularly the last three categories listed above.

2. United Nations High Commissioner for Human Rights (OHCHR), "General Recommendation No. 30: Discrimination against Non-citizens," October 1, 2004, Gen. Rec. no. 30, <http://www.unhchr.ch> (accessed June 15, 2009).

3. Convention on the Rights of the Child (CRC), art. 3.

4. Ibid., art. 2.

5. Separated Children in Europe Program (SCEP), "Statement of Good Practice," 3rd ed., 2004.

6. Treaty of Lisbon Amending the Treaty on the European Union and the Treaty Establishing the European Community, signed December 13, 2007, C 306, Official Journal of the European Union, <http://eur-lex.europa.eu> (accessed June 15, 2009).

7. The ECHR is the main European human-rights treaty of the Council of Europe (COE). The COE was founded in 1949, well before the foundation of the European Union. It currently counts forty-seven member states, compared to the EU's twenty-seven. The COE has a leading role in setting regional human-rights standards. On the one hand, the jurisprudence of the European Court of Human Rights (ECtHR), which enforces the ECHR, continuously advances the human-rights agenda in Europe. On the other hand, all states aspiring to join the EU must adhere to the ECHR.

8. Ibid., art 2(5).

9. Council of Europe, Convention on Action against Trafficking in Human Beings, adopted on May 16, 2005, art. 16(7), <http://conventions.coe.int> (accessed June 15, 2009).

10. See the Council of Europe Web site regarding key legal texts relating to children, <http://www.coe.int/t/transversalprojects/children/keyLegalTexts/Default_en.asp> (accessed June 15, 2009).

11. For more information, see <http://www.ombudsnet.org> (accessed April 1, 2009).

12. As noted in Save the Children Sweden's report on *Undocumented Children in Sweden* (Stockholm: Save the Children Sweden, March 2006–March 2007).

13. U.S. Department of State, "Country Report on Human Rights Practices in Greece," 2007, <http://www.state.gov> (accessed June 15, 2009).

14. "Overhauling Greek Citizenship Law," *Athens News,* February 29, 2008, <http://www.athensnews.gr> (accessed June 15, 2009).

15. See also 2006 Report of the Greek Ombudsman as National Equality Body, "Promoting Equal Treatment," <http://www.synigoros.gr> (accessed June 15, 2009).

16. In the introductory chapter, Jacqueline Bhabha defines *de jure* stateless persons according to the definition comprised in article 1 of the 1954 Convention Relating to the Status of Stateless Persons, which stipulates that a "stateless person means a person who is not considered as a national by any state under the operation of its law." By contrast, *de facto* stateless persons are stateless because of their irregular legal status in the current location.

17. Sven Goll, "Born in Norway, But Not a Citizen," *Afternposten*, August 7, 2008, <http://www.aftenposten.no> (accessed June 15, 2009).

18. UN General Assembly, Convention Relating to the Status of Stateless Persons, September 28, 1954, United Nations, *Treaty Series*, vol. 360, p. 117, <http://www.unhcr.org> (accessed June 15, 2009); Council of Europe, Convention on the Avoidance of Statelessness in Relation to State Succession, signed May 19, 2006, <http://conventions.coe.int/Treaty/EN/Treaties/Html/200.htm> (accessed June 15, 2009); and European Convention on Nationality, signed November 16, 1997, <http://conventions.coe.int/Treaty/en/Treaties/Html/166.htm> (accessed June 15, 2009).

19. Save the Children Sweden, "Undocumented Children: All I Want Is to Land," Stockholm, 2008. The report was issued by the Utanpapper.nu project, a helpline for undocumented children.

20. European Network of Ombudspeople for Children's Statement on State Obligations for the Treatment of Unaccompanied Children, approved in the Annual Meeting in Athens on September 26–28, 2006.

21. UN Committee on the Rights of the Child (CRC), "CRC General Comment No. 6 (2005): Treatment of Unaccompanied and Separated Children Outside Their Country of Origin," September 1, 2005, CRC/GC/2005/6, <http://www.unhcr.org> (accessed June 15, 2009).

22. See also the Detention in Europe Web site administered by the Jesuit Refugee Service (JRS), <http://www.detention-in-europe.org> (accessed June 15, 2009).

23. See the nonpunishment provision in Council of Europe, Convention on Action against Trafficking in Human Beings, art. 26.

24. Trafficked children are sometimes compelled to engage in criminal activities (such as stealing) and are then prosecuted and punished. A proposal for a revision of the EU Framework Decision addresses nonpunishment and suggests strengthening protections for trafficked children in these situations. Some states, such as the United Kingdom, have already issued guidelines to prosecutors instructing them on appropriate responses to children in these circumstances.

25. See chapters by Luca Bicocchi, Elena Rozzi, and Daniel Senovilla Hernández in this book.

26. See chapters by Elena Rozzi and Luca Bicocchi in this book.

27. See art. 41 of the Irish Constitution, <http://www.taoiseach.gov.ie> (accessed June 15, 2009).

28. "Supplementary additional information by the Government of Ireland concerning the List of Issues (CCPR/C/IRL/Q/3) taken up in connection with the consideration of the Third Periodic Report of Ireland under the International Covenant on Civil and Political Rights (CCPR/C/IRL/3)," 9, <http://www.eu2004.ie> (accessed June 15, 2009).

29. See also Jacqueline Bhabha's illustration of constructive deportation in "Arendt's Children: Do Today's Migrant Children Have a Right to Have Rights?," *Human Rights Quarterly* 31 (2009): 446.

30. See the chapter by David B. Thronson in this book.

31. The recent ECtHR ruling *Wallova and Walla v. The Czech Republic*, no. 23848/04, October 26, 2006, is interesting in this regard. The court ruled that it was a violation of the right to family life (art. 8) when the state removed the children to state institutions. In the court's opinion, the authorities should have addressed the problem of lack of means by adopting less onerous measures than the total separation of the family.

32. Save the Children Sweden, *Undocumented Children in Sweden,* 11–12.

33. See Save the Children/SCEP Position Paper, *Returns and Separated Children,* 2004, on the Dublin II Regulation and the best interests of the child.

34. A child born in the Irish Republic before January 1, 2005, was automatically an Irish citizen (*jus soli*). Following a referendum and constitutional change in 2004, this is no longer the case.

35. "Ireland's Invisible Children," *Metro Eireann,* April 17–23, 2008.

36. See the chapter by David B. Thronson in this book.

37. For more details, see Nalinie Mooten, *Making Separated Children Visible: The Need for a Child-Centred Approach* (Dublin: IRC, 2006). See also the chapter by Elena Rozzi in this book criticizing the inappropriate infantilization of undocumented separated children in care in Italy and the chapter by Daniel Senovilla Hernández highlighting the abusive techniques used within care institutions by the Spanish authorities.

38. CRC, art. 12.

39. CRC, art. 22.

40. See Jacqueline Bhabha, "Minors or Aliens? Inconsistent State Intervention and Separated Child Asylum Seekers," *European Journal of Migration and Law* 3 (2001): 283–314.

41. The preamble of the EU Qualification Directive states that "it is necessary, when assessing applications from minors for international protection, that Member States should have regard to child-specific forms of persecution" (see sec. 20). Article 9(2) clarifies that acts of persecution can take the form of acts of a gender-specific or child-specific nature. European Union: Council of the European Union, "Council Directive 2004/83/EC of 29 April 2004 on Minimum Standards for the Qualification and Status of Third Country Nationals or State-less Persons as Refugees or as Persons Who Otherwise Need International Protection and the Content of the Protection Granted," May 19, 2004, 2004/83/EC, <http://www.unhcr.org> (accessed June 15, 2009).

42. Kate Halvorsen, "Asylum Decisions on Child Applicants: Report on Four-Country Pilot Project," 2004, <http://www.regjeringen.no> (accessed June 15, 2009). See also Jacqueline Bhabha and Nadine Finch, "Seeking Asylum Alone: Unaccompanied and Separated Children and Refugee Protection in the U.K.," November 2006, <http://www.ilpa.org> (accessed June 15, 2009).

43. See Platform for International Cooperation on Undocumented Migrants (PICUM), *Book of Solidarity*, vols. 1–3 (Brussels: PICUM, 2002–2003).

44. For more information, see the Irish Social and Family Affairs Web site, <http://www.welfare.ie/EN/Publications/SW108/Pages/1WhatistheHabitualResi dencecondition.aspx> (accessed June 15, 2009).

45. Section 246 of the Social Welfare Consolidation Act 2005 provides that "it shall be presumed, until the contrary is shown, that a person is not habitually resident in the State at the date of the making of the application concerned unless he has been present in the State or any other part of the Common Travel Area for a continuous period of 2 years ending on that date."

46. Irish Ombudsman for Children's Act, no. 22, 2002, art. 11(e)(I), <http:// www.irishstatutebook.ie> (accessed June 15, 2009).

47. Ibid., art. 11(e)(iii).

48. See the Irish Society for the Prevention of Cruelty to Children (ISPCC) Web site, <http://www.ispcc.ie/Under-18/Service-Information/Leanbh.aspx> (accessed June 15, 2009).

49. In her chapter in this volume, Elena Rozzi describes other creative intervention strategies adopted in Italy.

50. See Utanpapper.nu Web site, <http://www.utanpapper.nu/en/startpage> (accessed June 15, 2009).

51. See Save the Children Norway's Web site for trafficked children, <http:// www.hvisk.no/English> (accessed June 15, 2009).

52. See Défense des Enfants International Web site, <http://www.dei-belgique. be/actions_dei_belgique.php> and Child Rights Information Network Web site, <http://www.crin.org/resources/infodetail.asp?id=16114> (both accessed June 15, 2009).

53. Irish Parliamentary Debates, <http://debates.oireachtas.ie/CommitteeMenu .aspx?Dail=30&Cid=CC> (accessed June 15, 2009).

54. Immigration, Residence and Protection Bill, 2008, <http://www.oireachtas .ie> (accessed June 15, 2009).

55. See more details on the Irish Refugee Council Web site, <http://www .refugeecouncil.org.U.K./news/press/2008/April/20080411.htm> (accessed June 15, 2009).

56. This includes the ESC's provisions in respect to the right to health (art. 11), the right to social and medical assistance (art. 13), the right to appropriate social, legal, and economic protection for the family (art. 16), and the right of children and young persons to appropriate social, legal, and economic protection (art. 17). They are to be read alone or in conjunction with Council of Europe, European Social Charter, May 3, 1996 (revised), art. E (nondiscrimination), <http:// conventions.coe.int/Treaty/en/Treaties/Html/163.htm> (accessed June 15, 2009).

57. UN High Commissioner for Refugees, "Best Interests Determination Children: Protection and Care Information Sheet," June 2008, 2, <http://www.unhcr .org> (accessed June 15, 2009).

7

Unaccompanied and Separated Children in Spain: A Policy of Institutional Mistreatment

Daniel Senovilla Hernández

Spain is one of the main destinations in Europe for migrating children,[1] most of whom are African. The challenges arising from their migration are numerous and reflect a range of complex factors, including migrant children's sociodemographic profiles and immigration status, unsatisfactory state policies relating to the reception of these children, and deficiencies in the public guardianship system. This chapter examines how Spanish authorities interpret international and national laws that are meant to protect children and avoid taking responsibility for migrant children who arrive on their shores.

For over a decade, national and regional authorities in Spain have chosen to return migrant children to their home country over other options, even if this return has not been to the child's family or even to foster care but to placement in a local care institution. Return to the country of origin is viewed as the best durable solution to the situation of unaccompanied and separated children and has been used to justify deterrent policies and practices that are targeted at potential new migrants to Spain.

Numerous entities have criticized this forced repatriation policy, including international human-rights bodies—such as the United Nations (UN) Committee on the Rights of the Child, the United Nations Children's Fund (UNICEF), the UN High Commissioner for Human Rights (UNHCHR), and the Special Rapporteur on the Human Rights of Migrants)—and national courts whose judgments increasingly overturn administrative decisions mandating forced return. In response, the concerned authorities have tried to find new strategies. Using different subterfuges, Andalusia, Catalonia, the Canary Islands, and the Madrid regional care authorities have avoided providing an adequate standard of care to many migrant children. The result of this new practice of institutional mistreatment is similar to the forced-return policy: children are often driven to leave the care facilities, thus becoming even more vulnerable and uprooted.

The Context and the Data

Several factors make Spain one of the main points of entry to the European Union (EU) and the destination for millions of migrants coming from Africa in search of a better future. Due to its geographical situation and significant economic development after integration in the European Union in 1986, Spain has moved from being the source country for large-scale worker emigration to northern Europe during the 1960s and the 1970s to being the second most popular global destination for international migrants after the United States.[2] Apart from geography and EU integration, the vast opportunities for undeclared work have also had a magnetic effect on migratory flows and account for their dramatic increase,[3] although the current sharp economic downturn is likely to reduce the number of future arrivals.

The migration of unaccompanied and separated children to Europe shares a number of common characteristics with the migration of adults (including routes, push factors, objectives) while preserving its own specificity at the same time. In Spain, the first cases of children migrating alone emerged in the mid-1990s (slightly later than in other European countries, like France, Italy, Belgium, and the United Kingdom), but the flow increased significantly by the end of the millennium and during the early years of the first decade. In contrast with the migratory flow of adults, the migration of unaccompanied minors is still a quantitatively modest phenomenon in Spain, although it is of great social and political importance.

Official statistics for Spain refer to the number of unaccompanied and separated children entering the care system over a given period. As figure 7.1 shows, residential child-care facilities have received an average of 4,000 to 6,000 new cases of unaccompanied and separated children annually since 2001 with a peak of more than 9,000 new cases in 2004. However, this flow decreased decidedly in 2008, probably as a result of both the harsh consequences of the economic downturn in Spain (the unemployment rate is close to 20 percent at the time of this writing)[4] and also the increasing effectiveness of the EU's repressive border-control measures, particularly the interception of boats with clandestine migrants close to African shores.

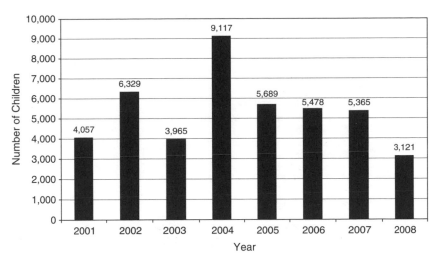

Figure 7.1
Unaccompanied and separated children in care in Spain, 2001 to 2008. *Source:* Data for 2001 to 2003 from Misión permanente de España ante la Oficina de Naciones Unidas en Ginebra;[a] data for 2004 to 2007 from *Boletín Oficial de las Cortes Generales*, July 2, 2008, ser. D, no. 45, p. 130;[b] data for 2008 from *Boletín Oficial de las Cortes Generales*, October 6, 2009, ser. D, no. 266, p. 27.
Notes:
a. United Nations Human Rights Commission, "Nota verbal de fecha 29 de enero de 2004 dirigida a la Oficina del Alto Comisionado de las Naciones Unidas para los Derechos Humanos por la Misión permanente de España ante la Oficina de las Naciones Unidas en Ginebra," 60th period of sessions, E/CN.4/2004/G/17, 2004.
b. The 2003 figures correspond to the number of children entering the care system until September 30. The rest (2001–2002 and 2004–2007) represent the annual number of unaccompanied children looked after.

The regions that were most exposed to the arrival of migrant children in 2004 and 2005 were Andalusia, Valencia, Catalonia, and Madrid, but by mid-2006 and 2007, the presence of unaccompanied children seemed to be more evenly distributed throughout the country. Only Andalusia still received a significantly higher number of migrant children than other regions, probably for geographical reasons. According to the data in figure 7.2, the Canary Islands, as of June 2006, were no longer one of the main reception regions for migrant children.

Nevertheless, throughout 2006, the Canary Islands became a key point of entry for an increasing number of unaccompanied and separated children coming mainly from West African countries. Of the 1,622 migrant children who arrived by boat during that year, 931 arrivals were

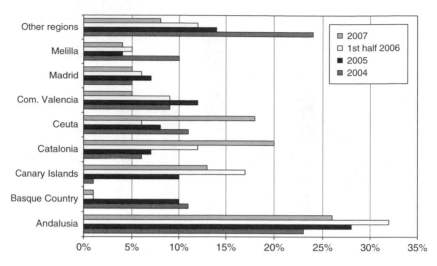

Figure 7.2
Unaccompanied and separated children in care in Spain, regional distribution, 2004 to 2007. *Source:* Data for 2004 to 2006 from *Boletin Oficial de las Cortes Generales*, March 21, 2007; data for 2007 from *Boletin Oficial de las Cortes Generales*, September 29, 2009.

reported in the Canary Islands, most coming from Senegal and, to a lesser extent, Mali.[5] This discrepancy with the previous figures can be explained by the fact that a significant number of children arriving in this region are eventually transferred to other Spanish regions and are therefore not included in the figures reported by the protection services of the Canary Islands.[6]

However, between 2000 and 2005, before the arrivals of sub-Saharan children to the Canary Islands started to increase, Morocco was the country of origin for a vast majority of migrant children under the care of Spain's protection services. Moroccan children represented 49 percent of the new receptions in 2004 and 79 percent in the first semester of 2005. In the preceding years, they constituted between 90 and 95 percent of the unaccompanied and separated children who were taken into care.[7]

Official data for 2004 show that a significant majority of migrant children are males (90 percent), even though the presence of girls is probably a cause for greater concern. Most girl migrants do not come to the attention of the authorities because they are victims of exploitative networks, mainly for prostitution.[8] There are no available figures regarding the average age of unaccompanied children, but it is reasonable to assume that most of them are teenagers age fifteen to seventeen.[9]

The Home Background of Unaccompanied and Separated African Children in Spain

Little research has been conducted on the home circumstances of independent migrant children, the social and economic conditions of their households and communities, and the motivations and reasons pushing them toward the migratory adventure. The few studies that are available on Spain as a destination point have focused on the geographical area of northern Morocco, particularly the municipality of Tangiers and its environs.[10]

These studies show that a significant majority of Moroccan migrant children come from households passing through serious financial difficulties. It is less clear whether the children come from stable or broken families. The studies also indicate, albeit to a lesser extent, a flow of former street children from the Tangiers area. Finally, the data suggest that migrant children from rural inland areas for the most part migrate with financial support from their families but that a minority lack this backing and travel to the port zone in Tangiers with the intent of crossing the border, typically ending up as "street children" there.[11]

No in-depth research has been conducted on the causes of the new migration of children originating from West African countries and crossing the sea to the Canary Islands. However, an unpublished survey looked at a sample of 475 children who were transferred from the Islands to continental Spain between 2006 and 2007.[12] The data from this study confirm that the majority of children coming to Spain via this route are Senegalese (66 percent), followed by Malians (19 percent) and Gambians (7.5 percent). Most of these children are close to adulthood (75 percent are sixteen or seventeen years old), and 60 percent come from rural areas. These children traveled to the Canary Islands by *cayuco* (colored boats used by fishermen in this African region). Their trips were financed by a variety of means: 25 percent did not pay for the crossing (these children were either already employed by the smugglers or were embroiled in other types of arrangements during the voyage), and of those who paid, 64 percent obtained financial support from their parents or siblings; and 11 percent financed themselves. The average cost of the journey varied between 500 to 1000 (about U.S. $750 to $1,500). Before starting the migration process, the vast majority of these children lived with their parents (70 percent with the father and 83 percent with the mother). A common attribute are large families of origin: more than half the children came from family units with more than ten members, and a significant number (eighty-four) said they had been living with more than twenty siblings. The household incomes were usually low, with 80 percent of the families surviving on less than 200 per month (about U.S. $300). The children agreed that low incomes and large families were key push factors motivating their migration. Additionally, education levels were low: more than 70 percent of the children in the sample had literacy problems (they were either illiterate or severely limited in their reading and writing ability). Finally, 79 percent had been employed in their homeland (although they received a very small income or nothing at all for their labor), but all children agreed that their main objective in migrating was to find a job and earn money to support their family.

Once in Spain: Reception Policies, Access to Care, and Public Guardianship

Unlike other European countries (France, Germany, or Italy), Spanish regulations do not allow unaccompanied children identified at a point of entry to be detained. Some children have been placed in detention centers, however, because they were initially identified as adults.[13] The relevant Spanish regulations concerning unaccompanied and separated migrant children, particularly section 35(1) of the Aliens Act Decree, authorize access to the territory for children who present themselves at a port of entry.[14]

However, all identified would-be migrant children first go through an age-determination process. A public prosecutor's Central Office Instruction makes it clear that the period during which a migrant is held for purposes of age determination must legally be considered a deprivation of liberty.[15] However, neither the prosecutor's instruction nor the law indicates a time limit within which the age test must be conducted, and in practice, children can remain in detention for several days with no support from a legal counselor.[16]

If the age-determination test confirms that the person is a minor, he or she is admitted to a reception facility, and the competent regional protection services are required to issue a declaration of "defenselessness" as defined by the Spanish Civil Code.[17] This declaration counts as a final official decision and initiates an obligation to establish public guardianship.[18] The advantage of this system is its speed: the guardianship has to be allocated almost immediately. The problem is that the public entity exerting guardianship does not always act in the child's interest.

The Policy of Forced Repatriations

The regulations on the status of unaccompanied migrant children clearly state that forced repatriation is the first and preferred solution for dealing with those who are on Spanish territory.[19] Remaining in Spain is considered as a secondary solution only when repatriation is not possible.

Although the regulations defining the competent body to initiate the repatriation process (and the ensuing search for the child's family and assessment of the family's social and economic situation)[20] are not clear, the final decision on repatriation clearly rests with the national immigration authorities. The regional protection services can express their views on the repatriation decision, and the children's prosecutor is to be informed throughout the process. The concerned child may also be heard, but this is not always done in an appropriate way.[21]

After the family has been located or the child-protection services in the country of origin have agreed to his or her return, the unaccompanied child is repatriated and placed under the custody of the border authorities of the country of repatriation. Repatriation is not meant to occur when a threat to the child's safety or to his or her family has been identified.[22]

The above paragraphs summarize the existing legal framework. The reality, however, is different. Over the years, numerous international organizations and children's advocates have criticized the Spanish authorities' practice of repatriating unaccompanied children with no respect for relevant national or international children's rights. In 2002, the United Nations Convention on the Rights of the Child (CRC) expressed "its concern at reports of . . . summary expulsions of children without ensuring that they are effectively returned to family or social welfare agencies in their country of origin."[23] The same year, Human Rights Watch extensively denounced the unlawful expulsions of unaccompanied children by Spanish authorities to Morocco. Citing a local nongovernmental organization (NGO), this international advocacy organization reported that between the end of July and mid-September 2001 there were at least thirty-two expulsions by delegated government authorities in Melilla (a Spanish territory situated in the north of Morocco[24]) of unaccompanied children. In 2004, the Special Rapporteur of the UNHCHR said the following:

The Special Rapporteur believes that because of the way in which some family "reunifications" have been carried out, allegedly leaving the minor in the hands of the Moroccan police without the presence of his family or the social services, these reunifications are interpreted as expulsions. Nevertheless, many "reunited" minors return to Spain and some speak of ill-treatment by the Moroccan police.[25]

At the national level, the Spanish ombudsman and the national public prosecutor have underlined that the blind implementation of a forced-return policy without any further considerations of the specific circumstances of the unaccompanied child is inconsistent with the principle of the best interests of the child.[26] Moreover, the ombudsman for the rights of children in the Madrid region has reported that many children who were returned had already achieved a high degree of integration and success in the Spanish educational or vocational training system.[27]

Despite these recent criticisms, Spain has made a strenuous effort over the past few years to establish bilateral agreements with the main countries of origin to facilitate repatriations. After the signature of the first memorandum of understanding with Morocco in March 2003, Spain signed bilateral agreements with Romania[28] and Senegal.[29] More recently, the memorandum with Morocco has been replaced with a bilateral agreement signed in March 2007.[30] These international legal instruments are relatively similar (particularly those concerning Morocco and Senegal), and all three dedicate a section to the return process. If there is a decision on return, authorities from both countries are required to ensure that there are satisfactory conditions for family reunification or reception of the affected child at an adequate care institution. However, none of the bilateral agreements provide further details or criteria for defining what conditions for family reunification or care institutions in the country of origin are to be considered satisfactory or adequate.

The 2007 Moroccan-Spanish agreement—the only one that is not yet in force—has, despite this, provided a legal basis for an initiative for the building and shared running of centers in Morocco dedicated to children returned from Spain. A 2005 announcement declared that eight centers were planned, but no information on the current state of this project is available.[31]

Completion of the plan to build reception centers in Morocco would follow logically from numerous Spanish court judgments ruling against administrative repatriation resolutions. Between September 2006 and February 2008, different regional courts have quashed either the decision or the way that the repatriation was carried out.[32] As Amnesty International highlights, Spanish magistrates reveal in these judgments the serious inadequacy of standard repatriation practices used by authorities. Some children are returned without even an attempt by the authorities to locate their family. Others do not receive a hearing or are never informed of the repatriation process.[33] Moreover, two recent decisions from the Spanish Constitutional Court have established the legal capacity of unaccompanied and separated children with an adequate degree of maturity to appeal a repatriation decision made without their consent.[34] When a child has not reached a sufficient degree of maturity, a representative (*defensor judicial*) must be appointed to defend the child's rights. Finally, the Constitutional Court recognizes the legal standing of advocacy organizations to represent a child and to appeal against an administrative resolution or measure that they consider a violation of the unaccompanied or separated child's fundamental rights. These recommendations from the Constitutional Court ensuring access to justice for children in claiming that their legal guardians face a conflict of interest are included in the new bill amending the 2000 Aliens Act currently under negotiation in the Spanish parliament.[35]

The policy of forced repatriations of unaccompanied and separated children is a real issue in Spain, but the number of implemented repatriations is extremely low (see figures 7.3 and 7.4).[36] Despite these low numbers and the shortcomings of the policy, the authorities still insist that repatriation is the best durable solution for unaccompanied and separated children in Spain. In practice, the authorities seem to use repatriation more as a permanent threat than as a real solution or response to children's situations. This practice is probably driven by the objective of reducing the flow of children's arrivals by disseminating the idea among those already in Spain that they will eventually be sent back home. The consequence of these practices is that a significant number of children abandon care facilities to become missing and legally invisible.

The Slim Chances of Getting Legal Immigration Status and Remaining in Spain

Section 35(4) of the Aliens Act of 2000 establishes that the residence of any foreign child under the guardianship of a public entity shall be considered legal. Regardless of his or her legal status, an unaccompanied child is eligible for a residence permit only after there is proof that return to the country of origin is impossible. Furthermore, a nine-month delay after the child enters into care is required before a residence permit can be issued.[37] However, in 2004, a legal amendment established the possibility of repatriating children even if they had already received legal documentation.[38]

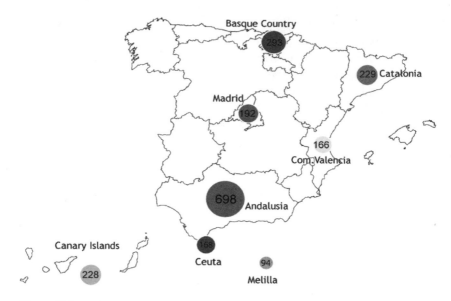

Figure 7.3
Unaccompanied and separated children in care in Spain, regional distribution, first half of 2006. *Source: Boletín Oficial de las Cortes Generales*, March 21, 2007, 23–25.

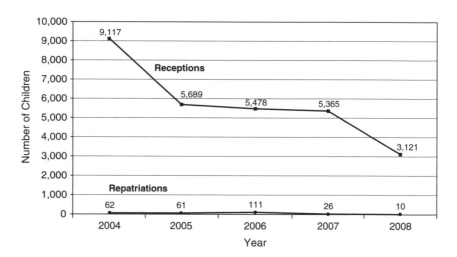

Figure 7.4
Unaccompanied and separated children in Spain, proportion between care and repatriation, 2004 to 2008. *Source:* Fiscalía General del Estado, *Informe* (2009), 737.

Regarding access to the labor market, immigration regulations provide a range of options that make regular employment possible for migrant children in care. Those age sixteen years or older and under the guardianship of regional protection institutions are exempted from the general obligation to obtain a work permit.[39] After they get a residence permit, they have preferential access to a work permit without the national labor-market situation being taken into consideration.[40]

Finally, when they turn eighteen, guardianship is canceled, and unaccompanied children must leave the care system. Although there are some local and regional programs that provide services to make the transition to adulthood easier, there is no general system of support to assist these young adults when they leave the protection system. Their chances of remaining in Spain depend on the status they had while under state protection. There are three different situations: (1) children who are documented with a residence permit that does not allow work and expires when they become of age (the renewal of this document is subject to its conversion into a work and residence permit, a potential problem since preferential access to employment runs out once the child turns age eighteen);[41] (2) children who are documented with a work and residence permit that a child is required to renew under general conditions set up for adults;[42] and (3) children who turn eighteen while undocumented and need to be supported by the institution providing guardianship to apply for a residence permit on humanitarian grounds (authorization of this document is subject to the discretionary evaluation of criteria regarding the child's participation and cooperation in the educational or training processes).[43] So the process of conversion from *de facto* stateless to regularized immigrant depends heavily on the exercise of official discretion.

Spanish regulations offer regularization options to unaccompanied children to facilitate residence and access to the labor market. In practice, however, there is a substantial gap between this theoretical option of regularization and the reality on the ground. Many regional protection services set up barriers that prevent unaccompanied children in their care from obtaining the documentation they need to regularize their status and obtain a residence permit. Typically, the responsible agency does not start the documentation procedure until a repatriation process has been frustrated. Even if they do not wait for this, many of the protection agencies delay embarking on the documentation process for several months after the requisite nine-month waiting period established by law. As a result, the majority of unaccompanied children have to wait to obtain a residence permit for periods of up to two years, and many are never documented.[44] Access to formal work for those over age sixteen is virtually impossible in practice, and hardly any minors are able to make use of the existing options provided by the law. Finally, after children turn eighteen, the harsh implementation of the rules translates into minimal opportunities for obtaining documentation or integrating into Spain, effectively condemning this already vulnerable population to a clandestine life. The conversion of *de facto* statelessness into a regular immigration status thus rarely takes place in practice.

Institutional Mistreatment: What Are the Consequences of the Laws and Policies in Practice?

Certain authors[45] have described the aforementioned policies and practices as a form of institutional mistreatment. Both the national authorities and several of the regional protection services exert a range of different forms of institutional pressure on the unaccompanied migrant children they are supposed to look after.

The manner in which many of the repatriations are executed is a good example of mistreatment. Sometimes police forces come to a reception center in the middle of the night, pull a child out of bed, and drive the child directly to the airport without allowing the child to take his or her personal belongings. Other children living in the center witness these practices, and the threat of being the next victim causes extreme stress and mistrust. At other times, police have come to schools or vocational training centers, taken children from their lessons, and treated them as delinquents in front of their colleagues.[46] The long waiting time to obtain a residence permit and the confiscation of the children's passports for the duration of the guardianship period are other common forms of mistreatment that are used by the child's care providers.

Children soon realize that there is no long-term benefit to be gained from their efforts to integrate, learn the Spanish language, acquire an education, or follow professional training. They message that they hear is that they are not welcome and that there is no future if they remain under the care of the regional protection services.

Seventeen-year-old Hussein arrived from West Africa and was received in a reception center in the Basque country. He describes how he spent the whole day wandering around the town and claims that he had no money and nothing to eat:

I go for lunch at a food pantry. Yesterday, they gave me some bread, a can of sardines, some milk, and a dessert. When it rains, I go under a bridge to eat what they give me.

The experience of Hussein is not isolated.[47] There are similar cases in the regions of Madrid, Catalonia, Andalusia, Canary Islands, Valencia, and Asturias. The national paper *El Mundo* published the story of Hicham. It provides a good example of the sort of institutional mistreatment meted out to well-integrated unaccompanied migrant children:

Hicham arrived in Spain when he was fourteen and was cared for by the protection services of Cantabria, northern Spain. He was luckier than others; he obtained a residence permit quite soon and qualified as a plumber. He also practiced sports and became Spanish vice champion of rowing in his category. He had just one dream left: to work as a plumber and earn his living. One September night, the immigration authorities sent two police officers to look for Hicham to take him back to Morocco and shatter his dream. Hicham got nervous, grabbed a knife, and climbed up to the roof of the reception center. He threatened to jump and also tried to injure himself. Fortunately, after a few hours of negotiation, he came down. The following day, he was back in Tangier.[48]

We agree with Pérez who argues that the main consequence of this institutional mistreatment is an increase in the number of children who live on the street.[49] The 2004–2005 official figures confirm that a significant number of children abandon care facilities.[50] Targeted institutional policies, therefore, result not so much in the invisibility of this population of children but rather in a guarantee of their long-term rightlessness.

What is the long-term fate of these unprotected children? Even though little information is available, [51] we can distinguish four common paths that are taken by those who abandon the protection system. They either (1) continue their voyage and move to another Spanish region or to another country,[52] (2) reunite with siblings or other members of their community, (3) come under the control of criminal networks of exploitation (unlike other European countries, this area remains completely unexplored in Spain), or (4) start a new independent life (alone or with a group of peers) by committing illegal activities (prostitution, begging, hawking) or crimes (mainly pickpocketing or drug dealing).[53]

Further Strategies of Institutional Mistreatment: Perspectives of a Close Future

Although the threat of forced repatriation to the country of origin continues to be used by national and regional Spanish authorities to control and reduce the flow of children migrating alone to Spain, this practice contradicts the position adopted by the Committee on the Rights of the Child—that return to the country of origin should take place only if it is in the best interests of the child. According to the Committee, the process of conducting the best-interest assessment should take into account several elements, including the safety, security, and the socio-economic conditions awaiting the child on return; the availability of care arrangements; the views of the child and those of the caretakers in the country of destination; and the child's level of integration in the host country and the duration of the absence from the home country.[54] There are cases where the return can turn out to be the best durable solution to respond to the situation of an unaccompanied minor. However, a coactive repatriation that does not involve family reunification or does not take into account the views of the child and those of the family seems unlikely to be in the best interests of the child. When implementing a policy of forced returns, Spanish authorities prioritize the right of the child to family life (or even an unexamined right to simply live in the country of origin where family reunification has not been established as a possibility). The authorities thus routinely forget to assess fundamental questions such as the right of the child to development and the conditions for accessing social rights to education or health care as well as the child's chance of reaching an adequate standard of living in the country of origin.[55]

Since 2006, numerous court decisions annulling repatriation orders against unaccompanied migrant children seem to have led the relevant authorities to search for new strategies of exclusion—new ways of perpetuating the children's *de facto* statelessness. To control the numbers of these children who enter their care systems, the regions most affected by child migrants have developed a range of exclusionary plans and tactics that take no account of national and international child-protection obligations.

A case in point is Andalusia, where traditionally no forced repatriations of children have been carried out. Officers at the Andalusia child-protection institution have repeatedly stated that most of the unaccompanied Moroccan children arriving in their region have stable family links and consequently no need for protection. According to the director of the childhood and family department in this region, the vast majority of unaccompanied minors now arriving in Andalusia are not children in need of protection under the terms of section 172 of the Spanish Civil Code. By their own account, these children receive adequate affection and material care from their parents and family members, in keeping with the socioeconomic conditions in their places of origin. In general, they are not children who have been abandoned, ill-treated, or neglected. Their families are not well-off and have little hope of seeing their situations improve. So although when they arrive in Spain they are no longer protected by their families, one might say these minors were the victims of "self-inflicted need."[56] Under the guise of designing a plan for forced family reunification in the child's country of origin, [57] Andalusia in practice implements a policy that facilitates the exclusion of migrant children from its protection system. The legal subterfuge used to achieve this goal is to thwart the establishment of public guardianship for the children by postponing the administrative order declaring the child defenseless, without which the guardianship cannot be established. Internal instructions to this effect have already been sent to different local administrative agencies. The Spanish ombudsman has denounced this practice as violating Spanish national regulations regarding the protection of children who are in a situation of abandonment.[58]

In Catalonia, regional authorities have created a specialized protection system that excludes most unaccompanied migrant minors from the mainstream facilities and centers for national children in need. The widespread institutional mistreatment in this region consists of a range of tactics for applying continuous pressure on the children. This includes threats of repatriation, placement in remote reception centers far from urban centers, and denial of educational or training opportunities.[59] As a result of these oppressive practices, many children "migrate" to other Spanish regions, initially the Basque country and, more recently, Asturias.[60] This region has also created an *ad hoc* program called "Catalonia-Maghreb" aimed at facilitating the voluntary return of Moroccan children to a new reception center in the Tangiers region.[61] Not surprisingly, the program was a failure: between 2006 and 2008, despite official predictions that about 200 children would opt into the program, in fact only seven children agreed to return to Morocco.[62]

In the Canary Islands region, authorities complain about the lack of resources for their protection system to avoid the responsibilities that they face as a result of the significant number of children migrating on their own from West Africa.[63] Most of the children legally represented by the Child Protection Institution of this region are eventually transferred to the Spanish mainland. Some of them are taken into custody by other regional protection services, and others are placed in *ad hoc* reception facilities that normally are managed by specialized NGOs. However, when these transfers are carried out, it is not clear whether the Canary Islands' institution remains the legal guardian of children who are thousands of miles from its territory or whether the authorities to whom the children are transferred assume their guardianship. These transfers were done in the framework of an *ad hoc* program called Programa Especial para traslado y atención de MENA desde Canarias.[64] Between October 5, 2006, and October 25, 2007, 497 children were transferred to thirteen different regions and the African enclave of Ceuta. Only the regions of Madrid and La Rioja did not accept any minors. The program cost 12 million, paid out of central government funds.[65]

Finally, in the Madrid region, forced repatriations were a common practice until the second half of 2007 (54 percent of the total national number in 2006). This figure demonstrates the critical decision-making role played by the regional child-protection services in initiating repatriations, despite the ultimate authority of the central authorities. Confirmation of this conclusion is provided by the fact that advocacy organizations working with this target group reveal that hardly a single unaccompanied child has been documented in this region since 2005.

Conclusion

Traditionally, the primary thrust of Spanish policy toward North African (particularly Moroccan) unaccompanied and separated children has been (and still is) to justify their forced repatriation on the grounds that it is in the children's best interests. In response to the ineffectiveness of this policy to date and the increasing arrival of children from other parts of the globe, during the last five years Spanish national and regional authorities have used a range of additional strategies and *ad hoc* practices to exclude these *de facto* stateless, unaccompanied migrant children from the protection systems and reception facilities to which they are entitled.

The combination of these policies leads to a problematic outcome. On the one hand, considerable numbers of unaccompanied and separated children keep on risking their lives to reach Europe and land on the Spanish coasts (1,622 arrivals by boat in 2006). On the other hand, a significant part of those admitted into care abandon the reception facilities to avoid the lack of opportunities offered and to look for better opportunities to make money.

The situation of those who abandon the care system is of particular concern because these now unprotected children experience the harsh consequences of *de facto* statelessness. Apart from the fact that after leaving care they do not have further access to housing support, access to education and medical care is also restricted. According to the law, every child in Spain is formally entitled to full access to health care and compulsory education, regardless of their immigration situation. However, unaccompanied and separated children outside the care system are often unable to make the most of this entitlement. In many cases, because these children lack any identification documents, their presence at an official establishment, such as a hospital, leads officials to notify the police, and the whole identification, admission into care, and abandonment process begins all over again.

What can be done? First of all, apart from some minor amendments that might be recommended, Spanish national legislation provides an adequate standard of care for unaccompanied and separated children, including full access to social rights, some routes to regularization of status, and access to employment for those above the age of sixteen. However, competent authorities have so far failed to interpret and implement this legislation in a child-sensitive and protective way. The law must not be implemented in a discretionary manner.

Second, central authorities in charge of immigration and regional authorities responsible for child care should coordinate their competences and actions and create a uniform national protocol of reception and treatment of unaccompanied and separated children to be implemented across Spain. The creation of this protocol would avoid the disparity of regional and local administrative practices that are currently a reality.

Third, repatriation should no longer be a standardized solution to be applied to every unaccompanied or separated minor irrespective of his or her personal circumstances. As the United Nations High Commissioner for Refugees (UNHCR) and the Committee on the Rights of the Child highlight,[66] every unaccompanied or separated child should pass through a formal best-interest determination process prior to identifying the best solution to respond to his or her situation—family reunification, voluntary return to the country of origin, or integration in Spain. None of these solutions must be adopted before evaluating and taking the particular situation of an unaccompanied or separated child into consideration.

Finally, how can we combine child-sensitive and protective reception measures with a decrease in the number of children migrating alone to Spain and Europe? So far, awareness campaigns in the countries of origin have been unable to erase the myth of El Dorado, which is shared by would-be migrant children and adults. Serious and long-term development assistance and cooperation programs to improve the situation of children, create employment opportunities, and develop improved living opportunities in the countries of origin are the only effective policies for reducing the flow of children migrating on their own in the near future and in the long term.

Notes

1. Although in Spanish regulations (and in practice) the official term used is *unaccompanied foreign minor* (*menor extranjero no acompañado*), this chapter uses the term *unaccompanied and separated migrant children* following the definitions of these two categories established by the United Nations (UN) Committee on the Rights of the Child (CRC), "CRC General Comment No. 6 (2005): Treatment of Unaccompanied and Separated Children outside Their Country of Origin," September 1, 2005, CRC/GC/2005/6, sec. 7–8, <http://www.unhcr.org> (accessed July 30, 2009.

2. C. Pereda, "Dos claves para comprender las migraciones internacionales. El caso de España," paper presented at the conference on Migrants de la Cité à la Citoyenneté: Etat des lieux des recherches européennes, Luxemburg, 2007. This author points out that from 2000 to 2006 the number of aliens documented with a residence permit in Spain increased 206 percent from less than 1 million to almost 3 million people.

3. A recent survey published by the European Commission shows that 33 percent of the respondents consider illegal immigrants to be the group most likely to carry out undeclared work, before unemployed (20 percent) and self-employed (16 percent). The survey states: "In Greece, Spain, France, Italy, Cyprus and Luxemburg, illegal immigrants are considered to be significantly active in the undeclared labor market. This result is not surprising as in most of these countries (with the exception of Luxemburg), illegal immigrants tend to find work in agriculture and tourism, two important sectors of those economies." European Commission, Directorate General, Employment, Social Affairs, and Equal Opportunities, "Undeclared Work in the European Union," European Commission, 2007.

4. Submission of manuscript to the publisher in December 2009.

5. "Dictamen de la Comisión de Estudio de Jóvenes y Menores de Canarias," *Boletín Oficial del Parlamento de Canarias*, March 28, 2007, 24.

6. See the last section in this chapter for further information about this practice.

7. According to a survey, 92 percent of the 1,651 unaccompanied children registered in the Catalonian region's protection services between January 1, 1998, and May 31, 2002, were from Morocco. In Andalusia, 90 percent of the children under protection were also Moroccan. Furthermore, as reported by Bermudez, many of them came from the same region or even the same borough. M. Capdevila and M. Ferrer, "Els menors estrangers indocumentats no acompanyats," *Invesbreu* no. 23, Centre d'Estudis Jurídics i Formació Especializada de la Generalitat de Catalunya (2003); Defensor del Menor de Andalucia, *Menores inmigrantes en Andalucía: La atención en los centros de protección de menores.*

Informe especial al Parlamento (Sevilla: Defensor del Pueblo Andaluz, 2003); M. Bermudez Gonzalez, *Los MINA: Niños de la calle en la España del siglo XXI* (Madrid: Ediciones Témpora, 2004).

8. The situation of unaccompanied female children living in Spain remains broadly unknown. A first approach to this phenomenon was the paper by María Luz Morante and María Auxiliadora Trujillo: "Las niñas y adolescentes que emigran solas a España. Las influencias o determinaciones derivadas de su condición de mujeres," paper presented at conference, "The Migration of Unaccompanied Minors in Europe: The Contexts of Origin, the Migration Routes, the Reception Systems," Poitiers, France, 2007.

9. To support this argument, we have extrapolated the data from the Catalonia region (74.3 percent of the children into care for the period 1998 to 2002 were of these ages) and from Andalusia (70 percent of the children between 2001 and 2002). Centre d'Estudis Juridics i Formació Especialitzada de la Generalitat de Catalunya, "Els menors estrangers indocumentats no acompanyat, 1998–2002," *Justdata* no. 35 (April 2003): 5; Defensor de menor de Andalucia, *Menores inmigrantes en Andalucía*, 419.

10. M. Jimenez Alvarez, *Buscarse la vida: Análisis transnacional de los procesos migratorios de los menores marroquíes no acompañados en Andalucía* (Madrid: Fundación Santa Maria, 2003); M. Serifi Villar and M. Jimenez Alvarez, *Nouveau visage de la migration, les mineurs non accompagnés: Analyze transnationale du phénomène migratoire des mineurs marocains vers l'Espagne* (Tangier: UNICEF Maroc, Fondation Jaume Bofill, Junta de Andalucía, 2005); Bermudez Gonzalez, *Los MINA*; S. Monteros, *La construcción social de un nuevo sujeto migratorio: Los menores migrantes marroquíes no acompañados. Condiciones de posibilidad para la agencia* (Madrid: Departamento de Antropología Social y Pensamiento Filosófico Español, Facultad de Filosofía y Letras, Universidad Autónoma de Madrid, 2007), 365.

11. Vacchiano has produced research on the profiles and characteristics of children from rural inland areas of Morocco. Most of these children come from the areas around the towns of Beni Mellal and Khourigba, and they migrate within a clearly defined household project: their parents consider the child's migration as an investment and expect income from them soon. F. Vacchiano, "Fi lghorba kebrit: Images et parcours des mineurs migrants entre Maroc et Italie," presented at the conference, "The Migration of Unaccompanied Minors in Europe: The Contexts of Origin, the Migration Routes, the Reception Systems," Poitiers: France, 2007; Serifi Villar and Jimenez Alvarez, *Nouveau visage de la migration*, 21.

12. All the information in this paragraph comes from the unreleased survey done within the *Proyecto Alondra de atención a menores no acompañados subsaharianos* and has been kindly made available by Fundación Nuevo Sol.

13. The Spanish ombudsman has recently reported the existence of this practice. On occasions, when undocumented migrants who appeared to be children arrived at the Canary Islands with adults, the authorities refused to do age-determination tests and instead considered them to be adults, opening a deportation process and taking them into detention. In most cases, as other adult

migrants, these children left the detention centers after the maximum authorized delay (forty days) and were transferred to the continent—mainly to the Madrid region—where they were finally legally recognized as children and entered the care system. Defenso del Pueblo Español, *Informe anual del Defensor del Pueblo 2006* (2007): 303–304.

14. Ley Orgánica *4/2000* de 11 de enero, reformada por Ley Orgánica 8/2000 de 22 de diciembre y por Ley Orgánica 14/2003 de 20 de noviembre, sobre los derechos y libertades de los extranjeros en España y su integración social (hereafter 2000 Aliens Act), sec. 35(1).

15. *Instrucción 2/2001 de la Fiscalía General del Estado*, on the interpretation of section 25 of the 2000 Aliens Act.

16. Several children interviewed by Human Rights Watch (HRW) in the Canary Islands stated they had been kept in detention from several hours to up to two weeks several times. S. Troller, *Unwelcome Responsibilities: Spain's Failure to Protect the Rights of Unaccompanied Migrant Children in the Canary Islands* (HRW, 2007), 26–28.

17. Spanish Civil Code, Alinea 2, sec. 172.

18. The legal basis of this public guardianship can be found in sections 172, 222.4, and 239 of the Civil Code, which determine that children living in a situation of special vulnerability, when their parents or legal representatives fail to accomplish their duties, should be subjected to the guardianship of the regional public authority competent for the protection of children in need. A. Duran Ayago, *La protección internacional del menor desamparado: Régimen jurídico* (Madrid: COLEX, 2004), 59.

19. 2000 Aliens Act, sec. 35, par. 4 (hereafter 2000 Aliens Act Decree);; Real Decreto 2393/2004 de 30 de diciembre por el que se aprueba el Reglamento de la Ley Orgánica 4/2000 de 11 de enero, de derechos y libertades de los extranjeros y su integración social (hereafter 2000 Aliens Act Decree), sec. 91, par. 3.

20. 2000 Aliens Act Decree, sec. 92, par. 4.

21. Ibid.

22. Ibid.

23. Committee on the Rights of the Child, "Concluding Observations of the Committee on the Rights of the Child: Spain," Consideration of Reports Submitted by States Parties under Article 44 of the Convention, 30th session, 2002, CRC/C/15/Add 185, June 13, 2002.

24. Human Rights Watch, *Nowhere to Turn: State Abuses of Unaccompanied Migrant Children by Spain and Morocco* (HRW, 2002).

25. United Nations Commission on Human Rights, "Report Submitted by Ms. Gabriela Rodríguez Pizarro, Special Rapporteur, in Conformity with Resolution 2003/46 of the Commission on Human Rights: Addendum. Visit to Spain," 60th session, E/CN.4/2004/76/Add.2 OF, 2004.

26. Defensor del Pueblo Español, Informe Anual del Defensor del Pueblo 2006, 305; and Instruction 6/2004 of November 26, 2007, issued by Fiscalía General del Estado.

27. Defensor del Menor en la Comunidad de Madrid, Informe Annual 2005, 70–81, esp. 73. Returning a child who is doing well destabilizes the other children in the reception centers when they discover that their efforts to integrate do not increase their chances of been allowed to stay in Spain. See also Stephen H. Legomsky's chapter in this book, which addresses the same issue in the U.S. context.

28. "Acuerdo entre Rumania y España sobre cooperación en el ámbito de la protección de los menores de edad rumanos no acompañados en España, su repatriación y lucha contra la explotación de los mismos, hecho en Madrid el 15 de diciembre de 2005," *Boletín Oficial del Estado* (August 16, 2006) (signed on December 15, 2005, and in force since August 2006).

29. "Acuerdo entre la República de Senegal y el Reino de España sobre cooperación en el ámbito de la prevención de la emigración ilegal de menores de edad senegaleses no acompañados, su protección, repatriación y reinserción, hecho en Dakar el 5 de diciembre de 2006," *Boletín Oficial del Estado* (July 18, 2008) (signed on December 5, 2006, and in force since July 2008).

30. "Acuerdo entre el Reino de España y el Reino de Marruecos sobre cooperación en el ámbito de la prevención de la emigración ilegal de menores no acompañados, su protección y su retorno concertado, hecho en Rabat el 6 de marzo de 2007," *Boletín Oficial de las Cortes Generales* (September 14, 2007).

31. A recent HRW report provides updated information from Moroccan, Spanish, and IOM representatives. According to these sources, six reception facilities (residential centers or apartments) are planned in the areas of Tangiers, Nador, Beni Mellal, Fahs Aujer, and Marrakesh with a capacity for 220 children. It is not clear if these facilities will be used exclusively for repatriated children or instead will be used to prevent would-be migrant children from leaving. According to the representatives interviewed by HRW, services will be provided to both focus groups. See S. Troller, *Returns at Any Cost: Spain's Push to Repatriate Unaccompanied Children in the Absence of Safeguards* (HRW, 2008), 5–7. Most recently, Consuelo Rumi, state secretary for immigration and emigration, stated at a press conference that two centers in Beni Mellal and Nador will be ready by June 2009. See *ABC* daily, electronic edition, November 12, 2008.

32. For example, Administrative Court no. 14, Madrid, ruling of September 25, 2006; Administrative Court no. 1, Huesca, ruling no 296 of October 13, 2006; Litigation/Administrative Court no 25, Madrid, Ruling no. 269 of November 6, 2006; High Court of Madrid, Chamber of administrative litigations no. 2, ruling no. 1987 of November 24, 2006; Administrative Court no 1, Santander, ruling no. 325 of December 27, 2006; High Court of Madrid, Chamber of Administrative Litigations no. 5, ruling no. 767 of April 26, 2007; Administrative Court no. 15, Madrid, ruling of April 27, 2007; Administrative Court no. 15, Madrid, ruling of May 31, 2007; High Court of Madrid, Chamber of Administrative Litigations no. 2, ruling no. 1495 of September 21, 2007; Administrative Court no. 26, Madrid, ruling of October 19, 2007; High Court of Madrid, Chamber of Administrative Litigations no. 4, ruling no. 1375 of November 23, 2007; High Court of the Bask Country, Chamber of Administrative Litigations, ruling no. 88 of February 14, 2008.

33. Amnesty International, "Amnistía Internacional denuncia expulsiones encubiertas de menores no acompañados," October 25, 2007, <http://www.es .amnesty.org> (accessed April 30, 2009).

34. Constitutional Court, First Chamber, 2008, rulings 114/06 and 114/08.

35. See section 35 of the new bill amending the 2000 Aliens Act, Proyecto de Ley Orgánica de reforma de la Ley Orgánica 4/2000, de 11 de enero, sobre derechos y libertades de los extranjeros en España y su integración social, Boletín Oficial de las Cortes Generales, November 6, 2009

36. See data in figures 7.3 and 7.4. The number of repatriation orders that are instigated but not achieved is much higher.

37. See 2000 Aliens Act, sec. 92(5), par. 1.

38. Ibid., sec. 92(5), par. 2.

39. Ibid., sec. 40(j).

40. Ibid., sec. 41(k). "National labor market situation" is the main criterion used in Spain, as in most European countries, to authorize the access of foreigners to a formal job. In Spain, the alien must present a formal and specific promise of employment from an employer. Competent labor authorities will examine this promise and issue a report indicating whether this employment is part of professional sectors with current unemployed national or resident aliens or not. In the former case, the authorization to work will be refused. For an extensive analysis of the requirements and conditions for migrants to access the labor market, see Lorenzo Cachon Rodriguez, *Colectivos desaventajados en el mercado de trabajo y políticas de empleo* (Madrid: Ministerio de Trabajo y Asuntos Sociales, 2004).

41. See note 38.

42. These conditions can be found in 2000 Aliens Act, sec. 54.

43. This rule is undetermined and does not define which criteria should be evaluated before issuing a residence permit: the regional care institution "could recommend" to central authorities the issuing of a residence permit when the child has participated in educational or training processes aiming to improve his or her social integration. See 2000 Aliens Act, sec. 92(5).

44. The United Nations Special Rapporteur denounces cases of delay on documentation of unaccompanied children, delays as long as twenty to twenty-five months. United Nations Commission on Human Rights, Report submitted by Gabriela Rodríguez Pizarro, Special Rapporteur, "Conformity with Resolution 2003/46 of the Commission on Human Rights: Addendum. Visit to Spain," 60th session, E/CN.4/2004/76/Add.2 OF, 2004; par. 58, p. 15.

45. P. Perez, "De náufragos y navegantes: los menores y jóvenes no acompañados," *Boletín Puntos de Vista*, no. 10 (2007), available at: <http://www.mugak .eu> (accessed July 19, 2010); N. Empez and V. Galea, "Menores no acompañados de Marruecos a Barcelona: Repaso histórico y la situación actual de los menores que migran solos," paper presented at conference, "The Migration of Unaccompanied Minors in Europe: The Contexts of Origin, the Migration Routes, the Reception Systems," Poitiers, France, 2007; S. Troller, *Unwelcome Responsibilities: Spain's Failure to Protect the Rights of Unaccompanied Migrant Children in the Canary Islands* (HRW, 2007).

46. Perez, "De náufragos y navegantes: los menores y jóvenes no acompañados."

47. Hussein's statement appeared in *El País*, Basque Country edition of Sunday, March 30, 2008, 7. *El País* is the most widely read newspaper in Spain. The translation is the author's.

48. The next chapter in Hicham's story shows the absurdity of the institutional practices. After arriving in Morocco, Hicham went to the border, showed his Spanish residence document, and came back into Spain. A lawyer took his case to court, and the magistrates repealed the repatriation order. But other children do not possess a residence permit or have less courage or personal skills than Hicham. Rafael J. Alvarez, "La vida en patera de plata," *El Mundo*, September 18, 2006, 23. *El Mundo* is nationally the second-most widely read paper in Spain. The translation is the author's.

49. Perez, "De náufragos y navegantes: los menores y jóvenes no acompañados." This author underlines other collateral effects linked to the principal one. We may highlight the fracture of the protection and educational system causing a lack of motivation of the staff working in this field. The increase of street children also has an influence on public opinion, which perceives unaccompanied migrant children as a problem and as potential delinquents.

50. According to Dirección General de Inmigración, Ministerio de Trabajo y Asuntos Sociales, *Informe estadístico sobre menores extranjeros no acompañados 2004–2005*, the number of children received in the different regional protection services was 9,117 between January 1 and 31, 2004. According to the same official source, the number of children who were still present on December 31 of the same year was 2004. Even by considering that several children leave the facilities because they come of age, the ratio between the received children and those staying in protection is too large to ignore. To reinforce this argument, a survey conducted in 2000 in the Andalusia region demonstrated how 58 percent of a sample of 232 unaccompanied migrant children had abandoned the care facility where they were received. E. Garcia España and F. Perez Jimenez, *Análisis de la delincuencia en Andalucía* (Malaga: Instituto Interuniversitario de Criminología, Universidad de Málaga, 2006), 103.

51. This constitutes one of the main research gaps on the issue of the situation of unaccompanied migrant children in the whole European continent and, by extension, in Spain.

52. This is the case with Moroccans who take a chance in France, Belgium, or Italy or the Romanians who are marked by a significant mobility between France, Italy, and Spain. N. Mai, *L'errance et la prostitution des mineurs et des jeunes majeurs migrants dans l'espace de l'Union européenne* (London: Institute for the Study of European Transformations, London Metropolitan University, 2008).

53. To date, few studies have rigorously analyzed this issue in the Spanish context. A. Rodriguez, "Reacciones y relaciones de menores y jóvenes ante la protección y la exclusión," paper presented at conference, "The Migration of Unaccompanied Minors in Europe: The Contexts of Origin, the Migration Routes, the Reception Systems," Poitiers: France, 2007; E. Ocariz y C. S. Juan, "Perfil criminológico del menor infractor inmigrante una investigacion retrospec-

tive," in *Menores extranjeros infractores en la Unión Europea: Teorías, perfiles y propuestas de intervención* (Bilbao: S. San Juan y J. L. De la Cuesta Arzamendi, Instituto Vasco de Criminología, Universidad del País Vasco), 59–68; M. Y. M. Ferrer, *Los menores extranjeros indocumentados no acompañados* (MEINA) (Barcelona: Formació i investigació social y criminologica, Generalitat de Catalunya, Center d'Estudis Jurídics i Formació Especialitzada).

54. Committee on the Rights of the Child (CRC), Regarding General Comment No. 6 (2005), sec. 84.

55. For a more extensive theoretical approach, see E. Rozzi, *The Evaluation of the Best Interests of the Child in the Choice between Remaining in the Host Country and Repatriation: A Reflection Based on the Convention on the Rights of the Child* (Save the Children Italy, 2002). See also D. Senovilla Hernández, "Implementation Practices of the CRC Best Interest Principle regarding Unaccompanied Asylum Seeking Migrant Minors in Europe: Cases of Forced Return in Italy and Spain," in *Focus on Children in Migration* (Warsaw, Poland: Save the Children Sweden, March 20–21, 2007).

56. C. Belinchon Sanchez, "Life Plans for Unaccompanied Migrant Minors and Co-operation between Countries of Origin, Transit and Destination," paper presented at conference, "The Migration of Unaccompanied Minors: Acting in the Best Interest of the Child," Malaga, Spain, 2005; Vasquez Murillo, "Los menores extranjeros no acompañados en Andalucía," paper presented at conference, "The Migration of Unaccompanied Minors in Europe: The Contexts of Origin, the Migration Routes, the Reception Systems," Poitiers, France, 2007. Vazquez Murillo is currently the regional representative of the Andalusia network of reception centers for children in need.

57. Murillo, "Los menores extranjeros no acompañados en Andalucía."

58. El Defensor al Día, "Los menores extranjeros no acompañados están en situación de desamparo y el Defensor del Pueblo recomienda su tutela por la Administración pública," *La revista del Defensor del Pueblo del Pueblo de España* 36 (March 2008): 9.

59. An extensive analysis on the Catalonian-specific protection system for unaccompanied children can be found at *La situación de los menores inmigrantes solos* (Barcelona: Sindic de Greuges de Catalunya, Febrero 2006); N. Empez and V. Galea, "Menores no acompañados de Marruecos a Barcelona."

60. Empez and Galea estimate that around 30 percent of the children under guardianship of protection services of Asturias region (north Spain) were previously cared for in Catalonia. Empez and Galea, "Menores no acompañados de Marruecos a Barcelona."

61. For more information, see Generalitat de Catalunya. Departament d'acció social i ciutadania, "Explicació del Programa Catalunya Magrib i el seu context als joves marroquins," leaflet, <http://www.catalunyamagrib.cat> (accessed October 1, 2008).

62. See F. Bassels, "Fracasa el plan retorno para menores inmigrantes," *El País* (daily), electronic edition, November 4, 2008.

63. The Canary Islands officer for social affairs states that the reception centers in this territory is receiving children at three times its maximum capacity. "Los centros de menores inmigrantes de Canarias están al triple de su capacidad," *El Mundo*, electronic edition, April 12, 2008.

64. Special Program for the Transfer and Reception of Unaccompanied Foreign Minors from the Canary Islands, Adopted by the Government (Consejo Superior de Política de Inmigración), September 18, 2006. The state secretary for immigration assumed the coordination of the program.

65. See *Boletín Oficial de las Cortes Generales*, January 16, 2008.

66. See, for instance, United Nations High Commissioner for Refugees (UNHCR), "UNHCR Guidelines on Determining the Best Interest of the Child," Geneva, 2005, general comment no. 6; Committee on the Rights of the Child, "Treatment of Unaccompanied and Separated Children outside Their Country of Origin," sec. 79ff.

8

Undocumented Migrant and Roma Children in Italy: Between Rights Protection and Control

Elena Rozzi

We will also take the fingerprints of children, derogating from the present law, just to avoid phenomena like begging. It will not be an ethnic booking but a real census for granting decent living conditions to those who have the right to stay. And for sending home those who do not have the right to stay in Italy.
—Roberto Maroni, Italian minister of the interior, June 25, 2008[1]

My dream is to have a document: think how beautiful it would be to be free to exist, to go where I like!
—Roma girl living in Rome[2]

Fingerprints for Protecting Children's Rights?

On May 30, 2008, Italy's Berlusconi government ordered the census and identification, including fingerprinting, of people who live in nomad settlements[3] in three Italian regions.[4] Children were included. The declared goals of the provision appeared ambiguous. On the one hand, it was intended to show the public that the state was tackling the problem of nomad camps by enacting harsh security and public-order policies, fighting crime and illegal migration, and removing unauthorized settlements. The census, in fact, was part of the extraordinary measures taken within the state of emergency declared by the government.[5] These measures equated the settlements of nomad communities with natural disasters and allowed the state to derogate from a large number of laws.[6] Special commissioners were appointed to carry out the necessary interventions, including—besides the census—the expulsion of persons with irregular status and the removal of illegal settlements. On the other hand, the provision was justified as a human-rights protection measure for the affected population. The government claimed that the fingerprinting policy was aimed at

guaranteeing the respect of fundamental rights and dignity of people, ensuring reliable means of identification . . . and structures that enabled access to essential social assistance and health services, taking into account children's need for protection from criminal subjects or organizations that use inadequate proof of identity or origin to carry out illicit trades and serious forms of exploitation.[7]

The census provoked strong criticism from international institutions, such as the European Union (EU) Parliament,[8] the European Commission, the Council of Europe, the Catholic Church and other religious organizations, several Italian and international nongovernmental organizations (NGOs), and opinion makers.[9] The Berlusconi government was accused of conducting an ethnic census that seriously discriminated against the Roma minority, both because the great majority of people living in nomad settlements are Roma[10] and because the census targeted not only undocumented people but also regular migrants with valid documents and even Italian citizens residing in nomad settlements.[11] Critics also stressed the coercive symbolic value of fingerprinting as a tool used by the state to exercise its control over criminals and other "potentially dangerous" people such as illegal migrants.[12]

Attention was drawn to the parallels between current events and those that had occurred on the eve of the introduction of racial laws in fascist Italy:

It started with an unexpected ethnic census in the summer of seventy years ago—the shameful history of Italian racial laws. A memorandum was sent to the prefectures on August 11, 1938, requiring an exact survey of Jews resident in the provinces of the country. In the country, 47,825 Jews were registered, of whom 8,713 were noncitizens who were immediately issued expulsion orders. In reality, the Viminale [ministry of the interior] was already in possession of this data. "The census was motivated more by the goal of subjecting than knowing, more of demonstrating than assessing," the French historian Marie-Anne Matard-Bonucci writes in *L'Italia fascista e la persecuzione degli ebrei* (il Mulino). In response to the criticism regarding the targeting of unfortunate citizens by such an ethnic census, the authorities claimed to have no persecutory intent but rather a protective mission.[13]

Among the recent anti-immigrant measures, which include stringent deportation and criminalization provisions, the fingerprinting of Roma children was one of the most controversial measures, both nationally and internationally. The government justified its policies by insisting they were necessary to guarantee Roma children's rights to education, decent living conditions, and protection from exploitation through begging, prostitution, and organ trafficking. According to the prime minister and his cabinet, "identification through fingerprinting is useful for granting them (Roma children) school and education. They have no discriminatory intent, just the positive will to integrate these European citizens."[14] According to the minister of the interior, Roberto Maroni, "the policies were necessary to take them away from *favelas* and to return to reality those 'shadow children' that by hundreds in Italy, and by tens of thousands in Europe, disappear every year. . . . The hypocrisy that everybody is in favor of children but everybody accepts that they live in these camps, sharing space with rats, must end."[15] This provision "is in the interest of children, of children without identity. If we leave them in this shameful abandonment, we do not act for their good,"[16] Franco Frattini, the minister of foreign affairs, declared on June 30, 2009. Mariastella Gelmini, the minister of education, said that "it is not discrimination but a form of protection, including protection against families that exploit them."[17]

Most of the Berlusconi government's justifications of fingerprinting as a necessary child-rights measure are false. Identification is not necessary to go to school, as the right to education under Italian law is granted to all children, even to those with no identity papers; and registration is not enough to guarantee adequate living conditions if effective social policies are not in place. Nevertheless, these arguments resonate because of a real problem: the lack of legal identity seriously hinders the protection of children's rights. It is no coincidence that international governmental organizations (IGOs) and NGOs often stress the importance of registration and documentation as measures to protect the rights of separated children and child victims of trafficking. For example, the United Nations (UN) Committee on the Rights of the Child recommends

prompt registration by means of an initial interview conducted in an age-appropriate and gender-sensitive manner, in a language the child understands, by professionally qualified persons to collect biodata and social history to ascertain the identity of the child, including, wherever possible, identity of both parents, other siblings, as well as the citizenship of the child, the siblings and the parents. . . . Unaccompanied and separated children should be provided with their own personal identity documentation as soon as possible.[18]

Registration and provision of legal identity documents to every child (whether the child is a migrant or a citizen) are recommended as key antitrafficking measures. For this reason, the Civil Liberties Committee of the EU Parliament recently approved a proposed amendment to European law requiring all EU citizen children to have their own passports, with fingerprints (from the age of twelve) and data on their parents.[19] So does registration violate children's rights or is it a useful, even necessary measure for protecting rights provided by the Convention on the Rights of the Child (CRC)?

Taking Italy as a case study, I first analyze the population of undocumented children living in Italy, defining some internal differences (such as EU/non-EU citizens and separated/accompanied children). I then analyze how the lack of documents jeopardizes the rights protection of these *de facto* stateless children in a number of areas—detention and return to the country of origin; access to education, health, and social services; protection from exploitation; and separation from parents against the child's best interests. Next, I argue that laws and policies affecting undocumented children are characterized by a deep and enduring ambivalence between child-rights protection and migration control. I consider some significant examples, such as the legal status of a child turning eighteen, the return of separated children, and the treatment of children accompanied by undocumented parents. I conclude with law and policy recommendations for protecting undocumented children's rights: promoting registration and documentation; protecting the rights of those children who remain undocumented; and taking measures aimed at building trust relationships with children and their parents and respecting their views and wishes.[20]

Who Are Undocumented Children in Italy?

Undocumented children are not a homogeneous group but rather one characterized by certain key differences. To start with, although all undocumented children, by definition, lack legal identity, this characteristic refers to two different conditions. One concerns the lack of a regular migration status in Italy because the child or the parents[21] do not fulfill the relevant legal criteria (they do not qualify for a legal migration status because they do not have a regular job, adequate accommodation, or a qualifying relationship to a legal resident).[22] The other condition refers to the lack of identity documents that prove eligibility for a legal status (such as a passport or an EU identity card).[23]

The two groups are conceptually distinct, but there are significant overlaps. Almost every child without identity documents is irregularly staying in Italy, as a valid identity document is generally required to get a regular migration status.[24] Conversely, many irregular migrant children lack valid identity documents for a number of reasons. For example, a regular migration status and residence are required to get an Italian identity card. Some consulates[25] issue passports only to citizens legally staying in the host country, thus creating a vicious cycle: if you do not have a passport, you cannot get a residence permit; but if you do not have a residence permit, you cannot get a passport. Some migrants do not have any identity documents because they were not registered at birth in their country of origin[26] or because they are legally stateless.[27]

Among undocumented children, we can further distinguish a number of different groups. Place of birth, nationality, family status, and ethnicity (in Italy, being a member of the Roma ethnic minority or not) are some of the most significant factors.

1. *Place of birth* Some undocumented children are born in Italy, while others have migrated from their country of origin. Children born in Italy to irregular migrants do not become Italian citizens at birth, as Italian citizenship law is based on *jus sanguinis* or nationality by descent. Since there are no special provisions to grant them a regular migration status by virtue of their place of birth, these children are ineligible for Italian citizenship even when they come of age.[28] Many children born in Italy to undocumented parents do not have an identity document issued by their parents' country of origin. Often the only document they have is a birth certificate because, as a matter of law, all children (including children born to irregular migrants) in Italy have the right to be registered at birth.[29] But problems arise in practice, especially if the parents are unmarried or do not have identity documents themselves.[30]

A change in immigration law that would prevent irregular non-EU migrants from registering their child at birth is currently under discussion in parliament.[31] The proposed provision has caused a lively debate. Both NGOs and some politicians have denounced the proposal for the serious rights violations it would entail:[32] these children would not be registered in any way and would therefore be confronted with the serious institutional handicap of having no legal identity. In many cases, they would be ineligible for their parents' citizenship, thus becoming legally stateless.[33] There is even a high risk that hospitals will separate the child from a parent who is unable to register him or her.[34] If this proposal is enacted, the result is likely to be that many undocumented women may choose not to risk giving birth in the hospital for fear of losing custody of their child.

2. *Nationality* Another important distinction concerns nationality, particularly between EU citizens and nationals of non-EU states. The requirements for getting a regular migration status are different for the two groups. EU citizens have the right of entry and residence in Italy for a period of up to three months with no conditions (except possession of an identity card or passport). To stay in Italy for more than three months, however, EU citizens need to prove that they have a regular job or

sufficient resources to prevent becoming a burden on the Italian social assistance system. Alternatively, they must show that they are a family member of an EU citizen who meets these requirements. They are also required to register their residence with the registry office.[35] EU citizens who are unable to comply with these qualifying criteria become irregular migrants (despite being EU citizens). By contrast, non-EU citizens need a visa to enter and reside in Italy legally, whether for employment purposes or for family reunification. There are limited annual quotas for employment visas, and eligibility for one of these visas depends on securing a job offer.[36] Moreover, although irregular EU citizens can regularize their position at any time once they meet the necessary requirements, non-EU citizens must apply for an entry visa from their country of origin (within the annual quotas) or wait to be granted amnesty. The consequences of irregular migration status on EU and non-EU citizens are different, too, particularly in respect to removal from Italy and return to the country of origin.[37] In general, the position of non-EU citizens is more precarious. However, even EU citizens can be returned in some circumstances. The limits on access to health and social services are similar for both groups.

3. *Family status*   Among undocumented children in Italy, a distinction is made between separated children and undocumented children who are accompanied by parents. Italian law provides that all undocumented children, simply by virtue of their minority, be issued a residence permit "for minor age,"[38] valid until the age of eighteen. However, in practice, this provision has a very different effect on the two groups of children. Children accompanied by undocumented parents are generally not issued any residence permit because only the parents can make the relevant application (no guardians are appointed for accompanied children). But since undocumented parents risk expulsion if they come into contact with the police authorities, these applications are rarely made.

By contrast, separated children have a guardian appointed and as a result are generally issued a residence permit "for minor age" as soon as the guardian applies, even if the child lacks a passport. In effect, this procedure means that in Italy there is a permanent, and potentially general, mechanism for regularizing separated children.[39] In practice, however, many separated children in Italy remain undocumented. There are several reasons for this. A high proportion of separated children never come into contact with any state or welfare institution. Among those that do, many leave the reception centers soon after they are placed and before a residence permit has been applied for, because the integration programs available do not meet their needs and wishes,[40] or they fear being repatriated by the authorities and so are reluctant to stay on, or because they are under pressure from traffickers or other abusive adults to return to the streets or to exploitative work situations. What is more, even separated children living in reception centers sometimes have no residence permit for months because of delays in the appointment of the guardian, who is responsible for applying for the residence permit.[41]

4. *Ethnicity*   Finally, there is a significant presence of undocumented migrants, both EU and non-EU citizens, among the Roma community. Depending on their circumstances, these migrants might be legally stateless, or they may find themselves in situations of *de facto* or *effective* statelessness. Little attention has so far been paid to the complex and rightless circumstances in which many members of this community live because most public comments simply focus on their interactions with the criminal justice system. In fact, however, Roma migrants face significant rights obstacles, which regularly precipitate precarious legal situations. Long-term irregular status, passed down from generation to generation, is a peculiarity of this group. It is not unusual for Roma children who are born in Italy to families that migrated decades ago from former Yugoslavia, whose parents or even grandparents were born in Italy, to be undocumented. Although most other irregular migrants manage to regularize their position sooner or later by proving they have a job and accommodation, Roma people are often unable to meet these requirements,[42] as they are seriously discriminated against in both labor and housing markets. Moreover, many Roma from the former Yugoslavia cannot get a residence permit because they do not have a passport. They are *de jure* stateless because they are not recognized as citizens by any state, and yet for a series of bureaucratic reasons the Italian authorities refuse to recognize their legal statelessness and therefore regularize their status.[43] There are other groups of Roma in Italy, including migrants from Romania, who are legal residents because they are EU citizens with a regular job but who nevertheless live in unauthorized camps and are not allowed in practice to register their residence with the registry office. They are *effectively* stateless, legally resident EU citizens who do not have access to health and social services and therefore have no state to rely on because of their lack of residence registration.

It is difficult to estimate the numbers of undocumented children living in Italy given the largely hidden character of this population and the absence of consistent and comprehensive data collection by state authorities. Some figures, however, have been published about separated children: 2,162 separated Romanian children were registered by the Committee for Foreign Minors, on December 31, 2006;[44] 7,548 separated children from non-EU countries (mainly northern Africa, eastern Europe, and the Middle East) were registered at the end of 2007; 75 percent of these children did not have a residence permit.[45] These estimates do not include the substantial but uncounted numbers of separated children who do not get in touch with any institution.

As for undocumented children accompanied by parents, no official data are available. There are estimated to be approximately 650,000 undocumented citizens from non-EU countries in Italy,[46] but no estimates exist for the number of children. Some tentative estimates can however be made for undocumented Roma children (who typically are accompanied by their parents): an estimated 45,000 to 70,000 non-Italian Roma, mainly from Romania and the former Yugoslavia, live in Italy.[47] As mentioned before, a significant proportion lacks a regular migration status. According to some censuses carried out at the local level (including the controversial census mentioned earlier), about half the Roma inhabitants of nomad camps are children,[48] so it is likely that several thousand undocumented Roma children are currently residing in Italy.

Lack of Documents, Lack of Rights

What are the consequences of the lack of documents (whether because of a complete absence of identity documents or because of irregular immigration status) on the life of a migrant child in Italy? Undocumented[49] children are *de facto* stateless: they do not have any state to turn to for protection of their rights, both in the sense of access to basic services (education, health care, shelter, and social services) and in terms of protection from exploitation and other serious child-rights violations. These children often encounter the state only as an agent of control and repression (through expulsion, detention, or separation from their parents against the best interests of the child).

The treatment of undocumented children varies considerably depending on their family status and citizenship. In general, non-EU citizens and children accompanied by undocumented parents are granted fewer rights than EU citizens and separated children.[50]

Return and Detention[51]
Italian immigration law for non-EU citizens provides that separated children must neither be expelled (except for reasons related to public

Box 8.1

Detention of Lily, six months old, with her mother: "We could not leave the center; they told us we had to stay there, in the container. . . . In the container, there was neither a cradle nor a high chair, so I had to hold Lily in my arms when she was awake. . . . We had to stay there. It was hot, but what could we do? As there were no trees in the center, this is what we did: we put the bed outside, in the container's shade, and we moved it as the shade turned."[a]

Letter of Mislim, detained in the Serraino Vulpitta detention center in Trapani because he was regarded as an adult despite his declarations: "I am a child, and I cannot stay here because all the people that stay here do not want me to stay with them because I am a child . . . and it is too bad to stay here. I've got to the point that I do not sleep at night, and my family is poor and I have relatives in Italy and I kindly ask you to let me go away as soon as possible. Thank you."[b]

Agrigento, July 8, 2005: "The Court of Agrigento confirmed the expulsion orders of migrants stopped in Lampedusa in the past weeks. . . . For two migrants, the judge had to resort to the health service to assess their age. The non-EU citizens claimed to be children to stop the expulsion. But x-ray exams that the youngsters underwent certified that they were adults, and for them, too, expulsion was ordered."[c]

Notes

a. Amnesty International (AI), *Invisibili: I diritti umani dei minori migranti e richiedenti asilo detenuti all'arrivo alla frontiera marittima italiana* (Roma: AI 2006), 68.

b. Ibid., 95.

c. Ibid., 91.

---

order and state security) nor held in detention centers.[52] Nevertheless, these provisions are not always applied. Some separated children with no documents proving they are minors are expelled or detained because they are wrongly identified as adults on the basis of inadequate age-assessment procedures.[53]

Although the expulsion of separated children is forbidden, they may be returned to their country of origin through assisted repatriation.[54] As a matter of law, this measure is different from expulsion. Adult migrants are expelled as a sanction for violating laws on immigration, with no assessment of the situation in the country of origin, while children can be repatriated only if return for family reunification purposes is considered to be in the best interests of the child, following investigations in the country of origin.[55] Moreover, the child must be properly accompanied during the return journey. Nevertheless, in the absence of clear criteria and procedures concerning repatriation decisions (for example, although the child has the right to be heard, his or her consent is not required) and given that the decision-making authority (the Committee for Foreign Minors) is a governmental, nonindependent body, in practice, separated children are sometimes returned against the child's best interests.[56] In the last few years, only a few children have been repatriated,[57] but the number is likely to increase, given the highly discretionary power of the Committee and the harsh position of the new government on illegal migration and deviance control. For example, a bill on prostitution was recently proposed by the government, providing assisted repatriation for all separated children practicing prostitution, with accelerated and simplified procedures.[58]

Non-EU children who are accompanied by undocumented parents are even less protected from return and detention than separated children. According to Italian law, children cannot be expelled unless they are exercising the right to follow their parents or caregivers.[59] The decision is taken by the police, and no procedures for the best-interest-of-the-child assessment are provided. Moreover, children can be detained in detention centers to guarantee the right to family unity, at the request of the parent or the juvenile judge.[60] In practice, the authorities rarely make a best-interest-of-the-child assessment when deciding whether to expel (or detain) the child with the parent or to separate him or her from the family. In some areas (such as northern Italy), the child is almost always separated from the parent, while in other areas (such as Sicily), children are usually detained with their parents. Finally, no specific guarantees (such as the use of trained staff) apply to the expulsion procedures involving children.

Legislation concerning the return of EU citizens is, in general,[61] much more favorable. Unless it is for reasons of public policy or public security, an EU citizen irregularly staying in Italy can be neither expelled immediately (at least one month's notice to leave Italy must be given) nor detained in detention centers. Even if returned to the country of origin, he or she can legally reenter Italy immediately.[62] Moreover, according to the law, children can be returned only if the expulsion is based on imperative grounds of public security that endanger state security or is necessary in the best interests of the child.[63]

An interesting illustration of the effects of nationality and family status on the treatment of undocumented children is the case of Romanian minors. In 2005 and 2006, most Romanian children facing criminal proceedings in Rome claimed to be separated children, even though they actually lived with their undocumented parents.[64] But when Romania entered the EU in 2007, these children revealed their true family status because they no longer feared expulsion for their parents and themselves. As far as accompanied children are concerned, EU citizens are more protected against return than non-EU citizens, but the same is not true for separated children. Romanian children are a case in point. Italy and Romania signed an agreement[65] permitting the return of separated Romanian children with fewer safeguards than those required for repatriating separated non-EU children. For example, the right of the child to express his or her views is less protected.[66] No reference is made to the best interests of the child, and no clear requirements for family tracing are indicated. Reports about the expected return of thousands of separated Romanian children have recently appeared in the media.[67]

Access to Education, Health, Social Services, and Adequate Living Conditions[68]

In Italy, a high proportion of separated children live outside reception centers. Between 2004 and 2006, almost two-thirds of children left reception centers within a month of placement.[69] These separated children, as well as children accompanied by undocumented parents, often live in inadequate accommodations (including overcrowded apartments, deserted factories, and huts). Particularly dramatic is the situation of Roma who live in unauthorized settlements with no basic services (water, sewage, and electricity,), are segregated from the rest of society, and are exposed to illegal settlement clearances and forced evictions. Several Roma children have died in nomad camps because of the lack of heat in the winter or because of fires (at least nine between 2006 and 2007).[70] Moreover, undocumented children (both children accompanied by undocumented parents and separated children living outside reception centers) face difficulties in acceding to social and health services and to education. The European Commission against Racism and Intolerance estimated that 20,000 Roma children were outside the compulsory school system in 2006.[71]

These rights violations are the result of several different factors, some due to legislation and some the product of practical obstacles, directly or indirectly resulting from undocumented status. According to Italian law, all foreign children, even those without a residence permit or identity documents, have the right to education (including the right to get

Box 8.2

Dear Europe, please help us . . . to have a place to sleep, a house, a job for my father . . . to go to school. . . . Small children live in the shacks, in that misery, and it stinks; among the mice, they can't eat. . . . Please help us, dear Europe, because we are very sad. My life is very sad; . . . help me so I can be happy.

—Letter entitled "Dear Europe" by Rebecca Covaciu, twelve-year-old Roma child[a]

At age twelve, Rebecca Covaciu—big eyes, white teeth, beautiful smile— has lived through and seen so much that she has enough material for a memoir. Rebecca is a Romanian girl of the Roma ethnic group, and she has spent half of her life out on the street. She has slept in a van, in a makeshift shelter, and on the floor. On some days, she has begged on the streets of Spain and Italy with her parents. At other times, she has seen her makeshift shelter destroyed. She has been attacked by Italian police officers. She listened (hiding under a blanket) as her father was beaten up after he attempted to defend her. She has seen babies and children die due to a lack of medicines. She shared the fear of the Roma people fleeing from Ponticelli (Naples) when their camp was set fire to. . . . The family had not slept under a proper roof for five years. "In Romania, we had a home, but we had nothing to eat," explains Rebecca. "We ate thanks to charity from our neighbors. Then in Milan, my parents were unable to find work," she continues, "and we had to go out and beg. We couldn't go to school because we didn't have a home. But now they tell me I'll be able to go to school. . . . We built a shelter from cardboard and plastic under a bridge in the Giambellino district." "To eat, we used to go out begging at the antiques market. Only for a few hours, to make enough for the children to eat," assures her mother lowering her gaze. As we can see from Rebecca's drawings, she too went out begging on "sad days." Her brother, whom they call Ioni, played the accordion. . . . On April 24, the police prefect of Lombardy sent the bulldozers to the Milanese district of Giambellino with a large number of policemen in antiriot gear. The tiny settlement where the Covacius lived was destroyed in one minute. . . . Rebecca adds: "They told us we couldn't gather our things together because with the new government in power we would have to leave Italy."[b]

They brought me to a reception center, but I escaped. . . . They didn't let us go out, and they told me I had to go to school, but I didn't go to school even in my country . . . ; imagine if I go here in Italy! And I have to help my family, and in centers, they don't allow us to work, and how can I make money?

—Romanian separated child living in Rome[c]

Notes

a. The letter, "Dear Europe," and the series of drawings, "The Mice and the Stars," by Rebecca Covaciu are available at <http://www.everyonegroup.com/it> (accessed May 1, 2009).

b. Miguel Mora, "Querida Europa," *El País*, July 13, 2008, <http://www.every onegroup.com> (accessed May 1, 2009).

c. Nicola Mai, *Opportunità e sfide per l'intervento sociale rivolto a minori migranti* (Rome: Save the Children Italia, 2008), 62.

the final school-leaving qualification) and the duty to attend compulsory school on the same conditions as Italian children.[72] Nonetheless, some argue that the right to education refers only to statutory primary education, excluding kindergarten, secondary school, and vocational training.[73] In December 2007, the Municipality of Milan issued an ordinance preventing children of irregular non-EU migrants from enrolling in kindergarten. This provoked a debate on the right to education of undocumented children. Eventually, the court of Milan declared the measure to be discriminatory and contrary to the right to education, protected by the CRC and by domestic Italian legislation. The court held that the right to education included all school grades and every child, irrespective of the parents' legal status.[74] Notwithstanding the court's judgment, this interpretation is not always implemented, and undocumented children are often not accepted outside the compulsory school system, particularly in vocational training courses.

The right of undocumented children to health care is much less protected by Italian law than the right to education. The norms applied to undocumented adults also apply to children: the latter have no special guarantees. Undocumented migrants are entitled to care for urgent or essential ongoing treatment and inclusion in preventive medicine programs,[75] but they cannot register with the national health system, and they do not have access to specialists (such as pediatricians and dentists). The scope of urgent or essential treatment is often the subject of controversy.

Finally, Italian law guarantees separated children the right to shelter and social assistance until the age of majority on the same conditions as Italian children. These rights are denied to children accompanied by undocumented parents. Administrative provisions vary significantly across localities. Many municipalities do not allow undocumented adult migrants in reception centers or authorized nomad camps, although exceptions are sometimes made for the most vulnerable subjects (such as mothers with very young children) or for limited periods (such as the coldest months). Access to the private housing market has been made more difficult by provisions recently introduced by the Berlusconi government. These provisions increase penalties for those who profiteer by renting accommodation to non-EU undocumented migrants and provide for confiscation of the property.

In addition to these legal restrictions, there are practical obstacles to the access of undocumented children to school, health, and social services. First, the law is not always applied (for example, some schools make it difficult for undocumented children to enroll). Even when the law is properly applied, clearings of illegal settlements and expulsions often prevent children from continuing to attend school or receiving health care and support from social services.

The main obstacle, however, is the undocumented migrants' fear of detection. Undocumented parents often avoid any contact with services for fear of detection and expulsion or for fear that their child may be separated from them because of their irregular status, the lack of documents proving the family relationship, or their economic conditions.[76] Fear of being returned to their country of origin also hinders the access of separated children to services in towns and areas where coercive assisted repatriations are carried out.

Italian law prohibits health services from reporting undocumented non-EU migrants to police authorities, except in cases where the report is also compulsory for nationals.[77] No analogous provisions exist as far as other services are concerned. Public officers working in schools and social services are neither forbidden nor obligated to report irregular migrants. Worrisome changes in immigration law for non-EU citizens, abolishing the above-mentioned provision regarding health services, making irregular migration a crime (thus imposing a duty to report irregular migrants on public officers), and requiring a residence permit to access public services (including education and social services), are currently under discussion in parliament.[78] Large campaigns against "spy doctors and school directors," which are aimed at promoting the right of undocumented migrants to health and education (with particular attention to undocumented children), have been launched by NGOs and some politicians.[79] Even though the new provisions have not yet been enacted, the fear of detection has spread. For example, a considerable decrease in the number of irregular migrants using health services has been registered in a number of cities.[80]

Finally, the limited access to education, health, and social services is caused by a number of factors that are not directly related to the condition of undocumented children but are particularly prevalent among this group. The most significant of these factors is poverty. Many undocumented children (both accompanied and separated) do not attend school because they need to earn money to support themselves and their families. The wish to send money home is one of the main reasons that many separated children immediately leave reception centers. In those centers, they are not allowed to work before completing statutory education or to practice illegal activities that are often more profitable than legal jobs.

Moreover, some children are prevented from attending school and having access to other services by abusive adults who do not want to lose the profits they make by exploiting the children in a variety of ways.

A last, fundamental factor impinging on undocumented children's access to protection is the inadequacy of many services. School, health, and social services are often perceived by undocumented children and their parents as closed, hostile, and unsuited to their needs and wishes: mutual understanding among education, health, and social workers and migrants is hindered by the lack of interpreters and cultural mediators; racist attitudes are not uncommon, particularly against some groups, such as Roma; and reception centers often treat separated children in an infantilizing way that is unsuitable for children who have experienced dangerous journeys and street life and who perceive themselves as adults in charge of maintaining their family.

Protection from Exploitation and Violence

The lack of documents exposes children to exploitation and violence in different ways.[81] First, undocumented children and parents usually do not report being victims of exploitation, violence, and other illegal actions by private citizens or public officers because they fear expulsion or removal.[82] The situation of Roma is particularly dramatic: in 2008, numerous violent acts committed against individuals (often children) or settlements failed to produce adequate protective intervention by authorities.[83] The attack on the Ponticelli camp, near Naples, is the most well-known case,[84] but there have been dozens of other attacks, fires, and police raids, including illegal destruction of Roma property by the authorities.

Second, according to Italian law, non-EU citizens can legally work only if they have a residence permit. Undocumented children who want to earn money for themselves and contribute to their family's livelihood cannot work in the legal and protected labor market. As a consequence, many of them end up being exploited in sweat shops, in begging, in illegal activities (such as stealing and drug-selling) or in prostitution. In some cases, these children are trafficked by criminal organizations.

Finally, the lack of identification prevents the authorities from reconstructing previous contacts between the child and the institutions and makes it more difficult to take effective measures to protect the child. This problem is particularly serious for child victims of trafficking and exploitation, who usually leave shelters shortly after placement and are moved by criminal organizations from one city to another. For example,

Romanian children are frequently moved from Rome to Milan or from Turin to Paris. In the absence of means of identification, it is difficult to reconstruct these children's movements and take protective measures.[85]

Separation from Parents[86]

More and more frequently, undocumented children (both Roma and non-Roma) are separated from their family without an adequate assessment of the best interests of the child for reasons related to the lack of documents, to socioeconomic conditions, or to cultural factors. Separation produces further trauma in children that have often already experienced severe difficulties related to migration and to poverty, discrimination, and other human-rights violations both in their country of origin and in Italy. Situations vary depending on local practices. Procedural safeguards provided by Italian law and international conventions are sometimes not respected. For example, lawyers in several cities[87] reported that parents are not always provided with interpretation services in court proceedings concerning separation, foster care, or adoption. Cases have also been reported where mothers in difficult situations have been persuaded to give their child to a foster family for a limited period of time but have then been unable to get their child back.

As mentioned before, many children are separated from parents in detention or facing expulsion. Sometimes these children are left completely alone, with no protection. For example, lawyers in Turin reported cases of women expelled to Nigeria while their children were left in Italy. In at least one case, this separation occurred against the explicit request of the mother. In other cases, children of deportees have been left alone or handed over to inadequate caregivers (in one case, to a woman that had exploited the child's mother in prostitution).[88]

Another reason for separation of parent and child is the lack of documents proving the family relationship. Because there are no consistent norms and procedures at the national level on this issue, practices differ. Usually no measures are taken, but sometimes the child is separated from the adult so that the relationship between them can be verified. The justification for these separations is usually the fight against child trafficking. For example, following child-trafficking investigations against Albanian adults who had brought dozens of children into Italy, presenting them as their own children at the border, the juvenile court of Ancona started separating all children accompanied by parents who had no documents proving the family relationship (including asylum seekers).

Box 8.3

R., a Roma child about twelve years old, was arrested by the police for stealing. The child said that he lived in a nomad camp with his family. The policeman in charge of the case decided not to return the child immediately to the family, suspecting he was a non-Roma Italian child kidnapped by Roma. This suspicion was founded just on the fact that R. was blonde and with a fair complexion. The child's grandmother showed the Italian birth certificate and the school documents to the police, as well as other grandchildren resembling R., but she was prevented from seeing the child. R. was placed in a child welfare center. He was afraid and depressed, did not eat, and continuously asked to go back home to his family. He was allowed to go home only after the DNA test confirmed that the woman was his grandmother.[a]

According to information gathered by OsservAzione, on October 5, 2007, several police officers threatened to forcibly remove a five-year-old Romanian Roma child from her parents' care after having found the family sleeping on the sidewalk outside the Florence railway station. The police warned the girl's father, Mr. D.S., that they would take her to a closed children's institution called "Safe Center" for abandoned or mistreated children. Mr. D.S. and his wife Ms. D.S. informed OsservAzione that they objected, telling the police that they had nowhere to go and asked the officers for help. According to Ms. D.S., the police issued them a written warning later that day, which stated, "D.S. as father of Caldararu L.S., born in Romania on October 31, 2002, is warned not to force his daughter to live in a condition of discomfort by having her sleep on the streets and bringing her up in unhealthy and dangerous places." Otherwise, Italian authorities "would take the said minor to a safe place, that is to the Safe Center on Viale Corsica 34/b." The following day, the police returned and found the girl still sleeping on the sidewalk and took her away. In spite of testimony from a social worker that "when the girl was brought to the Safe Center, she looked serene, not afraid," on October 16, the Juvenile Court of Florence ordered as a temporary measure that L.S. be placed in a children's home and forbade Mr. and Ms. S. from seeing her outside the home or without the presence of a social worker. As of November 28, Mr. and Ms. S. had not been able to see L.[b]

They don't know what living amid mice and rubbish, in the cold, without food means. When we children beg, they say that our parents are bad, because they don't know that if we don't help each other . . . , we die of hunger. It's a bad world for us gypsies.[c]

Notes

a. Report of a social worker working in a child welfare center in Rome, November 11, 2008.

b. ERRC, Center on Housing Rights and Evictions (COHRE) et al., *Written Comments Concerning Italy for Consideration by the United Nations Committee on the Elimination of Racial Discrimination at Its 72nd session*, 2008, 18.

c. Statement of Rebecca Covaciu, after receiving the UNICEF 2008 prize, May 26, 2008. <http://www.everyonegroup.com/it> (accessed May 1, 2009).

Children were placed in reception centers while the lengthy process of verifying family relationships through DNA was conducted.[89]

Separations of children from their parents because of suspicions relating to the relationship are particularly frequent in the case of Roma families. Thus, the authorities sometimes separate children who do not meet the physical stereotype of the Roma or who resemble disappeared Italian children, as they suspect them of being kidnapped children. The Italian media have recently given extensive publicity to allegations about children kidnapped by Roma women, producing disproportionate reactions by the population and institutions.[90]

In some cases, mere poverty is a sufficient cause for separation. If the family lives in inadequate material conditions (on the street, in nomad camps, or in deserted buildings), authorities sometimes separate the child from the parents instead of providing support measures to the family as a whole. This clearly contradicts the principles set out in Italian law and international conventions, according to which a child should never be separated from his or her parents against his or her will, except when it is in the best interests of the child. Binding legal obligations require the authorities to provide parents with support and assistance (particularly with regard to nutrition, clothing, and housing) to assist them in implementing the right of a child to an adequate standard of living.[91]

In other cases, children are separated from their family of origin because the parents are charged with exploitation, abuse, or neglect of the child. In 2008, politicians supported by the mainstream Italian media carried out a vigorous campaign on the exploitation of Roma children by their parents and called for the separation of these children from their family.[92] This is a complex issue that should always be considered on a case-by-case basis. There are some serious cases where parents exploit their children through prostitution[93] or force them, with violence, to commit crimes or to beg. In most of these cases, separation may be necessary in the best interests of the child (unfortunately, authorities do not always intervene in these cases, which results in serious consequences for the children). But there are many cases where the parents do not commit any violence or abuse, and their failure to protect the child's rights is merely a product of extreme poverty and social marginality. For example, many Roma women begging with babies love and care for their child. For these mothers, begging is their only way to deal with extreme poverty and discrimination. They bring along the child to the street, not to exploit him or her but because they cannot leave the child alone at the camp. In these cases, support to the family (such as social assistance, opportunity to send the child to kindergarten, and support in finding a job), instead of separation, is a more appropriate response to promote the best interests of the child.

Some cases have been reported where even situations such as "the child eats with his or her hands" or "does not wear pajamas when sleeping" were deemed sufficient reasons for considering the Roma family unable to take care of the child and for enforcing family separation.[94] Some judges and social workers seem to think that Roma culture is incompatible with adequate care and protection of the rights of the child.

Ambivalent Policies between Rights Protection and Control

Undocumented accompanied children have the right to attend school, but they can be expelled at any moment and detained in detention centers with their parents without any specific protection. Roma children living in nomad camps are registered and identified to protect them from exploitation and to promote their access to services but also to verify whether they have entitlements to stay in Italy and, if they do not, to expel them with their families. Separated children are protected from expulsion, but they can be repatriated against their will and against the will of their parents.

The deep ambivalence of policies concerning undocumented children is evident. On the one hand, states commit to promote children's rights and social inclusion by adopting a series of legal norms. State parties to the CRC must ensure the rights provided by the Convention to every child within their jurisdiction without discrimination of any kind, irrespective of their nationality, immigration status, or statelessness.[95] In all actions concerning children, including undocumented children, the best interests of the child must be a primary consideration:[96] "Non-rights-based arguments, such as those relating to general migration control, cannot override best-interest considerations."[97] On the other hand, in the last several decades, states have approached migration with control policies and repression of illegal migration by means of expulsions, detention centers, borders militarization, and punishment of illegal migration as a crime. A similar logic of control and repression marks more and more policies concerning deviance. For example, in Italy, laws and local policies have been adopted or are under discussion to increase the use of detention as a measure to control petty crime (including juvenile crime) and criminalize street prostitution and begging.

These two opposite logics—child-rights protection on the one hand and the control of illegal migration and deviance on the other—constantly clash with policies concerning undocumented children, producing their deeply ambivalent character. This ambivalence is inherent and cannot be fully overcome, as it characterizes our very view of these children. Separated children are minors deprived of their family, living alone in a foreign country, and in need of our protection. At the same time, they are also young migrants with adultlike attitudes illegally entering the country to escape poverty and dangerous youngsters pushing drugs or selling their bodies, endangering social order. Small Roma children, for instance, need protection from exploitation and abuse but are also considered "dirty beggars" and "thieves pick-pocketing and stealing from our homes." They are vulnerable children but also dangerous and disturbing subjects that we would like to remove, jail, or expel.

Inconsistency, gaps, and ambiguous legislation are indications of this ambivalence and also conveniently flexible, since they allow an interpretation of the law more inclined to one or other logic, depending on the political moment, on the local context, and on individuals. Sometimes shifts from one position to its opposite happen in a short time, quite schizophrenically. For example, to demonstrate the political will to protect Roma children's rights after the criticism provoked by the census, the minister of the interior, Roberto Maroni, proposed granting Italian citizenship to all children born in Italy who lacked consistent parenting:

As the great majority of these [Roma] children do not have ascertainable parents, I think that state institutions and the Italian government must maintain them, give them a future and even citizenship immediately as a concrete sign that we consider them as children of this land.[98]

Only two months later, the minister's position radically changed: from granting citizenship, the policy switched to mandatory returns. While declaring his support for a bill providing assisted repatriation of separated children practicing prostitution, with accelerated and simplified procedures, Maroni asserted that "about half of the people registered within Roma camps are separated children and often exploited in prostitution."[99] So does the Italian government propose to return separated and sexually exploited Roma children to their country of origin, or does it advocate in favor of granting them Italian citizenship?

Ambivalence leads to different results depending on the policy area. With reference to children's rights strictly conceived, such as the right to primary education and the right to the protection of children deprived of their family, the protective approach tends to trump the migration-control strategy. In Italy, as in many other European countries,[100] there is no real challenge to the principle that undocumented children have the right to attend primary school and that the state must ensure shelter and assistance to separated children. These rights, in fact, may be narrowly tailored to children in a double sense. First, no extension of these rights after the child has come of age is permitted (this is also true for citizen children when they age out). Second, undocumented parents are not directly involved, as the child is autonomously entitled to these rights.

By contrast, ambivalence is particularly strong in those areas and for those groups that are most contiguous to the world of undocumented migrant adults and to migration-control issues—the legal status when the child comes of age, the return of separated children, and the treatment of children accompanied by undocumented parents. Separated children coming from non-EU states can get a residence permit "for minor age", but what happens when the child comes of age? Immigration law provides that a separated child can be issued a residence permit for study or employment purposes at the age of eighteen if he or she has a job or attends school, has accommodation, and meets the following requirements—that a guardian has been appointed to care for the child or that the child entered Italy before the age of fifteen and has taken part in an integration program for at least two years.[101] Every separated child has the right to be assigned a guardian, while few separated children in Italy are able to meet the latter requirements.

The interpretation and application of these provisions vary depending on different political trends and approaches by national governments and local police authorities. When migration-control considerations prevail over the child-right-protection approach, a restrictive interpretation of the law is applied. Separated children that are not able to demonstrate the requirements concerning the date of entry and the participation in a two-year integration program are not issued any residence permit once they come of age, even if they have a job or attend school and have a guardian.[102] As a consequence, these youngsters become irregular migrants that can be expelled at any time.[103] This produces serious rights violations not only when the child turns eighteen but also during minority. Depriving separated children of any prospect of legal residence past the age of eighteen is one of the main factors driving these children to refuse integration programs, to leave reception centers, and thus to risk exploitation in prostitution and illegal activities.

On the contrary, in periods and towns where the child-rights-protec-
tion approach has prevailed over migration control, separated children
have been offered the prospect of long-term integration in Italy (including the issuance of a residence permit once they come of age), irrespective
of the date of their arrival in Italy. Many of them have stayed in reception centers, attended school and vocational training courses, and found
legal jobs.[104]

A range of different approaches also applies to the assisted repatriation of separated children. In some cases, the child's best interests guide
the decision-making process; in others, returns are coerced even when
they are clearly against the best interests of the child. For example, from
1998 to 1999, police authorities forcibly returned more than thirty separated Albanian children living in Turin to Albania, even though the
children strongly opposed repatriation and said they wanted to study
and find jobs in Italy to send money home. Many of the children's
parents had incurred debts to pay for their journey to Italy and also
opposed their repatriation.[105] Most of the children came from isolated
villages in the Albanian mountains, where the opportunities for education, health care, and social assistance were very limited compared with
their prospects in Turin, where they had attended school and vocational
training courses and had employment prospects. Of a research sample
of 256 Albanian children repatriated from Italy between 1998 and 2000,
only 98 were still in Albania at the beginning of 2001, while 155 children
had emigrated again. Some of the children surveyed had been repatriated
two or three times.[106] It is implausible to suggest that repatriation was
in these children's best interests.

Coercive returns are often justified by notions of child rights, particularly the child's right to family unity in his or her country of origin.
Repatriation, it is argued, is generally in the best interests of the child,
irrespective of the expressed wishes of the child or parent and independent of any assessment of the comparative opportunities available in the
destination as opposed to the host country.[107] According to repatriation
advocates, the right to family unity should always prevail over the child's
right to have his or her views taken into account and to have access to
basic social and economic rights (including education, health, and adequate standard of living). This position reflects a restricted interpretation
of children's rights. According to the CRC, the child's best interests
should always be assessed on a case-by-case basis, with a holistic
approach, taking into account the whole range of rights provided by the
Convention.[108]

On the other hand, it seems clear that coercive returns have also advanced other strategic goals. They act as a powerful deterrent message to children and their families, demonstrating that migration to Italy as a minor "is no longer a worthwhile strategy."[109] This has been the view propounded not only by police authorities but also by some municipal representatives. Since the latter are often appointed by judges as guardians of separated children, their views are taken into account in the repatriation decision. However, there is some conflict of interest inherent in the role of these municipal representatives, since municipalities are also financially responsible for the reception of separated children. This dual engagement, as some judges have pointed out,[110] results in an ambiguous role. Safeguarding the best interests of children may clash directly with reducing fiscal output for the care of separated migrant children within the municipality's jurisdiction.

The treatment of children accompanied by undocumented parents probably illustrates the migration-control approach most clearly. The most effective way of protecting this group of children is to protect their parents, too, by guaranteeing to the whole family the right to stay and to access necessary services. Expulsion of parents, by contrast, produces serious violations of children's rights, both directly (when the child is expelled with the parent or separated from the expelled parent) and indirectly (when the parents avoid contact with state authorities for fear of being detected). In practice, however, access to regularization of status and to fundamental rights is even more elusive for undocumented parents than it is for their children. International obligations toward irregular adult migrants are much more limited than those provided by the CRC and other international instruments toward children. For example, the best-interests and nondiscrimination principles apply to every child irrespective of migration status, whereas no such generic protections apply to irregular adult migrants. Second, regularization of undocumented parents on the basis of their children's presence within the jurisdiction would (unlike the regularization of only separated children) produce protections for almost the whole irregular migrant population, potentially undermining the whole system of migration control.

As regularization of parents is not a viable solution, states react in three different ways. Some simply ignore the problem by overlooking the effects of family expulsion on the children involved. By contrast with the relatively well publicized circumstances of separated children, the situation of accompanied children facing family deportation or being excluded from access to basic services scarcely features in research, data collection, or public-policy discussions. Other authorities adopt a compromise solution, singling out the child (but not the parent) for protection. This second option is typically not much more effective in protecting children's rights than the first. Without their parents, children are severely hampered in their ability to access essential state institutions, but undocumented parents usually avoid any contact with officials. A classic scenario is an irregular accompanied child who is eligible for a residence permit "for minor age," but the undocumented parent risks expulsion by applying to the police for a permit. Similar practical obstacles hinder the access of children of undocumented parents to education, health, and social services.

The third state strategy is to regularize the status of the child who needs protection by separating him or her from the undocumented parents, in effect turning the child from an accompanied to a separated child. This occurs where states afford accompanied children access to shelter and assistance or other protections to avoid detention with the parent that is to be expelled. This option imposes a painful choice between two sets of fundamental rights—family life but no access to essential social assistance (and where the parent is detained, deprivation of liberty) or the enjoyment of shelter and personal liberty but violation of the right to family unity.

As a result of the deep ambivalence that characterizes official attitudes toward undocumented children, even laws and policies intended to protect children's rights are at times used to exercise control and legitimize rights violations. An interesting example is the recent antitrafficking rhetoric. NGOs advocating for child rights have frequently represented separated children in general as being victims of trafficking. Although this may be an accurate characterization of some separated children, it is not generally helpful for describing the circumstances of accompanied undocumented children. In fact, this approach can precipitate rights violations—for example, when authorities separate children from parents who are unable to prove their relationship with the child and presume an intent to traffic (guilty until proven innocent, in other words).

Another problematic example of a protective strategy with negative consequences is a proposal concerning the registration and documentation of children that has been presented by the left-wing Italian opposition. This proposal is advanced as a nondiscriminatory measure aimed at protecting undocumented children's rights, unlike the census and fingerprinting of Roma children carried out by the Berlusconi government, which it is intended to replace. Issuing an identity card to every child, irrespective of nationality and status, was advocated as a means to protect the child's right to identity and as a means of avoiding child trafficking.[111] In practice, however, an identity card (particularly a mandatory one) might be used for sweeping checks to verify children's legal status in schools or other services. It might even trigger repressive measures, such as the insistence that children present their identity card as a precondition for accessing school. In a deeply ambivalent context, where protective goals compete with strong pressures in favor of immigration control and social conformity, caution needs to be exercised when proposing laws and policies that might be used for purposes other than those intended.

How to Protect Undocumented Children's Rights in Ambivalent Contexts?

In this context of deep, even inherent ambivalence, what can be done to protect undocumented children's rights? Can some good practices and some risks to avoid be identified?

Useful recommendations regarding separated children have been developed at an international level. They include the already mentioned General Comment by the CRC Committee on the "Treatment of Unaccompanied and Separated Children Outside their Country of Origin"[112] and the Separated Children in Europe Program's (SCEP) "Statement of Good Practice."[113] These documents thoroughly analyze the general principles (such as nondiscrimination, best interest of the child, participation, and the right to life and development) and the specific recommendations (such as the appointment of a guardian and access to education and health care) that should be adopted to protect separated children's rights, according to both the CRC and other international instruments. Yet IGOs and NGOs urgently need to broaden their attention to include undocumented *accompanied* children, too, and to extend the application of the recommendations developed for separated children where they are applicable. For circumstances that are peculiar to accompanied children (such as the child's treatment when the parent is expected to be expelled or detained and access to shelter and social assistance), special policies need to be crafted.

Taking the CRC Committee and SCEP recommendations as the starting point and extending their scope to accompanied children, I focus on two different issues—registration and documentation of undocumented children and rights protection for those children who remain undocumented.

Registration and Documentation

The first objective is to minimize the number of children who are undocumented. A real solution could be crafting laws and practices on migration and citizenship that are much less restrictive than those in force in most countries at the moment. In the absence of these radical reforms, some important interventions may be carried out anyway.

First, a residence permit (such as the residence permit "for minor age" provided by Italian law)[114] should be issued to all irregular migrants under age eighteen, whether accompanied or separated, simply because they are children. There should also be an option to convert this permit into a residence permit for employment or study when the child comes of age. As far as children accompanied by undocumented parents are concerned, the current approach by which the child follows the (irregular) position of the parent should be reversed. Instead, regularization of parental status should be permitted where this is appropriate and necessary to protect the best interests of the child. Italian law already authorizes the juvenile court to grant irregular migrants permission to remain in Italy in cases where there are serious reasons related to the psychological and physical development of the child.[115] In such cases, the parent is issued a temporary child-care residence permit.[116] Despite some local variation reflecting the more or less restrictive interpretation of the relevant juvenile court, this certainly is an example of good practice. If the parent does not qualify for a residence permit and is therefore in no position to approach the authorities on behalf of the child, alternatives should be provided. Social services or "semiguardians,"[117] for example, should be able to apply for the child's residence permit, just as guardians do for separated children.

Second, birth registration and the provision of identity documents for all children born to undocumented parents should be promoted. It is crucial that measures to ensure birth registration of these children take into account not only the legal provisions necessary to establish a binding obligation on the authorities but also the practical procedures essential to overcome relevant obstacles, such as parents' fear of detection. A good example is the Italian law that prohibits the expulsion of a woman and her husband within six months of a child's birth,[118] a measure introduced to assuage undocumented parents' fear of detection. Promoting birth registration and access to identity documents is not only the responsibility of the destination state. Countries of origin should also assist in the documentation of children of citizens by instructing their consulates to issue passports to irregular migrants, encourage birth registration, and record children born in the destination country on the citizen parent's passport.

Third, registration of undocumented children should promote access to legal identity and human rights and should not be an instrument of immigration control. Birth registration and provision of identity documents must therefore be the responsibility of agencies that are separate from and do not transmit information to migration-control authorities. For example, the residence permit "for minor age" is considered a child-protection measure and is issued to separated children to provide them with an identity document and guarantee them full access to health, education, social services, and employment. But the residence permit is issued by the police authorities, and the child is fingerprinted when applying for it. There are, at present, no guarantees that these data will not be used for facilitating coercive repatriation or expulsion once the child ages out. The risks related to the state's ambivalent stance toward undocumented children would be significantly reduced if the rights-promoting registration document were issued by an authority with no direct links to migration control enforcement, the registry office being one of them.

Fourth, procedures for registration and documentation must safeguard the child's dignity and not be discriminatory and stigmatizing. A political and cultural analysis of biometric registration (such as fingerprinting, retinal scans, and DNA) and its objectives, results, and risks (such as privacy violations and discrimination) is urgently needed. This would include a careful assessment of the social meaning of relevant official requirements. For example, fingerprinting is likely to be perceived as a discriminatory and stigmatizing procedure if it is associated with criminal suspects. Moreover, a technical analysis of the reliability of different measures, particularly when used on children, is necessary. Experts, for instance, debate whether child fingerprints are reliable as unique individual indicators and, if so, from what age. EU legislation requires fingerprints of third-country nationals from the age of six years for the issuance of residence permits. The European Parliament Civil Liberties Committee, however, suggests that children under age twelve should no longer have their fingerprints included on passports issued in the European Union, as "experience has shown that children's fingerprints are not of sufficient quality, especially those of the youngest children, which can change greatly as they grow older."[119]

Finally, to protect children's rights, registration should always be carried out in the presence of the child's parent or guardian, and child-friendly procedures should be used. Interviews to collect social histories from children should therefore be conducted by suitably trained social workers.

Rights Protection Irrespective of Possession of Legal Identity

Although registration and documentation should be promoted, it is also crucial to protect the rights of children who remain undocumented. Despite legal reforms and procedural improvements, some children will remain undocumented—as a result of implementation failures by the authorities, of lack of awareness by migrants, or of a choice by children and parents not to emerge from clandestine living. The following section discusses recommendations for the extension of fundamental rights protections already proposed for separated children (by the CRC Committee and by NGOs such as SCEP) to undocumented accompanied children.

Return and Detention   A child should never be returned to the country of origin unless it is in his or her best interests to do so and unless the necessary safeguards, including investigations in the country of origin, have been implemented. Moreover, children should never be detained solely for reasons related to their immigration status.

Specific recommendations on the return of and freedom from detention for children accompanied by undocumented parents should be developed. For example, procedures need to be established for determining whether it is in the best interests of the child to be returned and detained with his or her parents or separated from the family if the parents are to be removed. Consideration should also be given to the development of alternatives to the harsh choice between detention and separation from the parents. Furthermore, adequate age-assessment procedures (including consideration of psychological and cultural factors, benefit of the doubt, and holistic approaches) should be adopted to minimize the risk of treating children as adults.

Access to Education, Health, and Social Services and Adequate Living Conditions   First, every child should have the right to access education, health, and social services and adequate living conditions (including government support for family nutrition, clothing, and housing) on the same terms as national children and irrespective of the child's nationality, immigration status, or possession of identity documents. No distinctions, even concerning access to shelter and social services, should be made between separated children and undocumented accompanied children.

Second, measures should be taken to address the fear of detection and expulsion, which is one of the key practical obstacles preventing undocumented children from accessing services. An important step here would be to ensure that service agencies are instructed not to report undocumented migrants to the police simply because of their irregular migration status (Italian law already stipulates this for health services).[120] Moreover, providing a sort of semiguardianship for children accompanied by undocumented parents might be useful. A third person (such as a care worker) might represent the child in relations with education, health, and social services (for example, enrolling the child in school) without separating the child from his or her parents or depriving the latter of parental responsibility.[121]

Separation from Parents Children should never be separated from their parents if this is against their best interest for reasons solely related to migration status, lack of identity documents, or economic conditions. Procedural safeguards concerning separation provided by national law and international conventions (such as the right of the parent and the child to participate in the proceedings) should be fully respected.

When parents do not have documents proving the relationship, adequate procedures for assessing family relationship should be adopted. These should be based on psychosocial assessments, with DNA tests as a supplementary and voluntary tool. The automatic separation of children from parents should be avoided. Separation should be decided on a case-by-case basis—for example, where there is suspicion of abuse or exploitation of the child by the adult or where there are clear signs casting doubt on the relationship (such as when the child and the adult speak different languages). If the living conditions of the family are inadequate, support and assistance should be provided to the parents instead of separating them from the child.

Trust and Respect
Aside from the specific recommendations previously listed, the key for establishing more effective child-protection policies and interventions, given the radical ambivalence of the authorities toward this population,

is creating a relationship of trust and—as Jacqueline Bhabha stresses in her introduction—respecting the views and wishes of children and their parents. Trust is fundamental for children and their parents to overcome their fear of being detected and expelled when accessing education, health, and social services. Experience has demonstrated that undocumented children leave street life if they have built up trust in social workers (through outreach work) and if they are offered an integration program that meets their needs and wishes (the possibility of work, accommodation that is not infantilizing, and the prospect of legal residence after majority).[122] To promote communication, social workers need to leave traditional services and meet children and their families where they live and work (on the streets, in illegal settlements, and so on) and use cultural mediators.

Building a relationship of trust with undocumented children (and their families) and respecting their wishes are difficult given the ambivalent context, with its swings between rights protection and harsh migration control. For example, a group of separated children who agreed to be registered, to have their identity recorded, and to take part in an integration program were coercively repatriated by Italian authorities between 1998 and 2000. This incident ruptured the relationship of trust built up between social workers and the larger undocumented child population, and many who had been living in reception centers left and returned to living on the streets.[123] In this complex and unpredictable environment, it is often hard for children and their advisers to assess whether it is better to "come out" and be registered to qualify for rights or to remain underground and avoid the risks of return. Advisers have an obligation to inform undocumented migrants of the pros and cons in this situation and to respect the choice they make, even if it is to remain undocumented.[124]

Notes

1. See Italy's ministry of the interior, "Il ministro Maroni ha illustrato a Montecitorio le linee programmatiche del dicastero," August 25, 2008, <http://www.interno.it> (accessed May 1, 2009).

2. Vania Mancini, *Cheja' Celen: Ragazze che ballano* (Roma: Edizioni Sensibili alle Foglie, 2007), 43.

3. Large nomad camps were established by Italian municipalities beginning in the late 1970s to guarantee the right of Roma to a nomadic life style. Today, however, people living in these camps are mostly sedentary. In addition to authorized camps, many unauthorized settlements have appeared in the last ten years.

The great majority of people living in both authorized and unauthorized camps are Roma who either recently migrated from Romania, arrived from the former Yugoslavia in the 1960s or after the Balkan wars in the 1990s, or belong to groups that have lived in Italy for centuries and are therefore Italian citizens.

4. Ordinances of the President of the Council of Ministers, no. 3673, 3676, 3677, May 30, 2008, art. 1, sec. 2: Urgent Civil Protection Provisions to Tackle the State of Emergency in Relation to Settlements of Nomad Communities in the Regions of Campania, Lazio, and Lombardia.

5. Decree of the President of the Council of Ministers, Declaration of the State of Emergency with Regard to Settlements of Nomad Communities in the Regions of Campania, Lazio, and Lombardia, May 21, 2008. The decree applied the civil protection law that concerns emergency situations resulting from natural disasters. The Berlusconi government, elected in April 2008 following a xenophobic and racist campaign, justified the declaration of the state of emergency by referring to crimes that were heavily covered by the media and that were supposedly committed by Roma against Italian citizens. A good analysis of these provisions and xenophobic speeches by Italian politicians and the media may be found in European Roma Rights Centre (ERRC), Open Society Institute (OSI) et al., *Security a la Italiana: Fingerprinting, Extreme Violence and Harassment of Roma in Italy*, available at <http://www.errc.org> (accessed July 7, 2010).

6. Examples are the right to be informed when subject to an administrative procedure (such as fingerprinting) and the requirement that persons be dangerous or suspect or refuse to identify themselves before undergoing identity screening involving photographing, fingerprinting, and so on.

7. See preambles of the Ordinances of the President of the Council of Ministers, nos. 3673, 3676, 3677.

8. European Parliament, Resolution on the Census of the Roma on the Basis of Ethnicity in Italy, July 10, 2008, <http://www.europarl.europa.eu> (accessed May 1, 2009).

9. Some of the most important positions against the census of Roma in Italy are available on the Web site of Sucar Drom, an Italian nongovernmental organization (NGO), <http://www.sucardrom.blogspot.com> (accessed May 1, 2009).

10. The decree ordered the census of "people living in nomad settlements" with no reference to Roma ethnicity. Roma people who lived outside these settlements (no data are available) were not targeted by the census.

11. Besides the ethnic basis of the target, the provision was criticized as discriminatory for a number of other reasons. These included the use of emergency legislation by way of derogation from ordinary laws, the registration of information concerning ethnicity and religion, the lack of guarantees for privacy and protection of personal data, and the lack of specific provisions for registration of children (such as the need for authorization of parents or legal guardians). Following strong national and international criticism, the government revised initial provisions. The revisions provided that biometrics must be taken only where identification based on other means is not possible, ethnicity and religion must not be registered, and specific guarantees for personal data protection and

for identification of children must be taken. See Guidelines of the Ministry of the Interior for Implementing Ordinances no. 3676, 3677, 3673, July 17, 2008. These last provisions have been considered by the EU Commission as not in contrast with European legislation (statement by Jaques Barrot reported in "Impronte, la Ue assolve l'Italia. Maroni: Fa giustizia di tutte le accuse," *La Repubblica*, September 5, 2008, 2.

12. See, for example, Stefano Rodotà, "La società del controllo e la democrazia inquinata," *La Repubblica*, July 1, 2008, 1.

13. Gad Lerner, "Quel censimento etnico di settanta anni fa," *La Repubblica*, July 5, 2008, 1.

14. Silvio Berlusconi, prime minister, cited in *La Repubblica*, July 15, 2008, <http://www.repubblica.it> (accessed May 1, 2009).

15. Roberto Maroni, minister of the interior, cited in *La Repubblica*, June 29, 2009, and July 10, 2009, <http://www.repubblica.it> (accessed May 1, 2009).

16. Franco Frattini, minister of foreign affairs, cited in *La Repubblica*, June 30, 2009, <http://www.repubblica.it> (accessed May 1, 2009).

17. Mariastella Gelmini, minister of education, cited in *La Repubblica*, June 30, 2009, <http://www.repubblica.it> (accessed May 1, 2009).

18. United Nations (UN) Committee on the Rights of the Child, "CRC General Comment No. 6 (2005): Treatment of Unaccompanied and Separated Children outside Their Country of Origin," September 1, 2005, CRC/GC/2005/6, sec. 31, <http://www.unhcr.org> (accessed July 29, 2009).

19. European Parliament Civil Liberties Committee, "Biometric Passports: No Fingerprinting of under-Twelves," Press release, September 15, 2008, <http://www.europarl.europa.eu> (accessed May 1, 2009).

20. The sources of information and data reported in the following sections derive from various sources. First, I used research and analysis of laws and practices concerning separated children and child victims of trafficking and exploitation that I carried out or took part in as coordinator of "Migrant Children" for Save the Children Italia from 2001 to 2007. See Save the Children Web site, <http://www.savethechildren.it/2003/progetti.asp?id=102&n_pag=9> (accessed May 1, 2009); Gruppo Nazionale Enti e Servizi di Pronta Accoglienza Minori, "Le procedure e le buone prassi nei confronti dei minori stranieri non accompagnati," <http://www.grupponazionalepam.it> (accessed May 1, 2009); Elena Rozzi, "The Situation of EU and Non-EU Separated Children in Italy," *E-migrinter* 2 (2008), <http://www.mshs.univ-poitiers.fr> (accessed May 1, 2009). Second, I conducted informal interviews with social workers and lawyers who worked in different cities (Rome, Turin, Florence, Milan, Naples, and Genoa) in 2008. Third, I used reports and research produced by NGOs and institutions (references in footnotes); scientific articles published mostly in the reviews *Minori giustizia* and *Diritto, immigrazione e cittadinanza*; press releases and articles, most from *La Repubblica*, <http://www.repubblica.it>. And finally, I used legislation and case-law that are for the most part available on the Associazione per gli Studi Giuridici sull'Immigrazione Web site (ASGI) at <http://

www.asgi.it> (accessed May 1, 2009). This chapter was finished in May 2009, so changes to the law and practice after this date are not considered.

21. Hereafter, the word *parents* stands for "parents or other previous legal or customary primary caregivers."

22. I consider undocumented migrants who do not apply for asylum or had their asylum application rejected but do not analyze the asylum system. I also do not deal with legislation that specifically concerns people who have been victims of trafficking and exploitation.

23. Other documents, such as birth certificates, may be used for proving age, place of birth, or family relationships, although they are not considered identity documents.

24. Non-EU citizens are required to have a passport to get almost any kind of visa and residence permit (D.P.R. 394/99, arts. 5 and 9), with a few exceptions, such as asylum seekers and victims of trafficking and exploitation. EU citizens must have an identity card or passport to enter Italy and to register their residence (Legislative Decree n. 30/2007, arts. 7 and 9).

25. For example, Moroccan and Nigerian consulates in Italy.

26. This happens mostly in countries where there are no effective birth registration systems, such as some African states.

27. According to article 1 of the 1954 Convention Relating to the Status of Stateless Persons (hereafter 1954 Statelessness Convention), a legally or *de jure* stateless person is someone "who is not considered as a national by any State under the operation of its law." UN General Assembly, Convention Relating to the Status of Stateless Persons, September 28, 1954, United Nations, *Treaty Series*, vol. 360, p. 117, <http://www.unhcr.org> (accessed July 27, 2009).

28. According to the *ius sanguinis* principle, individuals acquire Italian citizenship at birth if they are children of Italian citizens (Law no. 91/92, art. 1, par. 1). Children born in Italy to foreign parents can get Italian citizenship when they come of age if they can prove they have legally resided in Italy from birth to the age of eighteen years with no interruptions (Law no. 91/92, art. 4, par. 2). Hence, undocumented children, who cannot prove the legal residence also cannot acquire citizenship when they come of age.

29. D.P.R. 396/2000, art. 30.

30. Some registry offices, such as those in Florence, do not allow foreign unmarried parents to recognize children at birth unless they have a certificate by the consulate of their country of origin allowing the recognition of illegitimate children. According to administrative provisions at the local level, such as those in Naples, irregular migrants are allowed to register their child at birth only if they have a valid identity document or accept being identified by two witnesses or by police authorities.

31. Bill "on security," A.C. 2180/2009, art. 45, par. 1, item f, Camera dei Deputati Web site, <http://www.camera.it> (accessed May 1, 2009).

32. See ASGI Web site, Conseguenze dell'art. 45, comma 1, lett. F) del ddl C. 2180 sul diritto del minore a essere registrato alla nascita, March 9, 2009 <www

.asgi.it> (accessed May 1, 2009); "Per i clandestini figli invisibili: non potranno registrarli," *La Repubblica*, March 12, 2009, 1.

33. According to the *ius sanguinis* principle, the child is ineligible for his or her parents' citizenship if he or she is not able to prove the family relationship.

34. A recently reported case refers to a child who was born in Naples to an undocumented woman and was separated from her mother because she lacked identity documents. See "Fermata dopo il parto, bufera a Napoli," *La Repubblica*, April 2, 2009, 15.

35. Legislative Decree no. 30/2007, arts. 7 and 9.

36. Legislative Decree, no. 286/98.

37. See the section titled Lack of Documents, Lack of Rights.

38. D.P.R. no. 394/99, art. 28, item a.

39. In some cases, non-EU separated children can get a residence permit for employment or study purposes when they come of age, but in other cases they cannot. The problem of the legal migration status when the child comes of age is dealt with in the section titled Ambivalent Policies between Rights Protection and Control.

40. For example, most separated children want to earn money immediately to send it home, but when they live in reception centers, they are not allowed to work before completing statutory education.

41. The issuing of a residence permit "for minor age" concerns non-EU children, while for separated EU children residence registration is provided. Most of the above-mentioned considerations concerning regularization of separated non-EU children can be extended to separated EU children.

42. Italian Government, *Report to the Committee on the Elimination of Racial Discrimination—CERD/C/ITA/15* (2006), sec. 175.

43. ERRC, Center on Housing Rights and Evictions (COHRE) et al., "Written Comments Concerning Italy for Consideration by the United Nations Committee on the Elimination of Racial Discrimination at Its 72nd session," 2008, 30.

44. The Committee for Foreign Minors is the authority responsible for the census of separated non-EU children at the national level. Since Romania became part of the EU on January 1 , 2007, data on separated Romanian children are no longer collected by the Committee for Foreign Minors. The most up-to-date data available are from December 31, 2006. See Associazione Nazionale Comuni d'Italia (ANCI), *Minori stranieri non accompagnat: Secondo Rapporto ANCI 2007* (Rome: ANCI, 2008), 16.

45. The most significant countries of origin are Morocco (19.8 percent), Albania (17.2 percent), Palestine (14 percent), Egypt (10.7 percent), and Afghanistan (7.1 percent). See Gruppo di Lavoro per la Convenzione sui Diritti dell'Infanzia e dell'Adolescenza (Gruppo di Lavoro per la CRC), *I diritti dell'infanzia e dell'adolescenza in Italia. 4° Rapporto di aggiornamento sul monitoraggio della Convenzione sui diritti dell'infanzia e dell'adolescenza in Italia 2007–2008* (Roma: Save the Children Italia, 2008), 111.

46. Estimate by Iniziative e studi sulla multietnicità (ISMU), "Record di irregolari nel 2008: Sono circa 650 mila," *ISMUnews newsletter* 6 (October 8, 2008), <http://www.ismu.org> (accessed May 1, 2009).

47. ERRC, COHRE et al., *Written Comments Concerning Italy*, 4.

48. Anticipated results from the 2008 census in Lazio, Lombardia, and Campania regions. See *La Repubblica*, "Censimento rom," October 16, 2008, 25. Similar data resulted in censuses carried out in other areas (for example, in the province of Turin).

49. The term *undocumented* is shorthand that covers both types of irregular situation—absence of identity documents and irregular migration status. As used in this chapter, the term applies to more than children who literally have no identity documents at all. We use this value-neutral term in preference to the term *illegal*, which we consider inappropriate as a qualifier for any person.

50. With a few exceptions, such as the return of separated EU-citizen children (see below).

51. Information on returns, detention, and age assessment can be found in Amnesty International (AI), *Invisibili: I diritti umani dei minori migranti e richiedenti asilo detenuti all'arrivo alla frontiera marittima italiana* (Roma: AI 2006); AI, *Fuori dal buio: Un anno dalla parte dei minori migranti* (Roma: AI, 2007); Commission Appointed by the Ministry of the Interior for Inspections and Strategies of the Centers, *Report* (Rome, 2007), 21; see Ministry of the Interior Web site, <http://www.interno.it/assets/files/1/2007131181826.pdf> (accessed May 1, 2009); Gruppo di Lavoro per la Convenzione sui Diritti dell'Infanzia e dell'Adolescenza, *I diritti dell'infanzia e dell'adolescenza in Italia*, 85–89. I focus on the situation of children who are already in the state and do not deal with serious rights violations concerning access to the territory (such as refoulements and the deaths of thousands of migrants trying to cross the Mediterranean Sea).

52. Legislative Decree no. 286/98, art. 19, par. 2, item a.

53. Usually age assessment is carried out only through wrist-bone X-ray or, less frequently, tooth examination, not taking into account the cultural and ethnic background of the child. Although these methods result in estimates with a certain margin of error, the benefit-of-the-doubt principle is rarely applied (Commission Appointed by the Ministry of the Interior for Inspections and Strategies of the Centers, *Report*, 21). As a consequence, many teenagers are wrongly identified and treated as adults. Amnesty International also reported cases of separated children, apparently much younger than age eighteen, who were detained.

54. Legislative Decree no. 286/98, art. 33; D.P.C.M. 535/99.

55. Family tracing and investigations in the country of origin are carried out by NGOs or intergovernmental organizations (IGOs). Currently, they are conducted by IOM.

56. This issue is analyzed in more detail in the section titled Ambivalent Policies between Rights Protection and Control.

57. The total number of assisted repatriations ordered by the Committee for foreign minors has decreased in the last years. After a peak in the biennium 2002–2003 (417 repatriation orders), the number decreased in 2004–2005 (234 orders) and reached almost zero in 2006 (8 orders). See ANCI, *Minori stranieri non accompagnati*, 24.

58. Bill on Prostitution, no. 1079/2008, art. 2, sec. 2.

59. Legislative Decree no. 286/98, art. 19, par. 2, item a.

60. Ministry of the Interior's Directive, August 30, 2000. Irregular migrants can be detained in detention centers up to two months, but an extension to six months is under discussion in parliament.

61. With the exception of separated Romanian children, as explained below.

62. Legislative Decree no. 30/2007, art. 21. The Berlusconi government tried to extend the possibility of detention and immediate expulsion to EU citizens staying irregularly (that is, not having registered their residence after three months), but the proposal was stopped by the European Commission in October 2008 as in contrast with Directive 2004/38/CE.

63. Legislative Decree no. 30/2007, art. 20, sec. 5.

64. Fifty-two out of a total number of seventy-six children registered as "separated children" by juvenile justice authorities confided to the peer educators and social workers of Save the Children Italia that they lived with their parents or close relatives in Rome. Save the Children Italia, *Rapporto annuale 2005–2006: Progetto "Orizzonti a colori"* (Rome: Save the Children Italia, 2006), 16.

65. Agreement between Italy and Romania on cooperation for the protection of Romanian separated children in Italy, signed June 9, 2008, <http://www1 .interno.it/mininterno/export/sites/default/it/assets/files/15/0287_accordo_ITA _ROM.pdf> (accessed May 1, 2009).

66. This right is not explicitly provided by the law. A ministry of the interior memorandum provides only that police authorities "register the wish of the child to return to his or her country of origin." Ministry of the Interior memorandum, no. 246, January 20, 2009.

67. "Da Natale i rimpatri bimbi romeni, migliaia in lista,," *Agenzia Giornalistica Italia (AGI)*, December 4, 2008.

68. Information on the access of undocumented migrants to services can be found in Gruppo di Lavoro per la CRC, *I diritti dell'infanzia e dell'adolescenza in Italia*, 81–83, 111–115, 144–147; ERRC, COHRE, et al., *Written Comments Concerning Italy*, 4–5, 12–14, 21–22; Nicola Mai, *Opportunità e sfide per l'intervento sociale rivolto a minori migranti* (Rome: Save the Children Italia, 2008); PICUM, *Undocumented Children in Europe: Invisible Victims of Immigration Restrictions* (Brussels: PICUM, 2008).

69. ANCI, *Minori stranieri non accompagnati*, 52. Save the Children Italy reported that one-third of the 1,117 separated children who arrived in Lampedusa and were placed in reception centers in Sicily left the centers almost immediately. Press release, October 29, 2008, <http://www.savethechildren.it> (accessed May 1, 2009).

70. ERRC, COHRE, et al., *Written Comments Concerning Italy*, 22–23.

71. Council of Europe, European Commission against Racism and Intolerance (ECRI), *Third Report on Italy, Adopted on 16 December 2005*, May 16, 2006, CRI(2006)19, sec. 97, <http://www.unhcr.org> (accessed July 29, 2009).

72. Legislative Decree no. 286/98, art. 38; D.P.R. no. 394/99, art. 45.

73. According to Italian law, school is compulsory for children from ages six through sixteen.

74. Court of Justice of Milan, I Civil Section, ordinance no. 2380, February 11, 2008, <http://www.meltingpot.org> (accessed May 1, 2009).

75. Legislative Decree no. 286/98, art. 35, par. 3.

76. See next paragraph on separation from parents.

77. Legislative Decree no. 286/98, art. 35, par. 5.

78. Bill on Security, A.C. 2180/2009, art. 21, par. 1, item a and art. 45, par. 1, item t.

79. See Divieto di segnalazione, <http://www.divietodisegnalazione.medicisen zafrontiere.it> (accessed May 1, 2009); "Fini: immorale la norma sui medici spia," *La Repubblica*, March 13, 2009, 9; "Presidi-spia, Fini frena Maroni," *La Repubblica*, May 5, 2009, 1. The above-mentioned changes were proposed and supported by the Lega Nord party, which is one of the most racist and xeno-phobic parties in Europe and has significant power within the Berlusconi govern-ment, while members of the postfascist party, Alleanza Nazionale, took the position against these proposals.

80. "I volontari: fuga già iniziata stranieri diminuiti del 20%," *La Repubblica*, February 10, 2009, 5.

81. I mention some aspects that *directly* relate to the lack of documents but do not address the entire range of complex issues concerning migrant and Roma children's vulnerability to exploitation, violence, and trafficking.

82. A residence permit "for social protection" can be issued to victims of traf-ficking, violence, and exploitation, but these provisions are applied in limited and discretionary ways.

83. ERRC, OSI et al., *Security a la Italiana*, 11–18.

84. On May 13–14, 2008, following the alleged kidnapping of an Italian child by a Roma girl, a group of about 400 people attacked a Roma camp in Ponticelli (Naples), and several Roma settlements were set on fire.

85. Information on child victims of trafficking and exploitation can be found in Francesca Borello, Valeria Ferraris, et al., *La strada dei diritti: Prassi e modelli di intervento per l'accoglienza e l'inclusione sociale dei minori di strada sfruttati e/o coinvolti in attività illegali* (Rome: Save the Children Italia, 2007); Salvatore Fachile, Elena Rozzi, et al., *Protocollo di identificazione e supporto dei minori vittime di tratta e di sfruttamento* (Rome: Save the Children Italia, 2007).

86. Information concerning the separation of Roma children from their parents is drawn from ERRC, OSI, et al., *Security a la Italiana*, 18–19; ERRC, COHRE, et al., *Written Comments Concerning Italy*, 18; and the summary of research

(still unedited) conducted by the Fondazione Migrantes (CEI) on adoption and fostering of Roma children over the last twenty years in Italy. Press release, Fondazione Migrantes, November 10, 2008. Other sources of information on the separation of both Roma and non-Roma children are informal interviews with lawyers and social workers in several cities.

87. Interviews with lawyers working in Florence, Rome, and Genoa, October 2008.

88. Interviews with lawyers working in Turin, October 2008.

89. Gruppo Nazionale Enti e Servizi di Pronta Accoglienza Minori, Save the Children Italia, Progetto Equal PALMS, *Le procedure e le buone prassi nei confronti dei minori stranieri non accompagnati* (Rome, 2006), 7.

90. An interesting analysis of cases of supposed kidnappings of children by Roma women in Italy over the last twenty years can be found in Sabrina Tosi Cambini, *La zingara rapitrice: Racconti, denunce, sentenze (1986–2007)* (Rome: CISU, 2008). According to this research, most of the cases reported by the media did not result in any criminal proceedings because there was not enough evidence. Very few proceedings ended with a conviction for attempted kidnapping, and no one was convicted for kidnapping.

91. See CRC, arts. 9 and 27.

92. See, for example, "Campi rom, la stretta di Maroni: Basta illegalità, li chiudiamo tutti," *La Repubblica*, June 17, 2008, 2.

93. For example, the inquiry called "Fiori nel Fango" (2006–2007) carried out by the police in Rome discovered about thirty children exploited in prostitution, some of them by or with the involvement of their parents. See Gruppo di Lavoro per la CRC, *I diritti dell'infanzia e dell'adolescenza in Italia*, 147.

94. Press release, Fondazione Migrantes, Rome, November 10, 2008.

95. Article 2 of the CRC stipulates: "States Parties shall respect and ensure the rights set forth in the present Convention to each child within their jurisdiction without discrimination of any kind, irrespective of the child's or his or her parent's or legal guardian's race, colour, sex, language, religion, political or other opinion, national, ethnic or social origin, property, disability, birth or other status." The CRC Committee has clarified that "[T]he enjoyment of rights stipulated in the Convention is not limited to children who are citizens of a state party and must therefore, if not explicitly stated otherwise in the Convention, also be available to all children—including asylum-seeking, refugee and migrant children—irrespective of their nationality, immigration status or statelessness." Committee on the Rights of the Child's General Comment no. 6, sec.12.

96. CRC, art. 3(1).

97. Committee on the Rights of the Child's General Comment no. 6, sec. 86.

98. "Maroni: daremo la cittadinanza ai bambini rom senza genitori," *La Repubblica*, July 22, 2008, 11.

99. "Prostituzione: ddl; Maroni, obiettivo più sicurezza urbana," ANSA, September 11, 2008.

100. PICUM, *Undocumented Children in Europe*, 16.

101. Legislative Decree no. 286/98, art. 32, amended by law no. 189/2002.

102. Notwithstanding case law by Corte Costituzionale (sentence no. 198/2003) and Consiglio di Stato (sentence no. 1681/2005) that says that this interpretation contravenes the Italian constitution, the ministry of the interior did not give instructions to police authorities to apply the law according to the Supreme Courts' case law until March 2008. Until that moment, many local police authorities applied the restrictive interpretation.

103. They can be even more easily expelled than other migrants, as they were identified (including fingerprints) when they were issued a residence permit "for minor age."

104. In my thesis, I analyzed the impact of different norms and practices regarding the issuance of a residence permit at age eighteen on social-inclusion processes of separated children in Turin. About the situation in Rome and Milan, see Mai, *Opportunità e sfide per l'intervento sociale rivolto a minori migranti*; Rita Bichi, ed., *Separated children: I minori stranieri non accompagnati* (Milano: Franco Angeli, 2008).

105. Data and information reported by juvenile judges, representatives of the municipality of Turin, and social workers. Similar cases are also reported in some repatriation orders provided by the Committee for Foreign Minors in 2001 concerning Albanian and Moroccan children living in Turin and in Trento that I could analyze during research and advocacy activities.

106. Servizio Sociale Internazionale Sezione italiana, Istituto Psicanalitico per le Ricerche Sociali, *I minori albanesi non accompagnati: Una ricerca coordinata fra Italia e Albania* (Rome: SSISI, 2001), 35–51.

107. For example, this position was expressed by the representative of the Committee for Foreign Minors, Mauro Valeri, in several conferences. See, e.g., Caritas, *Soli per il mondo: L'immigrazione minorile tra problemi e risorse* (Rome, 2001).

108. I do not mean that staying in the host country is always in the best interests of the child. I argue that several factors should be taken into account in a case-by-case, best-interest-of-the-child assessment, including the child's views, the available opportunities in the destination compared to the host country and the right to family unity. I analyze this issue in Elena Rozzi, "Evaluation de l'intérêt supérior de l'enfant dans le choix entre rester dans le pays d'accueil ou le repatriement: une réflexion basée sur la Convention des droits de l'enfant," *Journal du Droits des Jeunes*, no. 219 (2002): 22–37.

109. For example, police authorities, juvenile judges, and representatives of the municipality of Turin expressed this kind of position in 1998 and 1999. ASGI, *Atti del seminario "Minori stranieri irregolari: Quale tutela?"* (Turin, 1999).

110. For example, the juvenile attorney in Trento. See <http://www.garantemi nori.regione.marche.it/documenti/turri.doc> (accessed May 1, 2009).

111. Italian identity cards include a photograph of the person but not fingerprints. They are not considered stigmatizing but are less effective than identification cards that include fingerprints.

112. CRC Committee, no. 6 (2005).

113. SCEP, *Statement of Good Practice,* <http://www.separated-children-europe -programme.org> (accessed May 1, 2009).

114. D.P.R. no. 394/99, art. 28, item a.

115. Legislative Decree no. 286/98, art. 31, sec. 3. For more on the interpretation of this provision, see Maria Grazia Domanico, "I gravi motivi connessi con lo sviluppo del bambino per farlo rimanere in Italia," *Minori giustizia* 3 (2008): 52–59. This provision has considerable potential since the developmental needs of the child include access to healthy and stable care, not just access to medical intervention to address illness.

116. The child-care residence permit allows the parent to work, but it cannot be converted into a residence permit for employment reasons.

117. The proposal concerning "semiguardians" is explained below.

118. Legislative Decree no. 286/98, art. 19, par. 2, item d; sentence of the Corte Costituzionale no. 376/2000.

119. EP Civil Liberties Committee, "Biometric Passports: No Fingerprinting of Under-Twelves."

120. Legislative Decree no. 286/98, art. 35, sec. 5.

121. For example, according to Italian law on foster care, the foster person has the same powers as the parent concerning ordinary relations with school and health services but has to take into account parents' instructions where they have not been deprived of parental responsibility.

122. Mai, *Opportunità e sfide per l'intervento sociale,* 55–65; Borello, Ferraris, et al., *La strada dei diritti,* 15–48.

123. Servizio Sociale Internazionale Sezione Italiana, Istituto Psicanalitico per le Ricerche Sociali, 19.

124. I refer to children accompanied by their parents and to older separated children, while for younger separated children the need for protection generally prevails.

Undocumented Students, College Education, and Life Beyond

Stephen H. Legomsky

In her thoughtful introduction to this volume, Jacqueline Bhabha identifies three broad categories of stateless individuals—the legally stateless, the *de facto* stateless, and the effectively stateless. Bhabha's elaboration of the second category is particularly useful: "people who have a nationality but whose status where they reside is not legal because they are illegal, irregular, or undocumented migrants in their current location."

This chapter focuses on a population that fits squarely within that second category—undocumented immigrant children and their functional exclusion from postsecondary education in the United States. Undocumented immigrants are not literally stateless; they have not been stripped of the nationalities of their countries of origin. Functionally, however, their lack of a legally recognized status denies them practical access to the critical life opportunities that only a state can supply. The state taxes undocumented families, and the state simultaneously excludes undocumented children from both educational loans and the in-state-resident tuition subsidy that their families' taxes help fund. This combination of state actions imposes burdens that are hard to distinguish from those that attend legal statelessness. More broadly still, undocumented students' irregular legal status bars them from working, voting, and participating as self-sufficient adults in the kinds of social, economic, and political activities that constitute life in a modern society. A clearer example of *de facto* statelessness would be hard to find.

In 1982, the United States Supreme Court handed down its landmark decision in *Plyler v. Doe*.[1] The issue was whether a Texas statute that denied free elementary and secondary education to undocumented children violated the equal protection principle enshrined in the fourteenth amendment of the U.S. Constitution. Relying principally on the moral innocence of the children and the devastating effects of denying them elementary and secondary education, the Court struck down the Texas statute by a vote of five to four. In the process, it made clear that undocumented immigrants, like anyone else on U.S. soil, are protected by the Constitution generally and by the specific constitutional principle that all persons are entitled to the equal protection of the law.

Despite the decision in *Plyler*, the voters of California in 1994 passed proposition 187, which similarly sought to bar undocumented students from public elementary and secondary schools.[2] That law, too, was struck down, this time by a federal district court, on the grounds that the U.S. Supreme Court had spoken and that Congress had preempted the subject matter.[3]

Those court decisions have not ended the national debate over the educational rights of undocumented students, but the main battleground has shifted to postsecondary education. Since the Supreme Court has not addressed the constitutionality of excluding undocumented students from state postsecondary educational institutions, the legal issue remains open. So far, that possibility has had only limited traction. At this writing, only one state—South Carolina in 2008—has passed a law that bars undocumented students from its public colleges and universities entirely, although some individual state colleges or state college systems have achieved that end through their own admissions policies.[4]

Perhaps more important, therefore, are the financial barriers faced uniquely by undocumented youth who wish to attend college. These barriers are not merely a result of their frequently low family income. They are also a product of deliberate policy decisions enshrined in law. Two of these barriers are particularly noteworthy. First, undocumented students are legally ineligible for all federal and state educational financial aid.[5] Second, the laws of at least forty states require undocumented students who attend public postsecondary educational institutions to pay tuition at the higher rate reserved for nonstate residents.[6] Federal law *possibly* requires states to charge undocumented students the higher out-of-state rate, but the relevant statutory provision is ambiguous, and Michael Olivas and others have made strong arguments that federal law leaves states free to charge undocumented residents the lower in-state tuition rate.[7] Ten states have done so.

From the standpoint of the affected students, however, even actual access to postsecondary education, while critical, is not sufficient. Undocumented students who find ways to attend and graduate from college will remain undocumented unless they can qualify under either existing law or a future form of legalization. The former is highly unlikely. Even if the student fits within one of the categories of eligible immigrants—a possibility after graduation[8]—the law renders inadmissible for ten years anyone who has been unlawfully present for more than a year.[9] Consequently, several members of Congress from time to time have sponsored curative legislation known as the DREAM Act. These bills would not only permit certain undocumented students to qualify for in-state-resident tuition rates but simultaneously provide a path for eventual permanent resident status.[10] These efforts have not yet borne fruit. A growing literature addresses the legal implications of these federal and state provisions.[11]

The stakes are huge—for the undocumented students and their families but for the larger society as well. Moreover, the debate over this issue is a microcosm of the larger national debate over the appropriate treatment of undocumented immigrants.

This chapter does not revisit the legal arguments. My goal here is to articulate and synthesize the arguments that either have been or could be made on both sides of the *policy* debate. My personal preferences are probably transparent, but the intention is to give fair consideration to all of the relevant concerns and to identify the broader philosophies that drive them.

With that background, the debate can be framed in general terms: How should we conceptualize, and therefore how should we treat, undocumented immigrants generally and undocumented students in particular? This chapter first explores the theories typically asserted to justify the legally constructed practical barriers to access college education for undocumented students—their ineligibility for financial aid and their classification as out-of-state residents for purposes of tuition charges at state colleges. It then considers the challenges that they face after graduation and examines whether some form of legalization would make wise policy sense.

These issues are narrow and specific, but the value systems that inform their resolution are not. They stem mainly from two competing realities. One reality is that the individuals in question do in fact live in the state. The other is that their very presence in the United States is a violation of the immigration laws.

Access to College

Those who support both disqualifying undocumented students from federal and state financial aid and classifying them as out-of-state residents for college tuition purposes have marshaled an array of policy arguments. For the most part, the arguments apply equally to both policies, and they seem to fall under two broad headings. One is what I call the *justice theme*. It suggests that *we* (the taxpayers) shouldn't have to pay for *them* (the intruders) to attend college. The second is the *strategic theme*. It views these and other restrictions in instrumental terms. Maybe we can't round up and deport 12 million people,[12] the thinking goes, but if we make them feel unwelcome enough and make their daily lives miserable enough, a large number will leave on their own. At the least, more will think twice about coming. The remaining discussion examines these themes in more detail.

We the Taxpayers

Perhaps the most common refrain heard from those who wish to treat a state's undocumented residents as if they lived out of state is that lawful taxpayers should not have to subsidize the college educations of trespassers or intruders.[13] So articulated, that theme has two unstated premises. One premise is that taxpayers and undocumented residents are two distinct, nonoverlapping groups. The other premise is that undocumented students are trespassers.

The first premise is plainly false. Lawful residents of a state do pay a variety of taxes, but so, too, do residents who are unlawfully present. They pay the same kinds of sales taxes, gasoline taxes, and property taxes (indirectly through the rents charged by their landlords if they rent) that lawful residents pay. They also are subject to the same federal and state income tax obligations and federal social security taxes (the latter even though they are ineligible to receive the retirement benefits that those contributions fund) that lawful residents are required to pay.[14] Some undocumented residents, particularly some of those who work for small businesses or for homeowners, undoubtedly receive their salaries under the table and thereby avoid income taxes and social security taxes. But approximately 75 percent of those undocumented workers who are required to file federal income tax returns do so;[15] conversely, some lawfully present workers fail to pay their taxes. At any rate, neither documented nor undocumented workers can easily avoid their other tax liabilities.

Undocumented immigrants tend to be lower-wage workers, some will observe, and therefore they are unlikely to contribute as much per capita tax revenue as their lawfully present counterparts. One can assume that is true, but much of the rationale for state-subsidized higher education in the first place (admittedly not the only rationale) is to make it accessible to students who could not otherwise afford it. The philosophy that the low income of one's parents should be an argument *against* state subsidies of one's education would turn this principle on its head.

Charging undocumented students the much higher nonresident tuition thus means that undocumented families are *doubly* subsidizing documented families. The former help fund these institutions not only by paying taxes but also by paying the much higher tuition charges that enable documented resident students to receive their college educations below cost.

So the parents of undocumented students, even if undocumented themselves, are paying to support postsecondary education. Although this fact alone should cause the whole "We the taxpayers" theme to vanish, its persistence has outperformed its logic.

"But they're *illegal*," some will shout in protest. "Which part of *illegal* don't you understand?" Those who invoke that slogan believe they have delivered a simple, common sense, knockout punch. Their charge brings us to the second unstated premise, which is that the undocumented students are trespassers who should be denied in-state resident status whether or not their parents pay taxes.

To this, there are several responses. Perhaps the most compelling is the sheer silliness of ascribing any kind of moral culpability to those who were brought here as children by their parents. One could as easily question the morality of someone who was kidnapped and forcibly trafficked into the United States.

Indeed, one wonders what those who make these arguments imagine these children should have said to their parents. Perhaps they believe that a child whose parents are about to move the family to the United States should announce: "I know I'm only four years old, but I have carefully researched the U.S. immigration laws and have discovered that under 8 U.S.C. section 1182(a)(6)(A)(I), it is not permissible to enter the United States other than at a designated port of entry. I would very much like to accompany you, but it would be wrong. So I have decided to stay behind. Don't worry, though. I'm old enough to take care of myself."

Not all children who accompany their parents to the United States are as young as that hypothetical child. As the age of the child at the time of entry increases, the weight that this argument carries diminishes correspondingly. Even during the teenage years, however, when the child is more likely to understand that surreptitious entry violates U.S. law, I would suggest it is a rare child who would separate from the family and refuse to come. One who criticizes the child for failing to make that choice needs to ask whether he or she would have acted any differently under similar circumstances. The free will of the child at the time of entry cannot be assumed.

"Agreed," the critics might say. But now these children have grown up. They are adults who are old enough to start college. Innocent as they might have been when they first arrived, they understand that their continued presence is unlawful. They are old enough to get jobs and support themselves, and they could return to their home countries if they wished. Yet they don't. They have made the conscious decision to extend their unlawful stays in the United States. They can no longer be defended as innocent victims.

That argument has some theoretical appeal, but it ignores too many human realities. A person who has spent his or her formative years in the United States, whose family is here, whose friends are here, and who in every practical sense is a product of American culture does not normally choose to pull up stakes at age eighteen and move, permanently and alone, to an unfamiliar land in which the economic, educational, and other life opportunities are likely to be bleak. It is no answer to point out that billions of the world's people live out their daily lives in precisely such dismal conditions. That they must do so is tragic. It is still different, in kind as well as degree, to expect an eighteen-year-old who has been raised in the United States to be thrust suddenly and alone into a strange environment in which his or her life opportunities are drastically and voluntarily curtailed. One should think long and hard before assigning moral culpability to a person who does not elect that option.

That point aside, the claim that these individuals are themselves illegal requires thorough examination. What the accusation presumably means is that we are talking about people who have violated the federal immigration laws. In the overwhelming majority of these cases, the children have committed no criminal offense. A large percentage, though probably less than one-half, entered legally but overstayed. This is not a crime. A slight majority entered without inspection, and entry without inspection admittedly is a crime (ordinarily a misdemeanor, not a felony, which is a more serious crime).[16] Even in the latter group, however, the only children who would be committing crimes by entering are those who were then old enough to be criminal offenders; the age varies from state to state.

But suppose it were otherwise. Assume, contrary to reality, that the young people in question had committed criminal offenses by overstaying their visas or by allowing their parents to bring them here. Why, exactly, is that a reason to deny them the tuition rates that the state charges its other residents? Two arguments seem possible here, but both are problematic.

One argument for attaching significance to the allegation of criminality (assuming it were true) might be that their conduct diminishes their deservedness. One should not reward wrongdoers with a subsidized college education, some might say.

Surely, that argument proves too much. Should the thousands of people who exceed the posted speed limit when they drive—a far more dangerous violation than overstaying a visa, one would think, and indisputably a criminal offense—be punished with the denial of in-state tuition rates for their children? Even for murderers, rapists, and other violent criminals, the punishment does not entail the loss of in-state-resident tuition status for their children.

There is, however, a second argument for making violation of the immigration laws a ground not only for disqualification from in-state-resident status but also for exclusion from the federal and state financial aid programs available to other residents of the state. The argument would be that the undocumented are not really state residents because they are not supposed to *be* there.

But they *are* there. More important, they have been for a long time, and perhaps more important still, they intend to remain. Like any other residents, they might one day change their minds and leave the state. A small minority of them might even be apprehended one day and removed involuntarily.

They are still residents of the state, in every theoretical and practical sense. The well-settled understanding of residence rests on some combination of actual abode and future intentions.[17] Undocumented inhabitants of a state fit that understanding as well as any other state residents do. They work, pay taxes, study, attend religious services, play sports, participate in community activities, and socialize. They might be recent arrivals, or they might have lived in the state for many years—just as is true of their documented neighbors. As of January 1, 2006, some 64 percent of all undocumented immigrants had lived in the United States at least six years.[18] They might have future plans to leave, or they might intend to remain for the long haul—just like their documented neighbors. They have a range of different family statuses,[19] again just like their documented friends and neighbors. The states themselves do not seem troubled by treating them as real residents for tax-collection purposes.

in our state colleges as long as they are willing to pay nonresident tuition. They are also free to attend private colleges.

For many, if not most undocumented immigrants, none of these options is realistic. The admonition to go home for college ignores the reality, noted earlier, that the United States *is* home and that the country of birth is not. It also ignores the difficulty, if not the impossibility, of financing their education overseas. The options of attending either state college at nonresident tuition rates or private college are theoretically open and, in some cases, practically open as well. But at state colleges, the nonresident tuition is typically anywhere from two to three and a half times the resident tuition; undocumented students tend to be members of below-average-income families;[27] and they are ineligible for federal and state financial aid, including loans.[28] Unless one's family is wealthy, therefore, these options too are foreclosed.

Not everyone can, should, or needs to go to college. Whether one is a U.S. citizen, a lawful permanent resident, or an undocumented immigrant, college is not always the right choice. For a large number of people, however, it is very much the right choice. Even then, events beyond a person's control can sometimes thwart that choice. But we should not look for ways to add such events, because everyone loses when they occur. The bright, talented student who studies hard and prepares for college is the most direct victim when a college dream is shattered.

To all this, some will still respond that the issue is what is best for the larger society, not what is best for undocumented students. If denying in-state-resident status to undocumented students will save public funds and deter illegal immigration in the process, they might say, then the hardships on individuals who are unlawfully present are either irrelevant or at least outweighed by the interests of the lawfully present public. Even putting aside the moral question of what is owed to undocumented students, however, one would be hard-pressed to argue that putting insurmountable financial barriers in the way of bright, talented students who live in the state, study hard, and prepare for college is in the interests of the larger society. When such students are denied access to college, society is denied the social and economic contributions that a college education would have enabled those students to make. The economic loss is especially acute in a world in which higher education will become increasingly vital to the nation's long-term economic productivity. It is more acute still when one considers that undocumented students tend to be bilingual, another critical attribute in our increasingly global economy.

Studies show, too, that raising college graduation rates ultimately reduces public expenditures on health and welfare and increases workers' tax contributions.[28]

These arguments admittedly assume that the students in question will not only remain in the United States long enough to graduate but also enter the workforce. Because they are undocumented, neither assumption can be automatic. There is no guarantee they will continue to evade apprehension, and even if they do, they cannot legally work.[29]

Although there are no such guarantees, one similarly should not assume that a person who is undocumented today will always remain undocumented. As the Supreme Court said in *Plyler*, "the illegal alien of today may well be the legal alien of tomorrow."[30] Congress could enact legalization as part of a comprehensive package of immigration reform, or it could at least pass the DREAM Act. Or a person might individually regularize his or her status through marriage, employment, or discretionary relief from removal.[31]

Make Them Want to Leave

The laws that require undocumented residents of a state to pay nonresident tuition rates reflect a second broad theme. Unlike the justice theme, this one is instrumentalist. Recognizing the impracticality of rounding up and deporting 12 million undocumented immigrants, many of those who prioritize the removal of undocumented immigrants generally (not just undocumented students) have turned to strategies designed to induce self-deportation. Advocates of this strategy sometimes refer to it as "attrition through enforcement" or "the third way" (enforcement and legalization being the other two ways).[32] The idea is to get them to *want* to leave. It is a theory that resonates loudly in some quarters.

To be fair, some of the readier and more familiar responses fall short. "People are coming for jobs, not for education," it is often said. True enough, one would assume, but even when employment is the attraction, it does not follow that people would still come if they knew that doing so would prevent their children from receiving adequate educational opportunities. In the case of postsecondary education, however, the deterrent effect of relegating the children of prospective undocumented immigrants to nonresident status, perhaps several years down the road, does seem highly unlikely to offset the vastly enhanced economic opportunities that immigration is likely to bring—especially given the uncertainty as to whether college education would have been financially possible anyway in the country of origin.

To this, the critics of in-state-resident tuition for undocumented students might respond that the deterrent effect of this one strategy should not be assessed in isolation. It should be seen as just one in a bundle of deterrents that together will tip the balance in favor of leaving the United States or at least the state.[33] Other sticks in that bundle include such existing measures as the threat of removal, criminal prosecution, employer sanctions, enhanced border and interior enforcement, and ineligibility for the vast majority of public benefits. It also includes proposed measures, such as denial of birthright citizenship to the children of undocumented immigrants, denial of drivers' licenses, impediments to obtaining identification cards and credit cards, and penalties on landlords who rent housing to undocumented immigrants.[34]

In reality, it seems difficult to predict that, even in combination, these strategies would be a more powerful influence than the dramatic differential between the economic opportunities available here and those available in the major source countries of illegal immigration. As it is, most of the deterrents listed above have been in place for many years. Formidable as they are, they have not had their desired effect. Here I do not make the tenuous argument that during the time these policies have been in effect, illegal immigration has increased. I recognize that it is hard to identify cause and effect. We don't know whether the numbers would have been greater still without these policies. But it is clear that millions of people have voted with their feet. At the least, for these millions, the attractions of coming have outweighed the deterrents. One can only speculate, but if the current staggering array of existing deterrents has been inadequate, there seems little reason to expect the proposed new ones to add more than marginally to the mix.

Admittedly, too, that last point is not without irony. I have asserted, on the one hand, that the proposed new deterrents would do great harm to undocumented immigrants (in the present context, prospective college students). Now I am claiming that they are tame enough to add little additional deterrent. These positions might appear to be in tension. On close examination, however, the tension is easily resolved. The adverse effects of making college a practical impossibility for the talented, diligent, aspiring, and morally innocent undocumented children are powerful and permanent. But they still will not deter the parents from coming to the United States, illegally if necessary, because the parents have concluded that the alternatives, sadly, are worse still. The level of misery one would have to inflict on undocumented immigrants to tip the balance is so extreme that no morally or politically acceptable set of sanctions will ever be able to achieve that result as long as world conditions remain fundamentally unchanged.

Beyond College: Permanent Membership

As the introduction pointed out, access to college would not guarantee academically talented undocumented students or the larger society the full benefits that postsecondary education offers. If after graduation they still lack a legal status essential to the kinds of jobs in which they can fulfill their potential, both they and the larger society lose out. As the introduction explained, very few undocumented students would be able to attain eventual permanent residence under existing law. For that reason, many have proposed legislation generically known as the DREAM Act, in which certain qualified undocumented students who in fact live in the United States would be entitled to in-state resident tuition rates and, after graduation, put on a path to lawful permanent residence in the United States.[35]

Given the thorough writings of others on that subject,[36] an exhaustive discussion of the pros and cons of the DREAM Act is not necessary here. The only point I add is that all the familiar arguments for and against legalization generally apply to this debate, supplemented by the arguments specific to undocumented students. As this chapter has shown, the latter include the kinds of factors highlighted in *Plyler v. Doe*, albeit in the elementary and secondary education contexts—the moral innocence of those who were brought to the United States at a young age by their parents and the increased importance of education, for the students themselves and for the public, in this technological and global age.

Legalization is itself controversial. Some might feel that certain long-term residents have acquired a moral *right* to legalization. One who advocates open borders, for example, might believe that the same logic precludes deporting those who are already here. Short of that, one might argue that, as residents of the community, the interests of undocumented immigrants in remaining in the country grow with the passage of time and that, as their roots in their local, state, and national communities become deeper, there comes a point at which their individual interests so greatly outweigh society's interests in deporting them as to ripen into a moral right to remain. Finally, one might argue that the United States government's own conduct has created and nurtured the phenomenon of illegal immigration and therefore that the government is morally bound to accommodate the individual interests that have arisen as a result. Here, two types of government conduct are relevant. Today's undocumented population has its origins in the *Bracero* guest-worker program, which ultimately spawned a whole network of family and labor relationships that in turn have triggered and sustained illegal immigration.[37] In addition, the United States for decades has consciously adopted a visible policy of lax immigration enforcement. Generations of prospective undocumented immigrants have reasonably interpreted that policy as a signal that their presence would be effectively tolerated as long as they behaved themselves once they were here. That, it might be argued, was the unspoken deal, and it morally binds the government to give at least some effect to that reasonable reliance.

But these arguments based on a *right* to remain permanently are unlikely to persuade many. Arguments based on open borders, whatever moral force they are felt to command, are not within the realm of political plausibility. Nor, many would say, should the law allow a person to acquire a right to remain simply by entering unlawfully or overstaying and then evading apprehension for a specified period of time. As to the arguments based on government conduct and reasonable reliance, the counterargument would be that the government's decision, several decades ago, to import guest workers under a *legal* program should not be viewed as creating a right for others to enter or remain *unlawfully* many decades later. The subsequent lax enforcement raises additional issues, but governments always have to exercise some judgment in deciding what resources to invest in the enforcement of various laws. The fact that the government elects not to invest greater enforcement resources than it does should not be taken to create a right to violate that law.

Thus, the more persuasive case for legalization rests on a combination of compassion and pragmatism. For me, the most compelling reason for legalization of those undocumented immigrants who have lived in the United States a long time is the humanitarian one. They have sunk deep roots. There comes a point at which the decent thing to do is overlook the legal transgression when strict enforcement would destroy people's lives.

Legalization would end the need for whole families to hide in constant fear from the authorities. It would end the need to resort to subterfuge to get work. It would make exploitative wages or working conditions harder to accomplish. It would end the exclusions of undocumented immigrants from a variety of daily activities. It would offer the possibility for long-term residents to reunite, in the United States, with close family members. And it would provide an eventual path to naturalization and full participation in the civic and political life of their new homeland.

None of these individual benefits will necessarily persuade those whose sole goal is to remove undocumented immigrants from the country. For them, the point would be that undocumented immigrants could free themselves from this isolation by returning to their home countries. For those who hold this view, a showing that legalization would benefit the larger society would likely be required.

There are highly pragmatic, self-interested reasons for the United States to offer legalization to certain long-term undocumented immigrants. The overwhelming bulk of the undocumented population has no intention of leaving voluntarily, and there is no politically plausible way to identify, apprehend, arrest, detain, prosecute, and deport 12 million people. Legally or illegally, this population is here to stay.

Most important, an underground shadow population is not healthy for anyone. After legalization, people can operate transparently and above board. The government learns the names and addresses of the community's and the nation's inhabitants. By ending their vulnerability to exploitation, we raise the market wages and working conditions for everyone. We provide educational opportunities for their children, including their U.S. citizen children.

More generally, legalization would be the single most effective vehicle for integrating undocumented immigrants into American life. If people are going to live in the United States for substantial durations, we should want them to participate in the political life of the community. They can do this by becoming lawful permanent residents and eventually naturalized citizens. They also become a part of the social, educational, and economic fabric of the nation. All these things help them to be more productive. It is a win-win situation. The alternative is a lose-lose situation in which they continue to live here but remain vulnerable to ruthless employers, professional smugglers, dealers in false documents, violent criminals, and the like.

Opponents of legalization worry as well about the message that legalization would send to those immigrants who have applied for permanent resident status through the official legal channels, waiting patiently in the queue for years on end to reunite with their American family members. They have played by the rules. We should not signal them, it is argued, that they would have been better off entering clandestinely.

13. This is the main thrust of the policy arguments advanced in Kobach, "Immigration Notification," 498–503. Kobach makes little attempt to acknowledge (much less engage) most of the counterarguments included here.

14. 42 U.S.C. sec. 402(y). See, generally, Francine J. Lipman, "The Taxation of Undocumented Immigrants: Separate, Unequal, and without Representation," *Harvard Latino Law Review* 9 (2006): 1.

15. U.S. Congressional Budget Office, *The Impact of Undocumented Immigrants on State/Local Budgets* (December 2007), 7.

16. 8 U.S.C. sec. 1325.

17. See, e.g., *Black's Law Dictionary*, under "residence."

18. Michael Hoefer et al., U.S. Department of Homeland Security, "Estimates of the Undocumented Immigrant Population Residing in the United States: January 2006, Population Estimates" (August 2007), 3.

19. Jeffrey S. Passel, Pew Hispanic Center, "The Size and Characteristics of the Unauthorized Migrant Population in the U.S.: Estimates Based on the March 2005 Current Population Survey," March 7, 2006, 6–8.

20. Illegal Immigration Reform and Immigrant Responsibility Act (IIRAIRA) of 1996, Pub. L. 104-208, 110 Stat. 3009, Div. C (September 30, 1996); see 8 U.S.C. sec. 1623.

21. For thoughtful accounts of the evolution in the value of citizenship, see Peter H. Schuck, "The Re-Evaluation of American Citizenship," *Georgetown Immigration Law Journal* 12 (1997): 1; Peter H. Schuck, "Membership in the Liberal Polity: The Devaluation of American Citizenship," in *Immigration and the Politics of Citizenship in Europe and North America*, ed. William R. Brubaker (Lanham, Md.: University Press of America, 1989), 51 ff. For a normative account of the functions of citizenship, see Stephen H. Legomsky, "Why Citizenship?," *Virginia Journal of International Law* 35 (1994): 279.

22. See Stephen H. Legomsky, *Immigration and Refugee Law and Policy*, 4th ed. (New York: Foundation Press, 2005), 1350–1351.

23. Personal Responsibility and Work Opportunity Reconciliation Act of 1996, Pub. L. 104-193, 110 Stat. 2105 (August 22, 1996), sec. 411(b)(1), 8 U.S.C. sec. 1621(b)(1).

24. Foreign Affairs Reform and Restructuring Act of 1998, Pub. L. 105-277, Div. G, 112 Stat. 268, sec. 2242 (October 11, 1998).

25. Kobach, "Immigration Nullification," 500.

26. See Lipman, "The Taxation of Undocumented Immigrants," 6–18.

27. 8 U.S.C. secs. 1621(a)(c).

28. Gonzales, "Wasted Talent and Broken Dreams," 5.

29. This point is made by Kobach, "Lawmakers Gone Wild?," 502–503.

30. *Plyler*, 455 U.S. at 207 (quoting the district court).

31. See, e.g., 8 U.S.C. secs. 1151(a)(1)–(2) (family and employment preferences), 1158 (asylum), 1229b (cancellation of removal).

32. E.g., Mark Krikorian, "Downsizing Illegal Immigration: A Strategy of Attrition through Enforcement," *CIS Backgrounder* (May 2005), <http://cis.org> (accessed July 8, 2010); Jessica M. Vaughan, "Attrition through Enforcement: A Cost-Effective Strategy to Shrink the Illegal Population," *CIS Backgrounder* (April 2006), <http;//cis.org> (accessed July 8, 2010).

33. This last qualifier raises other issues. To the extent that these harsh measures are meant to encourage undocumented immigrants to move to other states within the United States, they create an unseemly race to the bottom. The issue then becomes whether these sorts of issues should be made by Congress and applied uniformly across the nation or made by each individual state. I do not take up the federalism question in this chapter.

34. See Legomsky, *Immigration Law and Refugee Policy*, ch. 12.

35. See generally Olivas, "Lawmakers Gone Wild?"

36. Ibid. and the writings cited therein.

37. See, e.g., Mae M. Ngai, *Impossible Subjects: Illegal Aliens and the Making of Modern America* (Princeton: Princeton University Press, 2004); Bill Ong Hing, "Immigration Policy: Thinking outside the (Big) Box," *Connecticut Law Review* 39 (2007): 1401, 1410–1429.

38. Much smaller legalization programs were enacted for Nicaraguans and Cubans in 1997. See Nicaraguan Adjustment and Central American Relief Act, Pub. L. 105-100, title II, 111 Stat. 2160 (November 19, 1997), sec. 202. For Haitians in 1998, see Haitian Refugee Immigration Fairness Act, Pub. L. 105-277, div. A, 112 Stat. 2681 (November 2, 1998).

39. Immigration Reform and Control Act, Pub. L. 99-603, 100 Stat. 3359, secs. 201, 202, 302 (November 5, 1986).

U.S. Immigration Law and the Devaluation of Children

From its basic framework to its minute details, U.S. immigration law devalues the interests of children. For one fundamental example, U.S. immigration law systemically devalues children by denying children agency throughout the principle frameworks of immigration law. In most jurisdictions and most legal contexts, decisions affecting children are guided by consideration of the child's best interests.[1] Yet the best-interest standard that serves as the hallmark of decisions affecting children is missing in the major frameworks of immigration law.[2] In fact, immigration law is designed not just to ignore the interests of children but rather to marginalize the role of children and thus the value placed on their interests.

In U.S. immigration law, the concept of family centers on parents, not children. Parents and their interests are recognized, while children and their interests in family integrity are ignored. To the extent that the statutory scheme of immigration law advances family integrity at all, it does so in the narrow sense of creating opportunities for parents to align their children's status with their own. Children, on the other hand, are denied agency and opportunity to extend immigration status to their parents. This is most apparent in the framework of family-sponsored immigration, the largest source of legal immigration.

The family-sponsored immigration framework allows legal permanent residents and citizens to petition for family members who fall within specified categories to be admitted to the United States as legal permanent residents.[3] Under this framework, the person having legal immigration status is the petitioner, and the person for whom a petition is filed is the principal beneficiary. If the beneficiary has a spouse or children, in some instances the spouse or children may acquire immigration status as derivatives.[4]

Petitions are given various levels of priority, depending on both the immigration status of the sponsoring petitioner, as either citizen or legal permanent resident, and the relationship between the beneficiary and the petitioner.[5] U.S. immigration law prioritizes petitions of citizens over those of legal permanent residents and favors the parent-child relationship of traditional nuclear families over other family relationships.[6] The highest-priority relationships, including the relationship between a citizen parent and a child, are not subject to numerical limitation and provide for the immediate availability of an immigrant visa.[7] Less favored relationships, such as that between a legal permanent resident parent and a child, are subject to numerical limitations that result in backlogs that can extend years. Immigration law does not recognize all family relationships, and the relationship given lowest priority by immigration law, the relationship between adult citizens and their siblings, includes backlogs of more than twenty years.

The parent-child relationship is favored in this statutory framework, but only when the parent holds legal immigration status. Although both citizen and legal permanent resident parents can petition for children, children may never petition for their parents. In fact, U.S. citizens may petition for their parents only when they are no longer children and have reached age twenty-one.[8]

The framework for family-sponsored and derivative immigration thus subordinates children's status to that of their parents. Parents who are successful in navigating the immigration system may include their children with them or may petition later for their children to join them. When parents' attempts to immigrate fail, the attempts of their derivative children fail as well. When parents are successful in navigating the immigration system, their children may benefit. In this way, children are passively advanced through the process by successful parents and are held back by unsuccessful parents.

Under this system, children with legal immigration status, such as children who are U.S. citizens based on their births in the United States, cannot extend family-based immigration benefits to a parent or other family members. The system facilitates the assimilation of children's status to that of their parents but does not provide for the assimilation of parents' status to that of a child.[9]

This asymmetry is not a reflection of the parent-child relationship involved as the same family relationship may allow an extension of immigration status if the legal status holder is the parent, not the child.[10] Yet unlike similarly situated adults, children who hold legal immigration or citizenship status are not permitted to extend that status to other family members. The pattern of disallowing the flow of immigration status from a child to other family members is prevalent in immigration law. A child, for example, cannot include a parent as a derivative if the child obtains legal immigration status.[11] Moreover, derivative status extends only one generation, so that persons who qualify as derivatives who are under age twenty-one and who have children of their own cannot extend immigration status to those children, the grandchildren of the principal immigrant.[12] Adult asylees and refugees may obtain derivative status for their spouses and children, but child asylees and refugees are not allowed to petition for derivative status for their parents.[13] Similarly, there is no statutory provision for a child granted protection from removal pursuant to the Convention against Torture to reunify with a parent.[14]

Children also face barriers in other major immigration law programs not directly related to family. For example, children generally are ineligible under a program known as the diversity visa lottery because applicants must be high school graduates or have equivalent education or work experience.[15] While children are not directly prohibited from applying for employment-based immigrant visas, it is highly unlikely that they would have the requisite education or job experience to qualify.[16]

In other instances, persons who are deemed inadmissible by immigration law may overcome this by showing hardship to adult family members but not by showing hardship to children. For example, immigration law provides the possibility of a waiver of inadmissibility based on prior unlawful presence if "the refusal of admission . . . would result in extreme hardship to [a] citizen or lawfully resident spouse or parent."[17] Hardship to children, however extreme, is statutorily irrelevant.

In U.S. immigration law, therefore, families centered on parents who have lawful immigration status are recognized and valued. The immigration scheme values the parents' interests in family integrity and provides for the possibility that such parents will choose to attempt to extend legal status to their children. But the family immigration provisions of immigration law reject children's interests so that children's interests in family integrity do not serve as a basis for possible extension of immigration status. This has profound implications for millions of children who find themselves in mixed-status families.

Mixed-Status Families and the Children of Immigrants

The inability of children to extend immigration status to parents contributes greatly to the rapid growth in the number of mixed-status families (families in which members do not share the same immigration or citizenship status) in the United States. Generally, children in immigrant families form "the fastest growing segment of the [United States] child population,"[18] and if current demographic trends persist, "children of immigrants will represent at least a quarter of all U.S. children by 2010."[19] Already, at least one child in ten in the United States lives in a mixed-status family where some family members do not share the same immigration or citizenship status.[20]

Many of these mixed-status families include parents who are not authorized to remain in the United States. In the United States, there are currently "over 5 million children living with unauthorized parents."[21] In fact, in the 6.6 million families with a parent who is not authorized to remain in the United States, two-thirds of all children are U.S. citizens.[22] Of these "unauthorized" parents, 1.5 million have only U.S.-born citizen children and no children who are not U.S. citizens.[23] Unsurprisingly, adolescent children in families with unauthorized parents are more likely to be unauthorized themselves in comparison with younger children.[24] Because more "younger children were born here, there are many mixed-status families in which the younger children are citizens but the older children—like their parents—are noncitizens."[25] Added to these children of immigrants are nearly 2 million children in the United States who themselves lack authorization to remain in the country.[26] In sum, millions of children are directly affected by decisions regarding immigration law and policy. As discussed below, many also pay a steep price for the happenstance of being born into a mixed-status family as their connections to unauthorized family members serve to devalue their citizenship and are exploited in the implementation of harsh immigration law-enforcement strategies.

Creating Effectively Stateless Children by Devaluing Their Citizenship

Even with immigration law enforcement considerations momentarily placed to the side, the children of immigrants face many barriers not contemplated in nonimmigrant families. Many "policies that advantage or disadvantage noncitizens are likely to have broad spillover effects on the citizen children who live in the great majority of immigrant families."[27] Unsurprisingly, mixed-status families "are more likely to be poor than other families."[28] They are "significantly less likely to be in any regular nonparental child care arrangement,"[29] and "[c]hildren in low-income working immigrant families were more than twice as likely as those in comparable native families to lack health insurance coverage in 2002."[30] Overall, "children of immigrants are substantially more likely than children with U.S.-born parents to be poor, have food-related problems, live in crowded housing, lack health insurance, and be in fair or poor health."[31]

Citizen children of immigrant parents access public benefits at a lower rate than citizen children of citizens, undermining myths that immigrants are drawn to the United States by the availability of public assistance.[32]

Because many social benefits laws now differentiate between citizens and noncitizens, even those noncitizens with legal immigration status, the overall availability of benefits to immigrant families is reduced.[33] The result is that while some citizen children live "in households with non citizens and suffer . . . the disadvantage of losing benefits and the reduced overall household resources that may result, . . . a second class of citizen children lives in households with only citizens and suffers no comparable disadvantage."[34]

Moreover, citizen children in immigrant families may not receive even needed benefits for which they are eligible as individuals: "[O]ften it is adults who claim citizenship rights for children and do so on their behalf and immigrant parents of citizen children may now find themselves in the position of requesting benefits for their children for which they (the parents) are not eligible."[35] When parents are less likely to seek benefits for their children, "inequalities in access within families have been created informally through the actions of parents and public program staff . . . resulting in a hierarchy of citizen children's access to social benefits, which is ordered by their parents citizenship and immigration status."[36] Often, the formal rights of children to social benefits are trumped by parents and program personnel who act on misinformed beliefs that the immigration status of parents extinguishes the rights of children. Although "citizen children of immigrant parents are formally 'insiders' and therefore are fully eligible for social benefits, their parents' non-citizen, 'outsider' status may eclipse their children's citizenship, resulting in citizen children informally taking on their parent's citizenship status."[37] Citizen children in mixed-status families thus are assimilated to the status of undocumented children.

The children of immigrants therefore often fail to receive the full promise of their citizenship and find themselves effectively stateless. The prevalence of this is high in part because of immigration law's prohibitions on children extending immigration status to their parents, perpetuating mixed-status families. As such, the role of immigration law extends well beyond the immigration context to inhibit children's full participation in the benefits of citizenship in a vast array of social contexts. Programs and benefits specifically designed to ensure the well-being of citizen children are undermined by the failure of immigration law to incorporate consideration of children's interests. Although this does much to disconnect children from the protection of their state, other aspects of immigration law challenge the very connection between children and parents that some areas of U.S. law and policy strive to preserve.

Expanding Immigration Enforcement and the Destabilization of Immigrant Families

The overwhelming focus of U.S. immigration law enforcement in recent decades has been at the border, leaving immigrants in the interior of the country relatively free from the threat of removal.[38] In a major shift, the enforcement of immigration laws in the interior of the nation has risen sharply since the creation of the U.S. Immigration and Customs Enforcement (ICE) in 2003.[39] This began with enhanced efforts to deport noncitizens removable on the basis of criminal convictions and unexecuted orders of removal.[40] The agency charged with interior enforcement of immigration laws asserts this focus as its ongoing priority.[41]

This shift has produced large numbers of deportations from the interior. Since 1996, "more than 650,000 immigrants—both undocumented and legal noncitizens—have been deported as criminal aliens, many after serving substantial prison time."[42] More than 90,000 individuals were removed as "criminal aliens" in 2004 and again in 2005.[43] However, as home raids ostensibly aim for this narrow target population, "[t]he conflation by ICE and others of 'illegal aliens,' 'criminal aliens,' and even 'terrorists' obscures the scope and function of the deportation system."[44] It is commonplace that raids on homes result in the arrests of persons outside the targeted categories such as family members and others living in the homes.[45]

These immigration raids on homes are dramatic and frightening events, and the legality of some often employed techniques has been challenged in many jurisdictions.[46] One complaint provides a succinct description of these raids:

ICE teams appear to have developed a practice of raiding residential homes in the dead of night, without warrant, in search of persons believed to have an outstanding deportation order. In a typical raid, multiple immigration agents surround a house and pound on the front door, announcing themselves as "police." In the belief that there is an emergency, an occupant opens the door. The immigration agents (often armed) then enter the home, without a search warrant and without securing informed consent for their entry. They move through the home in an intimidating manner, wake all occupants including children, and make them gather in a central location. The agents often announce that they are looking for an individual who is unknown to the occupants of the

on immigrant communities far exceeds the actual numbers of immigrants who are arrested. Even the sevenfold increase in workplace raid arrests during the first ten months of 2007 still resulted in only 3,600 arrests.[67] Relative to the overall unauthorized immigrant population or even to the overall population of persons deported, this is not a spectacularly high number. However, before declaring the raids a vindication of the theory that making life "difficult and unpleasant" for unauthorized immigrants works as an effective immigration law enforcement technique, it is important to look at where the effects of the raids actually fall and what fears the raids actually exploit.

The Effects of Immigration Raids on Children

Statistical estimates, corroborated by actual figures in several case studies, indicate that the number of children directly affected by the arrest of parents in workplace raids "would be equal to about half the number of adults arrested."[68] This means, by one count, that "at least 13,000 American children have seen one or both parents deported in the past two years after round-ups in factories and neighborhoods."[69] The number of separated families increases when extended families are considered.[70] The department of homeland security's office of inspector general reports that it does not require the collection of data on the status of children of those removed, which is remarkable in itself.[71] But existing data indicates at least 108,434 parents of U.S. citizen children were deported between fiscal years 1998 and 2007.[72]

Workplace immigration raids therefore have a pronounced effect on children in immigrant families. The effect of workplace raids is felt most acutely by younger children because "[t]he children of undocumented immigrants are predominantly young children, and many are infants, toddlers, and preschoolers."[73] Two-thirds of children with a parent arrested in one workplace raid were U.S. citizens.[74]

Unsurprisingly, "many children face traumatic circumstances and insecure care in the period after the raids."[75] According to "[c]hild psychology experts . . . children suffer most from the disruption of armed agents coming into their homes and taking away their parents—and sometimes themselves. Children can experience stress, depression, and anxiety disorders."[76] "The most destabilizing impact on the children of arrestees following worksite enforcement actions came from the separation and fragmentation of families."[77] For children, "emotional trauma

. . . followed separation from one or both parents."[78] For young children who do not understand the concept of immigration law, "sudden separation was considered personal abandonment."[79] Moreover, "children who witness their parents being taken into custody lose trust in their parents' ability to keep them safe and begin to see danger everywhere."[80] The harm to the parent-child relationship that flows from forced separation is not a new phenomenon and is not confined to the context of immigration. For example, "messages of parental vulnerability and subordination were repeatedly burned into the consciousness of slave parents and children, undermining their sense of worth, diminishing the sense of family security and authority, eroding the parents' function as a model of adult agency and independence."[81]

In the longer term, a parent's detention or deportation removes that parent's earnings from the household, creating "a more unstable home environment and remov[ing] one of the main strengths in immigrant families—the presence of two parents."[82] Commonly, the parent who is arrested in a workplace raid is the person in the family who is most integrated into U.S. society, so that the connection with broader society is diminished.[83]

In the wake of mass raids, children exhibit increased absenteeism in schools.[84] In many instances, immigration raids cause "some degree of polarization between Latino immigrants and other community residents."[85] Children can experience social isolation "when they were harassed by other children or branded as criminals because their parents were arrested."[86] Following one raid, at school "[m]any children exhibited outward signs of stress . . . and lost their appetites, ate less, and lost weight."[87]

These profound effects on children are troubling, yet they are hardly unexpected. Indeed, the predictable trauma to children is precisely the reason that such raids deeply affect immigrant communities. Raids into workplaces and homes exploit the connection between immigrant parents and their children to maximize their effects. As law and policy relating to children in other contexts strives to support family stability and promote the well-being of children, immigration law-enforcement policies intentionally work to create instability and fear. Immigrant families unequivocally understand the message that the state acts not as a source of protection but as an instrument of potential separation and loss.

The pronounced and predictable effects of mass workplace raids on children makes them untenable as a matter of public policy. Generally, "directing the onus of a parent's misconduct against his children does not comport with fundamental conceptions of justice."[88] Although immigration raids are formally targeted at adults, their ripple effects for children and families are an unmistakable message of loss and fear for immigrant families. This is not to say that immigration laws cannot be enforced. But at a time when the enforcement of immigration laws is highly selective, the decision to devote scarce enforcement resources in a manner that predictably and profoundly harms children is questionable at best. Practices that create crisis and discord in families place the enforcement of immigration law in direct opposition to widespread policies and significant government resources that are devoted to maintaining families and protecting children. When enforcement policies prioritize the desire to exclude unauthorized adults over the impulse to act in the best interests of vulnerable children, children effectively lose the ability to look to the state for protection.

Rethinking Children's Role in Immigration Law

If the logical result of the enforcement of existing immigration laws is that millions of children live in fear, thousands of children are traumatized by family separation, and social service agencies are strained beyond capacity to serve children left behind in communities that experience mass workplace raids, then the underlying laws that have constructed our current notions of illegality certainly warrant reexamination. Further, if the rights of citizen children to live within their country of citizenship with family are marginalized because the parents to whom the children are connected are not able to legalize their presence in the country, the limited ability of children to extend lawful immigration status to their parents is flawed.

Immigration law has never been constructed around the interests of children. The current policy and practice of immigrant raids is but one example of the extent to which immigration law embodies outright hostility to children and their interests. Yet there is no reason that a child's connection to a nation cannot serve as the basis for the creation of connection between a parent and the nation.[89] Immigration law need not stand in stark opposition to laws and policies directed at children and their welfare. Although it now serves as a powerful force in marginalizing children and separating them from the protection of their state, with reform it could as easily serve to empower children through recognition of their interests and needs.

Notes

1. D. Marianne Blair and Merle Weiner, "Resolving Parental Custody Disputes: A Comparative Exploration," *Family Law Quarterly* 39 (Summer 2005): 247.

2. Ibid. The best-interest-of-the-child principle appears in immigration law with respect to special immigrant juveniles—children dependent on a juvenile court for whom family reunification is not a viable option. 8 U.S.C.A. sec. 1101(a)(27) (J). The concept of "best interests of the child" is so unusual in immigration law that special factual findings with regard to the child's interest are made not in immigration proceedings but are delegated to state juvenile courts.

3. See ibid., secs. 1151(b)(2)(A)(i), 1153(a).

4. See ibid., sec. 1153(d).

5. See ibid.

6. See generally Nora V. Demleitner, "How Much Do Western Democracies Value Family and Marriage? Immigration Law's Conflicted Answer," *Hofstra Law Review* 32 (2003): 273; Linda Kelly, "Family Planning, American Style," *Alabama Law Review* 52, (2001): 943, 955–960; Hiroshi Motomura, "The Family and Immigration: A Roadmap for the Ruritanian Lawmaker," *American Journal of Comparative Law* 43 (1995): 511, 528; Victor C. Romero, "Asians, Gay Marriage and Immigration: Family Unification at a Crossroad," *Indiana International and Comparative Law Review* 15, (2005): 337.

7. See 8 U.S.C.A. sec. 1151(b)(2006). The immediate availability of an immigration visa should not be confused with the ability to immigrate immediately given processing times and bureaucratic delays that can be extensive.

8. Ibid., sec. 1151(b)(2)(A)(i).

9. See David B. Thronson, "Choiceless Choices: Deportation and the Parent-Child Relationship," *Nevada Law Journal* 6 (2006): 1165.

10. See Jacqueline Bhabha, "The 'Mere Fortuity' of Birth? Are Children Citizens?," *Journal of Feminist Cultural Studies* 15, no. 2 (2004): 91–117 (discussing the "striking asymmetry in the family reunification rights of similarly placed adults and minor children").

11. 8 U.S.C.A. sec.1153(d). For example, if a child immigrates on the basis of a parent-child relationship with one parent, immigration law does not then permit derivative status to extend to this child's other parent or siblings.

12. Ibid.

13. See ibid., secs. 1158(b)(3), 1157(c)(2).

14. See generally Lori A. Nessel, "Forced to Choose: Torture, Family Reunification and United States Immigration Policy," *Temple Law Review* 78 (2005): 897. Protection from removal under the Convention against Torture is available to those who do not qualify for or are barred from asylum who nevertheless can establish that it is more likely than not that they would be tortured if removed to the proposed country of removal. 8 C.F.R. sec. 208.16.

15. Ibid., 1153(c)(2).

16. Ibid., sec. 1153(b).

17. Ibid., sec. 1182(a)(9)(B)(v).

18. Valerie Leiter et al., "Challenges to Children's Independent Citizenship: Immigration, Family and the State, " *Childhood* 13 (2006): 11–27 (citation omitted).

19. Urban Institute, "Children of Immigrants: Facts and Figures," 2006, 1, <http://www.urban.org>. (accessed April 15, 2009).

20. Michael Fix et al., "The Integration of Immigrant Families in the United States," Urban Institute, 2001, 15, <http://www.urban.org> (accessed April 15, 2009).

21. Ibid., 2.

22. Jeffrey S. Passel, "The Size and Characteristics of the Unauthorized Migrant Population in the U.S.: Estimates Based on the March 2005 Current Population Survey," Pew Hispanic Center, 2006, ii, <http://pewhispanic.org> (accessed April 15, 2009).

23. Ibid., 8.

24. Randy Capps et al., National Council of La Raza, "Paying the Price: The Impact of Immigration Raids on America's Children," Urban Institute, 2007, 17, <http://www.urban.org> (accessed April 15, 2009).

25. Urban Institute, "Children of Immigrants."

26. Passel, "The Size and Characteristics of the Unauthorized Migrant Population in the U.S.," 7.

27. Michael E. Fix and Wendy Zimmermann, "All Under One Roof: Mixed-Status Families in an Era of Reform," Urban Institute, 1999, 2, <http://www.urban.org> (accessed April 15, 2009).

28. Ibid.

29. Randy Capps et al., "A Profile of Low-Income Working Immigrant Families, New Federalism: National Survey of American Families," Urban Institute, June 2005, 5 (citation omitted), <http://www.urban.org>. (accessed April 15, 2009).

30. Ibid., 4. This is in part the result of the U.S. health-care system that depends on employers to provide health insurance for their employees and the families of their employees. Immigrant parents in marginal or irregular employment are much less likely to have access to health insurance through employers that would extend to their children.

31. Capps, "A Profile of Low-Income Working Immigrant Families," 1.

32. Michael E. Fix and Jeffrey S. Passel, "Lessons of Welfare Reform for Immigrant Integration," March 8, 2002, <http://www.urban.org> (accessed April 15, 2009).

33. See Personal Responsibility and Work Opportunity Reconciliation Act of 1996, Pub. L. No. 104-193, sec. 412, 110 Stat. 2105, 2269–2270 (granting authority to states to determine eligibility of certain noncitizens for some public benefits such as Temporary Assistance for Needy Families and Food Stamps);

see also Leiter, "Challenges to Children's Independent Citizenship," 17 (noting that 1996 legal reforms "'target' social benefits to a more restricted scope of beneficiaries, and citizenship status is now one of the screens that is now used to determine eligibility") (citation omitted).

34. Leiter, "Challenges to Children's Independent Citizenship," 17.

35. Ibid.

36. Ibid.

37. Ibid., 17.

38. "One study found that between 1986 and 2002, about 60% of all appropriated enforcement resources went to border work, leaving only 10% for interior investigations and related enforcement." David A. Martin, "Eight Myths about Immigration Enforcement," *New York University Journal of Legislation and Public Policy* 10 (2006–2007): 525, 544. "The balance of enforcement spending went for detention and removal as well as intelligence." Ibid., n.84.

39. Dorsey & Whitney LLP, "Severing a Lifeline: The Neglect of Citizen Children in America's Immigration Enforcement Policy," Urban Institute, 2009, 26, <http://www.dorsey.com> (accessed April 15, 2009).

40. See Office of Inspector General, Department of Homeland Security, "An Assessment of United States Immigration and Customs Enforcement's Fugitive Operations Teams" (2007), 1.

41. See U.S. Immigration and Customs Enforcement, "Fact Sheets: ICE Fugitive Operations Program" (December 4, 2007), <http://www.ice.gov> (accessed April 15, 2009) ("ICE's Fugitive Operations Teams give top priority to cases involving aliens who pose a threat to national security and community safety, including members of transnational street gangs, child sex offenders, and aliens with prior convictions for violent crimes"); U.S. Immigration and Customs Enforcement, "News Releases: New Jersey ICE Fugitive Operations Teams Arrest More Than 2,000 in One Year," December 4, 2007), <http://www.ice.gov> (accessed April 15, 2009) (discussing "operations aimed at arresting criminal aliens and those who have defied the removal orders issued by immigration judges").

42. Capps, "Paying the Price," 10.

43. Ibid.

44. Daniel Kanstroom, "Post-Deportation Human Rights Law: Aspiration, Oxymoron, or Necessity?," *Stanford Journal of Civil Rights and Civil Liberties* 13 (2007): 195, 199.

45. See Tyche Hendricks, "The Human Face of Immigration Raids in Bay Area: Arrests of Parents Can Deeply Traumatize Children Caught in the Fray, Experts Argue,"*San Francisco Chronicle*, April 27, 2007, A1, <http://www.sfgate.com> (accessed April 15, 2009) ("The raids focus on illegal immigrants who have ignored deportation orders, but 37 percent of the 18,149 people arrested nationwide through Feb. 23 were not wanted fugitives").

46. See American Immigration Law Foundation Litigation Clearinghouse, <http://www.ailf.org/lac/clearinghouse_122106_ice.shtml> (accessed April 15, 2009).

83. Ibid.

84. "School Enrollment Down Following Swift Raids," WCCO.com, February 12, 2007, <http://wcco.com> (accessed April 15, 2009).

85. Capps, "Paying the Price," 51.

86. Ibid., 52.

87. Ibid.

88. *Plyler v. Doe*, 457 U.S. 202, 220 (1982).

89. The "assumption that children's immigration status must derive from that of their parents rather than vice versa recalls an earlier set of gendered assumptions—that women traveled with or followed their husbands, but not vice versa." Bhabha, "The 'Mere Fortuity' of Birth?," 96.

11

Birthright Citizenship: The Vulnerability and Resilience of an American Constitutional Principle

Linda K. Kerber

All persons born or naturalized in the United States and subject to the jurisdiction thereof, are citizens of the United States and of the state in which they reside.[1]

The fourteenth amendment to the U.S. Constitution was carefully crafted to deflect the former states of the Confederacy from reconstructing a civic order almost as oppressive as slavery had been.[2] That its majestic first clause—establishing *jus soli* (birth on U.S. soil) as central to citizenship—would quickly come to be understood as the heart of the Constitution and as the trigger for the incorporation of the Bill of Rights into the federal system, was not predicted. But as the last British governor of Massachusetts ruefully observed of Harvard College students on the eve of the American Revolution, "the spirit of liberty spread where it was not intended," and among the many significant outcomes of the Civil War amendments, the practices of universal birthright citizenship were stabilized in American law.[3]

Only a handful of other nations many, like the United States, nations whose political economy has depended on a dynamically increasing population and labor supply—take a similar position. Those with the longest and most stable histories of universal birthright citizenship are Latin American states. Canada established universal birthright citizenship only in 1977. It is not law in Australia. No European state now grants unconditional birthright citizenship.[4]

The fourteenth amendment goes on to promise the vague "privileges and immunities of citizens" and to promise "all persons" the somewhat more specific "due process of law" and "equal protection of the laws." What counts as due process and equal protection are notoriously unstable, and what the privileges and immunities of citizenship include are vague. But among the privileges that are not contested are some of the most protective—an unambivalent right to travel, to return to the nation from abroad, and to claim the assistance of a U.S. consul when in another country.

It is at the borders that citizenship generally meets its most stringent tests because there one faces the representative of the state alone, vulnerable, and exposed. Individuals approach consular officers singly or in family groups—that is, one or two adults and their own dependents—lacking any nest of community to which they can at that moment turn for advice and support. It is at the border that, in U.S. law and practice, claims to citizenship can be most readily denied; the plenary power claimed by Congress has long privileged those who would exclude.[5] Not until 1855 was it clear that children born overseas to American citizen parents were citizens at birth. Not until 1934 did married American women citizens gain the power to transmit citizenship to their foreign-born children. In 1952, the McCarran-Walter Act virtually restated the old English principle that the legal responsibility for a nonmarital child is the mother's alone. As Kristin Collins has put it informally, one of the generally unrecognized but firm obligations of women's citizenship remains the burden of care for a nonmarital child.[6]

Forty years ago, in 1971, the U.S. Supreme Court ruled for the first time that discrimination on the basis of sex might occasionally represent a denial of equal protection of the laws.[7] Despite the extraordinary developments in American law and social and cultural practices in the generation since then, gender—inflected by race and class—continues to be a significant component of the way that citizenship is experienced in the United States. I do not think that this asymmetry is a matter of chance or unreflective stereotype. Deep in American legal tradition and practice, antedating the early republic but continued into it, has been the conviction that married women's obligations to their husbands trump their civic obligations to the state. The assumption was embedded in the legal practice of coverture, which at marriage gave to a husband wide-ranging control over his wife's body (there was no recognition of marital rape until the late 1970s).[8] It seemed to follow logically that coverture also gave to the husband control over the property she brought to the marriage and her earnings during it and (since he could blackmail her so easily) denied her a public voice as voter or civil official.[9] In theory, the civic infirmities of married women should have had no effect on single women—the never-married, divorced, or widowed who make up at any moment a substantial proportion of the population, even at times when divorce was rare—but in practice all women were generally treated as if they were married or would be married.

The asymmetry examined in this chapter lies in the definitions of what counts as birthright citizenship. Although by far most Americans have claimed their citizenship through *jus soli,* certain categories of people born outside the United States to parents who are U.S. citizens have long been able to claim citizenship through the law of blood, *jus sanguinis.* The practices that define which children born abroad are to be considered citizens from birth and which must be naturalized have taken into account, with variations over the centuries, the status of the mother and the status of the father asymmetrically. The ways in which Americans have reasoned about this practice reveals something about our unspoken assumptions about belonging and protection.

In recent years, several appeals to federal courts have sought to widen the safety net of birthright citizenship. Generally, these appeals have been lost, and most commentary has focused on the extent to which—highlighted in the courtroom argument—these cases raised issues of equal protection for men and women parents. But they are also touchstones for an examination of Americans' complex understanding of the meanings of birthright citizenship and of our explicit practices of who is embraced as a citizen and who can be exposed to statelessness.

Their Mothers' Children

Joseph Boulais was an American who served in the peacetime army in Germany and after his discharge from service went to Vietnam in 1963 as a civilian employee of a construction company. In 1969, he had a son, Tuan Anh Nguyen, with a Vietnamese woman who abandoned them after giving birth. Boulais remained in Vietnam, married another Vietnamese woman (not Nguyen's mother), and cared for his son. When the North Vietnamese army captured Saigon in 1975 and, in effect, ended the war, the family made its way to the United States along with other refugees, and Nguyen grew up in Houston in his father's home.

If his birth parents had been married to each other, then U.S. law would have embraced Nguyen as a citizen from birth, requiring only that one parent have lived in the United States for ten years, at least five of which were after age fourteen. This rule was intended to ensure that the United States does not develop a class of citizens who, from one generation to the next, have never lived in the United States.[10] If his parents had not been married but his mother had been a citizen, then U.S. law would also have defined Nguyen as a citizen from birth if she had lived in the United States for twelve months before he was born.

But Joseph Boulais was the citizen, and to secure Nguyen's status as a citizen, Boulais was legally required formally to establish, by "clear and convincing evidence," the blood relationship between them; to agree to provide financial support until his son reached eighteen years of age; and before the child turned eighteen, to acknowledge his paternity.

So long as life moved along quietly and Boulais supported his son, what did formal paperwork matter? Once safely in Houston, Boulais and his family lived quietly in a modest house on the outskirts of town. But in 1992, Nguyen was convicted of two counts of sexual assault of a minor and served an eight-year prison sentence.[11] In 1996, responding to rising anti-immigrant sentiment, Congress tightened the rules controlling legal resident aliens like Nguyen: conviction of a felony now meant deportation.[12] As Nguyen's prison time neared its end, the Immigration and Naturalization Service (INS) moved to deport him. Because Boulais had not legitimized Nguyen, INS understood him to be a legal resident alien, and based on his felony conviction, the INS moved to deport him. Released from prison, Nguyen remained in confinement at the INS detention center in Houston.[13] Although the United States has now exchanged ambassadors with Vietnam, it has not signed a treaty that assures repatriation for crime, and Vietnam has no interest in welcoming Nguyen back. And Nguyen, with no family or other connections in Vietnam, was terrified at the prospect of involuntary return. He was, as Jacqueline Bhabha observes in the introduction to this volume, *de facto* stateless.

Nguyen and his father found their way to Nancy Falgout, a young lawyer who specialized in immigration cases, emphasizing political asylum, deportation, and violence against women. She had opened her office in the old Vietnamese neighborhood in the shadow of downtown Houston only a few years before. Nguyen had already had a deportation hearing where he first was represented by a staff counsel for inmates who withdrew and then appeared without a lawyer at all. In Falgout, they found a determined woman who had come to the law after more than a dozen years of working on various projects that supported and helped acclimate immigrants in Houston—first in Volunteers in Service to America (VISTA)[14] and then with service projects sponsored by the Red Cross and the Young Women's Christian Association. The citizenship claim was not made until Falgout assisted with their appeal to the Bureau of Immigration Affairs (BIA). Nguyen's comment in his initial deportation hearing that he thought he was a Vietnamese citizen would undermine his later claims.[15]

Frederick Lake of Brooklyn, who also appealed his deportation, had a somewhat happier story to tell, but his future also hung on the outcome of the Supreme Court's decision about Nguyen and the terms on which it would be enforced.[16] He, too, was born abroad to parents who never married. His mother was a Jamaican citizen, and his father an American who had a family in New York. Lake's father was attentive. He visited, sent money, toys, and clothing, and risked the anger of his wife by listing Frederick—although the child of another woman—in the family bible. But Lake's father, who died in 1997, never formally legitimized his son.

When he was in his early thirties, Lake made his way to New York, and by 2000, he was in his late forties, married, and a father of two young sons (both American citizens by virtue of their birth in the United States) and worked as an automobile mechanic. Like Nguyen, he was convicted and jailed for a felony.[17] Eight months after Lake was released on parole, he appeared for his regular meeting with his parole officer, and INS agents were there to greet him. As a legal resident alien who had been convicted of a felony, the 1996 Immigration Reform Act required that Lake be deported.[18]

Meanwhile, in the state of Washington, Ricardo Ahumada-Aguilar, the child of a Mexican mother and a U.S. citizen father, was also facing deportation. Abandoned by her lover when he learned she was pregnant, Ahumada-Aguilar's mother later gained legal residency and arranged for permanent legal resident alien status for her son Ricardo. In 1990, Ahumada-Aguilar was convicted for possession of cocaine, and as a resident alien he was deported. Insisting that the deportation was not legal, he reentered the U.S. illegally. When the attorney-general of California tried to deport him again, Ahumada-Aguilar claimed he was a U.S. citizen. Much of the reasoning behind the statute, said the U.S. Court of Appeals for the Ninth Circuit, relied "on outdated stereotypes" and "the generalization that mothers are more likely to have close ties to and care for their children than are fathers." The conviction was reversed and returned to a lower court for reconsideration.[19]

Frederick Lake and Tuan Anh Nguyen also appealed their deportation rulings. Their arguments were similar to Ricardo Ahumada-Aguilar's. All found themselves vulnerable to deportation because of the accident of the sex of their citizen parent. Had their parents been married, they would have been counted citizens at birth.[20] Flip the coin: had their unmarried citizen parent been their mother, they would have been citizens at birth and invulnerable to deportation.

the final decision, for example, on where a child should be apprenticed. After a divorce, fathers automatically got custody. A father had responsibility for financial support of the children born to his wife during a marriage.

But it is also a long tradition that a man had responsibility for the children he fathered *outside* of marriage only if he wished to claim it. The nonmarital child was the burden of its mother. American colonists also passed laws specifying that children of free fathers and enslaved mothers "followed the condition of the mother." Thomas Jefferson's father-in-law, John Wayles, used his own daughter by the enslaved Elizabeth Hemings as a slave. That daughter, Sally Hemings, was half-sister to Wayles's daughter by his free wife and accompanied Martha Wayles when she married Thomas Jefferson. Sally lived her life enslaved in the Jefferson household. After Martha Jefferson's death, Sally Hemings had a relationship with Jefferson that historian Annette Gordon-Reed characterizes as concubinage. She bore seven children, five of whom survived infancy. Jefferson freed them after they reached adulthood.[31] And slaves, even those born in the United States, had no citizenship or nationality whatsoever. They were legally stateless, in theory and in practice.

And when Congress confirmed this pattern in the McCarran-Walter Immigration Act of 1952, Americans knew what the implications of continuing this arrangement would be. Here is the dissenting Judge Andrew J. Kleinfeld in *Ahumada*:

This statute was passed during the Korean War. Members of Congress knew that American soldiers who went abroad to fight wars, and caused children to be conceived while they were abroad, were overwhelmingly male, because only males were drafted, so that the number of children born illegitimately of male citizens might be large enough to affect immigration policy, while the number of illegitimate children of female citizens would be negligible. They may also have sought to minimize the administrative burden on the Department of Defense for paternity and citizenship claims respectively by the women the soldiers left behind and their children. This may not be pretty, but it is a rational basis for the sex distinction. . . . Some non-custodial fathers of children born out of wedlock do not care to pay child support if it can be avoided.[32]

In other words, even those men representing the United States abroad have the Court's permission to father children out of wedlock and abandon them. "I expect very few of these are the children of female service personnel," Ruth Bader Ginsburg observed to the amusement of the audience during the oral argument in *Nguyen*; "there are these men out there who are being Johnny Appleseed."

There have been moments when the United States acknowledged a very limited collective responsibility for the children of military men and foreign women—for example, the 1975 airlifts of mixed-race Vietnamese orphans (known as *bui-doi*). Yet these children had no solid claim on American nationality. His father's loyalty had spared Tuan Anh Nguyen a future as *bui-doi*, but Nguyen's own crime catapulted him back into the realm of the marginal, *de facto* stateless.[33]

Other nations retain asymmetries of citizenship. A few years ago, a teenage boy was denied the Egyptian national tennis trophy for his age group on the grounds that the national trophy was only for Egyptian citizens. To his mother's surprise, it was explained that when an Egyptian woman marries a foreign man, she lost her citizenship. Uneven rules like these affect women's security and their children's nationality; in time of war, they can find themselves stateless. "It is very tribal," observed an Egyptian activist. "If you go to another tribe to marry, you are no longer one of us." Only in 2004 did Egypt change this law to enable mothers to apply to naturalize their children.[34]

Indeed, these were the asymmetries that the department of justice (DOJ) had in mind as it explained its commitment to protecting the mother's ability to transmit citizenship at birth to her nonmarital child. The citizen father's claim had less traction. The primary danger, the DOJ argued, was that "foreign born children of unwed citizen mothers might become stateless if they were not eligible for U.S. citizenship, because they would not be eligible for citizenship in the country of their birth or in the country of the unwed father."[35] The primary goal in drafting the basic 1940 statute had been that a child have a secure nationality at birth—whatever that nationality happened to be. Referring back to an argument that had been made in *Miller*, they emphasized that the drafters of the basic 1940 statute recognized that "the laws of some thirty foreign countries contain provisions for the nationality of illegitimate children . . . and in all but Turkey such children follow the mother's nationality." Thus, said the DOJ in *Miller*, "the illegitimate child of a United States citizen mother and a foreign father—unlike the illegitimate child of an American father and a foreign mother—might well not be recognized as a citizen or national by the country where the child was born (or the country of which the father was a citizen)." In a footnote, they elaborated on this point. Once again, the policy was built around the misbehaving serviceman abroad:

T]he Department of State . . . has consulted . . . with consular officers in six nations in which the United States has or has had a significant military presence and which, not coincidentally, account for a large proportion of citizenship claims by illegitimate children born abroad. The Department reports that the problem of foreign law . . . remains a clear concern today in at least Germany, Great Britain, South Korea and Vietnam. Recent legal changes in the Philippines and Thailand have allowed an illegitimate child born there of a non-national mother to acquire Philippine or Thai nationality, respectively, if the father is a Philippine or Thai national and complies with the requirements of local law. The possibility of statelessness remains, however, in all other cases, unless the mother can transmit her citizenship in accordance with the law of her own country.[36]

In short, the DOJ argued in *Nguyen*, "Congress minimized the burdens on unwed mothers who seek citizenship for their children . . . in order to advance its important interest in avoiding statelessness."[37] The DOJ went on: "The foreign-born child of an unwed American mother is at much greater risk of losing his or her 'status in organized society.'"[38]

Indeed, the appropriate comparison, it seemed to the DOJ, was not between citizen mothers and citizen fathers but rather between unmarried fathers and married fathers. By marrying, the father made in effect a commitment to future children—that he would acknowledge them, raise them as Americans, and support them. The unmarried father, by contrast, "typically will have no legally recognized rights or responsibilities toward his child."[39] The statute therefore "establishes reasonable steps an unwed father must take to equalize his status with that of a married father." This is not unlike requirements of domestic law in the United States. It is so simple that it "does not impose a substantial burden on the father." And without these requirements, the door was opened to fraud, "whereby men who were not natural fathers might claim paternity solely for the purpose of securing citizenship for the child."[40]

In the brief and in subsequent conversation, Edward Kneedler, who argued both *Miller* and *Nguyen* before the Supreme Court, stressed the lightness of the burden on nonmarital fathers. The burden was "minimal."[41] Having established a paternal relationship with his son, Joseph Boulais had needed merely to have claimed citizenship for his son at any time before Nguyen reached eighteen. After that, Nguyen, as a permanent resident alien, could have sought citizenship himself. The United States provides a much easier path to establishing birthright citizenship than other nations provide: "Congress cannot be faulted if petitioners did not take advantage of the benefit it extended."[42]

In June 2001, the Supreme Court ruled against Nguyen. The decision was five to four. The majority opinion, written by Justice Anthony Kennedy, emphasized (as the DOJ had done in oral argument) the reasonableness, even generosity of the rules. Citizen fathers have an extended period of time—eighteen years—to satisfy the requirements of the statute: "Fathers and mothers are not similarly situated with regard to the proof of biological parenthood"; "gender neutral language would have been hollow neutrality." Kennedy repeated the themes of *Miller* and the *Ahumada* dissent:

Given the 9-month interval between conception and birth, it is not always certain that a father will know that a child was conceived, nor is it always clear that even the mother will be sure of the father's identity. . . . One concern in this context has always been with young people, men for the most part, who are on duty with the Armed Forces in foreign countries. . . . [Moreover, considering] the conditions which prevail today, . . . the ease of travel and the willingness of Americans to visit foreign countries have resulted in numbers of trips abroad that must be of real concern when we contemplate the prospect of accepting petitioners' argument, which would mandate . . . citizenship by male parentage subject to no condition save the father's previous length of residence in this country.

To insist that citizenship must be consciously claimed, not "unwitting," was not, Kennedy insisted, a stereotype. Even the Court's opinion in *United States v. Virginia*[43] "does not make sex a proscribed classification. . . . Physical differences between men and women . . . are enduring."

Kennedy's opinion came as a disappointment to supporters of Nguyen who had trusted that, given facts different from those in *Miller*, Kennedy could be persuaded to focus on the similar situation of the newborn rather than the different situation of the mother and father. Still, as Gerald Neuman has pointed out, the opinion could also count as strengthening another important American tradition of citizenship—that descent alone should not be enough and that citizenship should be claimed. "U.S. citizenship isn't racial," Neuman observed. "We are not a descent group. We are tied together by something else. I think it may be useful not to lose sight of this positive aspect of the decision."[44]

The other vote that Nguyen supporters had hoped to swing swung. Justice Sandra Day O'Connor wrote an extensive dissent in which she was joined by Justices Ginsburg, Souter, and Breyer. She rejected the idea that the case was most significantly about immigration and naturalization; birthright citizenship was something quite different. Quoting an observation made in *J.E.B v. Alabama ex rel. T.B*, when, in 1994, the Supreme Court had ruled against the practice of using peremptory challenges to prospective jurors on the basis of gender, O'Connor situated Nguyen squarely "in the context of our Nation's 'long and unfortunate history of sex discrimination," a history that required "the application of heightened scrutiny" and the showing of "an exceedingly persuasive justification of the sex-based classification substantially relate[d] to the achievement of important governmental objectives." The majority had written an opinion as though *Reed* had not been decided: "The different statutory treatment is solely on account of the sex of the similarly situated individuals. This type of treatment is patently inconsistent with the promise of equal protection of the laws."[45] O'Connor clung to narrow readings of *Reed* and its successors. She was not prepared to be skeptical of *Washington v. Davis* (1976), even though its holding that "the differential impact of a facially neutral law does not trigger heightened scrutiny" has long upended other equal protection claims (including, most notably, the death penalty and also veterans' preference statutes) on the basis of race and gender.[46]

But she distrusted the arguments the DOJ had made. If the Court were truly interested in establishing that the citizen parent had a substantial relationship to the child, she thought, then it would logically have placed burdens of proof of parenthood on mothers as well as fathers. If it were interested primarily in biological connection, then it would not have shrugged off DNA testing so cavalierly. And so they were back to stereotypes. We are left with a "demonstrated opportunity" for a parent/ child relationship whether or not it has been fulfilled and with "the generalization that mothers are significantly more likely than fathers . . . to develop caring relationships with their children." The stereotype itself contradicted the facts: Boulais had raised Nguyen, not his birth mother.

O'Connor dismissed the government's assertion that the rules were intended to protect children from being stateless. Nguyen belonged in the "historic regime that left women with responsibility, and freed men from responsibility for non-marital children." She ended by castigating the majority for deviating from "a line of cases in which we have vigilantly applied heightened scrutiny" and by hoping "that today's error remains an aberration."

Deporting the Alien

When his prison term was completed, Ricardo Ahumada-Aguilar was deported to Mexico, where he remains.[47] Frederick Lake stayed in New York after *Nguyen,* while his lawyers—who had come to believe in his innocence of his original criminal charge—sought to deflect his deportation. In Houston, Nancy Falgout continued to try to keep Tuan Anh

Nguyen from deportation to Vietnam, where he had no family or personal connections, did not speak the language, and would have virtually no marketable skills.[48]

Now Lake and Nguyen joined thousands more permanent legal residents who were subject to deportation, especially after the expansive provisions of the Illegal Immigration Reform and Immigrant Responsibility Act (IIRAIRA) of 1996, which required deportation for felony convictions and defined as felonies an extended range of crimes. Among those facing deportation were hundreds who came from nations with which the United States has no treaty of reciprocity (Cambodia, Vietnam, Laos) and others whose birth nation refused to take them back, effectively rendering them stateless. In Seattle, Assistant Federal Public Defender Jay Stansell found an entire floor of the Federal Detention Center devoted to the nearly 200 prisoners who had prospect neither of freedom nor deportation. Among them were perhaps "a dozen Asian-American kids" whose hope of claiming birthright citizenship was dashed by the decision.[49]

In the spring of 2001, the Supreme Court heard arguments made by Stansell and by Lucas Guttentag, director of the ACLU Immigration Rights Project, challenging indefinite preventive detention. A week after handing down its decision in *Nguyen*, the Court ruled that although the attorney-general "may" continue to detain aliens who present risks to the community, it is not a "grant of unlimited discretion." Legal resident aliens have the right to *habeas corpus* proceedings as a challenge to postremoval period detention. The Court agreed that there was a presumptive limit to what counted as a reasonable duration of detention pending deportation. When there is good reason to believe that there is no significant likelihood of deportation in the "reasonably foreseeable future," the government must have evidence warranting further detention. It agreed that "permitting indefinite detention of an alien would raise a serious constitutional problem," and it reiterated that "once an alien enters the country, . . . the Due Process Clause applies to all 'persons' within the United States, including aliens, whether their presence here is lawful, unlawful, temporary or permanent."[50]

The Power of *Jus Soli*

Conceptions of birthright citizenship in the United States have deep roots in medieval England and were drawn into visibility in the early modern era after Elizabeth I's death, when James VI of Scotland became simul-

slippery slope, already claiming victims in the Dominican Republic, where, under the principle that "an illegal person cannot produce a legal person,"[60] citizenship is denied to the children of Haitian refugees. The Congressional Children's Rights Caucus held briefings on stateless children in 2007. As these children enter refugee flows, they become persons of concern to U.S. immigration authorities.[61]

Statelessness remains a problem in international relations, in administrative law, and most deeply in political philosophy. A refreshed electoral climate in the United States, signaled by the election of Barack Obama and Democratic majorities in Congress, is likely to deflate these efforts, at least temporarily. More significant counterforce may be exerted by the work of United Nations (UN) agencies—by the UN High Commissioner for Refugees (UNHCR), who now speaks of effective nationality and ineffective nationality and has broadened the definition of the stateless to include the unprotected;[62] by UNICEF, which has embarked on a worldwide effort to increase birth registrations; and by nongovernment organizations like Refugees International, which has a deep commitment to undermining statelessness.[63]

The framers of the fourteenth amendment were not romantics. They had lost their illusions in the Civil War, and they were addressing a vicious and widespread effort to undo its accomplishments. It is clear from the debate on the fourteenth amendment that many of them had to swallow hard before their vote, but they recognized that there could be no bright line between identities that they were prepared to approve (African Americans) and those that they were not (Asians). They did not give much, if any, thought to the special circumstances of children born to American citizens outside the territorial boundaries of the nation, but they knew that virtually all slave children were nonmarital children, whether their parents were two enslaved individuals or an enslaved mother and her white master.[64] They also knew that they could not rely on natural law to protect the freedpeople but instead had to stand with Edmund Burke, who was skeptical of the abstractions of the age of the democratic revolution. Children without birthright citizenship are in a weak position from which to claim the inalienable rights to which natural law entitles them. The Reconstruction Congress knew that citizenship was most safely grounded, literally, in *jus soli*.

Ever since 1863, when Edward Everett Hale published *The Man without a Country*, Americans have had our own cautionary tale about the nightmare of statelessness. Hale wrote it hoping to undermine Confederate sympathizer Clement Vallandigham's race for governor of Ohio and to support the Union. In the novella, Philip Nolan, a young officer, is tried for treason. When the chief judge asks him whether he has anything to say that will prove his loyalty to the United States, he blurts out, "Damn the United States! I wish I may never hear of the United States again!"[65] The shocked court grants his wish, condemning him to perpetual exile. He sails around the globe on American ships for the rest of his life, doomed never to return. The tale soon took on a life of its own. It was reprinted steadily throughout the nineteenth and twentieth centuries, with flurries of new editions during World War I and again during World War II. In 1973, a sympathetic made-for-TV version appeared, echoing the anxieties of the Vietnam War; and shortly after September 11, 2001, it was reprinted by the Naval Institute Press. Tuan Anh Nugyen's crime, followed by his slip of the tongue (not unlike Philip Nolan's), touched off a sequence of decisions that placed him in a situation as unstable as Nolan's sailing ships. But the publicity of his case may well have prompted other fathers to register the legitimacy of their children. Indeed, hundreds of thousands of people have multiple citizenships and multiple passports, which suggests that many are hedging their bets. Its framers informally spoke of the fourteenth as an "amendment to enforce the bill of rights," and it is still one of the most robust elements of the Constitution. To acknowledge it as a protection against statelessness is only to give it its due.

Notes

1. U.S. Constitution, 14th amend., 1868.

2. Although the thirteenth amendment was added to the U.S. Constitution immediately after the Civil War (1860–1865) to eliminate slavery, it quickly became clear that practices associated with slavery persisted and, indeed, were revitalized. Long-term labor contracts substituted for lifetime slavery, and severe limitations on African Americans' access to civil rights and legal protections substituted for the explicit denial of any rights at all. The Civil Rights Act of 1866 extended the legal security of the emancipated slaves, and it was stabilized by the fourteenth amendment (1868) guaranteeing equal citizenship and the fifteenth amendment (1870) guaranteeing the right to vote. On the significance of these three amendments, taken together, see Justice Thurgood Marshall's eloquent "Reflections on the Bicentennial of the U.S. Constitution," May 6, 1987.

3. Thomas Hutchinson, *The History of the Province of Massachusetts Bay: From 1749 to 1774*, vol. 3 (London: J. Murray, 1828), 187.

4. The United Kingdom abolished *jus soli* (citizenship by right of the soil) in the Nationality Act of 1981, requiring that a child born on British soil also have

parents who were citizens or "settled Immigrants" (thus shifting to *jus sanguinis,* citizenship by right of blood), unless the child is abandoned and otherwise would be stateless. Ireland abolished birthright citizenship as of January 1, 2005. As the Web site of the Irish Ministry of Foreign Affairs explains, "The citizenship of a person born on the island of Ireland on or after 1 January 2005 depends on the citizenship of the person's parents at the time of the person's birth or the residency history of one of the parents prior to the birth." <http://www.dfa.ie> (accessed June 1, 2009). I am grateful to Caroline Sawyer of the Faculty of Law, Victoria University of Wellington, New Zealand, for conversations on these points.

5. The doctrine of plenary power, first articulated in the *Chinese Exclusion Cases* of 1889, treats policy decisions about immigration by Congress and by the executive as binding on the judiciary. In *Mathews v. Diaz,* 426 U.S. 67 (1976), the Supreme Court observed, "In the exercise of its broad power over naturalization and immigration, Congress regularly makes rules that would be unacceptable if applied to citizens."

6. Kristin Collins, "When Fathers's Rights Are Mothers' Duties: The Failure of Equal Protection in *Miller v. Albright,*" *Yale Law Journal* 109 (2000): 101–142.

7. *Reed v. Reed,* 404 U.S. 71 (1971).

8. Traditionally, rape was defined as the sexual assault by a man of a woman not his wife. In 1975, the South Dakota legislature eliminated the marital exemption. Other states hesitantly convicted men of raping their wives (some only if the couple were estranged and living apart). Not until 1984 did a state court— the New York Court of Appeals in *People v. Liberta,* 64 N.Y.2d 152 (1984)— strike down the marital exemption as a denial of equal protection.

9. There are corollaries to this—that men and women are necessarily heterosexual, that married men are necessarily the head of the household, and that wives owe their husbands not only sexual service but also the physical work of caregiving (a principle still present in insurance coverage for worker's compensation today).

10. The number of years has since been reduced to five and two. See Immigration and Nationality Act (McCarran-Walter Act) of 1952, 8 U.S.C. 1409.

11. I have not been able to find the records of this case. It is likely that they were sealed to protect the privacy of the minor. Nguyen's family has claimed that the act was consensual.

12. Illegal Immigration Reform and Immigrant Responsibility Act (IIRAIRA) of 1996, 8 U.S.C. sec. 1101.

13. An unknown number of others were in the same position—vulnerable to deportation because of the accident of the sex of their citizen parent.

14. She had expected the Volunteers in Service to America (VISTA) would give her a chance to travel, but the refugee program in Houston "was like going to another place."

15. Interview with Nancy Falgout, Washington, D.C., January 11, 2001.

16. *Tuan Anh Nguyen v. Immigration and Service* (INS), 533 U.S. 53 (2001).

17. His attorney, John D. B. Lewis, met him in prison, where Lewis was conferring with another client. Lewis thinks himself no pushover for prisoners who claim their innocence, but he is persuaded that Lake was framed. There is substantial evidence that Lake was in Jamaica at the time of the crime. It persuaded Lewis, who thinks it also accounts for Lake's early parole. Interview with John D. B. Lewis, April 2000.

18. *Lake v. Reno*, 226 F.3d 141 (2d Cir. 2000).

19. *United States v. Ahumada-Aguilar*, 189 F.3d 1121 (9th Cir. 1999).

20. Boulais has provided DNA evidence of his paternity.

21. *Lorelyn Penero Miller v. Madeleine Albright*, 523 U.S. 420 (1998).

22. He did not say it, but a member of the medieval guild of fishwives had the right to be in the birthing room of Marie Antoinette, charged with the responsibility to witness that the heir to the French throne had actually emerged from the body of his mother.

23. *Miller v. Albright*, 1472.

24. This was a classic Catch-22. Her father had actually filed the original suit, and Justice O'Connor acknowledged that "he was wrongly dismissed from the action by the Eastern District of Texas" and that the arguments made by the government in that case had been "misguided." Still, since Charlie Miller had failed to appeal the "erroneous dismissal of his claim" (how was he to know?), it was he who was at fault.

25. *Nguyen v. INS*, 205 F.3d 528 (2000).

26. *Lake v. Reno*, 226 F.3d 141 (2d Cir. 2000). The chief judge, who wrote the opinion, was John M. Walker, Jr. Also on the bench was Judge Damon Keith. For his distinguished career, see Stanley I. Kutler, "Taking on Another President: Judge Damon Keith," in *History News Network*, September 16, 2002, <http://hnn.us> (accessed February 21, 2009).

27. *Benner v. Canada* (Secretary of State), 1 Can. S.C.R. 358 (1997).

28. I am indebted here to Kristin Collins, "When Fathers' Rights Are Mothers' Duties: The Failure of Equal Protection in *Miller v. Albright*," *Yale Law Journal*. 109 (2000): 101–142; and Cornelia T. L. Pillard and T. Alexander Aleinikoff, "Skeptical Scrutiny of Plenary Power: Judicial and Executive Branch Decision Making in *Miller v. Albright*," *Supreme Court Review* (1998): 1–70.

29. Nationality Act of 1855, 10 Stat. 604, sec. 2

30. See *Mackenzie v. Hare*, 239 U.S. 299 (1915), upholding the denationalization of American women who married aliens, and the splendid treatment of these matters in Candice Lewis Bredbenner, *A Nationality of Her Own: Women, Marriage, and the Law of Citizenship* (Berkeley: University of California Press, 1998). I have considered *Mackenzie v. Hare* in Linda K. Kerber, *No Constitutional Right to Be Ladies* (New York: Hill and Wang, 1998).

31. Annette Gordon-Reed, *The Hemingses of Monticello: An American Family* (New York: Norton, 2008), 24.

32. *United States. v. Ahumada-Aguilar,* 189 F.3d 1121 (9th Cir. 1999).

33. Some children had firmly established knowledge of fathers, and others had tradition or appearance but no specificity. These children eventually would have to establish their own citizenship by naturalization, but their moral claims on the United States were enacted in the airlift.

34. *New York Times,* May 14, 2001, 14. The 2004 revision is described on the Egypt State Information Service Web site, <http://www.sis.gov.eg/En/Pub/achievements/tweentyFiveyears/110301000000000002.htm> (accessed May 31, 2009). Even after World War II, the Japanese constitution provided that there should be no discrimination in political, economic, or social relations because of race, creed, sex, social status, or family origin," and the Civil Code of 1947 provided that marriage was to be "maintained through mutual cooperation with equal rights of the husband and wife as its basis." Not until 1985 was the Nationality Law revised to permit Japanese women to transmit Japanese nationality to their children. See Vera Mackie, "Feminist Critiques of Modern Japanese Politics," in *Global Feminisms since 1945,* ed. Bonnie Smith (London: Routledge, 2000), 182–183, 190.

35. *Nguyen v. INS,* 99–2071, Respondent's Brief, 8, see also 17–18.

36. *Miller v. Albright,* 1997 WL 433315, Respondent's Brief, 33–34 and n.18.

37. *Nguyen v. INS,* 99–2071, Respondent's Brief, 34.

38. Ibid., 42, quoting Trop v. Dulles, 356 U.S. 101.

39. Ibid., 9

40. Ibid., 21.

41. Ibid., 39.

42. Ibid., 40; interview with Edward Kneedler, January 13, 2001.

43. *United States v. Virginia,* 518 U.S. 515 (1996).

44. Gerald Neuman, immprof@lists.colorado.edu, January 13, 2001.

45. *Nguyen v. INS,* 533 U.S. 53 (2001).

46. *Washington v. Davis,* 426 U.S. 229 (1976). See Reva Siegel, "Why Equal Protection No Longer Protects: The Evolving Forms of Status-Enforcing State Action," *Stanford Law Review* 49 (1997): 1111 ff. Among examples of claims to equal protection upended by *Washington v. Davis,* 426 U.S. 229 (1976), are death penalty claims in *McCleskey v. Kemp,* 481 U.S. 279 (1987), and sex discrimination claims in *Personnel Administrator of Massachusetts et al. v. Feeney,* 442 U.S. 256 (1979).

47. Interview with Jay Stansell, January 12, 2001.

48. Interviews with Nancy Falgout, March 19 and 23, 2002, and April 2008.

49. Interview with Jay Stansell, January 12, 2001; Jonathan Simon, "Refugees in a Carceral Age: The Rebirth of Immigration Prisons in the United States," *Public Culture* 10 (1998): 577–607.

50. *Zadvydas v. Davis,* 533 U.S. 678 (2001); *INS v. St. Cyr,* 533 U.S. 289 (2001); and *Calcano v. INS* (533 U.S. 348 (2001).

51. *Coke Report,* 1a. 77 ER 377, 7 (1608). According to Polly J. Price, Coke claimed that he had no need to turn to precedent of other nations. The king ruled by natural law, and the natural-born subject naturally owed allegiance to their sovereign. Polly J. Price, "Natural Law and Birthright Citizenship in *Calvin's Case* (1608)," *Yale Journal of Law and the Humanities* 9 (1997): 73–145.

52. Ibid. The quotation is from *Inglis v. Trustees of the Sailor's Snug Harbor,* 28 U.S. (3 Pet) 99, 164 (1830).

53. 1866 Civil Rights Act, 14 Stat. 27-30, April 9, 1866, ch. 31.

54. I am indebted to the graceful formulations of Orville Vernon Burton, *The Age of Lincoln* (New York: Hill and Wang, 2007), 275.

55. *Congressional Globe,* 39th Cong., 1st sess., pt. 1, pp. 498, 573, 574.

56. *United States v. Wong Kim Ark,* 169 U.S. 649 (1898). Before his appointment to the U.S. Supreme Court, Gray had been chief justice of the Supreme Judicial Court of Massachusetts, where he had hired Louis Brandeis as his law clerk.

57. Shane Landrum of Brandeis University is at work on an interesting history of birth certificates in the United States.

58. Martha Gardner, *The Qualities of a Citizen: Women, Immigration, and Citizenship, 1870–1965* (Princeton: Princeton University Press, 2005), 164–165.

59. An effort to undermine birthright citizenship by statute was defeated in the immigration reform bill of December 2005 but reintroduced in April 2007 as H.R. 1940 by Representative Nathan Deal of Georgia. It had over 100 cosponsors.

60. Human Rights Watch, *Illegal People,* cited in Laura van Waas, "The Children of Irregular Migrants: A Stateless Generation?," *Netherlands Quarterly of Human Rights* 25, no. 3 (2007): 437–458 n. 36.

61. On the inability of noncitizen parents to benefit from the citizenship of their child, see 8 U.S.C. sec. 1151(b)(2)(A)(I). An argument for reinterpreting the fourteenth amendment was made by Peter H. Schuck and Rogers H. Smith in *Citizenship without Consent: Illegal Aliens in American Polity* (New Haven: Yale University Press, 1985). More recently, it was made in the "Brief of Amicus Curiae Eagle Forum Education and Legal Defense Fund in Support of Respondents" in *Yaser Esam Hamdi et al. v. Rumsfeld,* 542 U.S. 507 (2004). For an international overview, see Andrew Grossman, *Birthright Citizenship as Nationality of Convenience,* Proceedings of the Third Conference on Nationality, Council of Europe, October 2004, <http://uniset.ca> (accessed January 11, 2007).

62. The UNHCR Web page, <http://www.unhcr.org/protect/3b8265c7a.html> (accessed February 22, 2009), is framed as an answer to the question "Who is stateless?": "A stateless person is someone who is not recognized by any country as a citizen. Several million people globally are effectively trapped in this legal limbo, enjoying only minimal access to national or international legal protection or to such basic rights as health and education." "The Excluded: The Strange

Hidden World of the Stateless," *Refugees* 147, no. 3 (2007), is a convenient introduction to the problem.

63. Refugees International may be followed at its Web page, <http://www.refintl .org> (accessed February 22, 2009). See also Brad Blitz's International Observatory on Statelessness, a new Web site sponsored by the Refugee Studies Centre at the University of Oxford and Oxford Brookes University.

64. I am grateful to Kristin Collins for conversations on this point.

65. Edward Everett Hale, *Man without a Country* (Boston: J. Stilman Smith, 1897), 7.

III

Effective Statelessness

12

China: Ensuring Equal Access to Education and Health Care for Children of Internal Migrants

Kirsten Di Martino[1]

Since the 1990s, China has experienced rapid but highly uneven development that accentuates the divide between urban and rural communities. One of the key features of this development is large-scale migration from rural areas to urban centers. China's migrant workforce of 150 million represents the largest movement of people in modern history.

The Chinese government has embraced internal migration as essential to the national development strategy. If this migration is managed effectively, the government sees it as a means to increase rural incomes, restructure the economy, and level urban, rural, and regional disparities. However, maximizing the benefits of internal migration while mitigating its adverse effects is a difficult balancing act. Municipal and local governments face serious challenges in providing adequate social security and basic social services to migrant workers and their families.

This chapter examines the effects of internal migration on children in China and explores policy options for addressing the key challenges facing migrant children. Unlike local resident children who have an urban *hukou* (urban household registration), migrant children face extensive difficulties in accessing education and health-care services in urban areas as they only have a rural *hukou* (rural household registration), a prerequisite for accessing such services. Migrant children in China are effectively stateless: although citizens, they cannot access services to which they are eligible.[2] At the same time, they are also *de facto* stateless: as a rural *hukou* is very difficult to convert into an urban *hukou*, a situation not dissimilar to the one of undocumented migrant children in the United States and Western Europe described, for instance, by Stephen H.Legomsky and Luca Bicocchi elsewhere in the volume.

The *hukou* system was introduced in the late 1950s and continues to restrict the internal movement of the population. The *hukou* system effectively creates a two-tier system of citizens by identifying individuals at birth as either urban or rural residents based on their parents' *hukou* status. This social status is difficult to change. The majority of migrant workers who retain their original rural household registration are ineligible for the insurance and social welfare benefits (including unemployment, medical, and education benefits) that are granted to holders of urban household-registration permits. Similarly, their children who also hold a rural *hukou* cannot access public education and health-care services on a par with children of local urban residents.

Since the 1980s, the government has progressively relaxed the *hukou* system to allow millions of migrant rural workers to move to the cities. However, the system has not yet been completely reformed. Only a few migrants are granted the permanent official urban resident status that allows access to social services and other entitlements.

China is committed to achieving the millennium development goals (MDGs)[3] by 2015 and has ratified the United Nations Convention on the Rights of the Child (CRC).[4] The government's commitment to children is further articulated in the National Program of Action for Child Development (2001–2010), which sets clear goals to ensure the right of all children, including migrant children, to nine years of compulsory education and health-care coverage.

A human-rights-based approach to development identifies states as the main duty bearers. According to this approach, states should adapt their human-development policies to the reality of migration and improve the links among economic development, poverty-reduction strategies, and social development. Maximizing the benefits derived from migration while mitigating the harmful effects on the most vulnerable—especially children—remains a key challenge:

For where there is even distribution, there is no poverty. Where there is harmony, there is no scarcity. Where there is contentment, there is no revolt.
—Confucius, 551–479 BCE

Context

China has made remarkable progress in poverty alleviation since the start of the reforms in the late 1970s. Measured by the national poverty line, China's total official number of poor has dropped from 85 million in 1990 (9.6 percent of the rural population) to 14.79 million in 2007 (1.6 percent).[5] Unprecedented migration out of rural areas has contributed significantly to rural income growth, poverty reduction, and economic development.

Despite its rapid economic growth (averaging 9.5 percent annually in the fifteen years from 1990 to 2005, and more than 10 or 11 percent in recent years), China is still a developing country facing large and complex challenges in meeting the aspirations of all its people. Economic growth and accelerated industrialization and urbanization have generated uneven development and increased social demands for public services and goods. At the same time, labor-market discrimination and social exclusion are exposing migrants to many risks and vulnerabilities in the cities, where the urban migrant poor are on the increase. China now faces the dual challenge of sustaining economic development while ensuring the provision of basic and guaranteed public services for all.

China's Rapid But Highly Uneven Development

China's uneven development is accentuating the disparities between urban and rural citizens and widening the regional and personal income gap. The per capita gross domestic product (GDP) rose from U.S. $964 in 2000 to U.S. $3,328 in 2008.[6] However, development remains extremely uneven, with huge differences in income and levels of public services between the more developed coastal areas and the more backward remote interior areas as well as between urban and rural areas. In fact, the urban-rural income gap widened from 2.79 to 1 in 2000 to 3.33 to 1 in 2007[7] (see table 12.1). In 2007, the per capita GDP of urban Shanghai was 65,347 yuan, 9.55 times higher than that of rural Guizhou—one of the poorest western provinces of China—at 6,835 yuan.[8]

This, in turn, produces large disparities in tax revenue across the country and, given a weak fiscal-transfer system, large disparities in public expenditures per capita between rich and poor areas. Not surprisingly, the poorer rural areas have the worst social-development indicators. For example, the maternal mortality rate (MMR) in 2007 was 1.6 times higher in rural areas compared to urban areas and 2.5 times higher in remote areas compared to coastal areas. Mortality rates in rural type 3 and 4 areas[9] are two to five times higher compared to urban areas, and rural type 2 and 3 areas account for over 70 percent of all maternal and child deaths.[10]

Faced with these new economic and social contradictions, the Chinese government has called for "human-oriented development." Human development combined with economic and social development is seen as

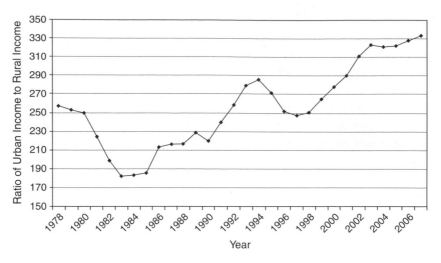

Figure 12.1
Ratio of urban income to rural income, China, 1978 to 2007. *Source: 2008 China Statistical Summary.*

the basis for the government's vision of a harmonious *Xiaokang* society for which addressing inequalities between the urban, rural, and migrant populations is a key priority. In recent years, the Chinese government has introduced a host of policy and legislative reforms to achieve gradual equalization of basic services and guarantee social justice and fairness. These reforms seek to achieve equal access by migrant workers and their families to compulsory education, public health and basic medical treatment, basic social security, and public-service employment. However, the size and complexity of the challenge means that progress remains gradual and uneven.

The Nature of Internal Migration

One of the key features of rapid economic growth and uneven development is large-scale migration from the county to the cities—possibly the largest movement of people in modern history.[11] For nearly five decades, China's unique household-registration system—*hukou*—restricted the movement of the population. The *hukou* system, which was introduced in China in 1958, required each household member to register with the local public security office as a legal resident, whether they were urban or rural.[12] This system was designed to prevent large numbers of poor rural workers from moving to urban areas. It required rural residents to provide documentation from an urban-based employer before they could legally reside in a city and to register with the urban police authorities. Migrant workers who retained their original rural household registration were ineligible for insurance and social welfare benefits granted to holders of urban household-registration permits.

Migration remained minimal and a highly controlled process until the period of reform in the early 1980s, when government policies relaxing the *hukou* system, high investment, and rapid urbanization created a huge demand for cheap, low-skilled workers in labor-intensive industries.[13] In 2003, the central government introduced the use of temporary household-registration certificates to facilitate the employment of rural migrants in cities.[14] The *hukou* system has since been further relaxed. Millions of migrant rural workers have moved to the cities in search of better opportunities, but the system has not yet been completely reformed.

China has a population of 1.32 billion people,[15] one-fifth of the global population and roughly three times the population of the European Union (EU). The number of migrant rural workers who have sought employment in the country's urban centers rose from just 2 million in the mid-1980s[16] to over 131 million in 2000,[17] accounting for over 10.6 percent of the population. At present, the internal migrant population is estimated to number some 150 million, comparable to the entire workforce of the United States.[18] In 2000, the number of migrant children was estimated at 23.6 million children,[19] 6.8 percent of all children in China and 18 percent of the total migrant population.[20] This figure increased to 25.25 million in 2005, accounting for 7.5 percent of all children in China.[21] The number of children left behind by parents who migrate has almost tripled in recent years from 22 million in 2000[22] to 58.61 million, and an estimated 48.48 million are under fourteen years of age.[23] Female migrants make up one-third of all migrants but constitute over half of those between sixteen and twenty-four years old.[24]

Over the next twenty years, the migrant population is expected to double as a shrinking agricultural sector and expanding industrial and service sectors will compel more surplus rural workers and new entrants to the rural labor force to find employment in towns and cities. In 2003, the proportion of urban population in China exceeded 40 percent for the first time. By 2007, it reached 44.94 percent (table 12.2).[25] The Eleventh Five-Year Plan for National Economic and Social Development (2006–2010) projects that the urbanization rate will increase to 47 percent in 2010. However, it is unclear how this projection may be affected by the global financial crisis. An estimated 20 million migrant

Table 12.1
Population data, China, 2000

	Number (million)	Percentage of total population	of child population	of migrant population	of migrant children
Total population	1,242.6	100.0			
Child population	345.3	27.8	100.0		
Male	182.6	14.7	52.9		
Female	162.7	13.1	47.1		
Migrant population	131.2	10.6		100.0	
Migrant children	23.6	1.9	6.8	18.0	100.0
Male	11.81	0.9	3.4	9.0	49.98
Female	11.82	0.9	3.4	9.0	50.02

Source: Tabulation on the *2000 Population Census of the People's Republic of China*, Population Census Office under the State Council and Department of Population, Social, Science, and Technology Statistics, National Bureau of Statistics, China Statistics Press, August 2002.

Table 12.2
The increased proportion of live births among migrant women in 2006

	Live births in 2005		M/P (percent) (2005)	Live births in 2006		M/P (percent) (2006)
	Migrant (M)	Permanent (P)		M	P	
Beijing	56,346	58,409	96.4%	65,899	63,120	104.40%
Tianjin	1,957	74,763	2.62%	20,738	75,349	27.53%
Shanghai	52,736	72,394	72.85%	75,030	62,980	119.13%
Jiangsu	38,493	532,714	7.23%	40,869	560,779	7.29%
Zhejiang	125,120	410,322	30.49%	153,522	378,909	40.50%
Guangdong	278,156	826,754	33.64%	350,084	856,020	40.90%

Source: MCH Annual Report, 2007.

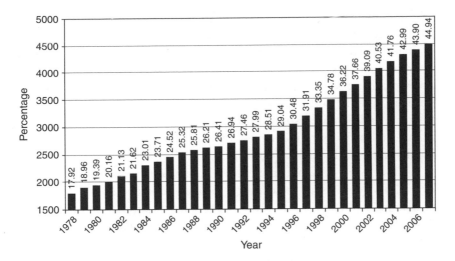

Figure 12.2
Rate of urbanization, China, 1978 to 2007 (percent). *Source: 2008 China Statistical Abstract.*

workers have already returned home to the countryside after losing their jobs in the cities.[26]

Limited Social Protection and Access to Basic Social Services

China's migrant workforce is fueling China's growth, but municipal and local governments are facing serious challenges in providing migrant workers and their families with social security and basic and guaranteed public services, including health care, education, and protection.

In 2005, the United Nations' Committee on Economic, Social, and Cultural Rights expressed its "deep concern" at "the *de facto* discrimination against internal migrants in the fields of employment, social security, health services, housing, and education that indirectly result from *inter alia*, the restrictive national household-registration system (*hukou*) which continues to be in place despite official announcements regarding reforms."[27] Temporary residence permits allow the government to monitor migrants in the cities while they continue to be denied many of the benefits of permanent urban household registration.

The *hukou* system also affects children of migrants, who are unable to access health-care and education services on a par with urban resident children because of their rural *hukou* permit. In 2005, the United Nations' Committee on the Rights of the Child expressed its concern about "discrimination against certain groups on the mainland, such as . . . internal migrant children." The Committee recommended that the Chinese government "strengthen efforts to eliminate discrimination against . . . internal migrant children" by "ensuring that these children have equal access to basic services, including health, education, and other social services, and that services used by these children are allocated sufficient financial and human resources" and by "enhancing monitoring of programs and services implemented by local authorities with a view to identifying and eliminating disparities."[28]

Although the migrant population contributes significantly to the overall development of the country, their working and living conditions remain markedly inferior to those of the resident population in receiving cities. Lack of permanent residence status—urban *hukou*—irregular and often informal employment patterns, financial insecurity, as well as the absence of nationwide territorial continuity in ensuring social protection exclude them from social security coverage and access to those public social services that are financed and delivered by local authorities to their own resident populations. Temporary household registration allows migrant workers to find work and housing strictly on a temporary basis. Many migrant workers are either unaware of the possibility of applying for such status or fear that any official contact with local public authorities may reduce their chances of staying in the cities for an extended period of time. Unscrupulous employers take advantage of this situation and continue to employ migrant workers illegally.

Eighty-four percent of migrants are working in low-paid and insecure jobs in the informal sector.[29] In 2006, the average living-quality index for migrant rural workers was 0.5, which was equivalent to 53 percent of the average level of urban residents. The social security index was only 0.3, which means that their social security coverage was only 25 percent of that of their urban counterparts.[30]

As a result, most migrant workers and their families are marginalized in their own country, excluded from the "harmonious society" that notably aims to avoid "polarization and social contradictions."

The Effect of Migration on Children

Most migrant workers are young and middle-aged and have school-aged children.[31] Many leave their children behind in villages to be brought up by their grandparents or relatives, but others migrate with their children to the cities.

Children of Migrants

As they move, children of migrants lose their traditional support structures and face economic hardship and discrimination as well as poor health and low rates of school enrollment and promotion. Many are not registered under the temporary household-registration system in their new place of residence and remain invisible to the local authorities as there is no requirement to collect data and register children under sixteen years of age in their new place of residence. Rather than the result of the authorities' inability to register children of migrants, their "invisibility" is a product of state policy to neglect one part of the child population.

This neglect has consequences, not least in respect to migrant children's access to education. Despite government policies and regulations (see below) barring discrimination against children of migrants, many of them are unable to attend public schools—38 percent in the case of migrant children in Beijing.[32] The reasons for this are twofold. First, children of migrants either lack the urban *hukou* or temporary household registration required to attend public schools. Second, in practice, public schools continue to collect extra fees from migrant workers to cover the costs of an increased intake of children of migrant workers.

As a result of these difficulties, many children of migrants are enrolled in low-quality private schools set up to cater to the migrant community. High fees and the entry of some older migrant children into the labor market result in higher dropout rates for migrant children than urban resident children.[33] The lack of health insurance coverage of migrants and their families—due partly to the completely separate nature of the schemes set up in urban and rural areas and the nontransferability of benefits because of the *hukou* system—leads to high medical expenses and access barriers to health services. Maternal and child mortality is significantly higher among migrants than urban residents (see below).[34]

Children Left Behind

The situation of children who are left behind, deprived of either one or both parents, is a matter of serious concern to the government. Left-behind children are concentrated in the densely populated and economically less developed counties in the provinces of Sichuan, Guangdong, Jiangxi, Anhui, Hunan, and Hainan, accounting for as much as 40 percent of all children in some counties. About 53 percent of them grow up with a single parent, and 47 percent are entrusted to the care of grandparents, other relatives, and in some cases even their siblings.

Nearly 40 percent of all left-behind children below the age of five live with their grandparents. Most left-behind children maintain irregular and limited contact with their parents and feel lonely, isolated, and deprived of support. Some see their parents only once a year during the spring festival. Their caregivers, especially grandparents, are often unable to provide them with adequate care—including emotional support, adequate hygiene and nutrition, and homework supervision. School retention rates are significantly lower for left-behind children, especially in junior high school,[35] and their relationships with their peers are often affected. This has a profound impact on both their physical, educational, and psychosocial development and well-being.

Limited Access to Education

China has the largest educated population[36] and the largest educational system in the world. As part of its development drive, the Chinese government has sought to improve the access to, and the quality of, education by increasing primary and secondary school enrollment. By the end of 2007, the net enrollment in primary education reached 99.5 percent, and the enrollment rate for junior high school reached 98 percent. According to the government, nine-year compulsory education now covers 99.3 percent of the school-age population nationwide, meeting the target of achieving universal primary education.[37]

Despite overall progress in primary and secondary school enrollment, in reality, many migrant children are not able to attend public schools. A 2003 UNICEF-supported survey in nine cities with a large influx of migrant workers found that only 90.7 percent of migrant children go to school. About 9.3 percent of migrant children are unable to attend school: 6.9 percent have never attended school, and 2.4 percent drop out before completing compulsory education. The older the age group, the higher the percentage of school dropouts. From the age of eight to the age of fourteen, the percentage of migrant children who are unable to go to school increases from 0.8 percent to 15.4 percent. The survey also found that those migrant children who do attend school are often over-aged. Nearly 47 percent of migrant children fail to go to school when they reach school age (six years of age), and some eleven- to fourteen-year-olds were still in the first and second grades. About 81 percent of migrant children are attending public schools, and 19 percent of them go to private schools for children of migrants.[38]

A more recent survey from 2006 by the National Bureau of Statistic indicates that only 72 percent of children of migrants are enrolled in public schools, 22 percent in private schools, and 1 percent cannot go to school or drop out for various reasons.[39] Of the migrant workers surveyed, 6.5 percent were satisfied with their children's education, 43.5 percent were fairly satisfied, 26 percent were neither satisfied nor dissatisfied, 19.6 percent were not quite satisfied, and 4.4 percent were very unsatisfied.[40]

Limited Access to Maternal and Child Health-Care Services

Although China has made significant progress in maternal and child health in recent years, the absolute number of maternal and child deaths remains high given China's large population, and a significant gap remains between rural and urban residents.[41]

Maternal Health

Between 2003 and 2007, the maternal mortality ratio (MMR) decreased from 51.3 to 36.6 per 100,000 live births. However, the MMR actually increased by 1.6 percent in urban areas from 2006 to 2007. Even more significantly, the MMR increased 5.7 percent in coastal areas from 2000 to 2007 but decreased 33.8 percent and 49 percent in inland and remote regions, respectively.[42] The rising MMR in coastal areas is attributed mainly to the increase in migrant workers who generally have lower access to health services.

The health-care behavior of migrant women is characterized by fewer antenatal checkups, low rate of hospital deliveries, low rate of postnatal visits, and a high rate of home deliveries.[43] The MMR among migrant women is significantly higher than that of women with permanent urban residences. In 2006, the MMR of migrant women was 38.3 compared to 30.2 among city-dwellers.[44]

Child Health

Between 2003 and 2007, the infant mortality ratio (IMR) declined from 25.5 to 15.3 per 1,000 live births and the under-age-five mortality rate decreased remarkably from 29.9 to 18.1 per 1,000 live births. However, the under-five mortality rate increased from 9.9 in 2005 to 10.4 in 2007 in coastal areas, a rise of 0.5 percent.[45] Again, this trend is explained by a growing migrant population in coastal areas. The proportion of children possessing regular physical examination cards in Beijing is 48 percent for migrant children, but over 90 percent among permanent residents.[46] Children of migrants are unable to access health services and obtain the physical examination card without an urban *hukou* or temporary household registration permit.

A UNICEF-supported study in 2003 found that average infant mortality for the resident population and the under-five mortality rate for the migrant population in seven of the nine cities surveyed (Beijing, Shenzhen, Wuhan, Chengdu, Xianyang, Shaoxing, and Zhuzhou—all cities with a large influx of migrant workers) was 13.8 per 1,000 and 24.8 per 1,000, respectively, the latter of which is significantly higher than the figures for the urban population with permanent residence.[47]

The proportion of live births among migrant women to permanent registered residents in several provinces containing large numbers of migrant workers is increasing (see table 12.2). Coverage data for migrant women and children has increased in each province, suggesting improved access by migrants to maternal health services. It may also point to an overall increase in numbers of migrant workers and a rising number of births among the migrant population.

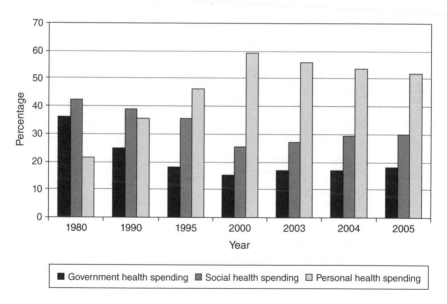

Figure 12.3
Ratios of health spending (percent) by government, society, and individuals. *Source:* The 1980 to 2004 data originate from the *2006 China Health Statistical Yearbook*, and the 2005 data are drawn from the *2006 Statistical Communique on the Development of China's Health Undertakings*.

The Government Response to Ensure Equal Access to Education and Health Care for Migrant Children

In recent years, China's government policy has evolved from restricting migration, to controlling migration, and now to facilitating migration.[48] This includes a host of policy and legislative reforms to ensure that children of migrants enjoy equal access to education and healthcare.

China is committed to achieving the millenium development goals (MDGs) by 2015, including providing universal primary education, reducing child mortality, and improving maternal health. It has also ratified the CRC and further articulated its commitment to children in the National Program of Action for Child Development (2001–2010), which sets clear goals to "guarantee children among the migrant population to basically receive nine years of compulsory education" and to "gradually raise the coverage of healthcare management for . . . children among the migrant population."

In relation to migrant women, the National Program of Action for Women's Development (2001–2010) states that they are to "enjoy the same healthcare service as the women with registered residence" in the urban areas and they are to be "integrated . . . in the maternal healthcare management system in their cities of destination."

In December 2006, the National People's Congress adopted the revised Law on the Protection of Minors.[49] Article 28 of the revised law stipulates that "people's governments at various levels shall ensure minors' right to education and take actions to guarantee access to education by minors from poor families . . . and migrant minors."

The government has also amended the compulsory education law,[50] which contains a new provision that ensures the right to education for children of migrant workers regardless of where they live. The law stipulates that when either parents or legal guardians are migrant workers living and working with their children in locations other than where the family is registered, local governments where they live and work must provide for the child's education. The law also eliminates for the first time fees for compulsory education through the allocation of resources from the government budget and the elimination of miscellaneous fees. It stipulates that "all school-aged children and adolescents shall receive compulsory education. Compulsory education is a public service that shall be guaranteed by the state. No tuition or miscellaneous fees may be charged for compulsory education." However, in view of the disparities in levels of economic development in different parts of the country, the law states in supplementary articles that "the implementation steps for not charging miscellaneous fees in compulsory education shall be stipulated by the State Council." The government has established inspection mechanisms under the legal office of the National People's Congress (NPC) and the ministry of education to ensure effective enforcement of these new legal provisions. Schools that continue charging illegal fees have been warned. However, in practice, it remains difficult to enforce these provisions systematically nationwide.

What Policy Options Ensure Equal Access to Education and Health Care for Children of Migrants?

Although China has introduced policy and legislative reforms to ensure equal access to education and health care for all children, including migrant children, several key factors still prevent children of migrants from accessing these services on a par with local resident children. These factors relate to fundamental institutional, administrative, and budgetary arrangements that continue to exclude the migrant population from enjoying the same rights as resident urban citizens.

Discrimination against migrants is not only enshrined in administrative barriers: "China's urban citizens commonly tend to see rural people as being of "low cultural level" and "low quality"; "The urbanization of rural populations thus challenges widespread and deeply held social prejudices."[51]

If migration is to be an effective tool in the fight against poverty, clear policy directions need to be formulated and pursued to ensure that migrant workers and their families derive the full benefits of economic development and are not excluded.

First, the *hukou* system needs to be reformed to eliminate the *de facto* institutional discrimination between rural and urban residents that prevents migrant workers with a rural *hukou* from enjoying the same rights and entitlements as persons with an urban *hukou*. Second, central government expenditure on education and health-care needs to be increased to ensure that public schools and local health services, which now heavily rely on funding from local budgets, receive sufficient resources to meet the growing demands of an increasing migrant population. Ensuring universal access to maternal and child health-care services and introducing one universal health insurance scheme for all regardless of their *hukou* status would also significantly improve access to health care for all, regardless of place of residence. Third, fiscal transfer payments need to be increased and equalized to cover both rural and urban poor and ensure adequate financing of social services. Fourth, all children of migrants below sixteen years of age need to be registered so that they obtain temporary household registration. This will enable local authorities to advocate for, monitor, and allocate adequate resources to ensure equal access to basic education, health, and protection services for children of migrants.

Reform the Household-Registration System (*Hukou*)

The underlying and most fundamental cause of unequal access to social security and public services for migrant workers and their children remains the *hukou* system. This system effectively identifies individuals at birth as either urban or rural residents based on their parents' *hukou* status. This social status is difficult to change for those with low education and income levels, thereby creating a *de facto* two-tier system of citizens. The majority of migrant workers who migrate to the cities are granted only temporary urban residence status and do not enjoy the same rights, services, and protection as urban-registered populations, including unemployment, medical, and education benefits guaranteed to residents with an urban *hukou*. Rather than creating an enabling environment, the *hukou* system has restricted migrants' access to social protection.

Criteria for qualifying for a permanent urban *hukou* vary considerably between large cities and subprovincial cities, which are eager to grow and expand and rely heavily on migrants. In subprovincial cities and towns, the threshold is usually much lower, and registered urban populations are growing rapidly. In these cities, evidence of fixed employment is usually sufficient to qualify for residency conversion from rural to urban *hukou*. However, in cities such as Beijing and Shanghai, the requirements are much more stringent, and migrants may be required to make cash payments in the form of bribes to invest in property or businesses and to have certain educational qualifications before qualifying for urban residency. In those cities, local governments have relaxed *hukou* restrictions on better-educated and wealthier migrants but have not granted similar concessions to poor migrant workers working under difficult conditions. Only 40 percent of today's estimated 150 million migrant workers living and working in cities obtain either a permanent urban *hukou* or a temporary residence permit. As a result of their social status, many migrants continue to endure harsh living conditions in marginalized urban communities, and most have no labor contracts. Recognition of this "plight" is growing; some are now calling for "universal citizenship" and major reforms in the household registration system.[52]

The government has indicated that it is committed to the gradual reform of the *hukou* system. These reforms include long-term plans to merge urban and rural health insurance schemes and equalize social entitlements to facilitate access to services and overcome disparities between rural and urban residents. In November 2007, the central government announced that it plans to "gradually commit to giving migrant workers in stable employment the opportunity for permanent residency status."[53] In January 2008, the National Development and Reform Commission, an official policy-formation organ of the government, indicated that the *hukou* system would be eliminated by 2020.[54]

However, these are huge and demanding reforms with large budgetary implications and will take many years to design and implement. In practice, *hukou* liberalization and population management are the responsibility of local governments. The financial and management challenges involved in reforming the *hukou* system dictate that developments must be gradual and experimental and reflect the conditions of a town or city. For example, when qualifications for permanent residence were relaxed in the city of Zhengzhou, the migrant population mushroomed tenfold to 150,000 in just three months. The rapid deterioration of social order forced authorities to reverse the decision.[55]

Increase Central Government Expenditures Relative to GDP on Education and Health Care

Government resources account for a relatively low share of total social sector expenditure, leaving individual households to assume much of the responsibility for paying for services, through fees and user charges. This has placed a heavy burden on the poor, particularly in the rural areas and among migrants in the cities.

Education   China spends only 2.8 percent of its GDP on education, which is far less than the international recommended average of 5 to 6 percent. Expenditures are tilted toward higher-education institutions at the expense of the institutions providing compulsory education.

Public schools therefore rely heavily on resources from local budgets. But local government cannot always allocate sufficient resources to schools in areas with a large influx of migrant children, thereby creating inequalities in educational opportunities. Including the children of migrants in the education system presents extremely high costs to the local authorities.[56] When residents in a city in Shandong province sought to extend free education to these children, they found that the necessary U.S. $1.2 million would be several times the total education budget.[57]

In 2005, the Committee on the Rights of the Child recommended that the government of China "increase the allocation of resources to education in step with increases in GDP, as directed by the Education Law, and target those resources towards ensuring that all children, in particular . . . migrant children, complete nine years of compulsory education."[58]

The government has begun to take some important steps to address this problem. In education, it has committed additional central government funds to back up the abolition of fees in primary and junior secondary schools in rural China (launched in the western region in 2006 and extended to the central and eastern regions in 2007) to promote the completion rate of rural compulsory education. The "two exemptions, one subsidy" policy circumscribes both the exemption from textbook payment, tuition, and miscellaneous fees and the subsidy to resident students as supplement for their living expenses. However, this policy does not yet extend to poor urban migrant families who do not have an urban *hukou*.

Health   The government spends only about 0.8 percent of its GDP on health. Government health expenditures in 2005 accounted for only 18 percent of total health expenditure (in contrast to over 50 percent of the total being attributed to individuals and about 30 percent to society) (see table 12.1). This places a heavy burden on the poor, including poor urban migrant workers.

These sectors need to receive high priority in the allocation of government resources. Budget policy should aim at quickly achieving the target of raising government education expenditure to 4 percent of the GDP, as was announced in 1993, as well as setting a longer-term goal of achieving the 6 percent international target. In health, efforts should be made to increase the share of government expenditure to total health expenditures (only 18 percent in 2006) and to raise the ratio of government health expenditures to 2 percent of the GDP. These targets are not impossible to achieve in China, as the rapid increase in government revenue provides an opportunity for the allocation of additional resources to the social sector.

A combination of an absolute and relative increase in central government budget for education and health care would help to improve access to public schools and health-care services for all children regardless the geographical location.

Increase and Equalize Fiscal Transfer Payments to Cover Both Rural and Urban Poor

Public expenditures are inequitably distributed both among regions and between urban and rural areas within a region due to the high degree of decentralization in the financing of social services and the large differences in local levels of economic development and tax revenues, which are insufficiently offset by intergovernmental transfer payments. For example, expenditure per primary school pupil was ten times higher in Shanghai than in the province of Henan in 2005.[59]

Fiscal decentralization and the nonequalization of fiscal transfers makes it difficult for rural areas to finance essential social services, including education and health care of rural children, but it also affects the fiscal capacity of municipal authorities in urban areas with a large influx of migrants. These authorities are not always able to meet the increasing demand for social services by the migrant population, including appropriate allocation of resources to public schools and health-care services for them to accommodate children of migrants. The migrant population should be considered a key determinant in government decisions on how many resources to allocate to local governments for basic service delivery.

Ensure Temporary Household Registration of All Children of Migrants below Sixteen Years of Age

There is currently no requirement for migrant parents to temporarily register children below sixteen years of age in their new place of residence to obtain temporary household registration. As a result, local governments often lack adequate information on the actual number of children of migrants who live in their localities.

Since 2001, UNICEF has been working with the National Working Committee for Children and Women (NWCCW) to pilot a system to register children of migrants below sixteen years of age in two cities with a large influx of migrants so that they can obtain temporary household registration. The system was initially tested in Shijiazhuang in Hebei province and Wuxi in Jiangsu province. In 2006, the initiative was extended to Beijing municipality. The project provides support to local public security bureaus and authorities to enable them to collect and maintain updated information on children of migrants and their families by using a dedicated management information system (MIS) linked to the temporary registration system for adult migrants. These systems recognize and publicize the existence of migrant children in their new home cities, and they also assist with the provision of protection and service referral. As a result of these efforts, 390,000 children of migrants below sixteen years of age have been registered by mid-2008 in the three NWCCW/UNICEF project sites.

Systematic registration of all migrant children under sixteen years of age would make migrant children more "visible" and improve the capacity of local government to advocate for, monitor, and allocate resources more efficiently to the provision of social services for children.

Reduce the Burden of Fees for Education and Health Care on the Urban Poor Migrant Population

Despite government efforts to promote equal rights in access to the nine-year compulsory education system for all of China's children and despite attempts to make it unlawful for cities to refuse to accept migrant children in public schools, migrant workers are still finding it difficult to get their children enrolled in urban school systems unless they can afford the exorbitant extra fees or agree to pay voluntary donations to the school.

Many municipal and local governments have introduced temporary school fees that are payable by transient students but not by local urban residents. A recent survey by the National Bureau of Statistics indicates that nearly 50 percent of migrants whose children moved to urban areas with them, had to pay "transient fees" and "supporting fees." The average per capita cost was 1,226 yuan (U.S. $153.25) per year.[60] The same survey also found that 36 percent of migrant workers believe that the biggest challenges in terms of their children's education are the high costs. About 27.6 percent of them said that their biggest challenge was not having an urban *hukou*, and 16.1 percent reported that their children were discriminated against in school.[61] Many migrant workers cannot afford these extra fees, and their children either have to go to schools run by other migrants—the so-called migrant schools—or not go to school at all. These schools charge much less, but most are unable to meet minimum standards due to inadequate government support and monitoring. Management and teacher quality are poor, there is high teacher turnover, conditions and infrastructure are not up to standard, and safety norms are not respected. In many instances, local authorities have responded by closing down such schools, thereby depriving these child migrants of any form of education.

Although many local governments have issued policies prohibiting the collection of education fees, the implementation of these policies is unsatisfactory. For instance, in 2004, the Beijing municipal government introduced regulations to eliminate temporary school fees for migrant children after the Beijing Education Commission specified that migrant children should pay the same fees as resident urban children.[62] In response, public schools are now introducing other "miscellaneous fees" to replace the "temporary fees." Lack of effective monitoring and enforcement mechanisms combined with an extremely competitive education system that drives parents to pay fees simply to secure a place for their child in a good school makes it difficult to enforce these regulations in practice.

The extra fees charged for the enrollment of migrant children and the financial difficulties of migrant families have resulted in lower enrollment rates for children of migrants compared to national average enrollment rates. Some are denied access to school because their parents do not have necessary documents, such as temporary residence permits, employment permits, and family-planning certificates.

Increased government expenditures on education would also help to reduce the need for the private, out-of pocket expenditures that affect the poorest, including migrant families. Similarly, the "two fees and one subsidy" policy, which aims at ensuring that children living in rural poor areas can complete compulsory education, should be extended to cover poor migrant children living in urban areas. If this policy were adequately applied and enforced, it would exempt children of migrants from paying miscellaneous fees and significantly increase their chances of accessing public schools.

Lift Restrictions on the Taking of Junior Secondary or College Exams by Migrant Children in Their New Home Cities

Even for those children of migrants who do receive education in the cities, the road to education is not problem-free. Due to the *hukou* system, children of migrants are obliged to go back to their hometown where their permanent residence is registered to take high school entrance exams and sit for the college entrance examination. They are therefore at a disadvantage compared to other children as there is often a gap between what they have learned in city schools and what they will be tested on in the examination. Relaxing this requirement would allow migrant children to take their examination where they attend school and to continue their education in their new place of residence.

Provide the Universal Delivery of an Essential Package of Maternal and Child Health-Care Services

The maternal and child health-care (MCH) system is still unable to cover marginal and vulnerable populations. Despite a well-developed MCH network, universal access to the services has not been achieved as the migrant population remains largely uncovered. Due to their *hukou* status, inadequate education, lack of awareness of self-care practices, and the high cost of medical and health services, migrant families frequently encounter problems obtaining adequate health care, and their needs are often neglected by the service network. This situation is aggravated by inadequate documentation of the maternal and child health-care needs and the status of the migrant population.

China has made significant progress in reducing maternal and child mortality. However, to ensure the achievement of the millennium development goals by 2015, maternal and child mortality in rural areas and among the poor migrant urban population must be significantly reduced.

Strategic MCH interventions need to be implemented to ensure equal access to quality MCH services for all. The government is prioritizing rural areas, but high priority should also be given to poor urban migrants because they account for a large proportion of maternal and child deaths in the urban areas.

Improve Health Insurance Coverage

The current social protection system reflects the approach underlying the *hukou* system. There are two completely separate insurance schemes for urban and rural residents, and this system makes it extremely difficult for migrant workers to gain access to urban social protection services.

Most migrant workers have no formal contracts or no contracts at all and can therefore not take part in the urban residents' basic medical insurance scheme. Without a permanent household residence in the city, they cannot get health insurance for themselves and their children. Lack of social security protection and the high cost of services make migrants reluctant to seek medical attention for themselves and their families, including maternal and child health-care services. About 33 percent of migrant workers are not satisfied with the available medical service.[63]

More than two-thirds of the migrant workers do not go to regular hospitals because the charges are too high. Nearly 75 percent of migrant rural workers are not covered by any insurance.[64]

In October 2003, the government launched a new Rural Cooperative Medical System (RCMS), a voluntary health insurance scheme that is financed primarily through central and local government funds (80 percent) as well as household contributions (20 percent). The RCMS currently covers about 90 percent of the rural population. The government has also been implementing a medical financial-assistance (MFA) scheme for both urban and rural poor. Under the new health-sector reform plan, the government has committed to full coverage of all urban employees in employee health insurance schemes as well as expansion of the urban residence health insurance scheme by the end of 2010. The number of urban employees participating in basic medical insurance (BMI), which is funded by central and local governments and individual contributions, has nearly doubled since 2002, reaching 180 million in 2007. Basic medical insurance for urban residents, initiated in eighty-eight cities in 2007 and funded by both government and individual contributions, covered nearly 100 million urban residents (including the elderly, children, and the unemployed) within fifteen provinces and municipalities in China by 2008.

The RCMS has helped to reduce rural residents' spending on medical care. Migrant workers, who are considered rural residents based on their *hukou,* can also benefit from this system. However, in practice, medical expenses incurred in the cities are far higher, and reimbursements of medical costs to migrant workers are limited to the rural rate. This means that these workers only recover a small percentage of the actual costs incurred. In addition, RCMS benefits are not transferable across locations, and migrant workers[65] have to return to their home counties to submit claims. Since many migrant workers return home only once a year during the spring festival, migrant workers are unable to recover any of the expenses incurred. Although the RCMS has in principle enabled many rural residents to get health insurance, in practice many migrant urban poor continue to be marginalized.

A new labor-contract law has recently come into force.[66] It provides stronger legal protections for migrant workers by requiring employers to issue formal contracts and introduce collective bargaining, which allows migrants to negotiate for better pay, working conditions, and social security coverage. However, ensuring effective enforcement of these new legal provisions remains a challenge.

Thus, while health insurance coverage is rapidly increasing, especially in rural areas, many people remain underinsured and continue to face high out-of-pocket costs. Increased government expenditure in the education and health fields would help to reduce the need for private, out-of pocket expenditures affecting the poorest, including migrant families. More important, however, the dual rural and urban social protection system needs to be reformed to ensure that the migrant population is adequately covered. Integration of the current RCMS and urban residents' basic medical insurance into one universal insurance scheme would ensure adequate coverage for all irrespective of the place of residence.

Conclusion

China has recorded significant development achievements and made remarkable progress toward achieving the millennium development goals by 2015. Two of the eight goals have already been met—halving poverty and achieving universal access to primary education.[67] Other goals are on track and likely to be met on time. However, MDG targets will be achieved only by addressing the persistent inequalities between the urban, rural, and migrant populations and investing in the most vulnerable. The government has several challenges—to align its vision of a harmonious *Xiaokang* society with the reality of migration and its economic and social consequences, to maximize the benefits that are derived from economic development and migration, and to mitigate the harmful effects of both these phenomena on the most vulnerable. It remains to be seen how much the current global economic downturn will affect China and its development progress. If recent development trends give way to a long-term slowdown in growth, the real challenge may be how to maintain harmonious development in the context of an economic recession.

Notes

1. The findings, interpretations, and conclusions expressed in this chapter are those of the author and do not necessarily reflect the policies or views of the United Nations Children's Fund (UNICEF).

2. This chapter is based on a review of recent research and documents available on this subject as well as UNICEF's in-country experiences since 2001 working with children affected by migration and their families, promoting innovative strategies, and scaling-up approaches by the government.

3. The millennium development goals (MDGs) are eight international development goals that 192 United Nations member-states and at least twenty-three
international organizations agreed to achieve by the year 2015. They include
reducing extreme poverty and hunger, achieving universal primary education,
promoting gender equality and empowering women, reducing child mortality,
improving maternal health, combating HIV/AIDS, malaria, and other major
diseases, ensuring environmental sustainability, and developing a global partner-
ship for development.

4. China ratified the United Nations Convention on the Rights of the Child
(CRC) in March 1992.

5. National Bureau of Statistics, "2008 China Statistical Summary," Beijing,
May 2008. The target has also been met as measured by the standard millennium
development goal (MDG) poverty line of U.S. $1 per day.

6. China Institute for Reform and Development and UNDP China, "Human
Development Report China 2007/08: Access for All: Basic Public Services for 1.3
Billion People," November 2008.

7. National Bureau of Statistics, "2008 China Statistical Summary," Beijing,
May 2008.

8. China Institute for Reform and Development and UNDP China.

9. Type 1 represents the most developed rural areas, and type 4 the least developed rural areas.

10. Ministry of Health, UNICEF, World Health Organization (WHO), and the
United Nations Population Fund (UNFPA), "Joint Review of the Maternal and
Child Survival Strategy in China, December 2006.

11. See Ted C. Fishman, "The Chinese Century," *New York Times*, July 4,
2004, <http://nytimes.com> (accessed July 8, 2010).

12. Household Registration Rules of the People's Republic of China, implemented January 1, 1958.

13. Yaohui Zhao , "Rural to Urban Labor Migration in China: The Past and
the Present," in *Chinese Rural Labor Flows*, ed. Lorraine West and Yaohui Zhao
(Berkeley: University of California, Institute for East Asian Studies, 2000), 2.

14. State Council Directive Permitting Rural Migrant Workers to Seek Jobs in
Cities, implemented January 5, 2003.

15. UNICEF, *The State of the World's Children 2009: Maternal and Newborn
Health* (New York: UNICEF, December 2008), 118.

16. Huang Ping, and F. Pieke, "China Migration Country Study," Paper presented at the Regional Conference on Migration, Development, and Pro-Poor
Policies in Asia, Dhaka, Bangladesh, June 22–24, 2003, 6.

17. According to the 2000 national census figures, the most comprehensive data
on migrants and migratory patterns available to date, 131 million people (10.6
percent of the population) were residing outside their places of household
registration.

18. Tang Jun, selections from the "Report on Poverty and Anti-Poverty in Urban
China," *Chinese Sociology and Anthropology* (Chinese Academy of Social Sci-

ences) (Winter–spring 2005). These figures were confirmed by the 2005 1 percent sampling census, which suggests that the number of floating population is 147.35 million. See the China Population Web site, *The Bulletin of Major Indexes of the 2005 National 1 Percent Sampling Census*, July 19, 2006.

19. In China, children are defined as persons under the age of eighteen, in accordance with the definition in the CRC as well as the Law on the Protection of Minors, in force since 1992. According to the population census in 2000, the total child population was 345 million, accounting for 27.8 percent of the total population. The *2005 China Population Statistics Yearbook* reports that in 2004 the total child population declined to 326 million, 19 million less than in 2000, accounting for 25.1 percent of the total population. The sex ratio in the child population was 53.4 percent male to 46.6 percent female.

20. National Bureau of Statistics, Department of Population Statistics, National Census, 2000.

21. Government of China and UNICEF, *2006–2010 Country Programme Mid-term Review Report*, December 2008. The estimate is based on the 2005 1 percent population-sampling census.

22. National Bureau of Statistics, Department of Population Statistics, National Census, 2000.

23. Office of Migrant Workers of the State Council and All China Women's Federation, "Research Report on Rural Left-Behind Children in China," February 2008. The figures were calculated based on the 2005 1 percent sampling census. Left-behind children account for 22 percent of China's total rural children from birth to age seventeen, almost one in every four rural children is left-behind. About 27 percent are under five years of age, 35 percent are six to eleven years old, 21 percent are twelve to fourteen years old, and 17 percent are fifteen to seventeen years old. About 54 percent are boys, and 46 percent are girls.

24. National Bureau of Statistics, Department of Population Statistics, *National Census*, 2000.

25. China Institute for Reform and Development and UNDP China.

26. Xinhua News agency, "Twenty Million Jobless Migrant Workers Return Home," February 2, 2009, <http://www.xinhuanet.com> (accessed May 30, 2009).

27. "Concluding Observations of the Committee on Economic, Social and Cultural Rights: People's Republic of China," E/C.12/1/Add.107, May 13, 2005, sec.15.

28. "Concluding Observations of the Committee on the Rights of the Child: People's Republic of China," CRC/C/CHN/CO/2, November 24, 2005, secs. 30 and 32.

29. China Urban Labor Survey, 2005.

30. Rural Development Research Institute of the Chinese Academy of Social Sciences and Rural Social Economy Survey Department of the National Bureau of Statistics, *2006–07: Analysis and Prediction on Rural Economic Situation of China* (Beijing: Social Sciences Academic Press, 2007).

31. National Bureau of Statistics, "An Investigative Report on the Migrant Rural Workers' Living Quality," *People's Daily*, October 24, 2006. According to this report, the migrant rural workers age sixteen to twenty-five, twenty-five to thirty-five, thirty-five to forty-five, and above forty-five, respectively, accounted for 30.43 percent, 35.86 percent, 25.54 percent, and 8.17 percent of the workers surveyed.

32. Yang Donping, "Children of Migrants Deserve Equal Education," *China Daily*, March 1, 2007. There were an estimated 375,000 children of migrant workers in Beijing in 2006. Only an estimated 62 percent of these children were studying in public schools.

33. National Working Committee on Children and Women, China National Children's Center, and UNICEF, "Let's Share the Sunshine: Survey Report on the Temporary Migrant Children in Nine Cities of China," 2003.

34. Ministry of Health, UNICEF, WHO, and UNFPA, "Joint Review of the Maternal and Child Survival Strategy in China," December 2006.

35. Duan Chengrong and Zhou Fulin, "Research on China's Left-behind Children," *Population Research* 2 (2005).

36. An estimated 230 million children.

37. Government of China and UNICEF, *2006–2010 Country Programme Mid-term Review Report* (Beijing: UNICEF, December 2008). Estimates are based on the 2005 1 percent population sampling census.

38. National Working Committee on Children and Women, China National Children's Center, and UNICEF.

39. China Statistical Information Network, "Survey No. 2 on Migrant Rural Workers' Living Quality: Living and Education," October 2006.

40. China Statistical Information Network, "Survey No. 3 on Migrant Rural Workers' Living Quality: Evaluation and Expectation of Urban Life," October 2006.

41. Ministry of Health, *China Health Statistical Yearbook 2008* (Beijing: Ministry of Health, 2008).

42. Ibid.

43. Ministry of Health, UNICEF, WHO, and UNFPA, "Joint Review of the Maternal and Child Survival Strategy in China."

44. Ministry of Health, *National Maternal and Child Health Annual Report*.

45. Ministry of Health, *National MCH Mortality Surveillance*, 2008.

46. Gao Yi, "Utilization of Maternal Healthcare in Designated Delivery Hospital for Rural Migrant Women," *Maternal and Child Healthcare of China* 1 (2008).

47. National Working Committee on Children and Women, China National Children's Center, and UNICEF.

48. Wang Dewen and Cai Fang, "Migration and Poverty Alleviation in China," Institute of Population and Labor Economics, China Academy of Social Sciences, 2006.

49. Law on the Protection of Minors, no. 50, adopted by the National People's Congress on September 4, 1991, and entered into force on January 1, 1992.

50. Compulsory Education Law of the People's Republic of China, no. 38, adopted by the National People's Congress on April 12, 1986, and amended in June 2006.

51. Nick Young, "How Much Inequality Can China Stand?," *China Development Brief*, February 2007.

52. Ibid.

53. "New Rules Designed to Help 140 Million Migrants," *Shanghai Daily* (Shanghai), November 21, 2007.

54. "Hukou Should Be Scrapped," *China Daily* (Beijing), January 23, 2008.

55. M. Liu, "Migrants' Rights: Opening Up the System," *Newsweek International*, January 31, 2005.

56. Ingrid Nielsen et al., "Determinants of School Attendance among Migrant Children: Survey Evidence from China's Jiangsu Province," Paper presented at the Conference on Globalization and Labor Mobility in India and China, Monash University, September 2005.

57. Liu, "Migrants' Rights."

58. "Concluding Observations of the Committee on the Rights of the Child: People's Republic of China," *CRC/C/CHN/CO/2*, November 24, 2005, sec. 77.

59. *China Education Expenditure Statistics Yearbook*, 2006.

60. China Statistical Information Network, "Survey No. 2 on Migrant Rural Workers' Quality of Life: Living and Education," 2006.

61. China Statistical Information Network, "Survey No. 4 on Migrant Rural Workers' Quality of Life: Problems and Suggestion on Work and Business," 2006.

62. Deng Jin, "Migrant Children Stay Bottom of Class," *China Daily*, November 4, 2004.

63. China Statistical Information Network, "Survey No. 3 on Rural Migrant Workers' Living Quality: Evaluation and Expectation of Urban Life," 2006.

64. China Statistical Information Network, "Survey No. 4 on Living Quality of Rural Migrant Workers: The Problems and Suggestions on Work and Business," 2006.

65. WHO-China, "WHO-China Country Cooperation Strategy (2008–2013)," May 2008.

66. Both entered into force on January 1, 2008.

67. Government of China and the United Nations System in China, "China's Progress toward the Millennium Development Goals," 2008.

13

To Register or Not to Register? Legal Identity, Birth Registration, and Inclusive Development

Caroline Vandenabeele

Legal identity—the right to have one's existence recognized—is a basic human right that few would question. *Legal identity*, for the purpose of this chapter, is defined as a person's legal—as opposed to physical— personality, which allows that person to enjoy the legal system's protection, to enforce his or her rights, and to demand redress for violations by accessing courts and other law-enforcement institutions. Legal identity, or the right to be recognized by the government of the country of which one is a citizen, is a primary right that exists regardless of whether one has a document to prove this citizenship. Proof of one's legal identity consists of official government-issued and -recognized documents that include basic information on the person's name, age, nationality, status, and legal relationships. These documents do not *confer* legal identity; they merely *confirm* it. But in day-to-day reality, the absence of this proof of legal identity can disqualify a citizen from access to rights or state protection flowing from his or her citizenship. This chapter thus deals with what Jacqueline Bhabha in her introductory chapter refers to as *effective statelessness*. It focuses on children who are legal citizens of their county but who cannot prove their nationality. The chapter also reflects on the different means through which such proof can be established.

Most countries issue a wide variety of identity-related documents that serve a range of different purposes. They include birth, citizenship, and marriage certificates, national identity cards, international passports, and some country-specific identity documents. *Birth registration*, defined by the United Nations Children's Fund (UNICEF) as "the official recording of the birth of a child by some administrative level of the state and coordinated by a particular branch of Government,"[1] is often hailed by the international community as the preferred standard for asserting legal identity. This is because birth certificates have the advantage of documenting age, place of birth, nationality, and family relations from the beginning of life. This approach is reflected in article 7 of the Convention on the Rights of the Child (CRC), which states: "The child shall be registered immediately after birth and shall have the right from birth to a name, the right to acquire a nationality, and, as far as possible, the right to know and be cared for by his or her parents." Because of the special focus on birth registration, the possession of a birth certificate is often equated with having legal identity, and not having a birth certificate with *not* having legal identity. Birth certification and legal identity are however not exclusive. Many documents can confirm a person's legal identity. In Nepal, for example, the main case study of this chapter, access to social and economic rights often depends on having a citizenship certificate rather than a birth certificate. As is illustrated in this chapter, an overreliance on birth registration as the sole means for establishing legal identity and as a prerequisite for accessing other rights and protections risks exacerbating poor and vulnerable groups' patterns of exclusion.

Civil registration is the means by which countries keep track of vital events affecting their citizens, such as births, deaths, and changes in marital status. In theory, a well-functioning civil registration system, in particular a comprehensive system of birth registration, should lead to improved access to service delivery and up-to-date demographic information. It should also yield improved and better targeted resource allocation and improved protection against violation of laws that have an age or relational element (such as laws on child labor, child marriage, or inheritance laws). Birth registration, according to this analysis, is a key tool in ensuring access to benefits and opportunities. This approach has led a number of countries and international actors to promote birth registration as a legal prerequisite for accessing rights such as education, a strategy that is aimed at increasing the demand for birth registration from citizens. This so-called demand-based approach is further described in this chapter.

It is worth noting that, in practice, improving access to better-targeted services and state protection depends on the realization of a set of assumptions that often do not hold true in developing countries. Although acknowledging that birth registration is a human right, this chapter examines some of these assumptions and the risks associated with a demand-based approach to birth registration. The apparent straightforwardness of international normative undertakings is contrasted with the complex realities of the domestic implementation of such guarantees.

Relevant policy and enforcement questions regarding legal identity and birth registration are addressed in the context of developing countries.

The chapter considers the questions of legal identity, birth registration, and access to goods and services from an empirical and pragmatic rather than a purely theoretical viewpoint. It is centered on Nepal, with comparative information drawn from Bangladesh and, to a lesser extent, Cambodia. The empirical information presented in this chapter is based on intensive research and experiences[2] over a period of four years in Bangladesh, Cambodia, and Nepal. It is worth reminding oneself that these countries rank 140, 131, and 142 (out of 179), respectively, in the United Nations Development Program's (UNDP) 2007/2008 Human Development Index (HDI).[3] The research findings presented in this chapter clearly reflect this low ranking and the related paucity of available government resources. Birth registration in Bangladesh was estimated to cover between 7 and 10 percent of the population in March 2007.[4] No more official up-to-date information is available. In Cambodia, an intensive mobile registration campaign undertaken by the government between 2005 and 2006 claimed to have distributed birth certificates to over 90 percent of the population, up from less than 10 percent of the population at the start of 2004. In Nepal, the numbers are disputed, but the Population Registrar puts the percentage of the population that had a birth certificate at the end of 2008 somewhere around 25 percent (see below).[5]

The first section of this chapter (with Nepal as its primary empirical source) describes the nexus between legal identity documentation and access to benefits and opportunities and between birth registration and human-rights protection. Obstacles to obtaining birth registration are also considered. Another section, drawing primarily on empirical data from Bangladesh, focuses on the risks associated with a demand-based approach to birth registration and the importance of the proper sequencing of interventions related to birth registration.

The Nepal Country Context

Nepal is a landlocked country nested in the Himalayas. It has a rugged terrain and is squeezed between India and China. Its population in 2008 was 27.02 million,[6] of which at least 80 percent lived in rural areas. Although poverty levels were reduced significantly from 42 percent in 1996 to 31 percent in 2004, Nepal remains one of the poorest countries in the world. In 2007, the World Bank estimated its annual per capita income at U.S. $363.7.[7] There are wide income disparities and a lack of access to basic services for a large portion of the population. Poverty is more acute in rural than urban areas and is much more pronounced among lower-caste and minority groups, such as Dalits, Janajatis, and Muslims (all above 40 percent) than in upper-caste groups (where poverty levels are below 20 percent).

Nepal has fifty-nine ethnic groups represented in its Constituent Assembly and more than a hundred groups altogether that seek representation as separate entities. There are about 125 documented languages, including six major ones. It is a multiethnic and multilingual society with complex variations in ethnicity, caste, language, and religion. Distinctions between groups are based on linguistic and sociocultural characteristics from the dominant Hindu caste. About two-thirds of the population are directly tied to the Hindu caste framework, and one-third comprises various noncaste ethnic and non-Hindu religious groups. *Dalit* is a collective term that is used to refer to disadvantaged castes (about 15 percent of Nepal's population) but is often used interchangeably with *untouchable*. The society is dominated by a complex unwritten system of rules, behavioral norms, traditions, and convictions. The caste system defines access to resources and opportunities, even though the Legal Code of 1964 officially did away with all castes. Upward mobility for the Dalits and other ethnic groups is, in general, limited. Large income disparities are related to gender, caste, and ethnicity.

Following the first People's Movement, Nepal introduced multiparty democracy in 1990 and became a constitutional monarchy. Notwithstanding the many pledges made in the period leading up to the restoration of democracy, the system did not bring stability or improvements in people's lives. There was a general lack of credibility of political parties, a continuous power struggle between parties, and a continued marginalization of large portions of Nepal's population. In 1994, the Communist Party of Nepal–Maoists (CPN-M) initiated a so-called People's War against what it termed the feudal state. In February 2005, the then king took over power and dissolved parliament. In April 2006, the seven major political parties, together with the CPN-M, formed an alliance to resist the king's direct rule that led to the reinstatement of the parliament. In November 2006, the seven-party alliance and the CPN-M signed a peace agreement that formally ended the armed conflict. In April 2008, elections were held for a Constituent Assembly, in which the CPN-M won the largest number of seats. The first session of the Constituent Assembly in May 2008 abolished the monarchy and declared the country to be a federal democratic republic.

The Nepalese legal framework for providing legal identity and proof thereof is a patchwork of laws, regulations, directives, and practices. Nepal ratified the CRC on October 14, 1990. In accordance with section 9 of the Nepal Treaty Act of 1990, provisions of international instruments are applicable as national laws, and in the case of inconsistency between the international treaty and national law, the international treaty prevails.[8] Article 22(1) of the Interim Constitution of Nepal of 2006 guarantees that "Every child shall have the right to his/her identity and name." The other main laws governing legal identity are the Birth, Death, and Other Personal Events (Registration) Act of 1976 (referred to as the Vital Events Registration Act); the Birth, Death, and Other Personal Events (Registration) Regulation of 1977; the Personal Events Registration Directives of 1999; the Nepal Citizenship Act of 2006; the Nepal Citizenship Rules of 2006; and the Citizenship Issuing Guidelines. The Vital Events Registration Act governs birth, marriage, divorce, migration, and death registrations. Although the act states that these events should be registered and certified, registration is not enforced. Other than the possibility of a fine for late registration, the act does not contain any provisions relating to the nonregistration of personal events.

The following are examples of identity documents that are *legally* required for accessing certain benefits and opportunities in Nepal. First, a *birth certificate* is needed to access government scholarships, get free schoolbooks, and sit for the school-leaving certificate examination. Second, a *citizenship certificate* is required to register one's marriage, receive allowances for senior citizens and internally displaced people, and receive compensation for victims of the armed conflict. A citizenship certificate is also required to purchase immovable property, register the ownership or transfer land, amend land-registration certificates, validate a tenant's registration, or measure the size of a parcel of land. It is also required to join the army, armed police, and civil police force and to sit for professional certification exams. Third, a widow must present her husband's death certificate, his citizenship certificate, and a relationship certificate to qualify for a widowhood allowance.[9] As these examples demonstrate, the citizenship certificate is the most essential legal-identity document for accessing benefits and opportunities. Nepalese citizenship can be obtained by descent, birth, or naturalization. Although the eligibility criteria for a citizenship certificate differ in each of these three cases, a *recommendation letter* from the local government office is required in all three. The law is silent on what is needed to obtain such a letter, but in practice, this usually requires the father's or husband's citizenship certificate, the applicant's birth certificate, a marriage certificate if citizenship is conferred by naturalization through marriage, and a migration certificate if the applicant has migrated. In the absence of these documents, the local body can prepare a deed of public inquiry for which seven witnesses are required, each of whom must submit a citizenship certificate.[10] Although there is currently no legal requirement for any document other than the application form to register a birth, in practice, the registering authority usually requests documents, such as marriage registration and the father's citizenship certificate. Ongoing discussions within the Ministry of Local Development suggest that in the very near future, a birth certificate is likely to become a legal requirement for obtaining a citizenship certificate.[11]

There are differing views on exactly how many people in Nepal have a birth certificate or a citizenship certificate. The cumulative number of registered births since 1978 is a little over 8 million.[12] Taking into account the present population of over 27 million, the maximum percentage of Nepalis that have a birth certificate cannot be more than 29.5 percent. After accounting for deaths in the ensuing years, the number is more likely to be around 25 percent, and the percentage is doubtless even lower for women, Dalits, ethnic minorities, internally displaced people, and other vulnerable groups in remote districts and regions.[13] Similarly, there is no agreement on the number of Nepalis over age sixteen, who, by law, are entitled to a citizenship certificate but do not have one. The cumulative number of citizenship certificates issued from the early 1960s until December 2008 is 17 million. However, this number does not account for deaths or people who relinquished their Nepali citizenship. Given the age structure of Nepal's population, a conservative estimate would suggest that between 3 and 5 million people who are age sixteen and above do not have a citizenship certificate though they are entitled to one. They are therefore excluded by law from benefits and opportunities for which a citizenship certificate is required.

The Nexus between Legal Identity Documentation and Access to Benefits and Opportunities

A major advantage generally associated with birth registration or other legal-identity documentation is that it enables access to benefits and opportunities. Empirical research by UNICEF in sixty-five countries demonstrates a strong correlation between birth registration and access to benefits. The research cross-tabulated birth-registration data with other socioeconomic characteristics and indicators. The resulting profile showed that unregistered children are generally delivered without the assistance of a health professional. They tend to be poor, live in rural areas, have limited access to health care and education, and suffer from higher levels of malnutrition and higher mortality rates. Often, their mothers are uneducated and lack knowledge regarding the signs of child-hood illness.[14]

Although there is no doubt that a strong correlation exists between the lack of proof of legal identity and patterns of exclusion from services, benefits, and opportunities, a more complex question is the one of causation. Is there a causal link between the lack of proof of legal identity and not having access to benefits and opportunities? And if these groups had the required legal-identity documentation, would they have meaningful access to benefits and opportunities? The causation question is an important one because birth registration, in particular, is often portrayed as the "gateway to life" or the "gateway to opportunities" such as education. Proponents of Universal Birth Registration UBR) argue that it opens up access to services and opportunities otherwise denied, thereby promoting birth registration as a right without which other rights cannot be fulfilled. Their aim is to ensure that as many births as possible are registered and that as many children as possible are provided with access to benefits and opportunities. Following this line of thought, these proponents, including international donors and the governments they advise, propose legislative changes to increase citizens' demand for birth registration by making the production of a birth certificate a legal requirement for accessing rights and opportunities. But these strategies often have an unintended consequence as they result in the legal exclusion of children without birth records from access to benefits and opportunities, making them worse off than registered children. This seems to be a counterproductive approach: children who might have had access to rights and services prior to the requirement of a birth certificate may now lose such access if they cannot obtain a birth certificate (see below on obstacles to birth registration).

The claim that there is a positive causal link between legal-identity documentation and access to benefits and opportunities relies on a number of problematic assumptions. They seem obvious at first glance but, perhaps for that reason, are often overlooked or taken for granted. These assumptions can be grouped as follows:

usually conditional on possession of a birth certificate. Requirements for accessing basic education vary between localities within the same country, and substitutes for a birth certificate may be accepted. These substitutes can vary in degree of formality. In Cambodia, for example, a family or lodging book[24] or a national identity card is generally interchangeable with a birth certificate. In Bangladesh, a statement by a local official who knows a child's family may be enough in some locations to enroll a child in school. In Nepal, traditional Hindu religious documents (such as astrologic charts that note the time and place of birth) have been used to establish age and thus to allow access to basic education. In many countries in Asia, particularly in rural areas, a child's ability to touch her ear while reaching over her head is considered sufficient proof that a child is of school-going age and enables a child to enroll in school. These alternatives do not have the same official value as birth certificates, but the research established that they are often accepted as a pragmatic substitute for the lack of formal identity documentation to enable access to basic education. Where the substitute identifiers are not accepted, this is usually because there are other, more fundamental grounds for refusing entry into schools, such as nationality, ethnicity, or caste.

Neither in Nepal nor in Cambodia is there a *legal* requirement to have a birth certificate to receive basic education. In Cambodia, the Ministry of Interior has stated that it will formally institute a policy of linking birth registration and school enrollment only after birth registration reaches 95 percent of the entire population. In Nepal, a 1996 circular from the Ministry of Local Development (MLD) instructed schools to require a birth certificate for school enrollment. Realizing that this deprived many children of their right to education, the MLD at the end of 2003 issued a new circular addressed to the local government, instructing local registrars that children without birth certificate were to be given access to education anyway. As these circulars were issued to different authorities and since many of the village development committees were not fully operational during the conflict, the two circulars have resulted in confusion, with some (but not all) authorities requiring birth certificates as a condition for enrollment in primary education. They have also created a perception in the public at large that a birth certificate is indeed a legal requirement. In the case of Bangladesh, the 2004 Birth and Death Registration Act required production of a birth certificate for admission to any educational institution. However, implementation of the act has been suspended ever since its enactment, and children have been able to enroll in primary education without a birth certificate. Both Bangladesh and Cambodia have taken the laudable step of not turning down children who come to enroll without a birth certificate and instead actively assist them in obtaining these certificates. Access to primary education is a fundamental human right that should not be made dependent on production of a birth certificate, even though having a certificate makes it easier to know a child's age and thus to know whether to enroll the child.

Access to basic health services such as immunization is not, according to the research, contingent on presenting a birth certificate or other formal identity documentation in Bangladesh, Cambodia, or Nepal. By contrast, the requirements for legal identity documentation in relation to property rights, land registration, and inheritance rights are considerably stricter.

Where a legal identity document is a strict requirement—as is the case for obtaining a passport in each of the three countries—alternative markets can often provide the prerequisite birth or citizenship certificate much faster than the official system and without any requirements other than payment. Each of the three countries under review has a black market for identity documents, with Nepal's being the most thriving. This is not surprising as Nepal also has the most stringent requirements for legal-identity documentation, in particular a citizenship certificate to access benefits and opportunities.

An important policy question concerns the level of priority and scale of resources that a government should devote to establishing a functioning civil registration system when the country has some other form of documentation that covers the overwhelming majority of the population. In those instances, should the government acknowledge the *de facto* situation and, at least for a transitional period, accept the available alternative documentation as sufficient for accessing benefits? In Cambodia, for example, about 90 percent[25] of the population is registered in both a family book and a lodging book.[26] This system of registration, designed to track the population's movements, was created by the tyrannical Khmer Rouge as a mechanism of social control. Although the origins of the system may be disreputable, the reality is that this form of registration is much more widely accepted by Cambodians than birth registration within the civil registration system.

There Must Be No Other More Fundamental Economic, Political, or Social Obstacles to Accessing Benefits and Opportunities

Having a birth certificate or any other form of legal identity will lead to increased access to goods, services, and opportunities if there are no other more fundamental obstacles to accessing those benefits and opportunities. In reality, traditional views (for example, on the role and position of women) or long-standing prejudices against minorities are often the real impediments to accessing benefits and opportunities for these groups. Consider Nepal, where discriminatory practices are embedded in the social structure through the caste system. Based on an age-old Hindu tradition, the 1854 Legal Code of Nepal divided society into four groups, with the lowest group being the "castes from whom water is not accepted and whose touch requires sprinkling of holy water." For these untouchable castes (Dalits), there was a different criminal justice system.[27] The new Legal Code of 1964 officially did away with that categorization, but socioeconomic conditions are still determined by the caste to which one belongs today. A 2002 study commissioned by Action Aid found 205 practices of caste-based discrimination, including in access to services.[28] Dalit students, for example, are still required to sit in separate parts of the classrooms and are often not allowed to eat with other students. There have been several reports of Dalit children not being allowed to use educational supplies and materials, enter recreational facilities, or participate in sports and other extracurricular activities. When discrimination is deeply embedded in a societal system, providing Dalit children with a birth certificate will not make much difference unless this is part of a more comprehensive nondiscrimination strategy.

Legal-Identity Documentation and Human-Rights Protection

Legal-identity documentation has the potential to play a key role in protecting human rights. In the context of child-rights protection, legal-identity documents, particularly birth certificates, provide a reliable and accurate means for establishing a child's age. Although child rights exist regardless of whether a child has a legal-identity document, having a birth certificate or other document seems to make it easier to enforce such rights. This is particularly important for problems such as child labor, including forced conscription into the armed forces, child marriages, crimes against minors, and juvenile justice. However, these problems are complex and require an integrated and multipronged reform agenda, of which birth registration is only one part. This section focuses briefly on child labor and child marriage.

According to a 2002–2003 study, Bangladesh has 4.9 million working children, which accounts for 14.2 percent of the total 35.06 million children in the age group of five to fourteen years.[29] In Cambodia, a 2006 report estimated that 40 percent of the children in the age group seven to seventeen (or 1.5 million) were involved in child labor, including 750,000 under the absolute minimum working age of twelve years.[30] The International Labor Organization—International Program on the Elimination of Child Labor (ILO-IPEC) estimated that there are more than 2.6 million child workers in Nepal.[31] Among them, many are employed in severely dangerous situations, including some who have been recruited as soldiers in Nepal's armed conflict.[32] The economic and political realities of these countries are such that few actors have an interest in enforcing child-labor legislation, even for those children who have a birth certificate. State enforcement and monitoring of child-labor standards face opposition from powerful business interests. Ministries of labor and labor inspectorates are severely underresourced. Because of widespread poverty in these countries, child laborers themselves and their families may find the enforcement of labor standards and laws against their interest and may prefer not to reveal their age. This is not to say that the right to legal identity, birth registration, and child rights can be derogated from in circumstances of acute socioeconomic deprivation. But it does mean that birth registration can be effective as a means for addressing child labor only if other obstacles against the elimination of child labor are addressed at the same time or even before.

Similarly, the absence of proper birth registration and of a functioning civil registration system are often considered contributory factors to child marriage, since registrars officiating at marriages have no basis for checking the age of the bride and groom. According to Nepal's population census of 2001, 55.5 percent of girls were married between the ages of fifteen and nineteen.[33] In addition, it was estimated that 34 percent of all marriages held in Nepal involve children below age fifteen.[34] And yet although the Legal Code of 1964 provides that the legal age for marriage is eighteen with parental consent and twenty without, between 1998 and 2005, only fourteen complaints against child marriage were registered with the Women and Children Service Center of the Nepalese police.[35] Child marriage is still considered normal and acceptable by a large portion of the population for whom arranged marriage at an early age is a way of reducing what is considered an economic burden on the family caused by girls and young women. Moreover, because a citizenship certificate is a prerequisite for registering a marriage and since many people do not have such a certificate, most marriages take place outside the formal system and are never registered. In such an environment, the promotion of birth registration is but one aspect of the battle against child marriages, albeit an important one.

Obstacles to Obtaining Birth Registration

Birth registration is often taken for granted by those who come from countries with well-functioning registration systems. In these countries, a child is generally registered automatically, and the registration itself tends to be a straightforward process. This experience makes it harder to understand why registration rates in developing countries are as low as they are. In fact, there are many reasons. They include financial, geographic, institutional, procedural, behavioral, legal, and political obstacles. Some of these barriers are discussed in further detail in the context of Nepal.

Financial Barriers

Provided that it is done within thirty-five days of the birth, birth registration in a local government office in Nepal is, in principle, free. Nevertheless, a wide range of expenses can make birth registration an expensive undertaking, particularly for the rural poor, who often have only a nominal income. To start with, few people register the birth within the specified thirty-five days. The topography of Nepal makes travel challenging, particularly during the winter. Moreover, the longstanding civil conflict has caused many village-level registration offices to close, and registration has had to be carried out at the district level, which may be several days' walk away. In such cases, registration requires extra expenses for travel, lodging, and food and possibly the loss of several days' income. Because of low levels of awareness and lack of clarity and consistency about the documentary requirements, people regularly find themselves at the registration office without the right papers. As a result, they may be unable to register their child or may have to pay extra to do so. Low-level corruption is common in countries with low salaries for government officials, and Nepal is no exception. There are also financial barriers on the supply side. For FY 2008–2009, the national budget included only NR 1.2 million, or about U.S. $14,000, for vital-event registration, along with a minimal additional allocation for local government bodies. In FY 2004–2005, 98 percent of the annual budget went for staff salaries and allowances, leaving only 2 percent for the actual registration process, including awareness-raising, production of application forms and birth certificates, and purchase of secure cabinets for safeguarding documents.

Institutional and Procedural Barriers

At the central level, the Population and Vital Event Registration Management section, headed by the registrar, has a total of eleven staff, including clerical and support staff. Although the registrar has the sole responsibility and authority to correct birth-registration certificates, the responsibility for registration and maintaining records and forwarding them to the central government lies with the secretary of the Village Development Committee (VDC) or municipality. In the wake of the armed conflict, the last elections at the VDC or municipality level took place in 1997, leaving elected positions vacant after the expiration of their term in 2002. This means that in addition to their normal workload, VDC secretaries or municipality officials have to do the work that normally would be done by elected representatives. This heavy workload, the low incentives, and the fact that local registrars can be held criminally liable for issuing certificates if the supporting documents or their contents are later found to be false (even if the official performed the duties in good faith) result in birth registration being regarded as a low-priority activity. This is aggravated by the fact that there is no midlevel administrative oversight over local registrars and the only person the public can turn to for guidance is the central registrar.

Moreover, the conflict significantly damaged VDC offices,[36] destroyed records, and forced many VDC secretaries to relocate to district headquarters, making the registration offices more difficult to reach. In Nangkhel and Chitapole, two VDCs in the Bakthapur district about a half hour drive from Kathmandu, all records were destroyed in 2002.[37] Even where offices still function, little logistical support in terms of application forms, copy machines, or record storage cabinets is available. On the procedural side, there are no clear guidelines on vital-events registration, with the result that procedures are made up by local registrars as they see fit. As a result, procedures are unpredictable and differ significantly from VDC to VDC and even from applicant to applicant. For example, although legally no longer required by the new Citizenship Act of 2006, many registrars still demand the father's citizenship certificate and the parents' marriage certificate to register a child. This makes it virtually impossible for single mothers, including widows, to register children. According to recurrent reports, relatives of a child's deceased father regularly refuse to provide the necessary documentation to a widow to cated staff, the Dhaka City Corporation—one of the more efficient and better-resourced local government entities in Bangladesh—accumulated a backlog of more than five years' worth of unprocessed registration data by 2007. In another case, notwithstanding donor-provided computers, staff at the Sylhet City Corporation still entered data in handwritten ledgers in 2007 due to a lack of computer skills.

To enhance the usefulness of birth registration for development planning and providing access to benefits and opportunities, the GOB has planned computerization of all birth records by 2010.[44] This will require, at a minimum, the following resources to start the process—about 5,500 dedicated computers, printers, and uninterrupted power supplies (UPS); a powerful central server and decentralized servers at the municipality and district levels; temporary staff to enter the data; and 140 million application forms, 140 million birth certificates, and 40,000 register books. As a comparison, in 2008, Brazil, with a population of 185 million and a birth registration rate of 90 percent, discussed a civil registration modernization project with the Inter-American Development Bank that was estimated to cost U.S. $1.8 billion .[45] Support provided by international actors to the GOB has covered at best 5 to 10 percent of the total cost of computerized UBR in Bangladesh and is primarily focused on children, neglecting the huge backlog of unregistered adults. Yet the overwhelming majority of benefits listed above for which birth registration has become mandatory are immediately relevant for adults, not children. As the end of 2008 has passed, it is obvious that the goal of UBR will not be reached, and the GOB, even with the support of international donors, does not have the logistical capacity to register the vast majority of Bangladeshis. If and when the 2004 Registration Act becomes fully effective, the vast majority of people will find themselves without the necessary documentary support to obtain services for which earlier no legal identity document was required. The effects of this poor sequencing of interventions will be many. They are likely to include further exclusion of vulnerable groups for whom obtaining a birth certificate is even more difficult; a lack of access to basic services such as utilities for the vast majority of Bangladeshis; an increase in speed money and bribes to either get a birth certificate or obtain the required services without a birth certificate; and increased public cynicism.

Conclusions

Legal identity is a primary right. It confers other rights, such as protection by the state to which an individual belongs and the right to make claims on the state for social and economic rights like education, health, and social protection. Birth registration is a primary means for ascertaining legal identity. As such, it can play a key role in the facilitation of a citizen's protection and rights access. The operative word, though, is *facilitation*. Contrary to what has been claimed in certain UBR campaigns, such as the one for Bangladesh, it is not the birth record itself that gives an individual the right to make claims on the state. Basic rights such as the right to education or protection against child labor are rights that exist in and of themselves and should not be made conditional on birth registration. Campaigns that center on universal and demand-based approaches to birth registration and that tie benefits and opportunities to a single document—as illustrated in the case of Bangladesh—not only miss the point (access to benefits and protection) but risk confirming existing patterns of exclusion or adding additional barriers to access and protection. The demand-based approach to birth registration thus risks becoming a self-fulfilling prophecy because people without a birth certificate start having less access than they had before the certificate was made a legal requirement.

Although there is a strong correlation between birth registration and patterns of exclusion, there is no uniform positive causal link between having a birth record—or other form of legal identity documentation— and having access to state protection and to social and economic rights. Nor does the absence of a birth record automatically preclude citizens from accessing these rights, although the absence of any form of legal identity documentation will make it more challenging to enforce those rights. The emerging picture is complex. The particular circumstances for each country and for each benefit and opportunity can differ dramatically. Failing to take these specificities into account when designing initiatives in the area of birth registration can lead to interventions that, at best, do not change people's lives for the better or, at worst, exclude them even more. Understanding the specific context of the country in which one tries to implement international normative human-rights standards, including the incentive structure of institutional actors, is key to successful domestic application of such international standards.

Establishing and maintaining a complete, effective, and accessible civil registration system requires sufficient funding, human resources, political priority, enforcement capacity, and administrative infrastructure. These essential inputs, however, cannot be taken for granted in developing countries. Given this reality, technical approaches that work in developed countries will not necessarily transfer to developing countries unless adjustments are made that take into account country-specific realities.

166 for the United Kingdom, 549 for the United States, and 240 for Singapore.

17. For comparative purposes, the per person expenditures in 2002 (in U.S. dollars) was $2,699 for Australia, $2,133 for Japan, $349 for Malaysia, $3,409 for Norway, $2,160 for the United Kingdom, $5,274 for the United States, and $1,105 for Singapore.

18. See Nepali Ministry of Finance Web site, <http://www.mof.gov.np/publica tion/speech/2008_1/index.php> (June 1, 2009).

19. See Nepal's Central Bank's Web site, <http://red.nrb.org.np/publications/study _reports/Study_Reports-Household%20Budget%20Survey20200820(Report) -NEW.pdf> (June 1, 2009).

20. To illustrate: Bangladesh received U.S. $4.81 billion in remittances for FY 2006. World Markets Research Center, *Global Insight,* July 6, 2006. Nepal received U.S. $1.1 billion remittances for FY 2005. ADB, *Asian Development Bank Outlook 2006: Economic Trends and Prospects in Developing Asia— South Asia,* 2006.

21. *Nepal Gazette* 41, October 19, 2005.

22. Section 4(1)(d) of the Vital Events Registration Act (Nepal), 1976; Birth, Death, and Other Personal Events (Registration) Regulations (Nepal), 1977.

23. Without comprehensive monitoring and registration, the estimates of inter-nally displaced people (IDP) in Nepal vary widely, from 20,000 to 2.4 million. In mid-2007, the Internal Displacement Monitoring Center (IDMC) estimated the number of IDPs at 50,000 to 70,000, <http://www.internal-displacement.org/ idmc/website/countries.nsf/(httpEnvelopes)/1949E98C81942B55C12571FE004 D8821?OpenDocument> (accessed June 1, 2009).

24. Historically, family and lodging books, which were both introduced at the time of the Khmer Rouge as a way of tracking the movements of people, have been Cambodia's most widespread, resilient, and useful form of identity docu-ment. Family books, which are issued by the commune police, track close family members of Cambodian descent, along with any adopted children. These books contain the names of each member of a family and may contain details on more than one nuclear family, as siblings or children with their own families may reside together. Lodging books record the number and identity of people residing in one household and track the numbers and locations of people in the country. Unlike family books, they do not identify familial relationships or nationality; they simply list the people living in a particular place. All heads of households must have one or are subject to a fine.

25. According to the Ministry of Interior's June 2005 statistics, 91 percent of Cambodia's population is accounted for in lodging books, and 88 percent is covered by family books.

26. See note 24.

27. For a description of the current status of Dalits, see, for example, Man B. Bishwakarma, *The Representation of Deprived People in State Governance in Nepal* (The Hague, Netherlands: Institute of Social Studies, 2004), <http://

nepaldalitinfo.20m.com> (accessed June 1, 2009); or see "Shadow Report by the International Dalit Solidarity Network (IDSN) on the 15th and 16th Periodic Report of the Government of Nepal on the Convention of Elimination of All Forms of Racial Discrimination (CERD)," <http://www.idsn.org> (accessed June 1, 2009).

28. Krishna B. Bhattachan,, Kamala Hemchuri, Yogendra B. Gurung, and Chakra M. Bishwkarma, *Existing Practices of Caste-Based Untouchability in Nepal and Strategy for a Campaign for Its Elimination (Final Report)* (Kathmandu: Action Aid Nepal, 2002).

29. International Labor Organization (ILO)–International Program on the Elimination of Child Labor (IPEC), Subregional Information System on Child Labor, Bangladesh, <http://www.ilo.org/public/english/region/asro/newdelhi/ipec/responses/bangladesh/index.htm> (accessed June 1, 2009).

30. Understanding Children's Work (UCW): An Inter-Agency Cooperation Project, *Children's Work in Cambodia: A Challenge for Growth and Poverty Reduction*, Country Report (Rome: UCW, 2006), <http://www.ucw-project.org> (accessed June 1, 2009).

31. ILO-IPEC, "Child Labor Situation in Nepal," Factsheet, 1996, Child Workers in Nepal Concerned Center (CWIN) Web site, <http://www.cwin.org.np> (June 1, 2009).

32. Nepal signed the optional protocol to the Convention on the Rights of the Child (CRC) on the Involvement of Children in Armed Conflict 2000, but no initiative has been taken to ratify it. According to the *Child Soldiers World Report*, around 30 percent of the Communist Party's Nepal-Maoist soldiers are children under the age of eighteen. According to Human Rights Watch, "Nepal: Child Soldier Use," 2003, there were "no indications of a policy of, or systematic recruitment below the age of 18 into the Royal Nepal Amy," <http://hrw.org/reports> (accessed June 1, 2009). However, anecdotal evidence suggests that children are used by government forces as informers.

33. Natural Census of Nepal, Central Bureau of Statistics of His Majesty's Government of Nepal, 2001.

34. See "Campaign to Create Child Marriage-Free Districts by 2009 Launched," *Nepal News*, October 20, 2008, <http://www.nepalnews.com.np/archive/2008/oct/oct20/news11.php> (accessed June 1, 2009).

35. Vandenabeele and Lao, *Legal Identity for Inclusive Development*, 28.

36. In Bhojpur District, for example, only thirty-three out of sixty-three VDCs were operational in 2007.

37. Discussions between VDC secretaries and the author on November 25, 2008.

38. Circular issued on January 10, 1999, for Tibetan children and circular issued on January 1, 2003 for Bhutanese children.

39. Quoted in the *Annapurna Post*, October 18, 2008, <http://www.annapurnapost.com> (accessed June 1, 2009).

40. As an example of this approach, see Plan International's problem statement of birth registration in Bangladesh at the occasion of the Fourth Asia and the Pacific Regional Conference on Birth Registration, Bangkok, March 2006, <http://www.plan-international.org/pdfs/bangladeshcp.pdf> (accessed June 1, 2009).

41. The demand approach is complemented by a supply-based approach by providing birth registration together with other services, in particular, education and health.

42. Universal Birth Registration (UBR) by the 2008 directives, Local Government Division, Local Government, Rural Development and Cooperatives Ministry, Dhaka, August 14, 2006.

43. These include official fees, fines for late registration, transportation and accommodation expenses, opportunity costs, bribes, and speed money. According to Transparency International Bangladesh, more than one in three service recipients are forced to pay a bribe for admission to schools, and nearly eight out of ten pay bribes for gaining police clearance. Low-income households spend about 10 percent of their household income on bribes.

44. The advantages of a computerized system include (1) more accurate and readily available information; (2) the storage of information in an electronic fashion rather than in handwritten ledgers that fade over time and are subject to destruction; (3) easier access to duplicates; (4) data-sharing with other databases and their use for generating voters' lists or lists for national identity cards; and (5) generation of lists by category (such as age groups, geographical areas, and gender) for use in development and related planning.

45. E-mail between author and IADB staff on file with the author.

14

Children with a (Local) State: Identity Registration at Birth in English History since 1538

Simon Szreter

As this volume's introduction points out, all children live under the imperfect realities of specific national state jurisdictions. This means that any examination of the human rights of children must grapple with a range of legal and practical problems. This subject cannot confine itself to matters of moral philosophy. The United Nations Convention on the Rights of the Child (CRC) has been ratified by virtually all the world's nations—apart from the broken state of Somalia and the scandalous exception of the United States, whose inexcusable failure to ratify has been the subject of an important new study.[1] However, the effectiveness of nation-states' internal social, economic, legal, and administrative arrangements in providing their most vulnerable citizens with the resources and support implied by ratification of the Convention varies enormously for many political, cultural, and historical reasons.

The highly undesirable condition of *statelessness* has previously been understood mainly to refer to those unfortunates caught in a legal limbo, typically as the victims of the military, political, or illegal activity of third parties. This leads to either *legal statelessness* (the absence of any nationality) or *de facto statelessness* (the absence of a legal migration status despite a legal nationality). However, Jacqueline Bhabha's introduction to this volume also proposes that a third widespread form of *effective statelessness* should be recognized. This embraces unregistered children within their own countries—amounting to hundreds of millions of persons today, given that UNICEF estimates that 36 percent of births are currently unregistered in the world.[2] Effective statelessness is significant and devastating for those afflicted, particularly in poor communities, including those ravaged by HIV-AIDS—which has left many households headed by twelve-year-olds in sub-Saharan Africa. This is because children are peculiarly dependent on states. There are two aspects to this dependency: first, all children depend on states for basic services, and second, many children depend on states when their families fail them.[3]

An efficient, state-organized universal registration system is not necessarily the only way to avoid this form of statelessness. As Caroline Vandenabeele shows in her chapter in this volume, alternative credentialing systems may be able to substitute satisfactorily for at least the principal human-rights functions of a birth-registration system, as in Cambodia or Bangladesh. But those who advocate establishing national identity-registration systems should not be content with anything less than a comprehensive vital-registration system (provided the state can be trusted by all its citizenry, an important and nontrivial proviso, as past and recent history shows). First, informal arrangements—such as those described in the chapter by Vandenabeele in Bangladesh, where local officials may validate children's identity for school enrollment—are satisfactory if the local official is honest; but informal systems are breeding grounds for bribery and sexual exploitation. If there is no universal system of registration at birth, the scope for corruption at all levels multiplies. For instance, in Kampala in 2008, officials were overheard taking phone calls from young adults who were seeking identity-registration documents so that they could enroll in higher education courses. The officials told the callers not to come to the government office but to meet them in other locations. A cynical comment on this corruption circulated in Kampala, claiming that the need for young women to obtain identity-registration documents from officials to further their education was an effective way of spreading HIV infection. Second, a comprehensive civil-identity-registration system simultaneously provides life-saving cause-of-death information, a vital flow of intelligence for effective preventive and curative health services.[4] Finally, in most countries, marriage registration is an important legal record that facilitates many forms of property inheritance and secures entitlements for wives, widows, and children in various circumstances. Advocating for the continuation of an informal system thus supports a system that provides only one of the three major functions of a fully operational civil identity-registration system that universally records births, deaths, and marriages.

Even so, simply creating by legislative fiat a comprehensive civic registration system does not automatically vanquish effective statelessness. As several of this book's chapters (such as those by Kirsten Di Martino on China, David B. Thronson on the United States, and Elena Rozzi on Italy) note, to achieve this, a society and its elected polity must also commit itself legally to an agreed set of practical and deliverable arrangements that provide the necessary social and economic supports that all vulnerable children need in all possible circumstances. To be in possession merely of a technically efficient national system of civic registration is not, on its own, enough.

Identity Registration: An Ambivalent History

Registration at birth (or its absence) is the outcome of an ancient historical legacy. Systems for recording the existence of persons have existed throughout history for a number of reasons, the most well-known being military and tax-related censuses. These include, for instance, the census taken over 2000 years ago by the Roman occupiers of what is today Israel and the census in operation in the Andean empire of the Incas when the Spanish arrived there.[5] This type of registration was conducted for purposes of state or imperial administration, not necessarily to register individuals' identities from birth but more often to count male adults. Identity-registration systems that recorded individual identities and familial relationships were also created in the distant past—often for the purposes of organized religions. Examples include the Confucian family registers of ancient China and early modern Japan and the late medieval parish registers of the Catholic Church in Spain. Children's names were recorded in these registers at or soon after birth.[6] The twentieth-century identity-registration system that supports individual legal and civil rights, which is the primary focus of this volume, is therefore one subset of historical identity-recording systems.

Systems of individual identity registration are not simply modern versions of older practices. The early modern and modern history of identity registration does not neatly advance chronologically with ideas about democracy and liberty. Such systems did not arise fully formed in either the eighteenth century as the product of Enlightenment ideals and principles or in the nineteenth century with the rise of liberal, increasingly democratic polities and their ideologies.[7] From 1790 onward in the United States, the first post-Enlightenment new state, the constitutional device of apportionment linked the new republic's electoral politics to a regular enumeration of its growing and geographically expanding citizenry. Every decade, the numbers of the states' electoral representatives to Congress were determined and reallocated by prorating them to population.[8] Yet despite this regular census and despite also its citizens' celebrated Bill of Rights, there was no equivalent interest in the United States in an efficient individual identity-registration service. In the end,

genuine and widespread social consent among the populace and to have recognized legitimacy, legal validity, and security from fraud.

The English Early Modern Identity-Registration System and the Poor Laws

England's system of parish registers of baptisms, burials, and marriages was neither intended nor used as a central state taxation or policing tool of surveillance, nor was it used as a private genealogical record, for religious purposes (as existed at that time in Japan), or as a confessional register (as in Roman Catholic France).[18] It was a public, local, and civic record that was created by the state in the mid-sixteenth century to be maintained for the legal and economic purposes of private individuals who were operating in England's nascent property markets. We know this because the system's instigator recorded his explanation for setting up the system. Thomas Cromwell, Henry VIII's vicar-general, introduced the nationwide system for the registration of all baptisms, burials, and marriages in 1538. He explained in the following terms the function of the new parish registers "for the avoiding of sundry strifes and processes and contentions arising from age, lineal descent, title of inheritance, legitimation of bastardy, and for knowledge, whether any person is our subject or no."[19]

Although insufficient literacy has been considered one of the reasons that it might be unviable for some of the poorest, least developed countries today to set up a comprehensive registration system, historians estimate that the English population's literacy rates in 1540 were no more than 20 percent for males and well under 10 percent for females—far below that of any country on the face of the globe today.[20] Nevertheless, the parochial registration system was soon a functioning reality throughout the land.[21] Indeed, registers were assiduously kept and preserved, and sufficient numbers survived to enable the Cambridge Group for the History of Population to analyze a 4 percent sample of 404 such registers , resulting in the group's groundbreaking study of the demographic history of England from 1538 through to 1870.[22]

After it was established, the parish registration system was efficiently maintained by the bishops, with the willing compliance of the great majority of the populace. It served the purposes of several distinct and powerful parties in British society as well as the vital interests of the poor. First, the needs of property-owners were spelled out by Cromwell in his statement of 1538. Although land ownership in much of western

Europe remained subject to the laws and customs of feudalism, since the late twelfth century in England it had been legal under the common law for free persons to buy and sell land as individual agents without reference to the interest of a feudal lord or to one's entail (other members of the nuclear family or the extended kin lineage).[23] As Michael T. Clanchy's classic study makes clear, the demand for legal records of such property transactions was increasingly socially widespread for at least three centuries before the 1538 act.[24] Property holding was relatively widely socially diffused. In 1436, nearly half of all land in England was owned neither by the Crown, the church, nor the great landowners, and by 1688, these middling and lesser gentry, yeomen farmers, and other small owners had increased their share to over 70 percent of the total.[25]

Second, in relation to the poor, sixty years after the parish registers were established in her father's reign, Elizabeth I enacted in 1598 and 1601 the famous Elizabethan Poor Laws, which mandated that each of England's 10,000 or so parishes should create a permanent fund "For the Relief of the Poor" to be maintained by a tax on local landowners and administered by independent local parish officials. Its fairness of operation was monitored by the locally sitting justices of the peace (magistrates), who were answerable to the Crown. This prototype local welfare state entitled all those born in a parish to support from its funds when ill, disabled, orphaned, widowed, old and infirm, or unemployed. On marriage, a woman's entitlement moved to the parish of birth of her spouse. Contrary to popular myth, the English working populace was highly mobile in the early modern period, as can be demonstrated by the finding that 60 to 90 percent of marriage registers show at least one of the two spouses not born in the parish where the marriage took place.[26] Thus, with the creation of a formal welfare-entitlement system in the form of the parish Poor Laws, records of place of birth and marriage (and of death of husbands for many claiming widows) became of considerable importance to the poor, as well as to those paying into the parish fund, and to those charged with administering the system and policing false claims. It is no surprise, therefore, to learn that in the year that the first of the Poor Laws were passed, 1598, the queen also gave her approval to the proposal that the records of vital events contained in all parish registers should henceforth be kept much more securely and permanently by having certified copies made at the level of each bishop's diocese.[27]

Thus, having created the law by statute, primarily for the sake of maintaining social order throughout the realm (particularly during times of economic hardship, as periodically occurred at this time with the vagaries of the harvest), the sovereign, who was head of the new Protestant Established Church, also had a significant and continuing interest in the efficiency of the parish registers. Hence, the universal identity-registration system created in 1538 soon acquired powerful additional institutional and political reasons for many different sections in society to support its maintenance and efficiency of operation. Indeed, such was the commonly perceived value of this system that the most organized among the nonconformist sections of English society, the Quaker brethren, who were aggrieved at having to use the Anglican registers, established their own parallel identity-registration system for exactly the same purposes as those served by the Anglican system—to provide themselves with property and inheritance records and to facilitate the working of their own social security funds for their members.[28]

But was this Old Poor Law really as extensive as the Elizabethan parliamentary statutes that set it up proclaimed it would be? Did it really work to assist the poor? Did the local landowners who were supposed to pay into the fund evade their financial obligations? Were the poor stigmatized and persecuted by the petty parish officials who exercised power over their lives? Did mendacity and cheating ruin the system? Historians of the Old Poor Laws have examined all of these questions and more, and although evidence of human folly, mendacity, and vindictiveness can certainly be found in the record of Poor Law history, the overall impression of this complex and evolving institution is surprisingly favorable in most of these respects. Its success has to do with political will and the impressive social capabilities of the early modern English state. As has been noted, a number of powerful parties genuinely wanted to see the system work. During the first half of the seventeenth century, the Crown, through the agency of the Privy Council, bore down relentlessly on parishes where local elites attempted to evade their responsibilities under the 1598 act by refusing to establish an adequate Poor Law fund.[29] The already existing and respected institution of local, cheap, and accessible recourse to justice—the petty sessions of the justices of the peace—also saw in this period a lot of litigation between parishes over liability for particular individual claimants and between parish officials and claimants over the fairness of claims or awards of relief that had been made in specific cases.[30] While these two constitutional and legal agencies of compliance and appeal were both kept busy, their industry maintained the integrity and political legitimacy of what would always be a labor-intensive and disputatious system, given its radically devolved, localized scale of operation into 10,000 separate parishes.

Furthermore, as Lynn Hollen Lees among others has shown, although the wealthy in each community found themselves compelled by statute and Privy Council to support the poor, the old, the disabled, the ill, and the orphaned, these laws did not "crowd out" voluntary initiative and charitable activity, as crude rational-choice models of human behavior might predict. In fact, they "crowded in" and enhanced such activity, creating, according to Lees, a welfare society in England.[31] Because members of the social and economic elites in each parish were directly financially responsible for alleviating the burden of poverty, illness, and human misfortune among fellow members of their local communities, they had plenty of incentives to use their wealth and ingenuity to attempt to minimize this financial burden on themselves by devising new agencies and institutions that would genuinely mitigate the long-term costs of such human problems. Thus, unable to evade their responsibilities, they turned their ingenuity instead to minimizing their costs in more constructive, legal ways. Successful merchants founded schools for the poor scholars of the community (the origins of several of England's oldest grammar schools, many of which over time evolved into elite private schools patronized by the wealthy for their own children's education); parishes devised schemes of apprenticeship to equip children of the very poor or orphans with income-earning work skills; alms houses were built to house the infirm elderly to rationalize the care and upkeep of this dependent section of the local populace; and in some parishes, cottages were built to house poor families.[32] There were many rough edges in the conduct of the Poor Laws—the apprenticeship of pauper children, espe cially where they were orphans, could be administered harshly by some officials—but it is difficult not to be impressed with the system's relative dynamism and diversity of provisions.

The most compelling evidence of the overall effectiveness of the Poor Laws comes from demographic historians' statistical analysis of the parish register data on death rates. These data can be compared with trends in the price of grain (a form of comparison that can also be mounted for a number of other western European populations during this period), which allows the consequences of the Poor Laws for the health of the population to be evaluated. These analyses confirm that in all of early modern Europe it was only among the English population, protected by the universal parish-based Poor Laws, that there was no longer any perceptible relationship between price spikes in the cost of grain (due to harvest fluctuations) and the national mortality rate. Until the early nineteenth century in Scotland, Ireland, France, Sweden, and all other countries for which adequate data can be found, sharp upward movements in the cost of food basics resulted in higher national death rates, but the English poor were almost entirely free from the shadow of harvest dearth a full century and a half earlier. By the mid-seventeenth century, with the Poor Laws properly established even in the most remote rural parishes, the English poor no longer died when harvests failed.[33]

As Peter M. Solar has pointed out, the English Poor Laws were probably as effective as they were because of their insistence on universality and a full extension into the countryside. [34] As today, most of the increased deaths that populations suffered during periods of food shortage were due to disease outbreaks, sometimes caused by unsuitable foods but also often due to the unplanned mobility that was required as people searched for food, resulting in water insecurities, lack of hygiene, crowding, and sanitation problems.[35] In early modern Europe, many cities and large towns had poor laws, but these never extended to the rural populations. As a result, in times of regional and geographically extensive famines, desperate rural refugees, often already diseased because of their privations, attempted to make their way to the towns where they believed some assistance could be found, frequently bringing disease with them and creating, through their movement, consequent mortality. Under the geographically comprehensive English parish Poor Laws, the rural poor had no reason to leave their parishes in times of food shortage.

However, after two centuries of effective operation by the late eighteenth century, the Anglican parish registration system began to experience serious difficulties. The rapid growth of urban parishes presented clerical incumbents with the impossible task of keeping up with the registration of all incomers and their children and many new dissenting congregations. A movement to renovate the nation's identity-registration system ensued, and it was spearheaded by those who wanted to protect their families' legal capacities to inherit and exchange property.[36] Meanwhile, after well over half a century of rapidly increasing expenditures on the poor (expenditures on Poor Laws rose tenfold in real terms between the 1750s and the 1810s), Parliament finally passed the 1834 Poor Law Amendment Act, an important transformation of the nation's social security system that established more restrictive Poor Laws. It was intended to respond to increasingly bitter complaints from sections of the landowning classes, who were footing all the bill and resented the new class of owners of industrial and financial capital, who did not hold large landholdings and therefore had rather fewer liabilities to pay for the poor.[37] After the 1834 Poor Law Amendment Act, expenditures were deliberately reduced by almost 50 percent, while administration was radically rationalized into just 650 unions (groupings of parishes). The unions were charged with building and staffing deterrent workhouses, and all those who needed support from the community would first face the *workhouse test*. As proof of their destitution, they were required to enter the workhouse, where they would perform menial work in return for meals of gruel and where the sexes were segregated. A central Poor Law Board in London was established to monitor the performance of the local management committees of the new unions—the Boards of Poor Law Guardians. Whereas during the seventeenth century, the Privy Council fought local parsimony to expand the system and establish its universality, after 1834, the central government advocated financial parsimony and the deterrent principle of the workhouse test. Many of the industrial employers in northern cities resisted for decades the building of these "bastilles" for their unemployed workers.[38]

The immediately ensuing 1836 Marriage and Registration Acts completely renovated the nation's identity-registration system. It was reborn as a universal civil registration system that was applicable to members of all religious denominations without exception and organized not by parish and diocese but by Poor Law union and department of state. Taken out of the hands of the bishops, civil registers now recorded the biological events of births and deaths and not the religious rites of baptisms and burials, as under the ecclesiastical system. The civil registers were to be collated and maintained by a staff of about 2,000 officials. Every month, these registrars and subregistrars sent copies of their records to the new General Register Office (GRO) in London, where they were compiled as a collective legal record under the Registrar-General, a high-ranking civil servant, in a single great new national registry. The GRO was located in Somerset House near to the inns of law of the legal profession, and each record was filed alphabetically by surname, as they still are to this day, reflecting the continuity of the primary legal usage envisaged for these records in relation to property claims and disputes of descent, inheritance, and legitimacy.[39]

Individual property ownership in the form of alienable land holding was never as widely diffused to a large proportion of the populace in early modern Scotland or neocolonial Ireland. However, the other major source of institutional support for a system of identity registration, the Poor Laws, did not exist in either country. Within the United Kingdom—which included Wales from 1301, Scotland from 1707, and Ireland from 1801—comprehensive Poor Law systems had never been created in either Scotland or Ireland, and by 1836, the populations in those territories never enjoyed identity-registration systems. However, by 1845, Poor Laws (along the lines of the New Poor Law of 1834) were enacted for both Ireland (1838) and Scotland (1845). Both countries then each acquired civil registration systems, as well (Scotland in 1854 and Ireland in 1864). Thus, although the creation of an English registration system in fact antedated that of a nationwide social security system, the impressive persistence and universality of the English parish register system probably depended as much on its functional utility to claimants, funders, and administrators within the nation's devolved social security system as on its utility to property-holding families.

Children in the English Identity-Registration System

The combination of Poor Law apparatus and a parish registration system combined to release the English populace from the long-standing relationship between famine and mortality. Even the most vulnerable in this society were apparently being protected from the most common form of periodic hardship, which throughout history has exerted a severe human penalty in most other comparable, less developed societies. The children of the rural poor would have been among the leading beneficiaries of this systematic difference.

The pre-1834 English Poor Laws also appear to have adopted a humane and nonjudgmental disposition toward an important category of vulnerable children and young mothers, who have been harshly treated for much of the twentieth century in many modern societies, including both the United Kingdom and the United States. Thomas W. Nutt's recent research has shown that before 1834, single unmarried mothers and nonmarital children did not receive stereotyped stigmatizing and victim-blaming treatment at the hands of the Old Poor Law officials and in the magistrates courts, which frequently oversaw such cases. (Mothers and children regularly came to court because of the legal requirement to establish paternity where possible so that Poor Law officers could pursue fathers for reimbursement of the parish's costs.)[40]

Nutt has found evidence for two contrasting regions, Essex near London and West Yorkshire in the industrial north, during the last half-century of the Old Poor Laws before the 1834 reforms. In both districts, Nutt shows, Poor Law officials and magistrates focused on identifying the father of the child. There was an unquestioned assumption by the authorities that the single unmarried mother would receive parish assistance to support the child. The only issue at stake for parish officials in the records of court proceedings was the practical one of recovery of costs from the father, provided that he could be identified and traced. Furthermore, Nutt shows that these northern parishes achieved extraordinary rates of recovery of up to 80 percent and more of their costs from fathers, who sometimes found themselves making regular payments for their nonmarital children for as long as ten years. Perhaps not surprisingly in these circumstances of determined pursuit of paternity by the Poor Law, nonmarital children were comparatively uncommon in early modern England—rarely above 3 percent of all births from 1550 to 1750.[41]

In fact, the early and mid-twentieth-century stigmatizing of single unmarried mothers, which remains a matter of living memory for older citizens, dates from the 1834 Poor Law reforms, at least in the British case. The Poor Law Amendment Act included the notorious "bastardy clauses," which had the practical effect of shifting all responsibility for nonmarital children onto the single unmarried mothers because it was henceforth impractical in law to trace absconding fathers.[42] The Poor Law authorities became extremely ill-disposed toward single unmarried mothers, who were cast as "delinquent" and irresponsible, as they represented an unrelievable burden on the poor rates. Unless their parents were prepared and able to support them (a great difficulty for the very poor), single unmarried mothers were now treated as morally deficient, like able-bodied men who would not work. Like such men, they had to enter a workhouse (with their children) and perform hard labor in return for their sustenance. Other categories of single adult women who required assistance because they had no male partner (such as widows or wives whose husbands were in military service or in jail, for instance) were entitled to live in their own homes and receive "outdoor relief" with no labor requirement.[43] Demographic trends indicate a strong popular reaction to this dramatic change of legal, institutional, and official attitudes toward unmarried motherhood. The average female age at marriage rose substantially during the 1830s and 1840s. In addition, after a trend toward an increase in national illegitimacy(associated with the incidence of unmarried motherhood) during the era of increasing generosity and spending under the Old Poor Laws from the 1750s to the 1810s, there was a long-term decline down to the first decade of the twentieth century, and the rates remained relatively low during the early decades of the twentieth century, as being born to unmarried parents came to be treated as a cultural taboo and a social disaster.[44]

Jacqueline Bhabha notes that the only reference to children's distinctive status or needs in the UDHR of 1948 was the statement in article 25(2) that "All children, whether born in or out of wedlock, shall enjoy the same social protection." In 1948, those framing the UDHR felt that it was an important, novel, and modern humanitarian issue to assert the equal rights of nonmarital children. However, in early modern England, an unusually comprehensive, local social security system had faced this issue in legal and administrative terms centuries earlier. Moreover, the legal and administrative principles adopted to guide practice in the era before the 1834 Poor Law Amendment Act anticipated the spirit of the 1948 UDHR. The denial of equal rights to this category of children and their single unmarried mothers should not necessarily be viewed as a long-standing Anglo-American practice, which only relatively modern ethical thought and principles has been able to dispel. In her excellent chapter in this volume, Linda K. Kerber writes of an "Anglo-American legal tradition—the law that Americans received as colonists and retained despite the Revolution." She also writes about certain constitutional legal principles that the United States and England held in common in relation to *jus soli* (nationality conferment by place of birth) ideas of citizenship, which can be traced to the era of Elizabeth I and her immediate successor, James I. Elsewhere, Kerber notes that U.S. law in the twentieth century has "virtually restated the old English principle that the legal responsibility for a nonmarital child is the mother's alone. . . . [O]ne of the generally unrecognized but firm obligations of women's citizenship remains the burden of care for a nonmarital child."[45] This is no doubt a correct reading of the English legal texts and their principles. However, it does not necessarily take into account the fact that England possessed an important social institution that was lacking in colonial America—the Old Poor Laws. Nutt's historical research on British pre-1834 Poor Law practice at the parish level emphasizes a crucial methodological point: when evaluating the legal position and treatment of potentially vulnerable categories (in this case, single unmarried mothers and nonmarital children), it is necessary to take into account all significant aspects of the sociolegal and institutional context, the realities of its administrative practices, and constitutional principles.

In England discriminatory treatments and practices toward single unmarried mothers and their children only became manifest over half a century after the American colonies had achieved their independence. After 1834, under the radically changed provisions of the New Poor Law, British society experienced industrialization, urbanization, and modernization. The early modern Elizabethan social security system was drastically modified in 1834 in conformity with the historically novel, supposedly rational and scientific principles of the post-Enlightenment "science" of classical economics. Adam Smith and Thomas Malthus each argued strenuously against the Poor Laws on the grounds of their economic irrationality.[46] Their new science of political economy was influential in pushing through this transformative change in the entitlements of the poor, who were now increasingly stigmatized as "paupers," which roughly translates as the contemporary notion of "scroungers"—people who supposedly lack the moral strength to support themselves independently in the market economy. Paupers and the children of paupers were not *effectively stateless*, but they were removed from civic society while they remained in the workhouses. They were free to leave at any time, but to do so, they needed access to a sufficient income to support themselves, something especially problematic for women lacking a male partner in a society that increasingly saw adult males as the sole workers who were entitled to a "family wage."[47]

Thus, government practices that are consistent with principles of equal human rights are not uniquely a product of the modern liberal democratic and humanitarian age.[48] Although early modern England was a hierarchical, monarchical, and aristocratic state, it committed itself to an effective social security system, and it did so not for liberal democratic or humanist reasons (an anachronistic notion) but for mercantilistic reasons to preserve social order and build up the size and strength of the national population.[49] Perhaps many different regimes with diverse ideologies can find compelling reasons to commit themselves to social policies that achieve similar practical effects as the principles announced by the UN Convention on the Rights of the Child (CRC). This may be partly why many states have signed and ratified this particular convention. However—and optimistically—the historical case study of early modern England also suggests that it may also be possible to encourage many different states and societies to deliver on a range of practical policies that ensure children's human rights while such societies remain diverse politically, culturally, and religiously.

Conclusion

This review of the history of English early modern social security and identity registration has indicated that the two institutions may be closely and functionally interlinked for twinned practical reasons— politico-fiscal legitimacy and administrative efficacy of a comprehensive social security system. A genuine national commitment to universal social security entitlements, rendered practically effective in this way, can provide powerful protections for registered children. Such a system need not be nationally (that is, centrally) organized. It was not in early modern England. But it does need to be nationally sanctioned by a credibly effective state that is capable of supporting the rule of law. The establishment of an efficient identity-registration system, however, may be of little value to children or adults in a society that has not committed itself to state-sanctioned entitlements for its poor citizens and their children.

In her chapter in this volume, Jacqueline Bhabha draws attention to the fact that unregistered children's statelessness is "jeopardizing their access to fundamental social protections and entitlements that many take for granted" as a matter of conventional public policy and law in affluent, democratic societies.[50] This points to the the close relationship between granting positive rights and entitlements to citizens from birth (in the historic form here of the English Old Poor Laws before 1834) and then identifying the people that those funding the system are liable to support. Furthermore, legitimate citizens also wish to be able, with as little inconvenience as possible, to access the resources that they are entitled to when and where they need them. This account indicates that *de facto* human rights for children existed as an administrative practice in England for several centuries before the full elaboration of such a notion in formal declarations, statutes, or texts produced by leading liberal theorists and thinkers. As Bhabha's question implies, in a world with all but two maverick states signed up to the CRC and with apparently almost unanimous cross-cultural and interreligious consensus on the idea of children's rights, what are human rights worth in practice for the world's most vulnerable children? They remain mere abstractions without practical systems of both identity registration and social services (such as education and health).

The details of English history show that it is unrealistic for today's activists simply to campaign for recognition of children's rights without simultaneously acknowledging the political, practical, administrative, and economic difficulties that are involved when states create systems of social support, which alone give substance to the official endorsement of such principles. In many ways, the human-rights problems of children without a state today are the direct consequences of there being many states in which children are born with virtually no practical rights or entitlements. This is partly because their governments offer little or nothing to ensure their social security and partly because their existence, as individuals with an identity, is officially unknown because it is unregistered. Reciprocally, there is no incentive for the poor and marginalized to volunteer themselves and their children for registration at birth since nothing is to be gained from doing so. Perhaps conversely, there is a real and legitimate fear that something will be lost if they provide information to a government that provides nothing of value in return. In such societies, unregistered individuals without *de jure* or *de facto* rights at birth too often grow into adults and parents without documented identities and rights.

The vulnerable, stateless children who may be detected at borders without papers too often simply conform to a normal pattern in their society of origin. The adults or caregivers who helped them to grow up were themselves unregistered people with few, if any, recognized entitlements. In many poor communities, parents cannot act as confident upholders of their children's rights—even in the country in which they and their ancestors have lived—since they lack any official recognition of their rights themselves, a process of omission that starts with the failure of the state to provide a trusted and secure identity-registration system. In many cases, parents of the poor, especially female parents and those who are themselves unregistered at birth, remain almost as disadvantaged, in human-rights terms, as their officially anonymous children.

Finally, the English early modern history of creating a practically functioning system of children's registration and rights (or at least practical entitlements) appears to have worked reasonably effectively for over two centuries. That history also indicates that any real system that is publicly accountable to its funding constituency needs to have a carefully worked-out and policed set of regulations and procedures regarding eligibility criteria and that it needs to be enforceable in a court of law. Bhabha refers to the tension for states in seeing children to protect them versus seeing children to control them. English early modern history, with its ten thousand parish states, suggests that the latter is partly a necessary and direct entailment when states take responsibility for the former. It is not necessarily intrinsically sinister but simply practically inevitable that states must "see" or register the people that they are protecting or giving resources to because otherwise the project of providing entitlements (resources that are provided by and paid for by other persons in the community) will become an indiscriminate form of unlimited liability, which none of the funders (other citizens) will willingly support in the long term. *Universality* cannot mean literally without strings attached in terms of defining eligibility and boundaries to the entitled population—unless there is to be a supplementary universal, globally collective fund to provide entitlements to all persons. This, it could be argued, might create the unintended moral hazard that such a universal provider of entitlements would potentially relieve nation states of the difficulty of living up to their obligations as signatories of the CRC (or perhaps more realistically might unintentionally facilitate the neglect or exclusion of certain categories, such as ethnic minorities).[51] Thus, in light of this volume's focus on the precariousness of the stateless child, the full implications, in terms of citizens' entitlements, of article 7(1) of the CRC are profound and onerous:

The child shall be registered immediately after birth and shall have the right from birth to a name, the right to acquire a nationality and, as far as possible, the right to know and be cared for by his or her parents.[52]

Notes

1. See Barbara Bennett Woodhouse, *Hidden in Plain Sight: The Tragedy of Children's Rights from Ben Franklin to Lionel Tate* (Princeton: Princeton University Press, 2008), on the extraordinary exceptionalism of the United States and the absence of any historical justification for this.

2. UNICEF, "The 'Rights' Start to Life: A Statistical Analysis of Birth Registration," UNICEF, 2005, 3, <http://www.unicef.org> (accessed August 31, 2009).

3. See Jacqueline Bhabha's introduction in this volume.

4. Prasanta Mahapatra et al., "Civil Registration Systems and Vital Statistics: Successes and Missed Opportunities," *Lancet*, October 29, 2007, DOI:10.1016/S0140-6736(07)61308-7.

5. P. Granville Edge, "Vital Registration in Europe: The Development of Official Statistics and Some Differences in Practice," *Journal of the Royal Statistical Society* 91 (1928): 346–379, 354–355.

6. Akira Hayami, *The Historical Demography of Pre-Modern Japan* (Tokyo: University of Tokyo Press, 2001), 18–21; on Spain, Edge, "Vital Registration," 354–355.

7. Lynn Hunt, *Inventing Human Rights: A History* (New York: Norton, 2007).

8. Margo J. Anderson, *The American Census: A Social History* (New Haven: Yale University Press, 1988).

9. Sam Shapiro, "Development of Birth Registration and Birth Statistics in the United States," *Population Studies* 4 (1950): 86–111.

10. Ibid.

11. See Bhabha's introduction to this volume.

12. Charles Steinwedel, "Making Social Groups, One Person at a Time: The Identification of Individuals by Estate, Religious Confession and Ethnicity in Late Imperial Russia," in *Documenting Individual Identity: The Development of State Practices,* ed. Jane Caplan and John Torpey (Princeton: Princeton University Press, 2001), 67–82.

13. Keith Breckenridge, "Verwoerd's Bureau of Proof: Total Information in the Making of Apartheid," *History Workshop Journal* 59 (2005): 83–108; Timothy Longman, "Identity Cards, Ethnic Self Perception and Genocide in Rwanda," in *Documenting Individual Identity,* ed. Caplan and Torpey, 345–357.

14. See, in particular, the excellent collection of studies in *Documenting Individual Identity,* ed. Caplan and Torpey.

15. Mark Harrison, *Disease and the Modern World: 1500 to the Present* (Cambridge: Polity Press 2004), chs. 5–6.

16. See Bhabha's introduction to this volume.

17. C. G. A. Clay, *Economic Expansion and Social Change: England 1500–1700,* vol. 2, *Industry, Trade and Government* (Cambridge: Cambridge University Press, 1984).

18. Edge, *Vital Registration,* 356–358.

19. G. R. Elton, *Policy and Police: The Enforcement of the Reformation in the Age of Thomas Cromwell* (Cambridge: Cambridge University Press, 1972), 259–260.

20. David Cressy, *Literacy and the Social Order: Reading and Writing in Tudor and Stuart England* (Cambridge: Cambridge University Press, 1980), 177.

21. Demonstrated most recently by Steve Hindle, *On the Parish? The Micro-Politics of Poor Relief in Rural England, c. 1550–1750* (Oxford: Clarendon Press, 2004).

22. E. A. Wrigley and R. S. Schofield, *The Population History of England, 1541–1871: A Reconstruction* (London: Edward Arnold, 1981).

23. Under customary law, this freedom was more nuanced since landlords were in theory able to intervene in land transactions or impose a levy. In practice, the underlying common law principles also applied more often than not, thereby facilitating active land markets with considerable security of tenure. I am grateful to R. M. Smith for advice on this. R. M. Smith, "The English Peasantry 1250–1650," in *The Peasantries of Europe from the Fourteenth to Eighteenth Centuries,* ed. Tom Scott (London: Longman, 1998), 339–371.

24. Michael T. Clanchy, *From Memory to Written Record: England 1066–1307* (London: Edward Arnold, 1979).

25. C. G. A. Clay, *Economic Expansion and Social Change: England 1500–1700*, vol. 1, *People, Land and Towns* (Cambridge: Cambridge University Press 1984), 143, table 5.

26. Peter Kitson, "Family Formation, Male Occupation and the Nature of Parochial Registration in England, c.1538–1837," PhD thesis, University of Cambridge, 2004, 183–200.

27. They were designed to be durable records; and examples of these leather-bound, high-quality parchment diocesan register books have survived over the centuries, enabling the scholars of the Cambridge Group to reconstruct the country's population history.

28. Richard T. Vann and David Eversley, *Friends in Life and Death: The British and Irish Quakers in the Demographic Transition* (Cambridge: Cambridge University Press, 1992), 15–16.

29. Steve Hindle, *On the Parish? The Micro-Politics of Poor Relief in Rural England c. 1550–1750* (New York: Oxford University Press, 2004); Paul Slack, *Poverty and Policy in Tudor and Stuart England* (London: Longman, 1998).

30. Documented in Hindle, *On the Parish?*, and Thomas Sokoll, *Essex Pauper Letters 1731–1837* (Oxford: Oxford University Press and British Academy, 2001).

31. Lyn Hollen Lees, *The Solidarities of Strangers: The English Poor Laws and the People, 1700–1948* (Cambridge: Cambridge University Press, 1998).

32. See Hindle *On the Parish?*, and, for instance, John Broad, "Housing the Rural Poor in Southern England, 1650–1850," *Agricultural History Review* 48 (2000): 151–170.

33. Patrick R. Galloway, "Basic Patterns in Annual Variations in Fertility, Nuptiality, Mortality, and Prices in Preindustrial Europe," *Population Studies* 42 (1988): 275–303.

34. Peter M. Solar, "Poor Relief and English Economic Development before the Industrial Revolution," *Economic History Review* 48 (1995): 1–22.

35. Cormac O'Grada, *Famine: A Short History* (Princeton: Princeton University Press 2009), 108–121.

36. Edward Higgs, *Life, Death and Statistics: Civil Registration, Censuses and the Work of the General Register Office, 1836–1952* (Hatfield: Local Population Studies 2004), 7–21.

37. Anthony Brundage, *The Making of the New Poor Law: The Politics of Inquiry, Enactment and Implementation, 1832–1839* (London: Hutchinson & Co., 1978); Peter Mandler, "The Making of the New Poor Law Redivivus," *Past and Present* 117 (1987): 131–157.

38. Nicholas C. Edsell, *The Anti-Poor Law Movement 1834–44* (Manchester: Manchester University Press, 1971); Margaret Anne Crowther, *The Workhouse System 1834–1929: The History of an English Social Institution* (London: Batsford Academic and Educational, 1981).

39. Higgs, *Life, Death and Statistics*, ch. 1.

40. Thomas W. Nutt, "The Paradox and Problems of Illegitimate Paternity in Old Poor Law Essex," in *Illegitimacy in Britain, 1700–1920*, ed. Alysa Levene, Thomas Nutt, and Samantha Williams (Basingstoke: Palgrave Macmillan, 2005), 101–121; and Thomas Nutt, "Illegitimacy and the Poor Law in Late Eighteenth and Early Nineteenth-Century England," PhD diss., University of Cambridge, 2005.

41. E. A. Wrigley, R. S. Davies, J. E. Oeppen, and R. S. Schofield, *English Population History from Family Reconstitution 1580–1837* (Cambridge: Cambridge University Press, 1997), 224.

42. Anthony Brundage, *The English Poor Laws 1700–1930* (Basingstoke: Palgrave, 2002), 68–69.

43. Lees, *The Solidarities of Strangers*, 142.

44. The *illegitimacy ratio* is defined by English historical demographers as the percentage of all baptisms described as "illegitimate" in those surviving parish registers where this information was consistently recorded (such registers comprise about one-quarter to one-third of all such surviving registers). Peter Laslett, *Family Life and Illicit Love in Earlier Generations* (Cambridge: Cambridge University Press, 1977), 112,120, 113 (fig. 3.1). On popular attitudes to illegitimacy from oral history sources in the early and mid-twentieth century, see John R. Gillis, *For Better, for Worse: British Marriages, 1600 to the Present* (New York: Oxford University Press, 1985), 238–241; Lucinda McCray Beier, *For Their Own Good: The Transformation of English Working-Class Health Culture, 1880–1970* (Columbus: Ohio State University Press, 2008), 221–228.

45. See Linda K. Kerber's chapter in this volume.

46. Adam Smith, *The Wealth of Nations* (Harmondsworth: Pelican, 1970; first published 1776), book 1, ch. 10; Thomas R. Malthus, *An Essay on the Principle of Population* (Harmondsworth: Pelican, 1970; first published 1798), ch. 5.

47. Lees, *The Solidarities of Strangers*, 135–144.

48. For this kind of view, see, for instance, Louis Henkin, *The Age of Rights* (New York: Columbia University Press, 1990).

49. Lars Magnusson, *Mercantilism: The Shaping of an Economic Language* (London: Routledge, 1994).

50. Bhabha, "Introduction," p. 2, this volume.

51. Article 7.2 of the CRC with its reference to "national law" may not be an entirely effective defense against this problem of internal discrimination: "States Parties shall ensure the implementation of these rights in accordance with their national law and their obligations under the relevant international instruments in this field, in particular where the child would otherwise be stateless." See UNICEF Web site, <http://www.unicef.org/crc/crc.htm> (accessed April 13, 2009).

52. Ibid.

Suggested Reading

General

Adjami, M., and J. Harrington. "The Scope and Content of Article 15 of the Universal Declaration of Human Rights." *Refugee Survey Quarterly* 27, no. 3 (2008): 93–109.

Aird, Sarah, Helen Harnett, and Punam Shah. *Stateless Children: Youth Who Are without Citizenship*. Washington, D.C.: Youth Advocate Program International, 2002.

Akram, Susan M. "Palestinian Refugees and Their Legal Status: Rights, Politics, and Implications for a Just Solution." *Journal of Palestine Studies* 31, no. 3 (Spring 2002): 36–51.

Aleinikoff, T. Alexander. *Semblances of Sovereignty—The Constitution, the State, and American Citizenship*. Cambridge, Mass.: Harvard University Press, 2002.

Aleinikoff, T. Alexander. "Between Principles and Politics: U.S. Citizenship Policy." In *From Migrants to Citizens: Membership in a Changing World*, ed. T. Alexander Aleinikoff and Douglas B. Klusmeyer, 119–172. Washington, D.C.: Carnegie Endowment for International Peace. 2000.

Aleinikoff, T. Alexander. "International Legal Norms and Migration: A Report." In *Migration and International Legal Norms*, ed. T. Alexander Aleinikoff and Vincent Chetail, 1–27. The Hague: Asser, 2003.

Aleinikoff, T. Alexander. "Policing Boundaries: Migration, Citizenship, and the State, in E Pluribus Unum?" In *Contemporary and Historical Perspectives on Immigrant Political Incorporation*, ed. Gary Gerstle and John H. Mollenkopf, 267–291. New York: Russell Sage Foundation, 2001.

Aleinikoff, T. Alexander. "Theories of Loss of Citizenship." *Michigan Law Review* 84, no. 1471 (1986): 1481.

Aleinikoff, Thomas, and Vincent Chetail. *Migration and International Legal Norms*. The Hague: Asser Press, 2003.

Aleinikoff, T. Alexander, and Douglas B. Klusmeyer, eds. *Citizenship Today: Global Perspectives and Practices*. Washington, D.C.: Brookings Institution Press, 2001.

Aleinikoff, T. Alexander, and Douglas Klusmeyer, eds. *From Migrants to Citizens: Membership in a Changing World*. Washington, D.C.: Carnegie Endowment for International Peace, 2000.

Aleinikoff, T. Alexander, and Douglas B. Klusmeyer. "Plural Nationality: Facing the Future in a Migratory World." In *Citizenship Today: Global Perspectives and Practices*, ed. T. Alexander Aleinikoff and Douglas B. Klusmeyer, 63–88. Washington, D.C.: Carnegie Endowment for International Peace, 2001.

Aleinikoff, T. Alexander, David A. Martin, and Hiroshi Motomura. *Immigration and Citizenship: Process and Policy*. 5th ed. St. Paul, Minn.: Thomson/West, 2003.

Aleinikoff, T. Alexander, David A. Martin, Hiroshi Motomura, and Maryellen Fullerton. *Forced Migration: Law and Policy*. St. Paul: Thomson/West, 2007.

Amnesty International. "Bhutan: Nationality, Expulsion, Statelessness and the Right to Return." ASA 14/001/2000. London, September 2000.

Amnesty International. *Down and Out in London*. London: Amnesty International, 2006. <http://www.amnesty.org.uk/content.asp?CategoryID=10682#report> (accessed January 5, 2010).

Amnesty International. "Perilous Plight: Burma's Rohingya Take to the Seas." May 2009, <http://www.hrw.org/sites/default/files/reports/burma0509_brochure_web.pdf> (accessed January 5, 2010).

Amnesty International. "The Rohingya Minority: Fundamental Rights Denied." ASA 16/005/2004. May 2004.

Amnesty International. "Slovenia: Amnesty International's Briefing to the UN Committee on Economic, Social and Cultural, Rights." 35th session, November 2005, <http://www.amnestyusa.org/document.php?lang=e&id=ENGEUR68002 2005> (accessed January 5, 2010).

Arendt, Hannah. *The Origins of Totalitarianism*. New York: Harcourt, 1951.

Bader, Veit. *Citizenship and Exclusion*. New York: MacMillan Press, 1997.

Barbieri, Patrick. "About Being Without: Bidun." Refugees International, Washington, D.C., October 2007.

Batchelor, Carol A. "Developments in International Law: The Avoidance of Statelessness through Positive Application of the Right to a Nationality." Paper presented at Council of Europe's Second Conference on Nationality, Strasbourg, October 9, 2001.

Batchelor, Carol A. "The International Legal Framework Concerning Statelessness and Access for Stateless Persons." Paper presented at the European Union Seminar on the Content and Scope of International Protection. UNHCR, January 8, 2002, <http://www.unhcr.org/refworld/docid/415c3be44.html> (accessed December 20, 2009).

Batchelor, Carol A. "The 1954 Convention Relating to the Status of Stateless Persons: Implementation within the European Union Member States and Recommendations for Harmonization." *Refuge: Canada's Periodical on Refugees* 22, no. 2 (September 2005): 31–58.

Batchelor, Carol A. "Statelessness and the Problem of Resolving Nationality Status." *International Journal of Refugee Law* 10 (1998): 156–183.

Batchelor, Carol A. "Stateless Persons: Some Gaps in International Protection." *International Journal of Refugee Law* 7 (1995): 232–259.

Batchelor, Carol A. "Transforming International Legal Principles into National Law: The Right to a Nationality and the Avoidance of Statelessness." *Refugee Survey Quarterly* 25 (2006): 8–25.

Batchelor, Carol A. "UNHCR and Issues Related to Nationality." *Refugee Survey Quarterly* 14, no. 3 (1995).

Bauboeck, Rainer. "Citizenship and National Identities in the European Union." Harvard Jean Monnet Chair Working Papers, Harvard Law School, Cambridge, 1997, <http://www.jeanmonnetprogram.org/papers/97/97-04-.rtf> (accessed on August 5, 2008).

Bhabha, Jacqueline. "Arendt's Children: Do Today's Migrant Children Have a Right to Have Rights?" *Human Rights Quarterly* 31 (2009): 410–451.

Bhabha, Jacqueline. "Belonging in Europe: Citizenship and Post-national Rights." *International Social Science Journal* 159 (1999): 11–23.

Bhabha, Jacqueline. "The Citizenship Deficit: On Being a Citizen Child." *Society and International Development* 46, no. 3 (2003): 53–59.

Bhabha, Jacqueline. "Un 'Vide Juridique'? Migrant Children: The Rights and Wrongs." In *Realizing the Rights of the Child*, ed. Carol Bellamy, Jean Zermatten, Peter G. Kirchschläger, and Thomas Kirchschläger. Swiss Human Rights Book, vol. 2. Zurich: Rüffer & Rub, 2007. 206–219.

Bhabha, Jacqueline, and Christina Alfirev. "The Identification and Referral of Trafficked Persons to Procedures for Determining International Protection Needs," UN High Commissioner for Refugees, October 2009, PPLAS/2009/03, 2009. <http://www.unhcr.org/refworld/docid/4ad317bc2.html> (accessed November 1, 2009).

Blackman, Jeffrey L. "State Successions and Statelessness: The Emerging Right to an Effective Nationality under International Law." *Michigan Journal of International Law* 19 (1998): 1141–1194.

Blake, Nicholas, and Laurie Fransman. *Immigration, Nationality, and Asylum under the Human Rights Act 1998*. London: Butterworths, 1999.

Blitz, Brad. "Statelessness and the Social (De)Construction of Citizenship: Political Restructuring and Ethnic Discrimination In Slovenia." *Journal of Human Rights* 5, no. 4 (2006): 1–27.

Blitz, Brad K. "Statelessness, Protection and Equality." U.K. Department of International Development and University of Oxford Refugee Studies Centre Policy Brief, September, 2009, <http://www.rsc.ox.ac.uk/PDFs/RSCPB3-Statelessness.pdf> (accessed January 5, 2010).

Blitz, Brad, and Maureen Lynch. *Statelessness and Citizenship: A Comparative Study on the Benefits of Nationality*. Cheltenham: Elgar, 2009.

Bloch, A. "Refugee Settlement in Britain: The Impact of Policy on Participation." *Journal of Ethnic and Migration Studies* 26, no. 1 (2006): 75–88.

Böcker, Anita, et al. *Migration and the Regulation of Social Integration.* Osnabrück, Germany: Institut für Migrationsforschung und Interkulturelle Studien (IMIS), Universität Osnabrück, 2004.

Bogusz, Barbara, et al. *Irregular Migration and Human Rights: Theoretical, European, and International Perspectives.* Leiden: Martinus Nijhoff, 2004.

Bosniak, Linda. "Being Here: Ethical Territoriality and the Rights of Immigrants." *Theoretical Inquiries in Law* 8, no. 2 (2007): 389–410.

Bosniak, Linda. *The Citizen and the Alien: Dilemmas of Contemporary Membership.* Princeton: Princeton University Press, 2006.

Bosniak, Linda. "Human Rights, State Sovereignty, and the Protection of Undocumented Migrants under the International Migrant Worker's Convention." In *Irregular Migration and Human Rights: Theoretical, European and International Perspectives,* ed. Barbara Bogusz, Ryszard Cholewinski, et al. Leiden: Martinus Nijhoff, 1994.

Brownlie, I. "The Relations of Nationality in Public International Law." *British Yearbook of International Law* 39 (1963): 284–364.

Brubaker, W. "Citizenship Struggles in Soviet Successor States." *International Migration Review* 26, no. 2 (Summer 1992): 269–291.

Calavita, Kitty. *Immigrants at the Margins: Law, Race, and Exclusion in Southern Europe.* New York: Cambridge University Press, 2005.

Chan, Johannes. "The Right to a Nationality as a Human Right." *Human Rights Law Journal* 12, no. 1–2 (1991): 1–14.

Chari, P. R., et al. *Missing Boundaries: Refugees, Migrants, Stateless and Internally Displaced Persons in South Asia.* New Delhi: Manohar Publishers, 2003.

Committee on the Elimination of Racial Discrimination. "General Recommendation 30: Discrimination against Non-citizens." New York, October 1, 2004, <http://www.unhchr.ch/tbs/doc.nsf/0/e3980a673769e229c1256f8d0057cd3d?Opendocument> (accessed January 5, 2010).

Cordova, R. "Nationality, Including Statelessness: Third Report on the Elimination or Reduction of Statelessness." A/CN.4/81, March 1954.

Council of Europe, Commissioner for Human Rights. "Memorandum by Thomas Hammarberg, Council of Europe Commissioner for Human Rights, Following His Visit to Italy, 19–20 June 2008," July 28, 2008. CommDH(2008)18, UNHCR Refworld, <http://www.unhcr.org/refworld/docid/48ce60372.html> (accessed December 3, 2008.

Coventry Peace House. *Statelessness: The Quiet Torture of Belonging Nowhere.* Coventry: Coventry Peace House, 2008.

Crawley, Heaven. *Child First, Migrant Second: Ensuring That Every Child Matters.* London: Immigration Law Practitioners Association, 2006.

Crawley, Heaven. *Moving Forward: The Provision of Accommodation for Travellers and Gypsies.* London: Institute for Public Policy Research, 2004.

Crawley, Heaven, and T. Lester. *No Place for a Child: Children in Immigration in the UK—Impacts, Alternatives and Safeguards.* London: Save the Children Fund UK, 2005.

Dedi , Jasminka. "Roma and Statelessness." European Parliament, Committee on Civil Liberties, Justice and Home Affairs, Brussels, June 26, 2007.

Dedic, J., V. Jalušic, and J. Zorn. *The Erased: Organized Innocence and the Politics of Exclusion.* Ljubljana: Peace Institute, 2003.

Deng, Francis. "Ethnic Marginalization as Statelessness: Lessons from the Great Lakes Region of Africa." In *Citizenship Today: Global Perspectives and Practices,* ed. Thomas Alexander Aleinikoff and Douglas Klusmeyer, 183–208. Washington, D.C.: Brookings Institution Press, 2001.

Dennis, J. *A Case for Change: How Refugee Children in England Are Missing Out.* London: Children's Society, Refugee Council and Save the Children, 2002.

Doebbler, Curtis F. "A Human Rights Approach to Statelessness in the Middle East." *Leiden Journal of International Law* 15 (2002): 527–552.

Doek, Jaap E. "The CRC and the Right to Acquire and to Preserve a Nationality." *Refugee Survey Quarterly* 25, no. 3 (2006): 26–32.

Donner, R. *The Regulation of Nationality in International Law.* New York: Transnational Publishers, 1994.

Duncan, W. "Nationality and the Protection of Children across Frontiers: The Case of Inter-country Adoption." Paper presented at the Third European Conference on Nationality: Nationality and the Child, Strasbourg, 2004.

Edwards, Alice, and Carla Ferstmann. *Human Security and Non-Citizens. Law, Policy and International Affairs.* Cambridge: Cambridge University Press, 2009.

Equal Rights Trust. "Testimony of a Stateless Child in Detention in Egypt." *Equal Rights Trust Review* 3 (2009): 56–62.

Fehervary, Andras. "Citizenship, Statelessness and Human Rights: Recent Developments in the Baltic States." *International Journal of Refugee Law* 5 (1993): 392–423.

Fransman, Laurie, et al. *Immigration and Asylum Emergency Procedures.* London: Legal Action Group, 1995.

Gelazis, N. "An Evaluation of the International Instruments That Address the Condition of Statelessness: A Case Study of Estonia and Latvia." In *International Migration Law,* ed. R. Cholewinski. The Hague: Asser Press, 2007.

Ghosh, Bimal. *Huddled Masses and Uncertain Shores: Insights into Irregular Migration.* The Hague: Martinus Nijhoff, 1998.

Goldston, James A. "Holes in the Rights Framework: Racial Discrimination, Citizenship and the Rights of Non-citizens." *Ethics and International Affairs* 20, no. 3 (2006): 321–347.

Goodwin-Gill, G. "The Rights of Refugees and Stateless Persons." In *Human Rights: Perspectives and Challenges,* ed. K. P. Saksena. New Delhi: Lancers Books, 1994.

Grant, S. "The Legal Protection of Stranded Migrants." In *International Migration Law,* ed. R. Cholewinksi. The Hague: Asser Press, 2007.

Groenendijk, Kees. "Nationality, Minorities and Statelessness: The Case of the Baltic States." *Helsinki Monitor* 4, no. 13 (1999): 16–17.

Grundy-Warr, C. and Wong, E. "Sanctuary under a Plastic Sheet: The Unresolved Problem of Rohingya Refugees." *IBRU Boundary and Security Bulletin* 5, no. 3 (Autumn 1997): 79–91.

Gupta, Parikrama. "De Facto Stateless: The Meshketian Turks." *Central Asia and the Caucasus* 5 (2006): 126–138.

Gyulai, G. "Forgotten without Reason: Protection of Non-Refugee Stateless Persons in Central Europe." Hungarian Helsinki Committee, June 2007.

Hammami, Rema, and Penny Johnson. "Equality with a Difference: Gender and Citizenship in Transitional Palestine." *Social Politics: International Studies in Gender, State and Society* 6, no. 3 (1999): 314–343.

Hayden, Patrick. "From Exclusion to Containment: Arendt, Sovereign Power, and Statelessness." *Societies without Borders* 3, no. 2 (2008): 248–269.

Helsinki Monitor of Slovenia. "Human Rights Problems in Slovenia." Statement No. 1, February 11, 1998, <http://www.fortunecity.com/meltingpot/iceland/363/Statement_No_1.htm> (accessed January 5, 2010).

Hess, Julia Meredith. "Statelessness and the State: Tibetan Citizenship, and Nationalist Activism in a Transnationalist World." *International Migration* 44, no. 1 (2006): 79–104.

Hodgson, Douglas. "The International Legal Protection of the Child's Right to a Legal Identity and the Problem of Statelessness." *International Journal of Law and the Family* 7 (1993): 255–270.

Hudson, Manley O. "Report on Nationality including Statelessness." A/CN.4/50. *Yearbook of the International Law Commission* 2 (1952): 2–24.

Human Rights Watch. "You Will Be Punished: Attacks on Civilians in Eastern Congo." Human Rights Watch, December 2009, <http://www.hrw.org/sites/default/files/reports/drc1209web_1.pdf> (accessed January 5, 2010).

Huntington, Samuel. *Who Are We? The Challenges to America's National Identity*. New York: Simon and Schuster, 2004.

Instituto Interamericano del Niño, la Niña, y Adolescentes. "El registro universal del nacimiento y el derecho a la identidad en América Latina y el Caribe: Desafíos y oportunidades." Paper presented at the Fourth Meeting of Directors of the Civil, Identity, and Vital Statistics Registries in Latin America, El Derecho a la Identitad: Oportunidad y Retos, Ciudad de México, July–August 2007, <http://www.iin.oea.org/IIN/Pdf/novedades/Registrouniversal.pdf> (accessed July 21, 2010).

Internal Displacement Monitoring Centre (IDMC). "India: Jammu and Kashmir—Displaced due to 1947 partition of Indian protest in Jammu to demand citizenship," 2007, <http://www.internal-displacement.org/idmc/website/countries.nsf/(httpEnvelopes)/f6e66d867c1f56b3c12572c30054b7b4!OpenDocument&Click => (accessed January 5, 2010).

International Law Commission. "Draft Articles on Nationality of Natural Persons in Relation to the Succession of States (with Commentaries)," April 3, 1999, Supplement No. 10 (A/54/10). <http://www.unhcr.org/refworld/docid/4512b6dd4.html> (accessed August 1, 2009).

International Law Commission. "Second Report on State Succession and Its Impact on the Nationality of Natural and Legal Persons, by Mr. Václav Mikulka, Special Rapporteur," April 17, 1996. A/CN.4/474, UNHCR Refworld, <http://www.unhcr.org/refworld/docid/3ae6b32e4.html> (accessed December 19, 2008).

Jackson, S. "Of 'Doubtful Nationality': Political Manipulation of Citizenship in the D.R. Congo." *Citizenship Studies* 11, no. 5 (November 2007): 481–500.

Jacobson, David. *The Immigration Reader: America in Multidisciplinary Perspective*. Malden, Mass.: Blackwell, 1998.

Jacobson, David. *Rights across Borders: Immigration and the Decline of Citizenship*. Baltimore: Johns Hopkins University Press, 1996.

Johnson, Kevin. *Opening the Floodgates: Why America Needs to Rethink Its Borders and Immigration Laws*. New York: New York University Press, 2007.

Jordan, Bill, and Franck Düvell. *Irregular Migration: The Dilemmas of Transnational Mobility*. Cheltenham: Elgar, 2002.

Kanstroom, Daniel. "Criminalizing the Undocumented: Ironic Boundaries of the Post-September 11th 'Pale of Law.'" *North Carolina Journal of International Law and Commercial Regulation* 29 (2004): 639–670.

Kanstroom, Daniel. *Deportation Nation: Outsiders in American History*. Cambridge: Harvard University Press, 2007.

Kartashkin, V. "The Rights of Women Married to Foreigners." Working Paper for the Sub-Commission on the Promotion and Protection of Human Rights, E/CN.4/Sub.2/2003/34, June 30, 2003.

Keely, Charles B. "How Nation-States Create and Respond to Refugee Flows." *International Migration Review* 30, no. 4 (1996): 1046–1066.

Kerber, Linda. "The Meanings of Citizenship." *Journal of American History* 84 (3) (December 1997): 833–854.

Kerber, Linda. *No Constitutional Right to Be Ladies: Women and the Obligations of Citizenship*. New York: Hill & Wang, 1998.

Kerber, Linda. ""The Stateless as the Citizen's Other: A View from the United States." Presidential Address. *American Historical Review* 112, no. 1 (February 2007): 1–34.

Kerber, Linda. "Toward a History of Statelessness in America." *American Quarterly* 57, no. 3 (September 2005): 727–751.

Kits, Harry J. "Betwixt and Between: Refugees and Stateless Persons in Limbo." *Refuge* 22, no. 2 (2005): 3–5.

Laczo, Mona. "Deprived of an Individual Identity: Citizenship and Women in Nepal." *Gender and Development* 11, no. 3 (November 2003): 76–82.

Lee, Tang Lay. "Refugees from Bhutan: Nationality, Statelessness and the Right to Return." *International Journal of Refugee Law* 10 (1998): 118–155.

Lee, Tang Lay. *Statelessness, Human Rights and Gender: Irregular Migrant Workers from Burma in Thailand*. Leiden: Martinus Nijhoff, 2005.

Lee, Tang Lay. "Stateless Persons, Stateless Refugees and the 1989 Comprehensive Plan of Action. Part 2, Chinese Nationality and the People's Republic of China." *International Journal of Refugee Law* 7 (1995): 482–500.

Legomsky, Stephen H. "Secondary Refugee Movements and the Return of Asylum Seekers to Third Countries: The Meaning of Effective Protection." *International Journal of Refugee Law* 15 (2003): 567–677.

Legomsky, Stephen H., and Cristina Rodríguez. *Immigration and Refugee Law and Policy.* 5th ed. New York: Foundation Press, 2009.

Lewa, Chris. "North Arakan: An Open Prison for the Rohingya in Burma." *Forced Migration Review* 32 (April 2009).

Liebich, Andre. "Plural Citizenship in Post-Communist States." *International Journal of Refugee Law* 12 (2000): 97–107.

Liddell, Zunetta. "Burma: Children's Rights and the Rule of Law." *Human Rights Watch* 9, no. 1 (January 1997).

Linde, Robyn. "Statelessness and Roma Communities in the Czech Republic: Competing Theories of State Compliance." *International Journal on Minority and Group Rights* 13 (2006): 341–365.

Loewenfeld, Erwin. "Status of Stateless Persons." *Transactions of the Grotius Society* 27 (1941): 59–112.

London Detainee Support Group. *Detained Lives: The Real Costs of Indefinite Immigration Detention.* London: London Detainee Support Group, 2009. <http://www.detainedlives.org/wp-content/uploads/detainedlives.pdf> (accessed January 5, 2010).

London Detainee Support Group. *Difficulties in Removal of Undocumented Algerian Nationals.* London: London Detainee Support Group, 2008. <http://www.ldsg.org.uk/files/uploads/dossierssummaries0708.pdf> (accessed January 5, 2010).

Lynch, Maureen. "Futures Denied: Statelessness among Infants, Children and Youth." Refugees International, Washington, D.C., 2008.

Lynch, Maureen. "Lives on Hold: The Human Cost of Statelessness." Refugees International, Washington, D.C., 2005.

Lynch, Maureen, and Perveen Ali. "Buried Alive: Stateless Kurds in Syria." Refugees International, Washington, D.C., 2006.

Lynch, Maureen, and Thatcher Cork. "Citizens of Nowhere: The Stateless Biharis of Bangladesh." Refugees International, Washinton, D.C., 2006.

Macklin, Audrey. "Who Is the Citizen's Other? Considering the Heft of Citizenship." *Theoretical Inquiries in Law* 8, no. 2 (July 2007): 333–366.

Mahapatra, Prasanta, Kenji Shibuya, Alan D. Lopez, Francesca Coullare, Francis C. Notzon, Chalapati Rao, and Simon Szreter, on Behalf of the Monitoring Vital Events Writing Group. "Civil Registration and Vital Statistics: Successes and Missed Opportunities." *Lancet* 370 (October 29, 2007): 1653–1663.

Manby, B. *Struggles for Citizenship in Africa.* London: Zed Books, 2009.

Martin, Susan F, and Elzbieta Gozdziak, eds. *Beyond the Gateway: Immigrants in a Changing America.* Lanham, Md.: Lexington Books, 2005.

Médecins sans Frontières Holland. "Ten Years for the Rohingya Refugees in Bangladesh: Past, Present and Future." Médecins sans Frontières, Geneva, 2002.

Mikulka, V. "Third Report on Nationality in Relation to the Succession of States." A/CN.4/480, Geneva, February 7, 1997.

Myers, John B. *Child Protection in America: Past, Present, and Future.* Oxford: Oxford University Press, 2006.

Nahajlo, Bohdan. "Forcible Population Transfers, Deportations and Ethnic Cleansing in the CIS: Problems in Search of Responses." *Refugee Survey Quarterly* 16 (1997): 26–76.

Neuman, Gerald L. *Strangers to the Constitution: Immigrants, Borders, and Fundamental Law.* Princeton: Princeton University Press, 1996.

Neuman, Gerald L. "*Wong Wing v. United States*: The Bill of Rights Protects Illegal Aliens." In *Immigration Stories*, ed. D. Martin and P. Schuck. New York: Foundation Press, 2005.

Ngai, Mae. *Impossible Subjects: Illegal Aliens and the Making of Modern America.* Princeton: Princeton University Press, 2004.

Olivas, Michael. "Plyler v. Doe: The Education of Undocumented Children, and the Polity." In *Immigration Stories*, ed. Peter Schuck, 197–218. New York: Foundation Press, 2005.

Onuma, Yasuaki. "Nationality and Territorial Change: In Search of the State of the Law." *Yale Journal of World Public Order* 8, no. 1 (1981): 1–35.

Open Society Justice Initiative. "Human Rights and Legal Identity: Approaches to Combating Statelessness and Arbitrary Deprivation of Nationality." Paper presented at the OSI conference, May 2006.

Oxford Refugee Studies Centre. "Stateless." *Forced Migration Review* 32 (April) 2009: 1–76.

Passel, Jeffrey. "Unauthorized Migrants in the United States: Estimates, Methods, and Characteristics." Organisation for Economic Co-operation and Development (OECD), DELSA/ELSA/WD/SEM(2007), September 2007.

Paulsen, Eric. "The Citizenship Status of the Urdu-Speakers/Biharis in Bangladesh." *Refugee Survey Quarterly* 25, no. 3 (2006): 54–69.

Peji, Jelena. "Citizenship and Statelessness in the Former Yugoslavia: The Legal Framework." *Refugee Survey Quarterly* 14, no. 3 (1995): 1–18.

Pentikäinen, Oscar, and Tom Tricr. "Between Integration and Resettlement: The Meshketian Turks." European Centre for Minorities Working Paper 21, ECMI, Flensburg, 2004.

Perks, K., and A. de Chickera. "The Silent Stateless and the Unhearing World: Can Equality Compel Us to Listen?" *Equal Rights Review* 3 (2009): 42–55.

Piotrowicz, R. "Victims of Trafficking and De Facto Statelessness." *Refugee Survey Quarterly* 21 (Special Issue) (2002): 50–59.

Platform for International Cooperation on Undocumented Migrants (PICUM). "Undocumented Children in Europe: Invisible Victims of Immigration Restrictions." PICUM, Brussels, 2008.

Pocock, J. G. A. "The Ideal of Citizenship in Classical Times." In *The Citizenship Debates*, ed. Gershon Shafir. Minneapolis: University of Minnesota Press, 1998. 31–42.

Reimers, Fernando. "Citizenship Education, Globalization and Education." *Prospects* 36 (September 2006): 275–294.

Reimers, Fernando, Cristian Cox, and Rosario Jaramillo. "Education for Democratic Citizenship in the Americas: An Agenda for Action." Inter-American Development Bank, August 2005.

Robinson, N. *Convention Relating to the Status of Stateless Persons: Its Origin, Significance, Application, and Interpretation*. New York: Institute of Jewish Affairs, 1958.

Saisoonthorn, Phunthip Kanchanachittra. "Development of Concepts on Nationality and the Efforts to Reduce Statelessness in Thailand." *Refugee Survey Quarterly* 25, no. 3 (2006): 40–53.

Sales, R. "The Deserving and Undeserving? Refugees, Asylum Seekers and Welfare in Britain." *Critical Social Policy* 22, no. 3 (2002): 456–478.

Sawyer, C., and P. Turpin. "Neither Here Nor There: Temporary Admission to the UK." *International Journal of Refugee Law* 17 (2005): 688–728.

Schärer, Roland. "The Council of Europe and the Reduction of Statelessness." *Refugee Survey Quarterly* 25 (2006): 33–39.

Schuck, Peter. *Citizens, Strangers and In-Betweens: Essays on Immigration and Citizenship*. Boulder: Westview Press, 1998.

Schuck, Peter, and David Martin. *Immigration Stories*. New York: Foundation Press, 2005.

Schuck, Peter, and Rogers Smith. *Citizenship without Consent: Illegal Aliens in the America Polity*. New Haven: Yale University Press, 1985.

Scott, James C. *Seeing Like a State: How Certain Schemes to Improve the Human Condition Have Failed*. New Haven: Yale University Press, 1998.

Seckler-Hudson, Catheryn S. *Statelessness: With Special Reference to the United States*. Washington, D.C.: Digest Press, 1934.

Sen, Sumit. "Stateless Refugees and the Right to Return: The Bihari Refugees of South Asia" (Parts 1–2). *International Journal of Refugee Law* 11, no. 4 (1999): 625–645 and 12, no. 1 (2000): 41–70.

Setel, Philip W., Sarah B. Macfalane, Simon Szreter, Lene Mikkelsen, Prabhat Jha, Susan Stout, and Carla Abouzahr. "A Scandal of Invisibility: Making Everyone Count by Counting Everyone." *Lancet* 370 (October 2007): 1569–1577.

Sokoloff, Constantine, and Richard Lewis. "Denial of Citizenship: A Challenge to Human Security." Paper prepared for the Advisory Board on Human Security, February 2005.

Southwick, Katherine, and Maureen Lynch. "Nationality Rights for All: A Progress Report and Global Survey on Statelessness." Refugees International, Washington, D.C., March 2009.

Soysal, Yasemin. *Limits of Citizenship: Migrants and Postcolonial Membership in Europe*. Chicago: University of Chicago Press, 1994.

Suarez-Orozco, Carola, and Marcelo M. Suarez-Orozco. *Children of Immigration*. The Developing Child Series. Cambridge, Mass.: Harvard University Press, 2001.

Suarez-Orozco, Carola, Marcelo M. Suarez-Orozco, and Desirée Baolian Qin. *New Immigration: An Interdisciplinary Reader*. New York: Routledge, 2005.

Thronson, David. "Choiceless Choices: Deportation and the Parent-Child Relationship." *Nevada Law Review* 6 (2006): 1165.

Tibet Justice Center. *Tibet's Stateless Nationals: Tibetan Refugees in Nepal*. Berkeley: Tibet Justice Center, 2002.

Tiburcio, C. *The Human Rights of Aliens under International and Comparative Law*. The Hague: Kluwer Law International, 2001.

Tienda, Marta, and Faith Mitchell, eds. *Hispanics and the Future of America*. Washington, D.C.: National Academy Press, 2006.

Tienda, Marta, and Faith Mitchell, eds. *Multiple Origins, Uncertain Destinies: Hispanics and the American Future*. Washington, D.C.: National Academy Press, 2006.

United Nations Children's Fund (UNICEF). *The State of the World's Children 2006: Excluded and Invisible*. New York: UNICEF, 2006.

United Nations Children's Fund (UNICEF). "Birth Registration and Armed Conflict." *Innocenti Insight*. Florence: Innocenti Research Centre, 2007.

United Nations Children's Fund (UNICEF). "Birth Registration: Right from the Start." *Innocenti Insight*. Florence: Innocenti Research Centre, 2002.

United Nations Committee on Economic, Social, and Cultural Rights (CESCR). "General Comment No. 4: The Right to Adequate Housing (Art. 11 (1) of the Covenant)." E/1992/23, December 13, 1991. <http://www.unhcr.org/refworld/docid/47a7079a1.html> (accessed February 2, 2010).

United Nations Department of Social Affairs. *A Study of Statelessness*. E/1112, February 1, 1949, E/1112/add. 1, May 19, 1949. Lake Success: United Nations, 1949.

United Nations General Assembly. "Children and Armed Conflict: Report of the Secretary-General." December 21, 2007. A/62/609–S/2007/757, <http://www.unhcr.org/refworld/docid/479f54592.html> (accessed February 2, 2010).

United Nations High Commissioner for Human Rights. *The Rights of Non-Citizens*. Geneva: United Nations, 2006.

United Nations High Commissioner for the Rights of Refugees (UNHCR). "2008 Global Trends: Refugees, Asylum-seekers, Returnees, Internally Displaced and Stateless Persons." UNHCR, June 2008.

United Nations High Commissioner for the Rights of Refugees (UNHCR). "Guidelines on International Protection. The Application of Article 1(A)2 of the 1951 Convention and/or 1967 Protocol Relating to the Status of Refugees to Victims of Trafficking and Persons at Risk of Being Trafficked." *International Journal of Refugee Law* 19, no. 2 (June 16, 2007): 372–390.

United Nations High Commissioner for the Rights of Refugees (UNHCR). "The Excluded: The Strange Hidden World of the Stateless." *Refugee Magazine* 3, no. 147 (September 2007).

United Nations High Commissioner for the Rights of Refugees (UNHCR). "The International Legal Framework Concerning Statelessness and Access for Stateless Persons." Paper prepared for the European Union Seminar on the Content and Scope of International Protection, January 8, 2002. <http://www.unhcr.org/refworld/docid/415c3be44.html> (accessed December 21, 2009).

United Nations High Commissioner for the Rights of Refugees (UNHCR). "Measuring Statelessness through Population Census." ECE/CES/AC.6/2008/SP/5, Geneva, May 13, 2008.

United Nations High Commissioner for the Rights of Refugees (UNHCR). "Overview of UNHCR's Citizenship Campaign in Crimea." Simferopol, December 2000.

United Nations High Commissioner for the Rights of Refugees (UNHCR) and Interparliamentary Union. *Nationality and Statelessness: A Handbook for Parliamentarians*. Lausanne: Presses Centrales de Lausanne, 2005 (updated in 2008).

United Nations High Commissioner for the Rights of Refugees (UNHCR). "Statelessness and Citizenship." In *The State of the World's Refugees: A Humanitarian Agenda*. Oxford: Oxford University Press, 1997.

United Nations High Commissioner for the Rights of Refugees (UNHCR). "Statelessness: Prevention and Reduction of Statelessness and Protection of Stateless Persons." Progress Report EC/57/SC/CRP.6, February 14, 2006." *Refugee Survey Quarterly* 25, no. 1 (2006): 127–131.

United Nations High Commissioner for the Rights of Refugees (UNHCR). "UNHCR's Activities in the Field of Statelessness: Progress Report." EC/55/SC/CRP.13/Rev.1, Geneva, June 30, 2005. "Progress Report on Statelessness 2009." EC/60/SC/CRP.10, Geneva, May 29, 2009.

Vandenabeele, Caroline, and Christine V. Lao. "Legal Identity for Inclusive Development." Asian Development Bank, 2007. <http://www.adp.org/documents/books/legal-identity/default.asp> (accessed June 1, 2009).

Van Schendel, Willem. "Stateless in South Asia: The Making of the India-Bangladesh Enclaves." *Journal of Asian Studies* 61, no. 1 (February 2002): 115–147.

Van Waas. Laura. "The Children of Irregular Migrants: A Stateless Generation?" *Netherlands Quarterly of Human Rights* 25, no. 3 (September 2007): 437–458.

Van Waas, Laura. *Nationality Matters: Statelessness under International Law*. Antwerp: Intersentia, 2008.

Vishniak, Marc. *The Legal Status of Stateless Persons.* New York: American Jewish Committee, 1945.

Warnke, Adam. "Vagabonds, Tinkers and Travelers: Statelessness among the East European Roma." *Indiana Journal of Global Legal Studies* 7 (1999): 335–368.

Waters, Mary, et al. *Inheriting the City: The Second Generation Comes of Age.* Boston: Harvard University, 2008.

Waters, Mary. *The New Americans: A Guide to Immigration since 1965.* Boston: Harvard University Press, 2007.

Weis, Paul. "The Convention Relating to the Status of Stateless Persons." *International and Comparative Law Quarterly* 10 (1961): 255–261.

Weis, Paul. *Nationality and Statelessness in International Law.* Alphen aan den Rijn: Sijthoff & Noordhoff, 1979.

Weis, Paul. *A Study on Statelessness.* Doc. E/1112 and add. 1. New York: United Nations, 1949.

Weis, Paul. "The United Nations Convention on the Reduction of Statelessness, 1961." *International and Comparative Law Quarterly* 11, no. 4 (October 1962): 1073–1096.

Weissbrodt, D. "Final Report on the Rights of Non-Citizens." UN Doc. E/CN.4/Sub.2/2003/23 UNHCR. 2003.

Weissbrodt, David, and Clay Collins. "The Human Rights of Stateless Persons." *Human Rights Quarterly* 28 (2006): 245–276.

Whitley, Andrew. "Minorities and the Stateless in Persian Gulf Politics." *Survival* 35, no. 4 (December 2003): 28–50.

Wright, Wendy. "Hannah Arendt and Enemy Combatants: New Implications of Statelessness." Paper presented at the annual meeting of the Midwest Political Science Association, Palmer House Hilton, Chicago, Illinois, June 2008.

Ziemele, I. *State Continuity and Nationality: The Baltic States and Russia.* Leiden: Martinus Nijhoff Publishers, 2005.

Zorn, J., and U. Lipovec ebron. *Once upon an Erasure: From Citizens to Illegal Residents in the Republic of Slovenia.* Ljubljana: Študentska Založba, 2008. <http://www.izbrisan17let.si/pdf/once_upon_an_erasure_combine.pdf> (accessed January 5, 2010).

Legal References

African Commission on Human and Peoples' Rights. *Case of John K. Modise v. Botswana.* Comm. No. 97/93, 2000.

Council of Europe. "Council of Europe Convention on the Avoidance of Statelessness in Relation to State Succession," March 15, 2006. CETS 200. Online. UNHCR Refworld. <http://www.unhcr.org/cgi-bin/texis/vtx/refworld/rwmain?docid=4444c8584> (accessed February 11, 2008).

Council of Europe. European Convention on Nationality. November 6, 1997, ETS 166. <http://www.unhcr.org/refworld/docid/3ae6b36618.html> (accessed October 2, 2009).

Council of Europe. European Convention for the Protection of Human Rights and Fundamental Freedoms. November 4, 1950, ETS 5. <http://www.unhcr.org/refworld/docid/3ae6b3b04.html> (accessed September 29, 2009).

European Union. Lisbon Treaty. *Brussels: Official Journal of the European Union,* C 306, vol. 50, December 17, 2007. <http://eur-lex.europa.eu/JOHtml.do?uri=OJ:C:2007:306:SOM:EN:HTML> (accessed November 27, 2008).

European Union. Treaty of the European Union (TEU). Brussels: Official Journal C 191, Jul7 29, 1992. <http://eur-lex.europa.eu/en/treaties/dat/11992M/htm/11992M.html> (accessed November 27, 2008).

High Court (Botswana). *Attorney General v. Unity Dow,* CA No. 4/91, July 3, 1992. <http://www.law-lib.utoronto.ca/Diana/fulltext/dow1.htm> (accessed January 5, 2010).

Inter-American Court for Human Rights. *Dilcia Yean and Violeta Bosico v. Dominican Republic,* I/A Court HR (ser. C), no. 134 (2005). <http://www.unhcr.org/refworld/docid/44e497d94.html> (accessed October 1, 2009).

International Court of Justice (ICJ). "Nationality Decrees Issued in Tunis and Morocco." Advisory Opinion No. 4, February 7, 1923. <http://www.unhcr.org/refworld/docid/44e5c9fc4.html> (accessed February 2, 2010).

International Court of Justice. Nottebohm Case (2nd phase), judgment of April 6. *I.C.J. Reports* (1955): 4.

League of Nations. Convention on Certain Questions Relating to the Conflict of Nationality Laws, April 13, 1930. League of Nations, *Treaty Series,* vol. 179, p. 89, no. 4137. UNHCR Refworld. <http://www.unhcr.org/refworld/docid/3ae6b3b00.html> accessed May 5, 2009).

Organization of American States. American Convention on Human Rights, "Pact of San Jose," Costa Rica, November 22, 1969. <http://www.unhcr.org/refworld/docid/3ae6b36510.html> (accessed October 2, 2009).

United Nations General Assembly. Convention on the Elimination of All Forms of Discrimination against Women. December 18, 1979. A/RES/34/180. <http://www.unhcr.org/refworld/docid/3b00f2244.html> (accessed October 2, 2009).

United Nations General Assembly. Convention of the Nationality of Married Women. January 29, 1957. A/RES/1040. <http://www.unhcr.org/refworld/docid/3b00f0674.html> (accessed October 2, 2009).

United Nations General Assembly. Convention Relating to the Status of Refugees. July 28, 1951. United Nations, *Treaty Series,* vol. 189, p. 137, UNHCR Refworld. <http://www.unhcr.org/cgi-bin/texis/vtx/refworld/rwmain?docid=3be01b964> (accessed February 11, 2008).

United Nations General Assembly. Convention Relating to the Status of Stateless Persons. September 28, 1954. United Nations, *Treaty Series,* vol. 360, p. 117, UNHCR Refworld. <http://www.unhcr.org/cgi-bin/texis/vtx/refworld/rwmain?docid=3ae6b3840> (accessed February 11, 2008).

United Nations General Assembly. Convention on the Reduction of Statelessness. August 30, 1961. United Nations, *Treaty Series*, vol. 989, p. 175, UNHCR Refworld. <http://www.unhcr.org/cgi-bin/texis/vtx/refworld/rwmain?docid=3ae 6b39620> (accessed February 11, 2008).

United Nations General Assembly. Convention on the Rights of the Child. November 20, 1989. United Nations, *Treaty Series*, vol. 1577, p. 3. <http://www .unhcr.org/refworld/docid/3ae6b38f0.html> (accessed October 2, 2009).

United Nations General Assembly. International Covenant on Civil and Political Rights. December 16, 1966. United Nations, *Treaty Series*, vol. 999, p. 171. <http://www.unhcr.org/refworld/docid/3ae6b3aa0.html> (accessed October 2, 2009).

United Nations General Assembly. International Covenant on Economic, Social and Cultural Rights, International Covenant on Civil and Political Rights and Optional Protocol to the International Covenant on Civil and Political Rights. December 16, 1966. A/RES/2200. <http://www.unhcr.org/refworld/docid/3b00 f47924.html> (accessed October 2, 2009).

United Nations General Assembly. Universal Declaration of Human Rights. December 10, 1948. UNHCR Refworld. <http://www.unhcr.org/cgi-bin/texis/ vtx/refworld/rwmain?docid=3ae6b3712c> (accessed May 13, 2008).

Contributors

Christina O. Alfirev   Christina Alfirev coordinated the book publication process of this edited volume during her master's degree studies at the Fletcher School of Law and Diplomacy at Tufts University. She has worked for various humanitarian organizations, including for the United Nations High Commissioner for Refugees (UNHCR) in Rwanda, the United Nations Development Program (UNDP) in Madagascar, and the Serbian Refugee Council in Belgrade.

Jacqueline Bhabha   Jacqueline Bhabha is the Jeremiah Smith Jr. Lecturer in Law at Harvard Law School, a lecturer in public policy at the Harvard Kennedy School, and the director of the Harvard University Committee on Human Rights Studies. Her writings on issues of child citizenship, migration, asylum, and trafficking in Europe and the United States include a coauthored book, *Women's Movement: Women under Immigration, Nationality and Refugee Law* (with Sue Shutter, 1994); an edited volume, *Asylum Law and Practice in Europe and North America: A Comparative Analysis* (with Geoffrey Coll, 1992); a cross-country analysis of child asylum seekers, *Seeking Asylum Alone: Unaccompanied and Separated Children and Refugee Protection in Australia, the U.K. and the U.S.—A Comparative Study* (with Mary Crock, Nadine Finch, and Susan Schmidt, 2007); and many articles.

Luca Bicocchi   Luca Bicocchi has a master's degree in immigration policies and social cohesion from the University of Rome "la Sapeienza" and has worked with NGOs in Rome and in Kathmandu, Nepal. He has also worked for the Platform for International Cooperation on Undocumented Migrants (PICUM) in Brussels, heading a European project (Daphne) that works to end discrimination-based violence against undocumented minors.

Brad K. Blitz   Brad K. Blitz is professor of human and political geography at Kingston University London and research associate in the department of international development at the University of Oxford. He is also director of the International Observatory on Statelessness (http://www.nationalityforall.org). Recent and forthcoming publications include a coedited book, *Statelessness in the European Union: Displaced, Undocumented, Unwanted* (with Caroline Sawyer, 2010); a coauthored book, *Statelessness and Citizenship: A Comparative Study on the Benefits of Nationality* (with Maureen Lynch, 2009); a research policy brief, *Statelessness, Protection and Equality* (2009); and *Freedom of Movement, Citizenship, and Exclusion* (2010).

Kirsten Di Martino   Kirsten Di Martino has been chief of the Child Protection Program for UNICEF China since May 2009. She has worked with UNICEF in China since July 2006 and previously held the position of chief of the Plans of Action and Promotion of Child Rights Program.

Daniel Senovilla Hernández   Daniel Senovilla Hernández is a PhD candidate at the Instituto de Estudios sobre Migraciones, Universidad de Comillas of Madrid, and has been hosted since 2004 by the research center MIGRINTER at the Université de Poitiers, CNRS.

Bela Hovy   Béla Hovy is chief of the migration section at the United Nations Population Division, Department of Economic and Social Affairs, New York.

Jyothi Kanics   Since August 2009, Jyothi Kanics has been working with UNICEF as an advocacy and policy specialist. From 2007 to 2009, she was separated children's officer with the Irish Refugee Council. Besides writing position papers and articles for several journals and organizations, she has provided expert input for various manuals, including UNICEF's *Reference Guide on Protecting the Rights of Child Victims of Trafficking in Europe* (2006) and the Separated Children in Europe Program's *Statement of Good Practice* (2004).

Linda K. Kerber   Linda K. Kerber is May Brodbeck Professor in the Liberal Arts, professor of history, and lecturer in the College of Law at the University of Iowa. In 2006, she served as president of the American Historical Association. She is also a past president of the Organization of American Historians (1996–1997) and of the American Studies Association (1988). Her paper "The Stateless as the Citizen's Other: A View from the United States" is the foundation of her current research and writing. She is the author of *No Constitutional Right to Be Ladies: Women and the Obligations of Citizenship* (1998), which won the Littleton-Griswold Prize for the best book in U.S. legal history and the Joan Kelley Prize for the best book in women's history (both awarded by the American Historical Association). Her other books include *Toward an Intellectual History of Women* (1997) and *Women of the Republic: Intellect and Ideology in Revolutionary America* (1980). She is coeditor of *U.S. History as Women's History: New Feminist Essays* (with Alice Kessler-Harris and Kathryn Kish Sklar, 1995) and of the anthology *Women's America: Refocusing the Past* (with Jane Sherron De Hart, seventh edition, 2010).

Stephen H. Legomsky   Stephen H. Legomsky is John S. Lehmann University Professor at Washington University School of Law in St. Louis and until 2002 was the founding director of the Harris World Law Institute at WUSL. He is the author of *Immigration and Refugee Law and Policy* (coauthored with Cristina Rodriguez, starting with the fifth edition, 2009). His other books include *Immigration and the Judiciary: Law and Politics in Britain and America* (1987) and *Specialized Justice: Courts, Administrative Tribunals, and a Cross-National Theory of Specialization* (1990).

Elena Rozzi   Since 2008, Elena Rozzi has been conducting research on Roma children in the social sciences department at Turin University. In the last decade, she has led the working group on children's rights at the Italian Association for Law Studies on Migration (ASGI).

Simon Szreter   Simon Szreter is Professor of History and Public Policy in the History faculty at the University of Cambridge and fellow of St John's College, Cambridge. He is a founding member of the History and Policy Network and coeditor of its electronic journal, *History & Policy* (<http://www.historyand policy.org>). His books include *Fertility, Class, and Gender in Britain 1860–1940* (1996) and *Health and Wealth: Studies in History and Policy* (2005). He is coauthor (with Kate Fisher) of *Sex before the Sexual Revolution: Intimate Life in England 1918–1963* (Cambridge University Press 2010). In 2009, he was awarded the Arthur Viseltear Prize by the American Public Health Association for distinguished contributions to the history of public health.

David B. Thronson   David B. Thronson is Professor of Law at Michigan State University College of Law.

Caroline Vandenabeele   Caroline Vandenabeele works with the United Nations in Nepal as head of the Resident Coordinator's Office and as strategic planning adviser. She coauthored *Legal Identity for Inclusive Development* (with Christine V. Lao, 2007) for the Asian Development Bank.

Index